ROMANS

ROMANS

A Theological and Pastoral Commentary

MICHAEL J. GORMAN

WILLIAM B. EERDMANS PUBLISHING COMPANY
GRAND RAPIDS, MICHIGAN

Wm. B. Eerdmans Publishing Co.
4035 Park East Court SE, Grand Rapids, Michigan 49546
www.eerdmans.com

28 27 26 25 24 23 22   1 2 3 4 5 6 7

ISBN 978-0-8028-7762-8

Library of Congress Cataloging-in-Publication Data

Names: Gorman, Michael J., 1955– author.
Title: Romans : a theological and pastoral commentary / Michael J. Gorman.
Description: Grand Rapids, Michigan : William B. Eerdmans Publishing Company,
    2022. | Includes bibliographical references and index. | Summary: "A theological
    commentary on Romans that provides the historical context for studying, teaching,
    and preaching Romans today"—Provided by publisher.
Identifiers: LCCN 2021035859 | ISBN 9780802877628
Subjects: LCSH: Bible. Romans—Commentaries. | BISAC: RELIGION / Biblical
    Commentary / New Testament / Paul's Letters | RELIGION / Biblical Studies /
    History & Culture
Classification: LCC BS2665.53 .G67 2022 | DDC 227/.107—dc23
LC record available at https://lccn.loc.gov/2021035859

The section of the commentary called "Introducing Paul: His Life, Theology, and Spirituality" has been adapted from "Paul, His Life and Theology" in the *Paulist Biblical Commentary* © 2018 Paulist Press. Used with permission. All rights reserved.

Portions of this work draw on material first published in Michael J. Gorman, *Apostle of the Crucified Lord: A Theological Introduction to Paul and His Letters*, 2nd ed. (Grand Rapids: Eerdmans, 2017).

Unless otherwise noted, Scripture quotations are from the New Revised Standard Version of the Bible.

Scripture quotations marked (CEB) are from the Common English Bible. Scripture quotations marked (NAB) are from the New American Bible, revised edition. Scripture quotations marked (NIV) are from the New International Version.

For the Church

Contents

Preface

This commentary has been prepared especially for pastors, students, and laypeople who want a careful exposition of Paul's letter to the Romans that stresses its theological content and considers its spiritual and pastoral implications for today. (Of course, I hope that biblical scholars and theologians will benefit from it as well.) This focus does not mean we will ignore the original message of Paul to his first audience. It simply means that I engage Romans as Christian Scripture.

"These things were written also for our sake" is Paul's basic principle for interpreting Scripture, and he would expect us to follow it in reading his own letters now that they are part of the Christian Bible.[1] I read, teach, and write about Romans as a Protestant Christian who has spent the last thirty years in a Catholic seminary that also has an ecumenical graduate school, in an ecumenical home Bible study, and in Methodist churches as a teacher of adults. In each place, we have studied Romans as a letter to and for us.

Furthermore, designating this commentary as "theological and pastoral" means, for me, that these two aspects are inextricably related, even hyphenated (theological-pastoral), because Paul is a pastoral theologian. Romans is a project of what Scot McKnight calls "lived theology."[2] Paul writes not merely about *thinking* Christianly but about *living* Christianly.

As a Christian and a scholar, I am quite enamored with the apostle Paul and his writings. At the same time, I recognize what 2 Peter lamented years ago: "There are some things in them [Paul's letters] hard to understand, which

---

1. See, e.g., Rom 4:23–24; 15:4; 1 Cor 9:10.
2. Scot McKnight, *Reading Romans Backwards: The Gospel of Peace in the Midst of Empire* (Waco: Baylor University Press, 2019). The essence of this lived theology, says McKnight, is "Christoformity," or Christlikeness.

the ignorant and unstable twist to their own destruction, as they do the other scriptures" (2 Pet 3:16). Sometime later, the church father Origen (d. 254) said that one reason Romans is so hard to understand is that Paul "makes use of expressions which sometimes are confused and insufficiently explicit."[3]

I therefore hope that this commentary will illumine Paul's message in Romans, identifying some misinterpretations and offering, I trust, some new and helpful ones along the way. (However, as I sometimes tell my students about biblical interpretation, let whoever is without sin cast the first stone!) My prayer is that it will help those who struggle with the letter to read it more intelligibly and charitably, and to embrace its call to participate in the life God offers in Christ by the Spirit more fully.

Unlike some commentaries, especially much longer ones (yes, they exist!), this commentary does not always deal with every word of every verse in sequence. It focuses on what scholars sometimes call *discourse units* and on the theological content and significance of those various sections of the letter. The commentary also has a minimum of footnotes and explicit references to other interpreters; the notes are mostly explanatory. The commentary also does not provide a list of all possible interpretations for every disputed word, verse, or topic. Rather, it offers a sustained interpretation of the letter as a whole, dialoguing with other interpreters primarily behind the scenes, rather than on the pages or in the notes (with some exceptions). That is, this commentary comments on the text, not on other commentators.

At the end of the introductory sections of the commentary and at the end of each section of comments are further reflections, questions, and suggested reading. The reflections are a significant aspect of this commentary and should be read along with the exposition of the text to which they are connected. Since this commentary is not aimed primarily at scholars, I have generally restricted the reading suggestions to resources intended for, or at least accessible by, a broad readership. (A few more technical works are included and indicated as such.) Furthermore, although I have recommended important books on the biblical and theological topics raised by the letter, I do not necessarily agree with everything in every book listed. Finally, summaries appear after the commentary on chapters 1–4, 5–8, 9–11, and 12–16.

The default Scripture translation used in this commentary is the NRSV, although there are many references to other versions, especially the NIV, NAB,

---

3. Origen, "Preface," in *Commentary on the Epistle to the Romans*, trans. Thomas P. Scheck, Fathers of the Church (Washington, DC: Catholic University Press of America, 2009), para. 1.

and CEB, as well as my own translations here and there. I have, of course, worked with the Greek text even though it is only occasionally cited (in transliteration, such as *charis*: "grace," "gift").

Of the making of books on Romans there is no end. As I was completing this commentary, I received notice of the option of buying an electronic package of more than ninety commentaries, plus another thirty-five scholarly studies and collections of sermons, totaling forty thousand pages. So, what is the distinctive contribution of this commentary? It is this: *if John is the gospel of life, as many have said, Romans is the epistle of life*. As Paul puts it, "Do you not know that all of us who have been baptized into Christ Jesus were baptized into his death? Therefore we have been buried with him by baptism into death, so that, just as Christ was raised from the dead by the glory of the Father, so we too might walk in newness of life" (Rom 6:3–4).

This newness of life takes shape—or should take shape—in multicultural communities of faithfulness and love; of holiness and hope; of harmony and hospitality; of worship and welcome; of mercy and mission; of peace, justice, and joy; and, yes, of suffering and solace. These aspects of Romans, and of Christian theology and practice, will all be emphasized in this commentary. Above all, Romans is a letter about Spirit-enabled participation and transformation in Christ and his story, and thus in the life and mission of God in the world.

Acknowledgments

In a very real sense, this commentary has been in the works for the better part of two decades. Various publications along the way have expressed some of the interpretations of Romans found in these pages. I am grateful to Eerdmans for encouraging and allowing me to expand the minicommentary on Romans in *Apostle of the Crucified Lord* into the present book-length commentary.[1] I am grateful also to Paulist Press for permission to use and expand the essay on Paul's life and theology from *The Paulist Biblical Commentary*.

I express my sincere gratitude as well to the pastors and others who made suggestions about what this commentary should look like and do. Likewise, I thank the members of my fall 2020 Romans Greek exegesis seminar for their feedback in the final stages of my writing this commentary. I mention in particular Rev. Dion Thompson, seminarian Peter Myers, and my co-instructor, Dr. Daniel Jackson. It was quite a gift to have in Daniel—a former student who had spent the last five years working on Romans—a conversation partner and friendly critic while I was completing this commentary and we were teaching the Greek text of Romans together. His knowledge of the text of Romans and of the secondary literature interpreting it is extraordinarily impressive and was helpful to me in many ways. Daniel's work on glory in Romans has been particularly influential on my own reading of the letter.[2] (I of course hold none of these fellow interpreters of Romans—or any other interpreter!—responsible for my own interpretations.)

1. Michael J. Gorman, *Apostle of the Crucified Lord: A Theological Introduction to Paul and His Letters*, 2nd ed. (Grand Rapids: Eerdmans, 2017), 395–481.
2. See W. Daniel Jackson, "The Logic of Divine Presence in Romans 3:23," *Catholic Biblical Quarterly* 80 (2018): 293–305.

Others who made contributions small and large to this commentary include especially my research assistants Luke Eshleman and Michelle Newman Rader. Luke checked the first round of scriptural references and citations, followed by Michelle for later rounds. Michelle also carefully read the entire manuscript, making helpful corrections and suggestions with an eagle's eye, scholarly insight, and pastoral vision. Her invaluable ideas for additional reflection questions and further reading were especially helpful.

Once again, I express my thanks to St. Mary's Seminary & University for its support of my teaching and research. I owe a particular debt to the president-rector, Fr. Phillip Brown, and to my deans, Dr. Brent Laytham and Fr. Gladstone Stephens. One recent class on Romans, taught in early 2019, particularly stands out. Offered in St. Mary's Ecumenical Institute, it had some seventy students, all connected to Agape Mission Church and its network of churches. I am grateful to Dean Laytham and the church pastors and members for that excellent experience, and to those advanced students and colleagues who assisted in the course: Brian Gorman, Dr. Jennifer McNeel, Michelle Rader, and Gary Staszak. I also want to thank my student Nicholas Mwai for various insights he offered in a class on Paul for Roman Catholic seminarians.

I am also grateful to Eerdmans for their belief in this project, with special thanks to James Ernest and Trevor Thompson, as well as Justin Howell and Laurel Draper.

Finally, I give thanks to and for my family, who are always supportive of my work: my adult children (Mark, Amy, and Brian), and especially my wife Nancy.

Abbreviations

alt.	altered
CEB	Common English Bible
e.g.	for example (Latin *exempli gratia*)
ESV	English Standard Version
Gk.	Greek
Heb.	Hebrew
i.e.	that is (Latin *id est*)
KJV	King James Version
KNT	Kingdom New Testament (N. T. Wright's translation)
lit.	literally
mg.	margin (indicating alternative translation)
MJG	author's translation
NAB	New American Bible (Revised Edition)
NASB	New American Standard Bible
NET	New English Translation (NET Bible)
NETS	New English Translation of the Septuagint
NIV	New International Version
NJB	New Jerusalem Bible
NLT	New Living Translation
NRSV	New Revised Standard Version
orig.	original
RSV	Revised Standard Version

Introductions

Introducing Paul

HIS LIFE, THEOLOGY, AND SPIRITUALITY

Paul, the Jew from Tarsus who had tried to destroy the fledgling Jesus-as-Messiah movement that became the Christian church, was early Christianity's most influential leader and thinker. His bequest to the church includes his apostolic example as well as his creative theology and profound spirituality. It is helpful to put his letter to the early Christian believers in Rome into the larger context of his life and convictions.

APPROACHING PAUL

There are various perspectives on Paul today, especially among scholars who have devoted their lives to studying the apostle. After listing and briefly describing some, I will highlight the approach taken in this commentary.[1]

- The *traditional perspective* on Paul, sometimes called the *traditional Protestant* or the *Lutheran* perspective, is the default position of many people. This perspective generally finds Paul stressing the individual's justification (right relationship with God) by faith rather than works; justification as a divine declaration of acquittal, as in a law court; substitutionary atonement, or Jesus' death in our place; and salvation history, or continuity between God's revelation to Israel and God's work in Christ. This approach to Paul is usually traced back (rightly or wrongly) to John Calvin and Martin Luther.
- The *new perspective* (or *perspectives*) on Paul emerged in the 1960s through the early 1980s in reaction to the traditional perspective. It continues today,

---

1. I draw heavily from my *Apostle of the Crucified Lord: A Theological Introduction to Paul and His Letters*, 2nd ed. (Grand Rapids: Eerdmans, 2017), 1–5, for this discussion.

in somewhat nuanced ways, due to critique from the traditional perspective and other quarters. Advocates have attempted to better understand first-century Judaism and Paul within it. Some new-perspective themes include the following:

> Paul did not have a modern introspective guilt complex.
> Judaism was not a religion of human effort, or works righteousness, but of *covenantal nomism*: keeping the law as a response to God's grace.
> The center of Paul's theology was not justification but participation in Christ.
> Justification is primarily about the inclusion of gentiles in the covenant community apart from keeping the Jewish law, especially the Jewish boundary markers of circumcision, kosher diet, and calendar (the Sabbath and other special days).

- The *narrative-intertextual perspective* emphasizes Paul as both a narrative theologian—that is, there are discernible stories within and behind his letters—and a scriptural theologian—that is, Paul is primarily an interpreter of Israel's Scriptures (the Christian Old Testament).
- The *apocalyptic perspective* stresses that for Paul, God's apocalypse (revelation) in Christ is God's unexpected incursion into human history to rescue people, and eventually entire cosmos, from the cosmic powers of Sin and Death. Thus, traditional law court imagery for justification and salvation is insufficient, and the language of a continuous salvation history is in need of modification.
- The *anti-imperial perspective* contends that Paul's proclamation of the gospel was a critique of and an alternative to Rome—its emperor, gods, good news (gospel), values, and so on. Proponents of this perspective contend that Paul consistently undermines Roman claims and practices, presenting Jesus rather than Caesar as the true lord, and the Christ-community as an alternative to the oppressive empire.
- Similarly, the *postcolonial perspective* emphasizes how Paul has been misused by colonial powers (and others in power) to oppress people, and works to reinterpret Paul in liberating ways.
- The *Paul within Judaism perspective* (sometimes called the *radical new perspective*) finds traditional and even new perspectives to be too influenced by their proponents' own Christian beliefs, thus failing to understand Paul and his communities adequately. They contend that Paul remained firmly within Judaism as a law-observant Jew, even as an apostle of the Messiah. One of the ongoing areas of exploration is how best to understand and identify non-Jews in Christ (gentiles) in relation to Paul's new form of Judaism.

- The *feminist perspective* (or *perspectives*) on Paul brings women's questions and concerns to the study of Paul and the Pauline letters. Feminist interpreters look both critically and constructively at views of women expressed in the letters in their ancient contexts, and in the interpretation of those views from antiquity to today.
- The *participationist perspective* stresses individual and community transformative participation "in Christ," especially in his death and resurrection, as the central dimension of Pauline theology. Its proponents resonate with early Christian interpreters of Paul and of salvation, who made statements like the following: "He [Christ/God] became what we are so that we could become what he is."

These various approaches to Paul (and there are more!) are not all mutually exclusive, though some are definitely in tension with others.

The present writer identifies with the participationist perspective but also shares the concerns of other approaches, especially the new perspective, the narrative-intertextual perspective, the apocalyptic perspective, and the anti-imperial perspective. Readers of the commentary will undoubtedly notice the emphasis on participation, but also, as indicated in the preface, on related themes, such as holiness, justice, peace, mission, and above all *life*.

PAUL'S LIFE AND MINISTRY

We have several kinds of sources for studying Paul. Nonetheless, dating the life and ministry of Paul with precision is notoriously difficult. At the same time, we can get a good general sense of the shape and character of his apostolic vocation.

Sources for Paul's Life and Theology

The most important sources for the apostle's life and theology are the seven letters he wrote that are universally agreed to be authored by him, including Romans (see further below). Supporting evidence comes from the other six letters attributed to him but whose actual authorship is debated by scholars. These writings may reflect less accurately or directly Paul's life and thought.

Another source is the Acts of the Apostles, written by Luke and thus more useful for Luke's own theology, and for his interpretation of Paul's life, than for Paul's theology per se. Scholars debate the degree of Luke's historical reliability, with some finding him more accurate in his description of the cities Paul evangelized than in his plotting of Paul's actual travels. (It is debated whether Luke was actually Paul's traveling companion.) Yet another kind of evidence is more general: ancient Jewish and pagan writings, inscriptions and other archaeological remains, and other sorts of historical information that help us understand Paul in his context.

Taken together, these sources reveal some highly significant aspects of Paul's life and theology, but they also leave open some questions. Although we cannot construct a full biography, and we cannot specify his precise position on every theological topic, there is sufficient evidence to describe and interpret both his life and his thought—sometimes quite precisely, sometimes more generally.

A General Chronology

Establishing a Pauline chronology is challenging, not only due to questions about the historical accuracy of Acts, but also due to the general absence of references to datable historical events in Acts and especially in the letters. Moreover, unfortunately, none of the letters bears a date stamp. The references in Acts 18:12–17 to Gallio, proconsul of Achaia from about AD 50 to 52, may help us date Paul's original ministry there to the early 50s, but even this date and text are subject to scholarly argument.

A very general outline of Paul's life and ministry is possible by drawing on what we can glean from the letters, Acts, and other sources. It looks something like the following, with a range of dates normally given to indicate something of the range of scholarly reconstructions:

DATES	EVENT
ca. 5 BC–AD 10	Birth in Tarsus (followed by education in Tarsus, then Jerusalem)
ca. 30–36	Persecution of the Jesus-as-Messiah movement (the church)
ca. 33–36	Call/conversion/commission
ca. 33–39	Three years in Arabia and Damascus (Gal 1:17)
ca. 36–39	Initial Jerusalem visit with Cephas and James (two weeks; Gal 1:18–19)
ca. 37–48	Early mission work in Syria, Cilicia, and possibly elsewhere (Gal 1:21; cf. Acts 9:30)
ca. 46–58	Evangelization especially in Asia Minor and Greece; writing of most canonical letters, including Romans (toward the end of this period)
ca. 47–51	Jerusalem meeting/council (Gal 2:1–10 = Acts 11:27–30? Acts 15?)
ca. 50–52	Corinth mission of eighteen months (Acts 18; see Acts 18:11)

Dates	Event
ca. 52–57	Ephesus mission of two to three years (Acts 19; see Acts 19:8, 10; 20:31), including possible imprisonment Additional three-month stay in Corinth (Acts 20:3), where Romans was written
ca. 54–59	Arrest in Jerusalem (Acts 21:27–36)
ca. 60–63	Imprisonment in Rome (Acts 28)
ca. 62–68	Possible release from Rome and further mission work and letter writing
ca. 62–68	Death

The transformation of Saul (his Jewish name)—or Paul (his primary secular name)—took place within a few years of Jesus' resurrection, but this sort of chronology suggests that we know very little of what happened to him for the next decade or so. It also places the main (undisputed) letters basically within the decade of the 50s. Depicted in Acts 13–21 as three mission trips, this period started with ministry in the region or province of Galatia (central Turkey). It then focused on the Roman provinces of Asia (western Turkey), Macedonia (northern Greece), and Achaia (southern Greece), all of which border the Aegean Sea (hence some call this period of Paul's life the Aegean mission). If Paul wrote some or all of the disputed letters, they would probably date from the 60s. (If he did not, some could derive from the late 60s to the 80s, and some from even later decades.)

From Persecutor to Apostle

According to both Acts and the Pauline letters, Paul was a Pharisee (Acts 23:6; 26:5; Phil 3:5), a devotee of the Jewish law, who persecuted the Jesus-as-Messiah movement (e.g., Acts 8:1–3; 9:1–5; 1 Cor 15:9; Gal 1:13–14, 23; Phil 3:6; 1 Tim 1:13). For reasons that are not completely clear, he found the movement, which he later called "the church of God," or the "assembly [Gk. *ekklēsia*] of God" (e.g., 1 Cor 15:9; Gal 1:13), to be both a threat to the law that Pharisees were committed to promote and a threat to the people of the covenant who were guided by that law.

It may have been the movement's message of a crucified Messiah, its relaxed attitude to the Jewish law, or both (and more) that led Saul/Paul to want to "destroy" the church (Gal 1:13)—to seek its demise. It is highly likely that Paul found a mentor for his particular form of sacred violence in the ancient figure of Phinehas (Num 25:6–13; Ps 106:30–31), who had killed an Israelite man and

7

his Midianite consort, thus ending God's wrath against Israel's idolatry and impurity. (This does not mean Paul actually committed murder.)

Again, both Acts and the Pauline letters relate (from different perspectives and with different details) Paul's unexpected encounter with the resurrected Jesus while in the midst of his persecuting activity: Jesus appeared to him (1 Cor 9:1; 15:8; Gal 1:15–16). This event took place, according to Acts 9 (retold in chs. 22 and 26), on the road to Damascus. It is generally known as Paul's conversion.

Many recent scholars, however, prefer to call the experience Paul's "call," since Paul did not cease being a Jew; he did not convert from Judaism to Christianity when he joined the Jesus-as-Messiah movement. Paul himself describes the experience as a prophetic call, echoing call narratives in Jeremiah and Isaiah (Gal 1:15–16; Jer 1:4–8; Isa 49:5–6). Nevertheless, if we define "conversion" as a radical transformation in belief, belonging, and behavior, then certainly Paul's call was also a conversion, as he himself implies (Phil 3:3–14). The initiative in this call/conversion was clearly not Paul's; Christ "took hold" of him (Phil 3:12 NJB).

Moreover, Paul's call/conversion was also a commission, a charge to preach the good news about Jesus as Messiah and Lord among the nations, or gentiles (the Greek word *ethnē* can mean either).[2] He was appointed an apostle, one sent with the authority of the sender. By virtue of God's grace, Paul believed, the former persecutor had been granted the privilege of seeing the resurrected Jesus and being called to apostleship (Rom 1:5; 1 Cor 15:9–10; Gal 1:15–17; Eph 3:7–8).

Some of the Hebrew prophets had promised a coming day in which YHWH's salvation would extend to the nations (e.g., Isa 2:2; 42:6; 49:6). Paul apparently saw the fulfillment of that promise above all in the ministry given to him and his colleagues. Although Paul's focus was to be the gentiles, the gospel was for both Jew and gentile (Rom 1:16–17). According to Acts, Paul frequently began his ministry in the synagogue, where he no doubt hoped to convince both Jews and Godfearers, gentiles who had affiliated with Judaism but had not become fully Jewish (i.e., for men, by circumcision). This meant, ironically, that Paul was sometimes rejected, and even persecuted, by his own people (e.g., Acts 17:1–9; 2 Cor 11:24–26).

Paul's life as an apostle was one of proclaiming the gospel by word and deed in unevangelized cities, which then served as epicenters of the gospel. Traveling on foot and by ship with co-workers, he was founder and then shepherd—often

---

2. See Acts 9:10–16; 13:47; Rom 1:5; 15:15–21; 16:26; Gal 1:16; 2:1–10; Eph 3:1, 8; 1 Tim 2:7; 3:16; 2 Tim 4:17.

from a distance—of a network of small communities of Christ-followers whose mission was to bear witness to the lordship of Jesus in their city and beyond. Each community, or assembly, met in a house, or perhaps occasionally in a workshop or tavern. The house church(es) in each city consisted of men and women, slaves and free, rich and poor, gentiles (mostly) and Jews (Gal 3:28).[3]

In order to imitate Christ's own self-emptying love, and to keep from being a burden to others, Paul worked with his hands as a tentmaker or leather worker (1 Cor 9:3–18; 1 Thess 2:9; 2 Thess 3:7–9; Acts 18:3). His apostolic life resembled Christ's in multiple ways, as he regularly suffered physical pain and deprivation, emotional distress, political torture, and imprisonment (Rom 8:35; 1 Cor 4:8–13; 2 Cor 4:7–12; 6:3–10; 11:23–33; 12:10). Paul's life became one of getting into what the late US congressman and civil rights activist John Lewis called "good trouble."

Paul the Letter-Writer

Paul's apostolic ministry meant he had ongoing concern for the churches he founded, as well as for other communities to which he was connected via associates, both men and women. In addition to occasional visits, Paul wrote letters in Greek (the common tongue in the Roman Empire) as a form of ongoing communal spiritual formation, pastoral care, and apostleship in absentia—sometimes even from jail (not unlike other political prisoners). As a self-described apostle, father figure, and mother figure (all at the same time), he corresponded expecting his addressees to read his letters aloud in the assembly and heed them.[4] Not everyone wanted to follow Paul, however, for he had opponents—who are often in view as he writes.

The New Testament contains thirteen letters bearing Paul's name. (Hebrews does not name its author, but it is almost certainly not by Paul despite its frequent association with him since the early years of the church.) Each letter is distinctive in terms of the situation addressed, rhetorical strategy employed, and theological content conveyed. As noted above, seven of the thirteen are sufficiently similar to one another to be called the undisputed, or uncontested, letters, meaning that scholars almost universally agree that Paul authored them: Romans (the longest), 1–2 Corinthians, Galatians, Philippians, 1 Thessalonians (probably the earliest, ca. 51), and Philemon.

---

3. It should be noted that a "house" could have been anything from tenement housing (Lat. *insulae*) to villas.

4. For Paul's maternal dimension, see 1 Cor 3:1–3; Gal 4:18–19; 1 Thess 2:5–8.

To many scholars, the other six seem to reflect a situation, style, or substance that does not correspond to the historical Paul of the undisputed letters. These letters—2 Thessalonians, Colossians and Ephesians, and the Pastoral Epistles (1–2 Timothy, Titus)—may have been written by friends or disciples in Paul's name to adapt his teachings to new situations.

There is, however, ongoing debate about which letters, if any, are authored by someone other than Paul. Although this is not the place to discuss the question of authorship in depth, it is important to note that the notion of *authorship* in antiquity covered a broad range of practices, including the use of secretaries, who sometimes had considerable freedom. Moreover, Paul's theology likely developed somewhat over time, and his pastoral approach varied from congregation to congregation. These factors, rather than non-Pauline authorship, may account for some of the unique features of the six contested letters.[5]

PAUL'S THEOLOGY AND SPIRITUALITY

Paul understood his message—his "gospel," or good news—to be the power of God at work in the world for the salvation of all people (Rom 1:16–17). This gospel was in continuity with the good news promised and proclaimed by Israel's prophets, and then taught and embodied by Jesus. Paul's gospel—what he called "the gospel of God" (Rom 1:1; 15:16; 1 Thess 2:2, 8–9)—also stood in stark contrast to the Roman "gospel" of peace and salvation promised by the empire and proclaimed by those who perceived in Augustus and his successors the means to human flourishing.

The gospel Paul announced, which he paradoxically received both by divine revelation (Gal 1:11–12) and from those before him (1 Cor 15:3–4), focused on the crucifixion and resurrection of Jesus as being God's saving act of faithfulness to Israel and mercy to all. Paul proclaimed this surprising gospel of a crucified Messiah (1 Cor 1:18–2:5) as God's apocalyptic (revelatory) and eschatological (end-time) act that brought about the prophetically promised new exodus, new covenant, new creation, and new age—the age of the Spirit.[6] Thus, N. T. Wright has rightly claimed that Paul's theology is a reconfiguration of Jewish theology in light of the Messiah and the Spirit.[7]

5. For Romans, Paul employed a scribe named Tertius (Rom 16:22), yet the letter's content is almost certainly thoroughly Paul's own.

6. Paul does not frequently use the precise phrase "new . . . ," but it is nonetheless clear that he sees these prophetic visions fulfilled or inaugurated through Christ. For "new creation," see 2 Cor 5:17; Gal 6:15. For "new covenant," see 1 Cor 11:25; 2 Cor 3:6.

7. See N. T. Wright, *Paul: In Fresh Perspective* (Minneapolis: Fortress, 2005); *Paul and the Faithfulness of God* (Minneapolis: Fortress, 2013).

Scholars have debated how best to organize this theology; what, if anything, is at its center; and whether and how it developed over time. In this introduction, we will take a narrative approach, laying out the reshaped scriptural story of salvation Paul tells and how people are incorporated into it. Romans will figure prominently, but not exclusively. As we consider this story, it is critical to remember that Paul was not an armchair theologian; he was always concerned about the real-life implications of the gospel. In the words of Scot McKnight, "pastor Paul" had one main goal: forming communities of "Christoformity," or Christlikeness.[8] The gospel is something to obey, not just accept; to "become" (in the sense of embody), not just believe. We should read, study, teach, and preach Paul's letters, including Romans, today for the same purposes.

Human Condition, Divine Response

According to Paul the faithful Jew, the one true Creator God chose Israel to be the covenant people and thus the vehicle of divine blessing among the nations (gentiles). This God is an impartial judge who expects obedience from all people, whether through the law of Moses or through the unwritten law inscribed on human hearts (Rom 2:14–16). However, like the prophets, Paul believes that God finds Israel faithless and disobedient, and the gentiles idolatrous and immoral (Rom 1:18–3:20). God has therefore promised to establish a new, effective covenant with Israel (Jer 31:31–34; cf. 1 Cor 11:25; 2 Cor. 3:6), and thus with and for all people, because Israel was called to be the source of blessing for all nations.

Paul characterizes the human condition as one marked by both sins (or transgressions) and Sin, a cosmic power that holds humanity captive (Rom 1:18–3:20). Being under the power of Sin is like having an addiction that manifests itself in concrete acts. Without an intervention, the result is death, both a living death in the present and a future, permanent separation from God. Death itself, then, is also a power.

Human beings need a solution that deals with both: forgiveness for sins and liberation (redemption) from Sin—both an act of atonement and a new exodus. Only such a solution will restore them to full and abundant life (cf. John 10:10), to right covenant relations with God and others: love of God and love of neighbor. The law of Moses, despite its divine origin, cannot bring about this abundant life (Rom 3:20; 4:13; 5:12–21; 7:7–8:4; Gal 3:21).

8. Scot McKnight, *Pastor Paul: Nurturing a Culture of Christoformity in the Church* (Grand Rapids: Baker Academic, 2019).

In faithfulness to Israel and mercy to the gentiles, God has acted in righteousness, that is, with saving restorative justice, by sending Jesus the Jewish Messiah ("Son of God"), to effect salvation via his death and resurrection (known later, especially among Roman Catholics, as the "paschal mystery"—a wonderful term for all Christians).

The Death and Resurrection of Jesus

The death of Jesus the Messiah by crucifixion—Rome's most degrading and shameful form of capital punishment—has rich and varied meaning for Paul. We can think of it in terms of four "Rs."

First of all, it is *revelatory*. It manifests the incarnate Son of God's faithful obedience to the Father and his freely chosen self-giving love for humanity (Rom 8:35–37; Phil 2:5–8; 2 Cor 5:14; Gal 2:20). It also discloses the Father's faithfulness and love, as well as God's counterintuitive and countercultural power and wisdom (Rom 5:1–11; 8:32, 39; 1 Cor 1:18–31). That is, the death of Jesus is both a Christophany (revelation of Christ) and a theophany (revelation of God).

Second, Jesus' death is *representative*. He dies as the faithful, obedient representative of God's covenant people and the single representative of all human beings. He is the second Adam, whose actions contrast with and counteract those of Adam (Rom 5:12–21). In his death, Jesus is the paradigmatic human, faithful to God and loving toward others. Moreover, Jesus dies not only as humanity's representative but also in their place and for their sins (Rom 5:8; 1 Cor 15:3; 2 Cor 5:14–15; Gal 1:4), fulfilling the role of Isaiah's suffering servant (Isa 52:13–53:12).

Third, Jesus' death is *redemptive*. Jesus died both to forgive sins and to liberate from the power of Sin (Rom 3:21–26). At the same time, as Paul knew from Scripture, it is the God of Israel who is the redeemer and liberator of the people of God. Jesus' death is ultimately an act of God.

Finally, Jesus' death, as an act of both God and God's Messiah, brings about human *reconciliation* with God (Rom 5:1–11; 2 Cor 5:11–21). In Christ's death, God has acted to restore humanity to that for which it was created: to right relations with God and others—to life! In doing so, God has kept the promise to Abraham that all the nations would be blessed through him (Gal 3:6–14). Above all, the death of Christ is God's act of amazing grace toward those who are God's enemies: sinful, rebellious people, unworthy of such love (Rom 5:1–11).

The death of Jesus is not a saving event, however, without the resurrection. The resurrection is God's act of vindicating and validating Jesus' death. Without it, Jesus is simply another crucified victim and would-be messiah whose death reveals Rome's victory, not God's. Without it, there is no forgiveness of sins, no eternal life, indeed no purpose to life other than hedonistic pleasure (1 Cor 15:12–34).

Although Paul can resolve to know nothing but a crucified Messiah (1 Cor 2:2), he also wants everyone to recognize that the crucified Jesus is now the resurrected and exalted Lord who lives in and among his people by his Spirit, infusing his life into his body. At the same time, the exalted Lord always remains the crucified Jesus, whose resurrection power is, ironically, cruciform (cross-shaped). It is *that* kind of power that Jesus conveys to his people as the Lord: the power of humble love and self-giving service. The resurrection means that human beings can participate in the life of God manifested in Jesus the Son—both now and eternally.

Jesus as Lord and the Gift of the Spirit

When Paul speaks of Jesus as "Lord," which he understands as the most basic affirmation of faith in the gospel (1 Cor 12:3), he once again means several things.

First, Jesus has been exalted to a position of participation in God's sovereignty, sharing the divine name, "Lord" (Gk. *kyrios*), and thus in the divine identity (Phil 2:9–11, interpreting Isa 45:23). Second, Jesus is the one on whom people must call for salvation (Rom 10:5–13, interpreting Joel 2:32[3:5]). Third, Jesus is worthy of obedience. To call on him and confess him as Lord means to pledge allegiance to him, to his way of faithfulness and love. Fourth, to name Jesus as Lord is to reject all other lords and gods and any participation in them (1 Cor 10). If Jesus is Lord, Caesar is not (as N. T. Wright has repeatedly put it), and neither is any other person or entity claiming rulership of the world, ultimate devotion, or both. And finally, to affirm the lordship of Jesus is to allow the shape of his life to become the shape of ours.

God's action in the death, resurrection, and exaltation of the Lord Jesus is the climax in history of God's promises to Israel (2 Cor 1:20). In him (to repeat for emphasis), the new exodus, covenant, age, and creation promised by the biblical prophets have been inaugurated, though in an utterly surprising way: via a crucified Messiah. Much Jewish thought at the time of Paul may be called *apocalyptic*, which is another term with many meanings. At the very least, however, it means that many Jews saw themselves as living in this age while anticipating the age to come. This age is characterized by sin, oppression, and injustice, while the age to come will be a time of righteousness, justice, and peace (Heb. *šālôm*, or shalom)—and these will be radically different from the righteousness, justice, and peace offered by the Roman Empire through its oppression and subjugation.

In Christ, Paul boldly claims, the new age has begun, but it is not yet here in its fullness. God's gift of the Holy Spirit—who is the Spirit of both the Father and the Son (Rom 8:9)—is at once the presence of God among the people of the Messiah and the promise of the fullness to come (2 Cor 1:22; 5:5; Eph 1:13–14). Scholars sometimes refer to this interim period, between Jesus' death/resurrection and his second coming (Gk. *parousia*), as the *overlap of the ages*. It is a time of *now but not yet*.

God's saving work will come to its ultimate conclusion, or telos, at the parousia. This does not mean either the removal of the church from this world (as in the popular notion of the rapture) or the destruction of the world. Rather, the parousia signals a series of eschatological events, including the resurrection of the dead, the final judgment, and the defeat of humanity's final enemy, Death (1 Cor 15:20–57; 1 Thess 4:13–18). It also signals the restoration of the entire cosmos to the wholeness intended by God (Rom 8:18–25; Col 1:15–20).

Human Response to the Gospel

We have thus far summarized Paul's understanding of God's redemptive action in Christ. Life comes to the spiritually dead only when there is a transformation—a resurrection, or revivification, as the prophet Ezekiel made clear (Ezek 37). But this grace and life do not convey automatically to human beings; there must be a response to the gospel of Christ crucified and raised.

For Paul (as today we say about real estate), location is everything. He understands humanity's sinful condition as being "in," or under the power of, Sin and thus being outside Christ and his sovereignty. When the gospel is proclaimed, the appropriate human response, enabled by God's grace, is twofold: faith and baptism. When faith and baptism occur, a person is brought from being outside Christ to being in Christ. Being "in Christ," Paul's basic term for what we would call being a Christian, means to be located within the resurrected Messiah by being in his body, the community or assembly of Christ-followers, and therefore under his lordship.

In both faith and baptism (which probably occurred right after the public confession of faith), people begin a lifelong participation in Christ and his story by dying and rising with him (Gal 2:15–21; Rom 6:1–11). That is, to believe the gospel is to share existentially in God's saving act—Christ's death and resurrection, by which a person dies to an old way of life (which was, actually, a way of death) and is raised to new life. Belief entails participation in that saving event; participation entails devotion to Christ the Lord; and devotion entails obedience. In Romans, Paul refers to all of this as the "obedience of faith" (Rom 1:5; 16:26), or what we might call believing allegiance.

Those who believe the gospel and are baptized into Christ the Lord undergo a transformation—a metamorphosis—that Paul describes in many ways: they are, for instance, washed, justified, and sanctified (1 Cor 6:11). That is, they are forgiven of their sins (washed), restored to right covenant relations with God in the midst of God's people (justified), and set apart to live as part of God's covenant people (sanctified).

This is not a series of spiritual experiences but a unified act of God, who does the washing, justifying, and sanctifying. This transformation occurs, then, not by virtue of anyone's status or good deeds but only by God's grace and the response of faith described above (Rom 3:27–31; 4:1–25; Gal 2:15–21; Eph 2:1–10). Paul was fully aware of his own unworthiness and of God's mercy (1 Cor 15:8–10; Gal 1:11–16; 1 Tim 1:12–17)—and we should be too.

Believers, the faithful,[9] are now part of a new creation, remade for lives of righteousness, or godly justice (2 Cor 5:14–21). They (we!) are called to leave behind idolatry, immorality, and injustice to experience the abundant life for which we were created. We are now in relationship with one God in three persons, as Christian theology would learn to say; we are

- children of God the Father ("*Abba*"; Rom 8:15; Gal 4:6);
- members of Christ and his body (1 Cor 6:15; 12:12–31), the "church" (*ekklēsia*) or "assembly of those in Christ"; and
- the temple of the Holy Spirit, both individually and corporately (1 Cor 3:16–17; 6:19).

This relational matrix is one of many dimensions of Paul's incipient Trinitarian theology—the conviction that God exists as one being in three persons.

The Holy Spirit supplies gifts for the *ekklēsia*'s common good (Rom 12:4–8; 1 Cor 12; Eph 4:7–16); produces "fruit," or Christlike virtues (Gal 5:16–26); and unites the community in faith, hope, and love (1 Cor 13:13; Gal 5:5–6; 1 Thess 1:3; 5:8) for faithful witness even in the face of opposition (e.g., Phil 1:3–2:18). The *ekklēsia* is a new family of brothers and sisters: male and female, slave and free, gentile and Jew (Gal 3:25–28). According to N. T. Wright, Paul

9. I will use these terms interchangeably, along with "Christians."

saw the church as a microcosmos, a little world, not simply as an alternative to the present one, an escapist's country cottage for those tired of city life, but as the prototype of what was to come . . . [when] the whole earth [would be filled] with his knowledge and glory, with his justice, peace and joy. Paul sees each *ekklēsia* as a sign of that future reality.[10]

Paul's Spirituality

Paul's spirituality, as we have already been seeing, is one of *participation* (location) and *transformation* (metamorphosis), both individual and corporate. Those who have died with Christ and have been raised with him to new life are also inhabited by him, that is, by the Spirit.

This is a relationship of *mutual indwelling*, or reciprocal residence: Christ/the Spirit inhabits us, and we inhabit Christ/the Spirit. This is true of both the *ekklēsia* as a community and each baptized individual (Gal 2:19–20; Rom 8:5–17). Paul refers to the resulting relationship in Greek as *koinōnia* with both the Lord and one another—communion, partnership, solidarity (1 Cor 1:9; 10:16; Phil 1:5; 2:1; 3:10). This *koinōnia* should come to special expression at the Lord's Supper (1 Cor 10:16–22; 11:17–34; later called the Eucharist, "thanksgiving"). The Lord's Supper is not specifically mentioned in Romans, though some interpreters believe it is part of the issue addressed in Rom 14:1–15:13.

For Paul, the indwelling Christ is the one who lovingly gave himself on the cross. This means that Christ-filled individuals and communities will be characterized by a cross-shaped existence, or *cruciformity*. Cruciformity, which expresses the "mind of Christ" (Phil 2:5), means especially a life of self-giving love that looks out for the needs of others rather than oneself—precisely what Christ did in his incarnation and crucifixion (Phil 2:1–11). Because this cross-shaped life conforms to the story of Christ, it can be described as a *narrative* spirituality and a narrative form of participation.

This transformation of thought and action, of mind and body (Rom 12:1–2) into Christlikeness is possible only by the activity of the Holy Spirit (Gal 5:13–26; 2 Cor 3:17–18) and only in a community of mutual instruction and care. Paul refers to all believers as "saints" or "holy ones" (depending on the Bible translation). His goal is for each individual and community in Christ to become holy (conformed to Christ) in anticipation of the final judgment (1 Thess 3:13; 5:23; 1 Cor 1:8).

10. Wright, *Paul and the Faithfulness of God*, 1492.

Holiness, then, is not reserved for a special class of saints but is for all. It means being set apart for God's purposes. Holiness is therefore the lifestyle of an alternative culture to that of the dominant culture (for Paul, the culture of Rome; for us, the dominant culture of the US or wherever we live), the culture of those who do not know God (1 Thess 4:5). Holiness means knowing Christ by sharing both in his death and in the power of his resurrection (Phil 3:10–14), thus participating in, and extending, God's saving mission.

CONCLUSION

As an apostle, Paul was simultaneously a community founder, a pastor, a spiritual guide or director, and a theologian—a pastoral theologian. At the end, moreover, he was probably a martyr who died at Rome in the 60s. In death as in life, his motto was, to paraphrase Phil 3:8–10, "I want to know Christ and be found in him." It is a motto for all times and places, for all Christians.

REFLECTIONS AND QUESTIONS FOR THE INTRODUCTION TO PAUL

Spiritual, Pastoral, and Theological Reflections

1. Paul was **simultaneously a pastor, a spiritual guide or director, and a theologian (and more)**. This multifaceted ministerial identity is worthy of study for those who fulfill any of those roles today, when the vocational complexity we see in Paul is often fragmented. He was also, obviously, a deeply spiritual person who saw his life and ministry as an offering to God, in Christ, enabled by the Spirit.

2. As a pastor, Paul is worthy of study because he carefully **addresses the concrete needs** of the communities to which he writes with the promises and demands of the gospel.

3. As a spiritual guide or director, Paul is worthy of study inasmuch as his goal is the **transformation and formation of individuals and communities** into the likeness of the faithful and loving Messiah Jesus.

4. As a (pastoral) theologian, Paul is worthy of study with respect to his being **both faithful to Scripture and creative** in interpreting it in light of the coming, death, and resurrection of Jesus—and applying that interpretation with contextual sensitivity to a variety of situations.

5. As a Christian, Paul is worthy of study because of his **profound sense of being in Christ and having Christ within**, which means a life guided by the Spirit in

daily worship of God and participation in God's mission, not as a lone ranger, but as part of the body of Christ.

Questions for Those Who Read, Teach, and Preach

1. With which big ideas has Paul been associated in your experience and, as far as you know, in the history of the church? Are they similar to or different from those discussed in this introduction? What presuppositions about Paul do you (or do those to whom you minister through teaching or preaching) bring to the study of Paul and of Romans?

2. What new information or perspectives about Paul did this introduction provide? How did you react to some of these? If you preach or teach, what challenges might you face in talking about these (or other) perspectives on the apostle offered here?

3. What is the historical and theological importance of understanding Paul's transformative experience as an appearance of Jesus? As a call and commission? As a conversion?

4. Which aspects of Paul's theology and spirituality do you find to be particularly significant in your context?

FOR FURTHER READING

Highly Accessible Books

Barclay, John M. G. *Paul: A Very Brief History*. London: SPCK, 2017.
———. *Paul and the Subversive Power of Grace*. Cambridge: Grove Books, 2016.
Burnett, Gary W. *Paul Distilled*. Eugene, OR: Wipf and Stock, 2021.
deSilva, David. *Transformation: The Heart of Paul's Gospel*. Bellingham, WA: Lexham, 2014.
Gorman, Michael J. *Participation: Paul's Vision of Life in Christ*. Cambridge: Grove Books, 2018.
———. *Reading Paul*. Eugene, OR: Cascade, 2008.
Kirk, J. R. Daniel. *Jesus Have I Loved, but Paul? A Narrative Approach to the Problem of Pauline Christianity*. Grand Rapids: Baker Academic, 2011.
Macaskill, Grant. *Living in Union with Christ: Paul's Gospel and Christian Moral Identity*. Grand Rapids: Baker Academic, 2019.
McKnight, Scot. *Pastor Paul: Nurturing a Culture of Christoformity in the Church*. Grand Rapids: Baker Academic, 2019.
Wright, N. T. *Paul: A Biography*. New York: HarperCollins, 2018.

Midlevel Books

Barclay, John M. G. *Paul and the Power of Grace*. Grand Rapids: Eerdmans, 2020.

Bowens, Lisa M. *African American Readings of Paul: Reception, Resistance, and Transformation*. Grand Rapids: Eerdmans, 2020.

Burroughs, Presian R., ed. *Practicing with Paul: Reflections on Paul and the Practice of Ministry in Honor of Susan G. Eastman*. Eugene, OR: Cascade, 2018.

Campbell, Douglas A. *Paul: An Apostle's Journey*. Grand Rapids: Eerdmans, 2018.

———. *Pauline Dogmatics: The Triumph of God's Love*. Grand Rapids: Eerdmans, 2020.

Fredriksen, Paula. *Paul: The Pagans' Apostle*. New Haven: Yale University Press, 2017.

Gorman, Michael J. *Apostle of the Crucified Lord: A Theological Introduction to Paul and His Letters*. 2nd ed. Grand Rapids: Eerdmans, 2017 (orig. 2004).

———. *Becoming the Gospel: Paul, Participation, and Mission*. Grand Rapids: Eerdmans, 2015.

———. *Cruciformity: Paul's Narrative Spirituality of the Cross*. Grand Rapids: Eerdmans, 2001.

Hill, Wesley. *Paul and the Trinity: Persons, Relations, and the Pauline Letters*. Grand Rapids: Eerdmans, 2015.

Longenecker, Bruce W., ed. *The New Cambridge Companion to St. Paul*. New York: Cambridge University Press, 2020.

Longenecker, Bruce W., and Todd D. Still. *Thinking through Paul: A Survey of His Life, Letters, and Theology*. Grand Rapids: Zondervan, 2014.

Matera, Frank J. *God's Saving Grace: A Pauline Theology*. Grand Rapids: Eerdmans, 2012.

McKnight, Scot, Lynn Cohick, and Nijay K. Gupta, eds. *Dictionary of Paul and His Letters*. 2nd ed. Downers Grove, IL: IVP Academic, 2022.

McKnight, Scot, and B. J. Oropeza. *Perspectives on Paul: Five Views*. Grand Rapids: Baker Academic, 2020.

Murphy-O'Connor, Jerome. *Paul: His Story*. New York: Oxford University Press, 2004.

Pitre, Brant, Michael P. Barber, and John A. Kincaid. *Paul: A New Covenant Jew: Rethinking Pauline Theology*. Grand Rapids: Eerdmans, 2019.

Reeves, Rodney. *Spirituality according to Paul: Imitating the Apostle of Christ*. Downers Grove, IL: InterVarsity, 2011.

Sanders, E. P. *Paul: The Apostle's Life, Letters, and Thought*. Minneapolis: Fortress, 2015.

Schnelle, Udo. *Apostle Paul: His Life and Theology*. Translated by M. Eugene Boring. Grand Rapids: Baker Academic, 2005.

Westerholm, Stephen, ed. *The Blackwell Companion to Paul*. Malden, MA: Blackwell, 2011.

Witherup, Ronald D. *101 Questions and Answers on Paul*. Mahwah, NJ: Paulist, 2003.

Wright, N. T. *Paul: In Fresh Perspective*. Minneapolis: Fortress, 2005.

More Technical Works

Barclay, John M. G. *Paul and the Gift*. Grand Rapids: Eerdmans, 2015.

Campbell, Douglas A. *The Deliverance of God: An Apocalyptic Rereading of Justification*. Grand Rapids: Eerdmans, 2009.

Dunn, James D. G. *The Theology of Paul the Apostle*. Grand Rapids: Eerdmans, 1998.

Gorman, Michael J. *Inhabiting the Cruciform God: Kenosis, Justification, and Theosis in Paul's Narrative Soteriology*. Grand Rapids: Eerdmans, 2009.

————. *Participating in Christ: Explorations in Paul's Theology and Spirituality*. Grand Rapids: Baker Academic, 2019.

Hays, Richard B. *Echoes of Scripture in the Letters of Paul*. New Haven: Yale University Press, 1989.

Johnson, Luke Timothy. *Constructing Paul*. Grand Rapids: Eerdmans, 2020.

Schnelle, Udo. *Apostle Paul: His Life and Theology*. Translated by M. Eugene Boring. Grand Rapids: Baker Academic, 2005.

Thate, Michael J., Kevin J. Vanhoozer, and Constantine R. Campbell, eds. *"In Christ" in Paul: Explorations in Paul's Theology of Union and Participation*. Grand Rapids: Eerdmans, 2018.

Wright, N. T. *Paul and the Faithfulness of God*. Minneapolis: Fortress, 2013.

Introducing Romans

L etters have played an important role in human life and culture for thousands of years. They have always been highly significant for the Christian faith. Most of the New Testament documents are letters, and many early church fathers wrote letters. Jumping across the centuries to more contemporary times, we cannot overestimate the impact of letters by Dietrich Bonhoeffer, C. S. Lewis (whose letters are both real and imaginary—*The Screwtape Letters*), and the Rev. Dr. Martin Luther King Jr. Furthermore, popes, bishops, pastors, and other church leaders continue to pen significant letters.

Paul's letter to the Romans is arguably the most influential letter ever written. It is certainly the most significant letter in the history of Christianity. It has spawned conversions, doctrines, disputations, and even a few reformations, and it has done so quite ecumenically and with a kind of domino effect. Here's what I mean:

- A text from Romans (13:13–14) provoked the conversion of Augustine as he picked up a Bible and opened to that page of Paul's letter.
- An Augustinian monk named Martin Luther had his theological furniture rearranged by reading Romans ("the chief part of the New Testament . . . the purest gospel"), which caused him to feel "reborn."[1]
- An Anglican priest called John Wesley, later to become the founder of Methodism, felt his heart "strangely warmed" in a church on Aldersgate Street in Oxford after hearing a reading of Luther's preface to Romans.

---

1. Martin Luther, "Preface to the Epistle of Saint Paul to the Romans," available in various editions.

There is more:

- A Swiss theologian named Karl Barth in the early twentieth century inaugurated a theological revival by dropping a bombshell on the playground of the liberal theologians (as someone has said)—with a commentary on Romans.
- The renewal of interest in Paul and Romans has sparked endless ecumenical conversations about faith and works, resulting in significant theological convergence and a joint 1999 Roman Catholic–Lutheran "Declaration on the Doctrine of Justification," later signed or commended by other global Christian bodies.
- The same Pauline letter has recently provoked various interpreters to offer strongly political, postcolonial, and peace-oriented readings that challenge empires both ancient and modern.

What should we conclude about reading Romans in light of all this? The reader (and commentator!) ought to approach this document with a mixture of anticipation and trepidation.

How and why has one letter made such an impact? That is a difficult, if not impossible, question to answer. The most obvious reply cites the theological breadth and depth of the document. In 1521, Martin Luther's colleague Melanchthon called Romans "a compendium of Christian doctrine," and it has often functioned as such.[2] It is certainly a very *long* document for a letter—more than seven thousand words.

Nevertheless, this traditional theological approach to Romans has been strongly questioned in recent decades. Augustine and Luther, it is often said, misread Romans, and perhaps, to some extent, they did. But who has not misread this very complex document? It is certainly the case that the letter is in fact *occasional*—that is, it was prompted by a specific situation in the house churches of Rome Paul addresses because the Roman faithful were real people with real problems. At the same time, Romans is also undeniably Paul's most systematic presentation of the gospel he proclaims—which he refers to as *God's* gospel. In fact, as we will see, its occasional and its systematic character are logically interconnected.

---

2. Philipp Melanchthon, *The Loci Communes of Philipp Melanchthon*, trans. C. L. Hill (Boston: Meador, 1944), 69, cited in Robert L. Plummer, "Melanchthon as Interpreter of the New Testament," *Westminster Theological Journal* 62 (2000): 257–65 (here 258). Plummer points out, however, that Melanchthon did not think Romans was actually a comprehensive systematic theology; it was a real letter outlining the main aspects of salvation.

Whatever its historical origins and specific contexts, Romans is truly a letter for all seasons. *If John is the gospel of life, Romans is the epistle of life.* It proclaims to us the gift of new life, narrating the saving grace of God toward sinful humanity, both Jews and gentiles. This grace creates, in Christ, a multicultural, cruciform (cross-shaped) community of obedient faith issuing in generous love and expectant hope. And that is just about the highest calling any letter by any Christian author can fulfill.

THE STORY BEHIND THE LETTER

When Paul wrote to the Roman believers from Corinth, sometime between AD 55 and 58 (probably in the winter or early spring of 55–56 or 56–57), he had never visited their city despite good intentions to do so (1:8–15; 15:14–33).[3] There had likely been assemblies of faithful Jesus-followers in the imperial hub that was Rome for a decade or more, perhaps even from the earliest days of the church, as especially Jewish believers traveled between Jerusalem and Rome (see Acts 2:10). As the gospel spread throughout the empire, believers of various backgrounds would have moved in and out of cosmopolitan Rome.

Although there are hints about the Christian community, or communities, in Rome throughout the letter, we are not given much explicit information until the last major section of the letter (chs. 12–16), and particularly in chapters 14–16. Chapter 16 names one specific house church (16:5) and infers the existence of others (see 16:10, 11, 14, 15).[4]

From chapter 16 we also learn that Paul knew some of the Roman faithful; the list of nearly thirty people in that chapter is impressive, including Paul's beloved, courageous co-workers from earlier times in Corinth, Priscilla (Prisca) and Aquila (16:3–4). Perhaps (and this is just an educated guess) Paul knew 10 to 15 percent of the believers in various house churches. Nonetheless, he was clearly not the churches' spiritual father. So why did Paul write this lengthy letter?

---

3. The precise date of Romans within this period is disputed but not generally held to be of great consequence. The correlation of Paul's travel plans, people's names (Phoebe, Gaius, and Erastus), and related data from Romans (15:25–26; 16:1–2, 23 [cf. 2 Tim 4:20]), 1 Corinthians (1:14), and Acts (19:22; 20:1–3) makes it virtually certain that Corinth (or its vicinity) was the place of composition.

4. Romans 16:10 and 16:11 imply households (see NIV, CEB, NET, NJB), while 16:14 and 16:15 imply small communities that are not members of a household. Some recent scholarship suggests that early Christian congregations may have met not only in houses of various sorts (from tenement apartments to villas) but also in workshops, in restaurants and taverns, in rented halls or other spaces, and even outdoors.

Reasons for Romans

The reasons-for-Romans debate is one of the longest and most complex within modern biblical scholarship. One scholar, Michael Bird, names several major proposals about the letter's purpose:[5]

1. a theological treatise
2. a summary of Paul's teaching
3. a letter of introduction to the multicultural churches in Rome[6]
4. a plea for support of his mission (i.e., a fundraising letter)
5. an effort at bringing unity to the Roman churches
6. an attempt to unify Christians and (non-Christian) Jews in Rome

Michael Bird's discussion concludes, as the present commentary will begin, by proposing an "eclectic" view of the purpose(s) of Romans. To such a proposal we now turn.

Paul's addressees were obviously in Rome. The significance of Rome as the capital of the empire may have been one factor in the letter's composition (see further below), but certainly not the only one, and probably not the most important. More substantive answers to the question *Why?* relate obviously to the situation of the house churches in Rome, the contents of the letter itself, and Paul's mission work.

A possible key to the letter may be the likelihood of some friction between gentile and Jewish believers in Rome. Many scholars think—though some, it must be mentioned, forcefully disagree—that something like the following scenario occurred in Rome in the years prior to Paul's writing of Romans:

- In AD 49 an edict of Claudius expelled the Jews, or at least some of them, from Rome because of their fighting about one *Chrestus*. This is in all likelihood an allusion to intra-Jewish debate over the identity and role of the Jewish Messiah and, perhaps, whether Jesus was the expected one. (For the edict, see the Roman historian Suetonius, *Claudius* 25.4 and Acts 18:2.)
- With the lack of Jewish believers for five years, gentiles temporarily consti-

5. See Michael F. Bird, "The Letter to the Romans," in *All Things to All Cultures: Paul among Jews, Greeks, and Romans*, ed. Mark Harding and Alanna Nobbs (Grand Rapids: Eerdmans, 2013), 177–204, esp. 183–92.

6. Focusing on this reason has led some to call Romans an "ambassadorial letter"—a letter of apostolic credentials—and may be closely connected to the next reason (fundraising).

tuted the bulk, if not the entirety, of the Roman churches, developing their
leadership, mission, and theology.

- Upon the death of Claudius and the return of the Jews to Rome, the gentile-
dominated churches were now poised for multicultural conflict as Jewish
believers tried to reconnect with their gentile siblings in faith.

- Gentile believers could have developed something of an independent spirit,
if not a superiority complex, while Jewish believers could now feel neglected
or marginalized. Differences in beliefs and practices would have likely quickly
emerged. Was unity possible? Necessary? Had the expulsion of the Jews been
some sort of divine judgment?

- The reality of this divergence and resulting tension is described by Paul in
Rom 14 and 15: Jewish believers (and perhaps more conservative gentiles)
and gentile believers (as well as more liberal Jews) are judging one another
over diet and calendar—matters that Paul finds incidental to the gospel and
the kingdom of God. The Stoics called such issues *adiaphora*—neutral, dis-
cretionary, and nonessential: things that don't matter. Paul seems to bring a
similar perspective to the table.

If this scenario is close to accurate, then Paul's letter to the Christ-
assemblies in Rome is meant at least to address this situation. One central
theme of Romans, God's grace to Jew and gentile alike, embodies Paul's deep-
est concerns and is therefore systematically unfolded. Indeed, the presentation
of the gospel might have been quite different if the churches had consisted only
of gentiles, or only of Jews.

Romans has four major sections: chapters 1–4, 5–8, 9–11, and 12–16 (or 15).
(See the detailed outline of the letter below.) One's reading of Romans depends to a significant degree on the part of the letter one sees as most theologically important and as most revealing of the story behind the letter.

- Some interpreters place most of their emphasis on chapters 1–8 (and maybe
some on the exhortations in 12–15, but little on 9–11), seeing Romans as a
theological treatise on justification, sanctification, and glorification. There
is no particular human story behind the letter, only the grand divine story
of salvation.
  - Interpreters who focus on justification may privilege chapters 1–4.
  - Interpreters who emphasize new life in Christ concentrate heavily on
  chapters 5–8.
- Other interpreters, especially more recently in light of the Holocaust and
developments in Jewish-Christian relations, find the focus of the letter in

chapters 9–11: Paul's concern about God's fidelity and Israel's fate. (In the past, these chapters were often neglected as largely irrelevant for the contemporary church. One popular Bible study guide I have, from the late twentieth century, skips these chapters entirely.)

- Still others find the key to the letter in the ethical consequences and community life depicted in 12:1–15:13. Special attention is often drawn specifically to 14:1–15:13, Paul's concern about factions and judgmentalism.
- Occasionally, the focus of interpreters is on 15:14–33, Paul's interest in the Romans' support for his ministry. This perspective turns the letter into a long appeal for spiritual and material backing.

Whatever their focus, interpreters try to relate the first part of the letter (chs. 1–8) to the second (chs. 9–16), and the letter as a whole to Paul's ministry. Most interpreters today think the letter must somehow further Paul's missionary and pastoral work.

This Commentary's Approach

In this commentary's reading of the story behind the letter, significant emphasis is placed on the second half of Romans (chs. 9–16, esp. 14–15) for understanding the entire letter—even though we will devote more space to the dense theological foundation that Paul provides in the first half (chs. 1–8). If there is Jewish-gentile conflict in the community, as I think there is, then the letter's profound theology about Jew and gentile must surely have as one of its primary goals the resolution of that discord. But in addition to addressing that conflict, Paul seeks to spell out what new life in Christ—which means in Christian community—looks like on the ground. Romans demonstrates, no less than any other Pauline letter, that Paul's theology always has a pastoral function; he has a formational, or transformational, agenda.

This does not mean, then, that Romans has no purpose other than to resolve Jewish-gentile friction. (In fact, some interpreters do not see conflict management as central to Paul's agenda, while others even doubt the existence of the conflict itself.) Most scholars agree that there is a variety of reasons for Romans. For instance, the letter serves as a splendid introduction to the apostle and his teaching so that the Romans will both accept him when he comes (regardless of whether there were already some critics of Paul in Rome) and, he no doubt hopes, support him in his mission work, especially as he heads for Spain.

In the meantime, Paul also wants support for the collection for the poor Jewish faithful in Jerusalem, and he undoubtedly desires a positive reception of the gospel as he proclaims it and this ministry when he actually goes to Jerusalem. The moral support of the Roman church would certainly help him in that regard. These goals, too, are part of Paul's commitment to the unity of gentile and Jew in one covenant community in Christ—whether locally (in Rome) or universally (from Jerusalem to Rome and beyond).

The complex scenario just described helps to account for the distinctive character of Romans among the Pauline letters. As the apostle writes to believers he has never visited, he composes a letter of great length, breadth, and depth. He remixes some of his best previous arguments and supports them with multiple appeals to Scripture and early Christian tradition, resulting in a pastoral letter in the form of a letter-essay (see further below).

But as Christian readers of Romans, we cannot stop with a proposal about Paul's original purposes in writing Romans, for Romans is now Scripture for us. This means that Romans is a word from God; it is divine address. Its theological claims about the gospel, and about the God of the gospel, are claims that we also need to take as part of the truthful witness of Scripture. Its teaching about sins and Sin, about grace and mercy, about justification and new life, about Israel, about life in Christ—these have become part of the church's theology, regardless of whether we are aware of those teachings.

The letter's claims on the Roman house churches are claims on us, too, claims about being transformed, claims about the work of the Spirit among us, claims about justice and peace and joy in the Holy Spirit. Today, for example, Romans continues to address the fractured body of Christ, both locally and globally, calling it to unity, peace, and hospitality in the midst of the gift of cultural diversity.

THE SHAPE OF THE LETTER

Romans is an amazingly complex piece of early Christian literature. As we consider the letter as a whole, we must first briefly look at its overall shape: its main themes, its "political" character, its literary genre, and its structure.

Themes in Romans

The breadth and length of this letter mean there is a rich variety of themes in Romans. It is completely understandable—and not altogether misguided—that some have called Romans a theological treatise. But what is the subject of this treatise, if we use that term? Some have called it a treatise on justification and sanctification, or on justice, or on peace, or on participation and transformation in Christ. It is probably all of these and more. Whichever theme or themes one considers to be the most significant will also affect, or reveal, one's perception of the letter's central message.

This tapestry of themes is due in part to Paul's theological genius, in part to the multidimensional occasion that generated the letter, and in part to Paul's borrowing from his own previous correspondence. One of my students once called Romans "Paul's greatest hits"! The letter draws on Galatians as well as both 1 and 2 Corinthians in major ways, though not without significant adaptation for a new situation.

So, for instance, justification, Abraham, the law, and the Spirit reappear from Galatians; the weak-strong divisions, spiritual gifts, and the body (individual and corporate) reemerge from 1 Corinthians; and reconciliation as well as Spirit-enabled transformation into the likeness of Christ, who is the image of God, find their way into Romans from 2 Corinthians. In fact, in many ways, Romans is an extended commentary on a key passage in 2 Corinthians:

> For the Messiah's love urges us on, because we are convinced that one has died for all; therefore all have died. And he died for all, so that those who live might live no longer for themselves, but for him who died for them and was raised. From now on, therefore, we regard no one from a human point of view; even though we once knew the Messiah from a human point of view, we know him no longer in that way. So if anyone is in the Messiah, new creation! everything old has passed away; see, everything has become new! All this is from God, who reconciled us to himself through the Messiah, and has given us the ministry of reconciliation; that is, God was in the Messiah reconciling the world to himself, not counting their trespasses against them, and entrusting the message of reconciliation to us. So we are ambassadors for the Messiah, since God is making his appeal through us; we entreat you on behalf of the Messiah, be reconciled to God. For our sake he made him (the Messiah Jesus) who did not know sin to *be* sin, so that in him we would become the righteousness, or justice, of God. (2 Cor 5:14–21 NRSV alt.)[7]

7. Similarities between 2 Cor 5:14–21 and Romans include the attention to Christ's love, his death for us, the pairing of Christ's death and resurrection, the reorientation of life toward Christ, being in Christ, reconciliation, the righteousness/justice of God, and more. It is likely that 2 Cor 5:14–21 is a reworking of Gal 2:15–21 for a new audience. Thus, Romans also owes a great deal to that Galatians passage too.

In addition to the previously noted theme of saving grace for Jews and gentiles, other key motifs in Romans, many drawn from Paul's previous correspondence, include the following:

- Jesus as God's Messiah
- the righteousness of God, a rich term that refers to God's fidelity, integrity, impartiality, saving power, and restorative justice
- justification by faith and its corollary, obedience (cf. "the obedience of faith"—or believing allegiance—as bookends in 1:5 and 16:26), for believing means pledging and practicing allegiance[8]
- the death and resurrection of Jesus, and of believers with him, that brings about life before God
- salvation as God's restoration of humanity's lost glory and righteousness (Gk. *doxa* and *dikaiosynē*) by identification with and conformity to Christ (Christoformity or Christification or even deification/theosis)[9]
- the multicultural character of God's people and the unity of gentiles and Jews in Christ[10]
- participation in Christ as participation in the Spirit within his body/community and as conformity to Christ and his story
- the gospel as God's peacemaking initiative (Heb. *šālôm*, or shalom)
- the gospel's challenge to Rome and its values
- justification, salvation, participation, and shalom as interrelated dimensions of *life*—both present and future (eternal)

8. The theme of obedience is frequently overlooked in Romans; see also 2:8, 25; 5:19; 6:12, 16–17; 10:16; 11:30–31; 15:18; 16:19.

9. Some or all of these terms in parentheses may be unfamiliar to readers. "Christoformity" is the term of James Dunn and Scot McKnight that they use to mean Christlikeness. Along with "Christification" and "Christosis," "Christoformity" can also refer to the process that leads to that goal. Because Christians affirm that Christ is God incarnate, some have used the terms "deification" or "theosis" to mean becoming like God (Latin *deus*; Gk. *theos*) by becoming like Christ. There is some overlap between these terms and the term "sanctification," or growth in holiness, but it is important to remember that Paul believes all believers are already sanctified—set apart for God's purposes—even if they are not (yet) fully Christlike. A working definition of theosis for our purposes is this: transformative participation in the character, life, glory, and mission of God through Spirit-enabled conformity to the incarnate, crucified, and resurrected/glorified Messiah Jesus. It includes as one process what has often been seen in the West as separate realities: justification, sanctification, and glorification.

10. See especially the "Jews and gentiles/Greeks" refrain that appears in 1:16; 2:9–10; 3:9, 29; 9:24; 10:12.

We will explore a few of these a bit more fully later.

Some interpreters want us to choose between a theological and a pastoral, or practical, reading of Romans. Others want us to choose between a theological and a political reading of the letter. Romans is, however, both pastoral/practical and theological, and it is both theological and political (in the sense we will define below). The complex story *behind* the letter yields the comprehensive shape of the story *within* the letter, as well as its many interwoven themes. Yet this multilayered letter possesses a real, if complex, unity summarized in one word: "gospel" (Gk. *euangelion*).

This gospel is not merely a set of propositions but a dynamic, life-changing force in the world: "the power of God for salvation," as Paul says in 1:16. For this reason, the gospel narrated in Romans challenges not only individuals but also communities and larger bodies, even social and political structures. Such social and especially political bodies do two primary things that Romans (and the rest of the New Testament) confronts and subverts: they demand devotion, including sometimes even self-sacrifice to the point of dying or killing on their behalf; and, in exchange, they promise abundant life in the form of peace, justice, victory, fecundity, and so on—what we might call salvation.

It is in this sense that Romans is political: it undermines these sorts of social and political demands and promises, offering an alternative demand for devotion and an alternative gift of life. We can briefly examine some aspects of how this relates to Rome and Romans itself (the last theme listed above).

The Gospel's Challenge to Imperial Values

Roman society was a culture of honor and shame, and it was also agonistic—meaning highly competitive. Humility was not a virtue, and the highly stratified culture was built on the principle of seeking honor for oneself and one's social and political superiors, not looking out for the weak and lowly.

Roman culture was also extremely religious, and this religiosity was polytheistic. This religiosity was also practiced both at home and in public spaces. In addition to the many traditional gods of the pantheon (Jupiter, Neptune, Venus, etc.), Roman religion included household deities honored with in-home shrines. More important for our purposes, religious rites were associated with most clubs and guilds where hardworking people (mostly men) gathered for social purposes. To abandon the patron deities of these organizations could spell social and even economic disaster.

Furthermore, Roman religion was inseparable from politics. The political aspects of Roman religion included a whole set of convictions about the role of Rome and its emperors in the plan of the gods. It was believed that the gods had established Rome as the vehicle for bringing peace and justice to the world—through conquest and enslavement as necessary. In the various forms of what is called the imperial cult, emperors themselves were hailed as saviors, lords, and gods, and in some cases their birth and activity were portrayed as good news—as "gospel."[11]

People were expected to be faithful to the Roman deities, a quality known as *fides* (faithfulness) that was demonstrated, for instance, in temple sacrifices. Temples were dedicated not only to gods like Jupiter, but also to emperors and to imperial virtues such as *Victoria* (similar to Gk. *Nikē*), *Pax, Concordia, Securitas, Libertas, Felicitas, Clementia, Pietas, Fides*, and *Iustitia*: victory, peace, harmony, security, liberty, happiness/good luck, mercy, piety, faith, and justice. Justice, said Cicero, was "the crowning glory of the virtues" (*On Duties* 1.20). Such deified virtues made Roman social and political values into sacred entities, and the worship of them was therefore often naturally associated with the emperors, their particular strengths, and the imperial cult.

Paul's gospel—the gospel of God—confronted all of this, sometimes implicitly, sometimes explicitly. Like Jesus, Paul was announcing a new, divinely established political order: not new political parties and governments but a new way of being human together in the world, under a completely different kind of Lord, with very different values. As N. T. Wright has often said, "If Jesus is Lord, Caesar is not."

In other words, the gospel of Rome—or of any other empire, superpower, or political figure—is not the gospel of God. Moreover, in the empire of God, the Roman practice of seeking honor for the self and the strong is replaced with practices such as seeking honor for the least and the last, and serving with humility. Deified virtues like peace and victory are thoroughly recast in terms of God's peace initiative in the crucified and resurrected Messiah Jesus. *The power, peace, and justice of Rome have met their match in the power, peace, and justice of God.*

Once again, we cannot stop with the past and limit Paul's alternative gospel to the first century. Still today there are gospels on offer from various political

---

11. Inscriptions from 9 BC in various parts of what is now western Turkey contained the following words about the "savior" (Gk. *sōtēr*) Caesar Augustus, whom "providence" sent to end war and establish peace: "Since Caesar when revealed surpassed the hopes of all who had anticipated the good news [Gk. *euangelia*], not only going beyond the benefits of those who had preceded him, but rather leaving no hope of surpassing him for those who will come, because of him the birthday of God began good news [*euangelia*] for the world."

and social bodies and their leaders. Romans will offer a critique of them, too, one that is powerful and robust, but also one that may take careful reflection and conversation to discern.

The Genre of Romans

The complexity of Romans noted earlier, with its many themes, strong theological claims and arguments, and challenging questions of interpretation, raises the question of its genre, or literary form. Though it bears witness to the gospel, it is obviously not a gospel like the Gospel of Mark or of John. It presents itself, rather, as a letter. But is Romans in fact a letter?

On the one hand, Romans—like the rest of the New Testament writings—is an interpretation of the Scriptures of Israel in light of the coming, ministry, death, and resurrection of Jesus. There are some fifty scriptural citations in Romans, plus many more allusions to and echoes of biblical texts and figures. Following Paul's use of these scriptural quotations can give the careful hearer or reader a good sense of the flow of his argument.

The word "argument," however, suggests another dimension of Romans. It does in fact contain an argument, or rather a series of arguments within an overall careful plan, that is not common in ordinary letters. This is true of many Pauline letters, but Romans is particularly rich—and dense. It is not difficult to see why Melanchthon (Luther's colleague) and others have seen Romans as a theological handbook or treatise.

Romans is, indeed, a powerful rhetorical gem. There are many aspects of Paul's rhetoric that could be mentioned: his appeal to emotion as well as reason, his usage of Jewish as well as secular rhetorical devices, and much more. But one fascinating feature to note is Paul's fondness in Romans for groups of words and phrases in biblically significant numbers: three of this and four or five of that; seven of one thing and ten of another. For instance, in Rom 8 there are first precisely seven and then exactly ten things that cannot separate us from God's love in Christ (8:35, 38-39).[12] These groupings indicate both care in planning the argument and sensitivity to the spiritual symbolism of certain numbers.

If we put all of this together, it is probably best to classify Romans as a pastoral letter-essay. It is a sustained treatise, or persuasive argument, that is nonetheless a real letter to a real group of people addressing a real situation. Paul's

---

12. This rhetorical feature of Romans is noted at great length by Robert Jewett, *Romans*, Hermeneia (Minneapolis: Fortress, 2007), 32-39.

goal is community spiritual formation and re-formation. He is in teaching mode, and he frequently employs, as we will see in the commentary proper, the ancient technique of diatribe. This was not a rant or complaint (the common meaning of the term today) but a method of argumentation and instruction using an imaginary conversation partner, the interlocutor, who is addressed directly.

Romans, then, invites participation in the drama of this Pauline dialogue and compels us to respond to the gospel that it powerfully proclaims. For those who do respond, the result is life indeed—life in Christ and life in community, life shaped by the cross and life suffused with the resurrection, newness of life now and eternal life to come.

The Letter's Structure

The story of Romans—the story of the gospel for Jew and gentile alike that Romans narrates—may be outlined as follows:

1:1–17   **Opening and Theme: The Gospel of God's Son, Power, and Justice for the Salvation of All**
> **1:1–15**   Opening
>> **1:1–7**   Salutation and Theme: Paul, the Romans, and the Gospel of God's Son
>> **1:8–15**   Thanksgiving, Intercession, and Hope
>> **1:16–17**   Theme: The Gospel as God's Power and Justice for the Salvation of All

1:18–4:25   **God's Faithful, Merciful, and Just Response to Human Sin**
> **1:18–3:20**   Divine Impartiality and Human Accountability
>> **1:18–32**   The Gentile Predicament
>> **2:1–16**   God's Impartial Judgment according to Deeds
>> **2:17–3:8**   The Jewish Predicament
>> **3:9–20**   Humanity under the Power of Sin
> **3:21–31**   God's Faithfulness, Mercy, and Justice in Christ
>> **3:21–26**   Justification by Faith: God's, Christ's, Believers'
>> **3:27–31**   The Exclusion of Pride
> **4:1–25**   The Witness of Scripture in the Story of Abraham
>> **4:1–15**   Abraham's Justification by Faith without Circumcision or the Law
>> **4:16–25**   Abraham's Justification as Resurrection from the Dead

THE STORY WITHIN THE LETTER

Before examining the several parts of the letter in the commentary itself, we will briefly knit together the themes noted above as a way of approaching the story of God in Romans that unfolds according to the proposed outline. We will then look briefly at two overarching themes in Romans: (1) participation in Christ and (2) peace (shalom), with its corollary, justice.

The Story as a Whole

To examine the story we find in Romans as a whole, it is first necessary to say a word about a misguided understanding of that story. In some churches and traditions, the Letter to the Romans is associated with something called the Roman (or Romans) Road. This consists of a selection of verses taken from Romans that allegedly present the plan of salvation. These verses focus in a very individualistic way on the universality of sin (e.g., 3:10, 23), death as the wages of sin (e.g., 6:23), Jesus' substitutionary death for sinners (e.g., 5:8), and the promise that all who call on the Lord will be saved (e.g., 10:9–10, 13).

While each of these is arguably a component of Romans, the overall path of this road is, unfortunately, a dead end. For one thing, the Roman Road misses the mark by failing to center on the centerpiece of Romans: God. For another, it fails to recognize that what God is up to is not merely the rescue of individuals so they will have everlasting life when they die. Paul is focused on communities and on life in Christ now. Various themes manifest this focus.

One major theme of Romans, as already noted, is God's grace—God's impartial faithfulness and mercy—toward Jews and gentiles that creates a new community through the "obedience of faith," or believing obedience (1:5; 16:26). This community is the community of the new covenant that prophets like Ezekiel and Jeremiah promised God would bring about in the future.

For Paul, that future is now.[13] This theme of divine grace is announced at the outset, using the language of God's saving righteousness, or restorative justice (Gk. *dikaiosynē*), in what many interpreters have thought to be the thesis or theme statement of the letter:

> For I am not ashamed of the gospel; it is the power of God for salvation to everyone who has faith, to the Jew first and also to the Greek. For in it the righteousness of God is revealed through faith for faith; as it is written, "The one who is righteous will live by faith." (1:16–17)

This is a description of the gospel Paul proclaimed, stressing its effect more than its content. Recent interpreters have pointed as well to the letter opening, in which the word "gospel" also appears, as equally important for understanding the letter's theme. Paul says he is an apostle of

> the gospel of God, which he promised beforehand through his prophets in the holy scriptures, the gospel concerning his Son, who was descended from David according to the flesh and was declared to be Son of God with power according to the spirit of holiness by resurrection from the dead, Jesus Christ our Lord. (1:1b–4)

Under this banner of God's righteousness, or saving justice, powerfully displayed in the royal Messiah Jesus, the letter proceeds to tell the story of God's faithful response to faithless humanity (chs. 1–4); the resulting new situation for those who are justified by grace through faith, thereby dying and rising with Christ and living in the Spirit (chs. 5–8); the question of the future fate of ethnic Israel in light of the failure of most Jews to accept the gospel (chs. 9–11); the need for the community at Rome to embody this gospel as they live cruciform (cross-shaped) lives of holiness and hospitality (chs. 12–15); and finally, the relationship of all this to God's great story of salvation and Paul's mission within it (chs. 15–16).

We can say, then, that the subject of Romans is God's gospel of salvation (Gk. *sōtēria*), but we must be careful to let Paul define for us what salvation means. It is much more than just the forgiveness of sins. Humans have turned

---

13. The technical term for events associated with the future culmination of God's plans for his people and the world is "eschatological"—meaning "referring to the last days and the restoration of humanity and creation." Paul does not use the term "new covenant" in Romans (though see 1 Cor 11:25 and 2 Cor 3:6), but the concept is present.

from God and from others, and the result is a lack of both righteousness, or justice (Gk. *dikaiosynē*; 1:18), and glory (Gk. *doxa*; 3:23). Interestingly, these are both divine traits that can be shared with humans. The result is life—newness of life and eternal life.

We have already noted that Romans is the epistle of life. The *last* Greek word of the letter's thematic statement in 1:16–17 is *zēsetai*, "will live," and it is the letter's *first* specific reference to life, with nearly forty to follow.[14] The verb "live" will occur a total of twenty-three times in Romans, the noun "life" fourteen times, and the verb "give life" ("make alive") twice. Many of these occurrences are paired with references to the opposite of life, that is, death. A few additional texts embodying this central theme of life are the following:

- To those who by patiently doing good seek for glory and honor and immortality, he will give **eternal life**. (2:7)
- [God] gives **life** to the dead and calls into existence the things that do not exist. (4:17b)
- If, because of the one man's trespass, death exercised dominion through that one, much more surely will those who receive the abundance of grace and the free gift of righteousness exercise dominion in **life** through the one man, Jesus Christ. (5:17)
- Therefore we have been buried with him by baptism into death, so that, just as Christ was raised from the dead by the glory of the Father, so we too might walk in newness of **life**. (6:4)
- But if we have died with Christ, we believe that we will also **live** with him. (6:8)
- So you also must consider yourselves dead to sin and **alive** to God in Christ Jesus. (6:11)
- For the wages of sin is death, but the free gift of God is **eternal life** in Christ Jesus our Lord. (6:23)
- I was once **alive** apart from the law, but when the commandment came, sin revived and I died, and the very commandment that promised **life** proved to be death to me. (7:9–10)
- To set the mind on the flesh is death, but to set the mind on the Spirit is life and peace. (8:6)
- If you **live** according to the flesh, you will die; but if by the Spirit you put to death the deeds of the body, you will **live**. (8:13)

14. Most translations place "by faith" at the end of the English sentence, but see, e.g., the NET: "'The righteous by faith will live'"; cf. NJB.

- For if their rejection is the reconciliation of the world, what will their acceptance be but **life** from the dead! (11:15)
- I appeal to you therefore, brothers and sisters, by the mercies of God, to present your bodies as a **living** sacrifice, holy and acceptable to God, which is your spiritual worship. (12:1)
- We do not **live** to ourselves, and we do not die to ourselves. If we **live**, we **live** to the Lord, and if we die, we die to the Lord; so then, whether we **live** or whether we die, we are the Lord's. For to this end Christ died and **lived** again, so that he might be Lord of both the dead and the **living**. (14:7–9)

For Paul, then, salvation means rescue from death and entry into life: God's restoration of righteousness/justice and glory to unrighteous/unjust and gloryless humanity. Salvation means participation and transformation; it means life through death and resurrection; it means becoming more and more Godlike by becoming more and more Christlike.[15] Paul's understanding of the restoration of God's *dikaiosynē* and *doxa* to humans is that it occurs by grace-enabled participation in the saving death and resurrection of the Messiah Jesus, God's righteous and now glorified Son. This participation is not vaguely mystical but narrative in character: new life as conformity to Christ and his story.

Central to this story of life are Jesus' death and resurrection. In the death of Jesus, God has made peace with his enemies—the human race—and begun the project of reconciling all people to himself and to one another. This peacemaking mission includes the gift of God's own self, and thus of the divine attributes of righteousness/justice and glory, in the reality of the indwelling Spirit of God (5:1–11; ch. 8).

Paul offers this interpretation of salvation explicitly as the fulfillment of Israel's hope for life—salvation, righteousness/justice, peace, and glory—extended now to the gentiles, the nations. It is a salvation that creates a multicultural community, the renewed people of God. At the same time, as noted earlier, Paul holds out this message of salvation as the true gospel of God in contrast to the pseudo-gospel of Rome's salvation, righteousness/justice, peace (Latin *pax*), and glory.

Paul's missional goal was to expand the presence of God's life, God's *dikaiosynē* and *doxa* and shalom, throughout the nations, and therefore also throughout the existing Roman house churches—right under the nose of the emperor, so to speak. Paul believed that the gospel would establish an international (empire-

---

15. As noted earlier, this process is therefore sometimes called deification or theosis and Christification or Christosis. Theosis principally means taking on certain divine attributes, partially in the present and fully in the age to come.

wide) network of transformed, multicultural communities obeying, glorifying, and bearing public witness to the one true God of Israel by conformity to God's Son in the power of the Spirit. What better place to see that gospel take deeper and further root than at the center of Rome's (so-called) power, glory, and justice!

The story that unfolds within Romans, therefore, is an implicit invitation both to join in and to help spread the ultimate divine project: the fulfillment of God's promise to allow Israel and the nations to share in the justice/righteousness and glory of God—and to live out those divine attributes in the real world in anticipation of full and final salvation to come.

The West's fixation on sin and guilt has sometimes hampered us from seeing how central to Paul's understanding of human nature (anthropology) and his understanding of salvation (soteriology) are the themes of glory, life, peace, and immortality—both the absence of these for those in Adam and their restored presence for those who are "in Christ."

This phrase "in Christ" leads us to consider the theme of participation in Romans, for the salvation and life of which Paul speaks is a life of participation in the life of God.

Participation in Christ in Romans

Some of Paul's most significant sentences in his letters, including Romans, contain the phrase "in Christ" (i.e., "in the Messiah") or a variant of that phrase ("in Christ Jesus," "in the Lord," "in him"). For example, in Romans we find sentences such as these (emphasis added):

- So you also must consider yourselves dead to sin and **alive to God in Christ Jesus.** (6:11)
- There is therefore now no condemnation for those who are **in Christ Jesus.** (8:1)
- We, who are many, are **one body in Christ**, and individually we are members one of another. (12:5)
- Greet Prisca and Aquila, who work with me **in Christ Jesus.** . . . Greet Andronicus and Junia . . . ; they were **in Christ** before I was. Greet Ampliatus, my beloved **in the Lord.** Greet Urbanus, our co-worker **in Christ.** (16:3, 7–9a)

Being in Christ is not anyone's default location. Life in the Messiah begins when, through faith and baptism, a person is transferred from being outside Christ to being in him, which means also being in his body, the *ekklēsia*:[16]

16. In Romans, Paul uses the term *ekklēsia* itself only in ch. 16 (five times), but he

> Do you not know that all of us who have been **baptized into Christ Jesus** were **baptized into his death**? (6:3)

Whatever else "in Christ" signifies, it means that Christian believers and communities are located within the sphere of Christ's personal presence and power.

Not only are believers in Christ, however; Christ is also in, and among, them. There is a *mutual indwelling* of Christ and the faithful, both individually and corporately. This mutual indwelling takes place by means of the Spirit, so Paul can use the language of mutual indwelling with respect to both Christ and the Spirit in the same breath:

> But you are not in the flesh; you are **in the Spirit**, since **the Spirit of God dwells in** [or **among**] you. Anyone who does not have the Spirit of Christ does not belong to him. But if **Christ is in** [or **among**] you, though the body is dead because of sin, the Spirit is life because of righteousness. If the **Spirit of him who raised Jesus from the dead dwells in you**, he who raised Christ from the dead will give life to your mortal bodies also through **his Spirit that dwells in you**. (8:9–11)[17]

This sort of affirmation about the indwelling of Christ/the Spirit stands in stark contrast to Paul's assessment of the human condition outside of Christ, where Sin, understood as a malevolent apocalyptic power, inhabits people, and they inhabit it:

- Now if I do what I do not want, it is no longer I that do it, but **Sin that dwells within me**. (7:20)[18]
- What then are we to say? Should we continue **in Sin** in order that grace may abound? (6:1)

In addition to "in" language to express participation, Paul also uses "with," or "co-" language. A few of the texts in Romans are these:

---

clearly articulates a theology of the church throughout the letter. He speaks of the body of Christ in 12:4–5.

17. See also 5:5 for the presence of the Spirit within believers' hearts: "Hope does not disappoint us, because God's love has been **poured into our hearts** through **the Holy Spirit that has been given to us**."

18. Here and elsewhere, I will alter the NRSV by capitalizing the words "sin," "death," and "grace" when they indicate a personified power (Sin, Death, Grace).

- We know that **our old self was co-crucified with him** [in baptism] so that the body dominated by Sin would be done away with, and we would no longer be enslaved to sin. (6:6 MJG; see also 6:4–5)
- But if we have **died with Christ**, we believe that **we will also live with him.** (6:8)
- If [we are God's] children, then [we are also] heirs, heirs of God and co-heirs with Christ—if, in fact, we **co-suffer with him** so that we may **also be co-glorified with him.** (8:17 MJG)

Furthermore, this participation in and with Christ does not happen in isolation, but in community. For instance, the pronouns and verbs in chapter 8 about being in Christ/in the Spirit are plural forms of those Greek words: you all are in Christ, together. And Paul expresses key aspects of community by using various forms of "with," or "co-," language. He anticipates a time of being co-encouraged and co-refreshed when he finally visits the Roman Christians (1:12; 15:32), and he expects all of them to "associate with the lowly"—to co-join with them (12:16). He also refers to colleagues with the Greek terms for "co-prisoners" (16:7) and "co-worker(s)" (16:3, 9, 21), though English translations do not always capture this nuance, especially for "co-prisoner."

Paul's participation language is indebted to the prophets Ezekiel and Jeremiah (Ezek 36:26–27; Jer 4:4; 9:23–26; cf. Deut. 10:16). They saw that what God's people needed, God would supply: a transformed heart inhabited by the Spirit and empowered to keep their covenant obligations and become increasingly holy like the Holy Spirit of God within them. For Paul, this Spirit of God is also the Spirit of Christ (Rom 8:9).

Accordingly, as we will see throughout the commentary, being in Christ and having Christ within is the key to becoming what God intended all people, Jews and gentiles, to be. Participation in Christ is where transformation occurs, where ungodly values and practices are undone, and where the life, glory, joy, justice, and peace of God are found. It is *in* Christ that people become *like* Christ, conformed to him and his story. It is where the *doxa* and *dikaiosynē* of God—God's glory and righteousness/justice—are restored to humanity. *Humans experience the glory of God as they give glory to God in a community of people being transformed into the likeness of God manifested in his Son Jesus.* "Eternal life" refers to the time and place when the divine traits humans are privileged to share are perfected in a state of bodily resurrection and immortality.

The early Christian theologians Irenaeus and Athanasius proclaimed that Christ became what we are so that we would become what he is. Similarly, but more metaphorically, the Byzantine theologian Maximus the Confessor, in the seventh century, compared our transformative participation in the life of God by comparing it to putting an iron sword into a fire; it remains an iron sword but also takes on certain properties of the fire—light and heat—by participating in it.[19]

God's Peace, God's Justice

One aspect of the story of participation in Romans that demands special attention in our contemporary violent world is shalom—God's peace. For Paul, peace means the fullness of life promised by God in Israel's Scripture, incarnated in Jesus the Messiah, and actualized for us by the ongoing power of the Spirit. Peace means healing and wholeness, including right relations both with God and with others, and even with the rest of the created order.

We can easily see the theme of peace in a standard English translation of Romans (NRSV) in the following table:[20]

HUMAN VIOLENCE	GOD'S SHALOM FOR THOSE IN CHRIST
They were filled with every kind of wickedness, evil, covetousness, malice. Full of envy, **murder**, **strife**, deceit, craftiness, they are gossips, slanderers, God-haters, insolent, haughty, boastful, inventors of evil, rebellious toward parents, foolish, faithless, heartless, ruthless. (1:29–31)	There will be anguish and distress for everyone who does evil, the Jew first and also the Greek, but glory and honor and **peace** for everyone who does good, the Jew first and also the Greek. (2:9–10)
	Therefore, since we are justified by faith, we have **peace** with God through our Lord Jesus Christ. (5:1)
	To set the mind on the flesh is death, but to set the mind on the Spirit is life and **peace**. (8:6)
"All have turned aside, together they have become worthless; there is **no one who shows kindness**, there is not even one." "**Their throats are opened graves**; they use their tongues to deceive." "**The venom of vipers is under their lips.**" "**Their mouths are full of cursing and bitterness.**" "**Their feet are swift to shed blood**; ruin and misery are in their paths, and **the way of peace they have not known**." (3:12–17)	If it is possible, so far as it depends on you, live **peaceably** [practice peace] with all. (12:18)
	For the kingdom of God is not food and drink but righteousness and **peace** and joy in the Holy Spirit. . . . Let us then pursue what makes for **peace** and for mutual upbuilding. (14:17, 19)
	May the God of hope fill you with all joy and **peace** in believing, so that you may abound in hope by the power of the Holy Spirit. (15:13)

19. Irenaeus, *Against Heresies* 5, preface 1; Athanasius, *Incarnation of the Word* 54; Maximus the Confessor, *Ambiguum* 7; cf. Opuscule 16.

20. For more detailed discussion of peace in Romans, see my *Becoming the Gospel: Paul, Participation, and Mission* (Grand Rapids: Eerdmans, 2015), 169–79.

It is much more difficult, however, to perceive the inseparably related theme of justice in most English translations of Romans. The issue revolves around the translation of one Greek word-family, *dik-*. In English (as this introduction has already hinted), this one word-family has been translated with two different word-families: "right-" and "just-." We see this in words like "righteousness," on the one hand, and "justification," "justice," and "just," on the other. The most important questions, as we will see in more depth in the commentary, is whether and how to show relationships among the realities of injustice, justification, and justice—both divine and human.

This commentary argues for close connections among these words and the realities they signify. Not all commentators or translations agree. Interestingly, some (not all) Roman Catholic translations capture this aspect of the letter better than most ecumenical and evangelical Protestant versions, with N. T. Wright's *Kingdom New Testament* being the exception to that rule. The table of representative translations on pages 44–45 illustrates the situation.

The point here is not to defend one translation. Suffice it to say at this juncture that it should not surprise even those who rely on English translations that there is a theme of justice in Romans. After all, even in English, the words "injustice," "justification," and "justice" are part of the same word-family.

The challenge has been, as the table reveals, showing these connections when there has been a predisposition to mix "righteousness" rather than "justice" language with "justification" language. The commentary will show that justification is not simply about being forgiven or pronounced righteous, but about being made just/righteous. This is often thought to be a Catholic rather than a Protestant view of justification. As a Protestant, however, I contend that it is a *Pauline* view of justification. If this is correct, it should have a huge impact on how we understand Paul's theology in Romans and its consequences for us. One aspect of those consequences will be our understanding of Christian mission to include devotion to biblically shaped justice.

THE STORY IN FRONT OF THE LETTER

It would take a much longer book, or an additional one, to consider at length the effect Romans has had on Christian faith and practice. I will, however, say something brief about three important topics that are not always discussed in commentaries on Romans: Christian mission, ecumenical relations, and interfaith relations. I also include a note about terminology as it relates to connections between Paul's language and ours.

		ECUMENICAL NRSV (NEW REVISED STANDARD)	EVANGELICAL NIV (NEW INTERNATIONAL)
1:17 GOD		For in it [the gospel] **the righteousness of God** is revealed through faith for faith; as it is written, "**The one who is righteous** will live by faith."	For in the gospel **the righteousness of God** is revealed—**a righteousness** that is by faith from first to last, just as it is written: "**The righteous** will live by faith."
1:18 HUMAN SIN		For the wrath of God is revealed from heaven against all ungodliness and **wickedness** of those who by their **wickedness** suppress the truth.	The wrath of God is being revealed from heaven against all the godlessness and **wickedness** of people, who suppress the truth by their **wickedness**.
3:4–5 GOD VS. HUMAN SIN		Although everyone is a liar, let God be proved true, as it is written, "So that **you may be justified in your words**, and prevail in your judging." But if **our injustice** serves to confirm **the justice of God**, what should we say? That God is **unjust** to inflict wrath on us? (I speak in a human way.)	Let God be true, and every human being a liar. As it is written: "So that **you may be proved right** when you speak and prevail when you judge." But if **our unrighteousness** brings out **God's righteousness** more clearly, what shall we say? That God is **unjust** in bringing his wrath on us? (I am using a human argument.)
3:21–22, 25 JUSTIFICATION		But now, apart from law, **the righteousness of God** has been disclosed, and is attested by the law and the prophets, **the righteousness of God** through faith in Jesus Christ for all who believe. . . . whom God put forward as a sacrifice of atonement by his blood, effective through faith. He did this to show **his righteousness**, because in his divine forbearance he had passed over the sins previously committed.	But now apart from the law **the righteousness of God** has been made known, to which the Law and the Prophets testify. **This righteousness is given** through faith in Jesus Christ to all who believe. . . . God presented Christ as a sacrifice of atonement, through the shedding of his blood—to be received by faith. He did this to demonstrate **his righteousness**, because in his forbearance he had left the sins committed beforehand unpunished.
5:17, 21 GOD'S GIFT IN CHRIST		much more surely will those who receive the abundance of grace and **the free gift of righteousness** exercise dominion in life through the one man, Jesus Christ. . . . so that, just as sin exercised dominion in death, so grace might also exercise dominion **through justification** leading to eternal life through Jesus Christ our Lord.	how much more will those who receive God's abundant provision of grace and of **the gift of righteousness** reign in life through the one man, Jesus Christ! . . . so that, just as sin reigned in death, so also grace might reign **through righteousness** to bring eternal life through Jesus Christ our Lord.
6:18 NEW LIFE IN CHRIST		And that you, having been set free from sin, have become **slaves of righteousness**.	You have been set free from sin and **have become slaves to righteousness**.

Roman Catholic NJB (New Jerusalem)	Wright's Kingdom New Testament (KNT)
for in it [the gospel] is revealed **the saving justice of God**: a **justice** based on faith and addressed to faith. As it says in scripture: **Anyone who is upright** through faith will live.	This is because **God's covenant justice** is unveiled in it [the gospel], from faithfulness to faithfulness. As it says in the Bible, "**the just** shall live by faith."
The retribution of God from heaven is being revealed against the ungodliness and **injustice of human beings** who in their **injustice** hold back the truth.	For the anger of God is unveiled from heaven against all the ungodliness and **injustice** performed by people who use **injustice** to suppress the truth.
God will always be true even if no human being can be relied on. As scripture says: That **you may show your saving justice** when you pass sentence and your victory may appear when you give judgment. But if **our injustice** serves to bring **God's saving justice** into view, can we say that God is **unjust** when—to use human terms—he brings his retribution down on us?	Let God be true, and every human being false! As the Bible says, So that **you may be found in the right** in what you say, and may win the victory when you come to court. But **if our being in the wrong** proves that **God is in the right**, what are we going to say? That God is **unjust** to inflict anger on people? (I'm reducing things to a human scale!)
God's saving justice was witnessed by the Law and the Prophets, but now it has been revealed altogether apart from law: **God's saving justice** given through faith in Jesus Christ to all who believe. . . . God appointed him as a sacrifice for reconciliation, through faith, by the shedding of his blood, and so showed **his justness**; first for the past, when sins went unpunished because he held his hand.	But now, quite apart from the law (though the law and the prophets bore witness to it), **God's covenant justice** has been displayed. **God's covenant justice** comes into operation through the faithfulness of Jesus the Messiah, for the benefit of all who have faith. . . . God put Jesus forth as the place of mercy, through faithfulness, by means of his blood. He did this to demonstrate **his covenant justice**, because of the passing over (in divine forbearance) of sins committed beforehand.
how much greater the reign in life of those who receive the fullness of grace and **the gift of saving justice**, through the one man, Jesus Christ. . . . so that as sin's reign brought death, so grace was to rule **through saving justice** that leads to eternal life through Jesus Christ our Lord.	how much more will those who receive the abundance of grace, and of **the gift of covenant membership, of "being in the right,"** reign in life through the one man Jesus the Messiah. . . . so that, just as sin reigned in death, even so, through **God's faithful covenant justice**, grace might reign to the life of the age to come, through Jesus the Messiah, our Lord.
And so, being freed from serving sin, you took **uprightness as your master**.	You were freed from sin, and now you have been **enslaved to God's covenant justice**.

Romans and the Mission of the Church

Romans has played a major part in the history and theology of Christian mission, not least because of chapters 9–11 and the end of chapter 15. For some, their reading of Rom 9–11 has relieved anxiety about evangelization because they are sure Romans teaches the election of some and the damnation of others, and thus the certainty of the salvation of the elect. As we will see in the commentary proper, this is a misreading of the letter.

Others, more appropriately, have seen in Paul's missionary zeal (15:14–33)—especially his desire to take the gospel to Spain—an example for them. The theology for this missionary zeal comes in large measure from chapter 10, with lines like these:

> "Everyone who calls on the name of the Lord shall be saved." But how are they to call on one in whom they have not believed? And how are they to believe in one of whom they have never heard? And how are they to hear without someone to proclaim him? And how are they to proclaim him unless they are sent? As it is written, "How beautiful are the feet of those who bring good news!" (10:13–15)

This traditional understanding of Romans and Christian mission is certainly a valid and important one. Recently, however, it has been supplemented with interpretations of Romans that understand the mission of the church in more comprehensive terms that include not only preaching the gospel in words and in personal relationships but also in deeds and in the community's life together.

In other words, Romans calls the church to *embody* the gospel that permeates its pages and to *participate* in God's missional activity. Since God desires all to confess Jesus as Lord, this participation is critical to Christian mission. Since God is forming a people in Christ, Christian community of various kinds is itself a form of mission. Since God in Christ is bringing shalom (peace, justice, and abundant life) to the world, practicing peace, justice, and other life-giving spiritual disciplines is essential to Christian mission. If God intends to liberate and redeem the *entire* creation (8:18–25), then creation care is likewise indispensable to Christian mission.

The challenge to contemporary Christians in reading Romans is to allow the text, and the Spirit speaking in and through the text, to convert our imaginations, as Richard Hays would put it.[21] That is, we may need to break free of

---

21. "The conversion of the imagination" is a term Hays has used often; it became the

narrow readings of Romans, not only with respect to mission, but also more generally, in order to allow this letter once again to spark conversions, movements, and transformations.

Romans and Ecumenical Relations

It is sometimes said that Protestants focus on Paul while Catholics focus on Jesus, or on the Gospels. There is a grain of truth in this claim, but there is also a significant error of both fact and perspective. The alleged Protestant prioritizing of Paul is due to the emphasis on the Pauline letters, especially Romans and Galatians, in some of the key Reformers, such as Luther and Calvin. But for a variety of reasons, Paul has fallen out of favor among some contemporary Protestant laypeople and clergy, even as scholarly work continues unabated among both Protestants and Catholics and, increasingly, among Orthodox Christians. In fact, Catholic scholars have produced many important commentaries on Paul. In addition, it will surprise many people, both Protestant and Catholic, to learn that in the Catechism of the Catholic Church, full of official Catholic teaching, Romans is the fourth most-referenced biblical book, surpassed only by the gospels of Matthew, Luke, and John.

Furthermore, Orthodox Christians (Greek and Russian Orthodox, etc.) bring a unique perspective to Romans, especially passages about justification, because Orthodoxy stresses a unified and holistic understanding of salvation as transformation into Christlikeness (theosis/Christosis). This sort of perspective on Paul has had significant influence on a good number of Pauline scholars, including the author of this commentary.

If Romans was written in part, if not primarily, to unify Christians of different cultural backgrounds and perspectives, then certainly one of its ongoing contributions is, or ought to be, effecting greater unity among Christians of different traditions, ethnicities, and theological perspectives.

Romans and Interfaith Relations: The Two-Ways Interpretation

Before proceeding to the letter itself, we must acknowledge but respectfully reject one particular reading of Paul in general and Romans in particular. This interpretation had originally been put forth by a very small but vocal minority of New Testament scholars and has recently been revived by a few proponents

---

title of a book of his essays: Richard B. Hays, *The Conversion of the Imagination: Paul as Interpreter of Israel's Scripture* (Grand Rapids: Eerdmans, 2005).

of what is called the *Paul within Judaism* perspective. Such scholars read Paul and Romans as offering a way for gentiles, but not Jews, to be justified and to become part of God's people—namely, faith in Christ. Ethnic Jews, they argue, not only remain God's people but are justified by their keeping the law, apart from faith in the Jewish Messiah.

The concern of these scholars to rescue Paul (and eventually, they hope, Christianity) from anti-Judaism and supersessionism (the idea that Christianity replaces Judaism) may be understandable. However, as one *Jewish* scholar of Paul put it succinctly, "Keeping the Law was for Paul adiaphora [nonessential]; faith in Jesus was most certainly not!"[22] The two-ways interpretation contradicts nearly everything we know about Paul's convictions, behavior, and communities.

Nothing could be clearer than the fact that Romans heralds one gospel for Jew and gentile alike, as Paul had announced in Gal 3:28. Romans is a tapestry of texts and themes attesting to this reality: from the thematic statement about the gospel as the power of salvation for all (1:16–17), to the impartial criterion of judgment according to deeds (2:9–11), to the theme of the one God of all (e.g., 3:29; 10:12), to the charge of universal enslavement to Sin (3:9), to the offer of justification and salvation and life to all by grace through faith (3:22, 28–30; 10:12), to the multicultural character of the church (9:24, and all of chs. 9–11 and 14–15), to the need for Jewish and gentile believers to embrace cultural differences and welcome one another (14:1–15:13), to the notion of mutual benefit between gentile and Jewish believers in the diaspora and in Jerusalem (15:22–29).

In all these texts and themes, Romans offers one gospel for all—specifically for both Jews and gentiles (indeed, says 1:16, Jews first! cf. 2:9–10)—creating one people of God that calls upon the name of the Lord (Jesus). Paul's efforts among the gentiles (primarily) are to ensure that God's promise is extended to them; however, the promises and claims of the gospel he proclaims in no way exclude Jews.

This does not make either Paul or Romans anti-Jewish or supersessionist, at least not as those terms are normally used. Paul is a Jew participating in first-century Jewish debates about what constitutes genuine Jewishness, about the true Israel, and about what God is up to in history among the chosen people and the nations. Paul offers a prophetic critique of the Judaism(s) of his day and a simultaneous reinterpretation of the Jewish story to include

22. Daniel Boyarin, *A Radical Jew: Paul and the Politics of Identity* (Berkeley: University of California Press, 1994), 42.

gentiles—but that makes him only as anti-Jewish as Isaiah, Hosea, Amos, Jeremiah, and Jesus.

Paul is convinced that, in and through Jesus the Jewish Messiah, God has reconstituted Israel as his eschatological people of both Jews and non-Jews who are endowed with the Spirit, circumcised in the heart, and thus able to live in covenant with God and others (fulfill the law)—the very blessing to all nations for which Abraham had been chosen and for which the prophets hoped. Thus, Israel is not *replaced* but *reconstituted*. Yet this reconfiguration of Israel as an eschatologically inclusive people is not fundamentally due, in Paul's mind, to some fatal flaw in Israel (though Israel has in fact "stumbled," according to Romans),[23] but rather to the eternal promises and purposes of God.

The history of Christianity means it is critical that we read Romans carefully, and that we make sure we do not allow a misreading of the letter to perpetuate any anti-Jewish sentiment. At the same time, we must not allow that history or our legitimate theological and interfaith concerns to cause another sort of misreading.

A NOTE ABOUT TWO KEY TERMS: *CHURCH* AND *BELIEVERS*

The word *ekklēsia*, basically meaning "assembly" and often translated as "church" when it occurs in the New Testament, occurs only five times in Romans. All of these are in chapter 16 (16:1, 4, 5, 16, 23), and only one of them refers to a Christian group in Rome (16:5). Throughout this commentary, however, we will use words like "church" and "house church," in both singular and plural forms, to refer to the Roman believers as a group or as several groups.

But how should we refer to the people who are part of these groups in Rome? We could call them "the siblings," since Paul calls them "brothers" (Gk. *adelphoi*) meaning "brothers and sisters."[24] That approach is not common, however, in biblical scholarship. A few scholars have suggested terms like "messianists" (followers of the Messiah Jesus) or even "loyalists" (those loyal to Jesus), both of which are appealing but, again, not commonly used.

23. See 9:32–33; 11:11.

24. The Greek word for "brother" (*adelphos*), usually in the plural (*adelphoi*), occurs in 1:13; 7:1, 4; 8:12, 29; 9:3; 10:1; 11:25; 12:1; 14:10 (twice), 13, 15, 21; 15:14, 30; 16:14, 17, 23. Translations differ in how they treat the word in various texts ("brothers," "brothers and sisters," "friends," etc.). "Sister" (*adelphē*) occurs in 16:1, 15.

Given this commentary's emphasis on participation in Christ, it is tempting to use "co-participants," but (once again), that term is not frequently used (and certainly does not roll off the tongue!).

I will use words like "believers," "the faithful," "Christ-followers," and "Christians" interchangeably. In doing so, I want to stress that for Paul, believing means being faithful (following and obeying). Furthermore, being a "Christ-follower" means following Jesus the Jewish Messiah, and being a Christian—a term Paul never uses—means, at its core, the same thing. Although some interpreters think using the term "Christian" is anachronistic and misleading, others also use it in the way I suggest here.

Summary

To summarize this introduction to the letter, I return to a sentence used earlier: *if John is the gospel of life, as many have said, Romans is the epistle of life*. It depicts and calls for Spirit-enabled participation and transformation in Christ and thus in the life and mission of God in the world. It depicts and calls for multicultural communities of God's shalom in the midst of a world characterized by conflict and violence: Paul's world—and ours.

Reflections and Questions for the Introduction to Romans

Spiritual, Pastoral, and Theological Reflections

1. As a letter that has had such an impact and is a **letter for all seasons**, Romans needs to be read, taught, and preached as if handling something powerful, like the gospel it presents.
2. Paul's thick (robust) portrayal of believers as those who are faithful, those who pledge allegiance to Jesus, **challenges all thin forms of Christian faith.**
3. The claim that Romans **challenges the political status quo** and offers Christians a new kind of politics will be new to some readers and may be resisted at first. But if it is true, the claim will have much to say about and to Christians who find themselves in a wide variety of political contexts.
4. **Participation is a largely untapped dimension** of understanding Paul and of understanding the Christian life, yet it is one with great promise. It needs to be unpacked and developed for those very reasons.
5. The **themes of peace and justice** are not modern or liberal additions to the gospel but are actually at the very heart of the gospel.
6. The **multicultural/multiethnic dimension** of Romans is one that speaks especially prophetically to nearly all times and places.

7. Most Christians are **unaware of many of the themes in Romans** and will be surprised at some of them. Some, however, are aware of certain texts that have frequently been misunderstood or misused. The preacher/teacher (and commentator!) must exhibit patience and sensitivity in presenting these aspects of Romans—and there are many.

Questions for Those Who Read, Teach, and Preach

1. What are some of the advantages and disadvantages of communicating about sensitive issues, whether in the church or elsewhere, by letter?

2. What presuppositions about Romans do you (or do those to whom you minister through teaching or preaching) bring to the text?

3. Why do you think Romans has been such an important part of the life of the church?

4. When you think of Romans, what words or verses come to mind?

5. What other "gospels"—all-encompassing ways of thinking and living that demand allegiance and offer the promise of life/salvation in some sense—are on offer in your culture that compete with the Christian gospel?

6. What new information or perspectives about Romans did this introduction provide? How did you react to some of these, such as the discussions of Romans and politics, participation in Christ and his story, peace, and Christian mission? If you preach or teach, what challenges might you face in talking about these, or other, perspectives on the letter offered here?

7. · How does the prospect of having our imaginations converted as we read Romans affect you as you start the study of this letter?

8. How might your study of Romans be an occasion to seek greater understanding and unity among Christians?

9. How might your study of Romans be an occasion to appreciate more deeply the place of the Jewish people in the plan of God?

FOR FURTHER READING AND STUDY

Highly Accessible Commentaries and Books

Gaventa, Beverly Roberts. *When in Romans: An Invitation to Linger with the Gospel according to Paul.* Grand Rapids: Baker Academic, 2016. Focuses on salvation, identity, ethics, and community in the letter.

Hahn, Scott W. *Romans.* Catholic Commentary on Sacred Scripture. Grand Rapids: Baker Academic, 2017. Perceptive theological interpretation by a leading Catholic scholar.

Kaylor, R. David. *Paul's Covenant Community: Jew and Gentile in Romans.* Atlanta: John Knox, 1988. Focuses on the pervasive theme of covenant.

Keener, Craig S. *Romans.* New Covenant Commentary Series. Eugene, OR: Cascade, 2009. Concise but insightful analysis of Paul's literary and social worlds, theological claims, and contemporary relevance.

Matera, Frank J. *Preaching Romans: Proclaiming God's Saving Grace.* Collegeville, MN: Liturgical, 2010. Comments for preaching from the Sunday and daily readings in the Roman Catholic lectionary.

McKnight, Scot, and Joseph B. Modica, eds. *Preaching Romans: Four Perspectives.* Grand Rapids: Eerdmans, 2019. Presents readable essays and sermons from different basic takes on Paul.

Rutledge, Fleming. *Not Ashamed of the Gospel: Sermons from Paul's Letter to the Romans.* Grand Rapids: Eerdmans, 2007. Compelling sermons on nearly every text in the letter.

Stegman, Thomas D. *Written for Our Instruction: Theological and Spiritual Riches in Romans.* Mahwah, NJ: Paulist, 2017. A brief but rich treatment of five aspects of the letter, with reflection questions.

Westerholm, Stephen. *Understanding Paul: The Early Christian Worldview of the Letter to the Romans.* 2nd ed. Grand Rapids: Baker, 2004 (orig. *Preface to the Study of Paul.* Grand Rapids: Eerdmans, 1997). Beautifully written reflections on Romans, written to captivate the intelligent contemporary reader.

Wright, Tom. *Paul for Everyone: Romans.* 2 vols. Louisville: Westminster John Knox, 2004. Perceptive commentary with personal and practical insights.

Midlevel Commentaries and Books

Bird, Michael F. "The Letter to the Romans." Pages 177–204 in *All Things to All Cultures: Paul among Jews, Greeks, and Romans.* Edited by Mark Harding and Alanna Nobbs. Grand Rapids: Eerdmans, 2013. Helpful overview of interpretive issues and options.

———. *Romans.* The Story of God Bible Commentary. Grand Rapids: Zondervan, 2016. Romans as a theological, pastoral, and missional text.

Blackwell, Ben C., John K. Goodrich, and Jason Maston, eds. *Reading Romans in Context: Paul and Second Temple Judaism.* Grand Rapids: Zondervan, 2015. Short, insightful essays on the connections between the various sections of Romans and selected Jewish texts.

Byrne, Brendan. *Romans.* Sacra Pagina. Collegeville, MN: Liturgical, 1996. Excellent rhetorical and theological analysis, stressing divine faithfulness and inclusivity.

Calvin, John. *Calvin's Commentaries: The Epistles of Paul the Apostle to the Romans and Thessalonians*. Translated by R. Mackenzie. Grand Rapids: Eerdmans, 1960. The magisterial reformer's interpretation "for the common good of the church."

Chrysostom, John. "The Homilies of St. John Chrysostom: Epistle of St. Paul the Apostle to the Romans." Pages 329–564 in vol. 11 of *Nicene and Post-Nicene Fathers*. Edited by Philip Schaff. Buffalo: Christian Literature, 1886. Exegetical sermons by the great church father (d. 407). Available in multiple editions and online.

Gaventa, Beverly Roberts. *Romans*. New Testament Library. Louisville: Westminster John Knox, forthcoming. Theocentric emphasis from within the apocalyptic perspective.

Greenman, Jeffrey P., and Timothy Larsen, eds. *Reading Romans through the Centuries: From the Early Church to Karl Barth*. Grand Rapids: Brazos, 2005. Essays on significant interpreters of Romans in church history.

Grieb, A. Katherine. *The Story of Romans: A Narrative Defense of God's Righteousness*. Louisville: Westminster John Knox, 2002. Compelling interpretation that identifies God's righteousness with Jesus' faithfulness, with provocative questions for reflection.

Haacker, Klaus. *The Theology of Paul's Letter to the Romans*. Cambridge: Cambridge University Press, 2003. The letter's message in its Roman context and beyond, stressing peace and reconciliation.

Harink, Douglas. *Resurrecting Justice: Reading Romans for the Life of the World*. Downers Grove, IL: IVP Academic, 2020. A readable treatment of the theme of God's life-giving justice narrated in Romans.

Jewett, Robert. *Romans: A Short Commentary*. Minneapolis: Fortress, 2013. Distillation of the technical commentary described below.

Johnson, Luke Timothy. *Reading Romans: A Literary and Theological Commentary*. Macon, GA: Smyth & Helwys, 2001 (orig. New York: Crossroad, 1997). Insightful interpretation, highlighting God's oneness and fairness, and Christ's faith(fulness); stresses letter's fundraising purpose.

Keck, Leander E. *Romans*. Abingdon New Testament Commentaries. Nashville: Abingdon, 2005. Attention to the letter's rhetoric and theology, with special focus on God's character and activity.

Keesmaat, Sylvia C., and Brian J. Walsh. *Romans Disarmed*. Grand Rapids: Brazos, 2017. Creative, counterimperial interpretation.

Kirk, J. R. Daniel. *Unlocking Romans: Resurrection and the Justification of God*. Grand Rapids: Eerdmans, 2009. Commentary-like analysis focusing on the theme of resurrection.

Longenecker, Richard N. *Introducing Romans: Critical Issues in Paul's Most Famous Letter*. Grand Rapids: Eerdmans, 2011. In-depth but readable exploration of issues such as date, purpose, structure, etc.

Matera, Frank J. *Romans*. Paideia Commentaries on the New Testament. Grand Rapids: Baker Academic, 2010. The rhetorical structure, pastoral concerns, theology, and ongoing relevance of each section of the letter.

McKnight, Scot. *Reading Romans Backwards: The Gospel of Peace in the Midst of Empire*. Waco: Baylor University Press, 2019. An interpretation that focuses on the last part of the letter and reads the rest of the letter as supporting the last section.

Oakes, Peter. *Reading Romans in Pompeii: Paul's Letter at Ground Level*. Minneapolis: Fortress, 2009. Creative, insightful historical reading of the letter as an address to a house church of craftworkers.

Origen. *Commentary on the Epistle to the Romans*. Translated by Thomas Scheck. The Fathers of the Church 103–4. Washington, DC: Catholic University of America Press, 2001–2002. Influential interpretation by the third-century theologian.

Reardon, Patrick Henry. *Romans: An Orthodox Commentary*. Yonkers, NY: St. Vladimir's Seminary Press, 2018. Theological interpretation from an Eastern Orthodox perspective, with special attention to the church fathers.

Reasoner, Mark. *Romans in Full Circle: A History of Interpretation*. Louisville: Westminster John Knox, 2005. Major interpretations of main passages over the centuries.

Rodriguez, Rafael. *If You Call Yourself a Jew: Reappraising Paul's Letter to the Romans*. Eugene, OR: Cascade, 2015. Sees Romans as a dialogue with a gentile convert to Judaism and to Jesus, intended to convince gentile believers to worship Israel's God through the faithful Messiah without recourse to torah.

Sumney, Jerry L., ed. *Reading Paul's Letter to the Romans*. Atlanta: Society of Biblical Literature, 2012. Essays representing various perspectives on the letter as a whole and on key aspects of it.

Talbert, Charles H. *Romans*. Smyth & Helwys Bible Commentary. Macon, GA: Smyth & Helwys, 2002. Special emphasis on parallel texts and ideas in the ancient world.

Tonstad, Sigve K. *The Letter to the Romans: Paul among the Ecologists*. Sheffield: Sheffield Phoenix, 2017. A reading of the letter through the lens of ancient and contemporary relationships between the human and nonhuman creation.

Thiselton, Anthony C. *Discovering Romans: Content, Interpretation, Reception*. Grand Rapids: Eerdmans, 2016. Perceptive introduction to the text and its interpretation.

Wright, N. T. "Romans." Pages 393–770 in vol. 10 of *The New Interpreter's Bible*. Edited by Leander E. Keck et al. Nashville: Abingdon, 2002. Creative theological analysis that pays close attention to the social and political realities that Paul confronts and challenges.

Wu, Jackson. *Reading Romans with Eastern Eyes: Honor and Shame in Paul's Message and Mission*. Downers Grove, IL: IVP Academic, 2019. An interpretation that pays close attention to cultural values such as honor and shame and collective identity.

Technical Commentaries and Books

Cranfield, C. E. B. *A Critical and Exegetical Commentary on the Epistle to the Romans*. International Critical Commentary. 2 vols. Edinburgh: T&T Clark, 1975, 1979. Thorough, if traditional, exposition that presents and evaluates many interpretive options.

Dunn, James D. G. *Romans*. Word Biblical Commentary 38A–B. 2 vols. Waco: Word, 1988. Sophisticated, detailed treatment from the new perspective on Paul.

Elliott, Neil. *The Arrogance of Nations: Reading Romans in the Context of Empire*. Minneapolis: Fortress, 2008. Interprets Romans as offering an alternative to imperial values and practices, both ancient and contemporary.

Fitzmyer, Joseph A. *Romans*. Anchor Yale Bible 33. Garden City, NY: Doubleday, 1993. Technically thorough and learned analysis of the letter with a fairly traditional interpretation.

Gaventa, Beverly Roberts, ed. *Apocalyptic Paul: Cosmos and Anthropos in Romans 5–8*. Waco: Baylor University Press, 2013. Leading experts explore the human and cosmic dimensions of God's action in Christ.

Hultgren, Arland J. *Paul's Letter to the Romans: A Commentary*. Grand Rapids: Eerdmans, 2011. Detailed exposition that interacts with other interpreters, ancient sources, and key theological issues.

Jewett, Robert. *Romans*. Hermeneia. Minneapolis: Fortress, 2007. Massive study arguing that Romans is intended to gather support for the mission to Spain; its main themes are overcoming the Roman culture of honor and practicing radical hospitality.

Käsemann, Ernst. *Commentary on Romans*. Translated by Geoffrey W. Bromiley. Grand Rapids: Eerdmans, 1980. Classic theological analysis stressing the righteousness of God as God's saving power.

Longenecker, Richard W. *Romans*. The New International Greek Testament Commentary. Grand Rapids: Eerdmans, 2016. Careful, detailed analysis of the Greek text.

Moo, Douglas J. *The Letter to the Romans.* New International Commentary on the New Testament. 2nd ed. Grand Rapids: Eerdmans, 2018. Careful analysis of the Greek text from within the more traditional perspective.

Porter, Stanley E., and Francis G. H. Pang, eds. *The Letter to the Romans: Exegesis and Application.* Eugene, OR: Wipf & Stock, 2018. Essays on various aspects of the letter.

Wu, Siu Fung. *Suffering in Romans.* Eugene, OR: Pickwick, 2015. A careful study, stressing Rom 5 and 8, with far-reaching implications.

Commentary with Reflections and Questions

1:1–17
OPENING AND THEME: THE GOSPEL OF GOD'S SON, POWER, AND JUSTICE FOR THE SALVATION OF ALL

Ancient letters, like contemporary correspondence, had a certain predictable structure. Paul both follows and modifies that format, and this is evident in the first seventeen verses of Romans. Theologically speaking, Paul Christianizes standard elements of the ancient letter, such as the identification of the sender and recipients and the greeting. Pastorally speaking, he writes with authority and conviction, but also with humility and warmth. Rhetorically speaking, Paul expands the letter's standard elements because Romans is a pastoral letter-essay. It has a theme and even a thesis, a *propositio*. Accordingly, although the sustained argument of the letter begins at 1:18, there is much of great significance in 1:1–17.

1:1–15. OPENING

How a piece of correspondence begins is important. The very first words of a letter generally establish or reestablish a relationship. Unknown, except by reputation, to many of the Roman believers, Paul uses the salutation and thanksgiving to set forth his distinctive apostolic identity and to articulate his respect for, and bond with, the Roman faithful. He also whets their appetite to hear the gospel he has been commissioned to proclaim (1:1, 15). This gospel is the letter's theme, and Paul will spell it out in the following chapters, since he has so far "been prevented" from a personal visit to do so (1:13).[1]

1:1–7. Salutation and Theme: Paul, the Romans, and the Gospel of God's Son

Paul writes this letter alone (1:1), unlike the other undisputed letters. Perhaps this is because he has not visited Rome and needs to establish his apostolic integrity, though we learn in chapter 16 that he is already known by quite a few in the imperial capital. His rather lengthy self-identification (1:1–5) focuses on both his call to apostleship and the gospel he proclaims, while his identification of the Roman recipients (1:6–7) centers on their calling.

---

1. All biblical quotations in the commentary, unless otherwise indicated, are from the NRSV. A few manuscripts omit "in Rome" from 1:7, probably in an attempt to make the letter serve a wider audience. But both historically and theologically speaking, the particular audience is important for good interpretation.

Paul and the Roman Believers

Paul is first of all a "servant" (Gk. *doulos*, "slave") of Christ, through whom he has received the common believers' experience of grace (cf. 5:2) as well as the particular grace to be an apostle (1:1, 5). Ultimately the source of each aspect of his identity is God, who has called him and set him apart to be an apostle (1:1; cf. Gal 1:15), one sent with the authority of the sender as the sender's representative and agent. Paul understands "apostle" to include not only Jesus' original disciples (1 Cor 15:7) but also those like himself, Barnabas (1 Cor 9:5–6), and even, it seems, a husband-wife team, Andronicus and Junia (Rom 16:7). Having seen the resurrected Lord (1 Cor 9:1; 15:8–9) and having been commissioned by him seem to be the two basic requirements for apostleship, in Paul's view. He summarizes his apostolic ministry as being a witness to, and agent of, God's amazing grace and peace (1:7).

The same God has called the Roman believers (1:6–7) to be "beloved" (children) and set them apart to be "saints," or, better, "his holy people" (NIV) who "belong to Jesus Christ." To be holy is to be marked out for God's purposes; it is to be part of an alternative culture, a different way of being human: in the world but not of the world. Paul will have much more to say about this holiness in chapter 6 and especially chapters 12–15. (What he says needs to be heard by contemporary Christians who, in the words of Jesus in Rev 3:16, are sometimes more "lukewarm" than they are holy.)

The word "saints," then, does not refer to a special class of people but to all who belong to Christ: God's holy ones (Gk. *hagioi*). Holiness with respect to humans is the scriptural language of covenant relationship, now reconfigured around Jesus, who makes a new covenant possible. The children of Israel were called to be holy because God is holy (Lev 11:45; 19:2; 20:26). So also Christians are called to be holy, sharing in the holiness of God by being reshaped into the image of Christ, God's son and our elder brother (Rom 8:14–17, 29). The Roman believers demonstrate the meaning and impact of the gospel (despite Paul's not being their spiritual parent) as exemplars of "the obedience of faith among all the Gentiles," or "nations" (1:5; Gk. *ethnē*). (We will return to this phrase momentarily.)

The Gospel

The link between the writer and the recipients of this letter is "the gospel of God . . . concerning his Son" (1:1, 3), the letter's subject matter. The gospel is what ultimately binds all Christians together. It is critical for Paul and for us that this gospel, this good news, is "the gospel of God." God, not Paul, is its source, its author.[2] The key terms—*Son of God, Lord, grace, peace, faith, obedience*—in these first verses of the letter are drawn directly from the language Paul uses to articulate the gospel in Romans and elsewhere. Many of these words could also be found in both the Scriptures of Israel and in the gospel, or ideology, of Rome. Paul's gospel stands in continuity with the former and in contrast to the latter.

The word "grace" (Gk. *charis*, meaning "favor," "benevolence," "gift") in 1:5 and 1:7 refers to God's completely unmerited and unearned favor. But a gift in antiquity required reciprocation. For Paul, as John Barclay has demonstrated, God's grace is *unconditioned* (given to the unworthy) but not *unconditional*. Those who have received such grace are expected to be transformed by the Spirit; grace implies obligation.[3]

"Peace" (1:7) summarizes the gospel as much as "grace" does (e.g., 5:1; 8:6; 14:17). It represents the Hebrew word *šālôm* (shalom), meaning not merely the absence of conflict but also wholeness: having right relations with God, one another, and all creation. The architect of true peace is not Caesar or any other political power; it is the God of peace (15:33; 16:20; Phil 4:9; 1 Thess 5:23).

The phrase "the obedience of faith" (1:5) is also particularly important to Romans, which not only begins but also ends with a reference to it (16:26). As the letter unfolds, it will become clear that faith and obedience are not two separate responses to the gospel, one requiring or generating the other, but one unified response of obedient faith. Recent ways of rendering this phrase include "faithful obedience" (CEB), "believing obedience" (KNT), "believing allegiance," and "covenantal believing allegiance."[4]

This unity of faith and obedience is grounded in the fact that the gospel is a divine and royal announcement: it is the good news from God (1:1), promised in Scripture through the prophets (1:2), about God's Son (1:3). Although Paul does not identify which prophets or which specific promises he has in mind, it is clear from Romans that he finds Scripture as a whole, and the prophet Isaiah in particular, as a multifaceted witness to the gospel he proclaims. The prophets Jeremiah, Ezekiel, Hosea, and Habakkuk also figure significantly in Romans, as does the entire Torah, and the Psalms also have a prominent place.

2. When Paul does call the gospel "my gospel" (2:16; 16:25; cf. 2 Tim 2:8), he means the gospel of God as he proclaims it, not something he has invented, owns, or controls.
3. See John M. G. Barclay, *Paul and the Gift* (Grand Rapids: Eerdmans, 2015); *Paul and the Power of Grace* (Grand Rapids: Eerdmans, 2020). For a short overview, see his *Paul and the Subversive Power of Grace* (Cambridge: Grove Books, 2016).
4. On obedience in Romans, see also 2:8, 25; 5:19; 6:12, 16–17; 10:16; 11:30–31; 15:18; 16:19.

For Paul, the entirety of Israel's Scripture points toward the arrival and reign of Jesus as Messiah and Lord.

"The obedience of faith" may well be a phrase Paul coined to connect Jesus' experience to that of believers. Jesus, God's Son and the focal subject of the gospel, was both obedient and faithful to his Father (3:22, 26; 5:19).[5] The gospel, therefore, is not simply to be *believed* but to be *obeyed* (Rom 10:16). To believe is to share in the Son's obedience, which (as we will see) means to share in his death and resurrection (Rom 6). Paul proclaims Christ's obedience/faithfulness in order to elicit a similar obedience/faithfulness from his hearers and readers, both ancient and contemporary.[6] Jesus is "our Lord" (1:4; cf. 1:7), a title that also clearly implies a call to allegiance and obedience.

Jesus our Lord is also Jesus God's Son (1:3–4). The Son Paul names here was not merely a Davidic *descendant* but is revealed, by God's resurrection of him (cf. Gal 1:1), to be the promised Davidic *Messiah*, or royal Son of God (a messianic designation). The "Spirit of holiness" (1:4) powerfully at work in Christ's resurrection is the same Spirit at work in all believers, as Paul will discuss at length in chapter 8.

It is likely that in 1:3–4 Paul is citing part of an early Christian creedal tradition that speaks of Christ's exaltation. Neither the tradition nor Paul, however, holds an adoptionist Christology, as some interpreters have suggested: the belief that Christ was not the eternal, preexistent Son of God but a man who became Son of God through adoption at some later point (his baptism or his resurrection). The declaration (NRSV) of Jesus' messiahship/sonship, sometimes understood as his appointment (NIV, NET) to messiahship/sonship, is a way of describing the resurrection as God's vindication of Christ's death and the commencement of his royal messianic reign. His nature has not changed, but his role in God the Father's salvation project has been publicly announced with clarity.

This sort of confession about the significance of Christ's resurrection and exaltation, as Phil 2:6–11 shows, does not contradict a belief in Christ's preexistent divine status (see also Gal 4:4), even though preexistence is not explicitly mentioned by Paul (or the tradition he cites and affirms) in 1:3–4. The citation of early Christian tradition and the reference to Scripture (1:2) lend authority to Paul's proclamation of the gospel and put him on common ground with the teachers and believers in Rome.

---

5. As we will see in the discussion of 3:21–26, this commentary understands the Pauline phrase that is often translated as "faith in Jesus Christ" to mean the faith, or faithfulness, of Jesus Christ.

6. See also 6:15–20; 15:18.

Summary

The importance of these first few lines of the letter, with their brief but poignant summary of the gospel, should not be underestimated. The emphasis is on Jesus' royalty and resurrection. In conjunction with 1:16–17, which focuses on God's righteousness, they tell us in summary form what the gospel is and what it does. References to Jesus as Son of God and Messiah (Christ) mean that he is the prophetically promised king who has inaugurated God's salvation, righteousness, and justice in the world.

Such claims are implicitly a challenge to Rome, with its own claims to being the good news of universal sovereignty, salvation, and justice, embodied especially in its own royal figure, the emperor. Such claims about Jesus also implicitly invite Paul's audience to participate in the universal dissemination of God's gospel as the truly good news humanity needs and the proper alternative to any other alleged gospel of salvation, ancient or contemporary.

Having identified himself, the content of the gospel, and his letter's recipients, Paul offers the Romans grace and peace (1:7b). In these first seven verses, then, Paul lets his addressees know that they and he—despite their different callings—share a common gospel experience of grace and a common response of believing allegiance that relates them to God the Father, Jesus the Messiah/ Son and Lord, and the Spirit of holiness. The stage is set for Paul to narrate the saving work of the triune God and the human joy of benefiting from and participating in that salvation.[7] But first, Paul needs to create a more personal rapport with his addressees, which he does in the following verses.

1:8–15. Thanksgiving, Intercession, and Hope

Most of Paul's letters include a thanksgiving after the salutation. Paul does three main things in this particular thanksgiving, all of which help to establish his relationship with the Roman faithful. He speaks of gratitude, prayer, and hope rooted in a sense of Christian mutuality.

First, Paul expresses gratitude for the Roman believers and the worldwide reputation of their faith, or faithfulness (1:8, referring to the global Christian community). We find a similar joy in believers' faithfulness expressed in other letters (e.g., 1 Thess 1:2–10; Col 1:6–7). This is not mere rhetorical flattery.

---

7. Some readers may find the word "triune" anachronistic or out of place here, but as Paul's letters clearly demonstrate, he experiences and describes God in terms of Father, Son, and Spirit. We will see this come to expression in various parts of Romans.

Historically and today, certain Christian communities are worthy of special recognition, especially for their fidelity in challenging situations.

Second, Paul says he constantly prays for the Roman Christians (1:9), as he does for all the churches in his care and his co-workers (Eph 1:15–21; Phil 1:3–5; Col 1:3–7; 1 Thess 1:2; 3:10; 2 Thess 1:11; 2 Tim 1:3; Phlm 4). Later in the letter (15:30–32) and elsewhere, in the spirit of mutuality manifested in the following verses, Paul invites prayer for himself and his ministry (see also 2 Cor 1:10–11; Eph 6:19–20; Phil 1:18–19; Col 4:3–4; 1 Thess 5:25).

Third, and above all, Paul expresses his prayer and desire to visit the Roman faithful both as a fellow believer and as an apostle (1:10–15). As an apostle, Paul is still a brother, so ministry for him is a two-way street. He anticipates not only imparting a "spiritual gift" (Gk. *charisma*; see also 12:6) to strengthen the Romans, but also engaging in mutual, or co-, encouragement (Gk. *symparaklēthēnai*) while among them (1:11–12).

Paul explains that his failure to visit Rome thus far has not been due to his own desire or decision but to his having been "prevented" (1:13; cf. 15:22–24). This is almost certainly a reference to God's intervention and guidance, especially given Paul's sense of being sent to places where Christ has not been "named" (15:20).[8] Paul believes that Christian ministry—and the Christian life more generally—means going where and when God leads, not when and where people expect. Nonetheless, it is altogether appropriate to express "eagerness" for ministry (1:15) while patiently waiting for God's timing.

Thus, while clearly acknowledging divine providence, Paul cannot help but also envision a future apostolic mission of reaping some "harvest" (or bearing fruit) in Rome as he does in all the gentile lands, paying his debt to cultured persons (the "Greeks"; the "wise") and uncultured people (the "barbarians"; the "foolish") alike (1:13b–15; cf. 1 Cor 9:19–23).[9] That is, even though his general mode of operating is only to go to the unevangelized, Paul feels an obligation to "gospelize" the whole world. As John Wesley would later say, "The world is my parish."

---

8. It is far less likely in this situation that Paul attributes his being prevented to mere humans or to Satan (though see a different scenario in 1 Thess 2:18).

9. Like most Jews of his day, Paul generally divides the world in a binary fashion into Jews and non-Jews, the latter called either "Greeks" or "the gentiles" (= "the nations"). Here he also follows the convention of Greeks and then Romans referring to those perceived to be uncivilized as "barbarians," an onomatopoeic word for those who babble ("bar . . . bar"). Cf. Col 3:11. Both the gospel and the *ekklēsia*, however, are for all people, even barbarians and worse.

Since Paul is writing to believers, preaching the gospel to (or perhaps among) those in Rome means teaching the converted as well as converting unbelievers (1:15). Christian believers always need to encounter afresh the promises and demands of the gospel. Walter Brueggemann's understanding of evangelism is not unlike Paul's: "evangelism means inviting people into . . . [the scriptural] stories as the definitional story of our life."[10] Paul wants to proclaim the gospel to the Roman believers too—not to effect their initial conversion but to deepen their understanding of the gospel so they can embody it more fully.

Prayer has been Paul's substitute for presence thus far in his relationship with the Roman house churches. Now that intercession will be supplemented with a letter as a prelude to an anticipated visit. With these words of introduction, gratitude, and explanation written, Paul proceeds to "proclaim the gospel" to those in Rome.

1:16–17. Theme: The Gospel as God's Power and Justice for the Salvation of All

By many accounts, these two dense verses (1:16–17), especially read in conjunction with 1:1–4 about the Son, contain the theme or thesis (Latin *propositio*) of Romans. They are therefore worthy of careful attention. In them, as in 1:1–7, we find another, even richer minilexicon of Paul's vocabulary as well as a host of grammatical and other interpretive issues. The key terms include *ashamed, gospel, power, God, salvation, believe/faith* (they have the same root, *pist-,* in Greek), *Jew and Greek (gentile), righteousness/justice of God, revealed, written, the one who is righteous/just,* and *live.*

What is noticeably absent from 1:16–17, however, has confused some people—no direct reference to Christ. This absence points to at least two of the major interpretive issues. Is this justifying faith oriented to Christ? And is there any implicit, if not explicit, reference to Christ?

1:16. Not Ashamed of the Gospel, the Power of God for Salvation

The first thing Paul says in 1:16 is that he is "not ashamed of the gospel" because it is "the power of God for salvation to everyone who has faith" (1:16). This

---

10. Walter Brueggemann, *Biblical Perspectives on Evangelism: Living in a Three-Storied Universe* (Nashville: Abingdon, 1993), 10.

gospel can be none other than the one already announced in 1:1–4 and soon to be described in detail over the next fifteen chapters. It must be, therefore, a thoroughly Christocentric (Christ-centered) gospel and revelation (1:17).

For Paul, one cannot simply have faith—even faith toward the God of Israel—as if the Messiah had never come. The words "ashamed," "power," and "salvation" indicate immediately that Paul is indeed thinking of the gospel of the crucified Messiah. Writing from Corinth to the Romans, he may even be deliberately alluding to his own words sent earlier to, rather than from, Corinth:

> For the message about the cross is *foolishness* to those who are perishing, but to us who are being *saved* it is the *power* of God. . . . God decided, through the *foolishness* of our proclamation, to save those who believe. For *Jews* demand signs and *Greeks* desire wisdom, but we proclaim Christ crucified, a stumbling block to *Jews* and foolishness to *Gentiles*, but to those who are the called, both *Jews* and *Greeks*, Christ the *power* of God and the wisdom of God. . . . "Let the one who *boasts, boast* in the Lord." (1 Cor 1:18, 21b–24, 31b; emphasis added)[11]

That Paul is not ashamed of the gospel of Christ crucified, not embarrassed by it, is a deliberate understatement. He means that he *boasts* in the crucified Lord Christ and therefore in the gospel. In an honor-shame culture, this is an incredibly significant but utterly counterintuitive and countercultural perspective.

Western Christians, for whom honor and shame are less defining cultural characteristics than they were in Paul's world (or still are today outside the West), may have trouble fully grasping the nature of this embrace of the crucified Messiah, even if certain Western hymns use the language of shame and glory. Non-Western Christians, however, are generally better able to understand Paul here because they often inhabit a similar honor-shame culture; Western Christians can learn from them. (This is an example of the necessary mutual edification and instruction Paul has noted in the thanksgiving.)

The gospel, Paul announces, is a power—a "force unleashed" in the world.[12] As such, it accomplishes its divine task of salvation, of revealing and establish-

---

11. See also 2 Tim 1:11–12: "For this gospel I was appointed a herald and an apostle and a teacher, and for this reason I suffer as I do. But I am not ashamed, for I know the one in whom I have put my trust, and I am sure that he is able to guard until that day what I have entrusted to him."

12. Joseph A. Fitzmyer, *Romans*, Yale Anchor Bible 33 (Garden City, NY: Doubleday, 1993), 254.

ing God's righteousness/justice, not returning void or empty (see Isa 55:11). It is what linguists and others call a performative utterance: a speech-act that makes something happen, that causes a transformation. This can be the case only if the crucified Messiah Jesus is also the resurrected, vindicated Son of God narrated in 1:1–4.

Significantly, this gospel-power is revealing God's righteousness (or jus-tice—see below) *now*—present tense (Gk. *apokalyptetai*; 1:17). Any under-standing of Paul as an apocalyptic theologian must include the reality that God's powerful revelation, or apocalypse, in human history did not end with Christ's death and resurrection; it continues in the ongoing work of the proc-lamation of the gospel.

Paul clearly views God's gospel and salvation as oriented to all people: "to the Jew first and also to the Greek" (1:16). He knows that the one God of all humanity (3:29–30) has indeed chosen Israel, to whom and through whom came God's law (torah, or instruction), promises, and Messiah (3:2; 9:4–5). But the divine election of Israel was ultimately for the blessing or salvation of all nations (see Rom 9–11; Gal 3:6–9; Gen 12:3; 18:18).

Salvation—God's deliverance of Israel, according to the Scriptures—is thus offered universally in this good news, and this universality is a strong thematic emphasis in Romans. The only condition for the receipt of this salvation, or divine rescue, is faith. We are wise as readers not to import our own precon-ceptions of words like "salvation" and "faith" into these texts. The letter itself will unpack their meaning.

For now, all we need to say is that both terms are rather comprehensive in scope. Salvation for Paul, though oriented toward the future day of deliv-erance, is the total experience of being put into right covenant relationship with God now, being one day raised from the dead and acquitted at the divine judgment, and therefore having eternal life. Faith, for the hearers, is the total response of believing obedience to the gospel (1:5). It includes the mind, heart, and body.

The term "faith," however, leads us also to 1:17, and to the possibility that the notion of faith in Paul's proclamation of the gospel applies to more than just believers.

1:17. *The Revelation of God's Righteousness/Justice and the Meaning of Faith*

Romans 1:16 links salvation and faith, and now 1:17 will connect righteousness, or justice, and faith.

The Righteousness/Justice of God

The phrase "the righteousness of God" (Gk. *dikaiosynē theou*) in 1:17 and else-where in Paul has been the subject of unending debates.[13] This is also the case with a few other key New Testament phrases containing "of . . ." in English, such as "faith of Christ" and "love of God." Whatever the phrase precisely sig-nifies, we know two things for sure from 1:17. First of all, the righteousness of God is not something we can figure out on our own, or give it any meaning we want. It must be, and is being, *revealed*. Like the gospel described in 1:1–7, the righteousness of God is not a matter of human imagination. Second, it is in fact the gospel that contains and reveals the righteousness of God. God's righteous-ness is a gospel-shaped righteousness. Once again, we cannot imagine or think our way to God's righteousness; we must, instead, look for it in the gospel.

That said, the interpretation of this important Pauline phrase in 1:17 has raised the following question among interpreters: Does "the righteousness of God" refer to (a) something that *originates in* God (e.g., "righteousness from God")[14] or (b) something that is *characteristic of* God (e.g., "God's righteous-ness"), either a divine quality or a divine activity, or both?

Despite the long-standing prevalence of the "righteousness from God" in-terpretation, especially among Protestant interpreters, many recent scholars have argued persuasively that the translation "God's righteousness" is more often correct, including here in 1:17. (The phrase may have different senses in different contexts.) This is the interpretation adopted here: Paul is not speaking primarily of something God *gives* but of something God *has* and *does*. (Nonetheless, as we will see, humans can, in Christ, share in this divine attribute and activity.)

That is, "the righteousness of God" refers to one of the most prominent divine characteristics and corollary actions in the Bible—*God's covenant fi-delity to Israel demonstrated in saving power to make things right*. In a word, the *righteousness* of God is the *justice* of God. Certain sorts of scriptural texts informed Paul's perspective on God's righteousness/justice:

- Paul seems especially to have Ps 98:1–3 (LXX 97:1–3) in mind. The psalmist declares that God's victory and faithfulness have been manifested to both Israel and the ends of the earth. The Greek text of verses 2–3 refers twice to God's "salvation" (*sōtērion*) and also to God's "justice/righteousness" (*dikaio-*

---

13. See also Rom 3:21, 22; 2 Cor 5:21.

14. This was the interpretation in the original 1984 NIV, though it was changed in the 2011 edition.

synē). Paul uses both terms in 1:16–17.[15] Psalm 98:3 also refers to God's mercy and truthfulness (= fidelity).[16]

- In Ps 143:1 (LXX 142:1), the psalmist says, "Hear my prayer, O LORD; give ear to my supplications in your faithfulness; answer me in your righteousness" (LXX *dikaiosynē*)—that is, God's "justice" (NET) or "saving justice" (NJB).
- And in Isaiah, the prophet presents God's righteousness/justice and God's salvation as parallel realities: "My righteousness [*dikaiosynē*] draws near swiftly; my salvation [*sōtēria*] will go out, and the nations will hope in my arm" (LXX Isa 51:5a NETS).

We might say that God *does* what God *is*: the righteous God acts righteously; the God of justice creates justice; the faithful God practices fidelity; God the savior saves. God's faithful, saving, justice-making power makes right that which is wrong and out of kilter with God's intentions. It is *restorative*, establishing that which ought to be but is not. It is thus *justice*, not in the sense of vengeance but in the sense of making right. The New Jerusalem Bible therefore appropriately translates the phrase as "the justice of God." The gospel is about God's justice, God's making-things-rightness. The just God acts justly, establishing justice, and this justice is gospel-shaped.

It is important to note here, and to keep in mind throughout the letter, that the words translated "righteousness" or "justice," as well as "justification" and "justified," are all part of the same Greek word-family, whose root is *dik-*. (See the sidebar below.) We must keep this in mind in order to see the relationship between God's righteousness/justice and the justification of human beings, which (the commentary will show later) makes human beings righteous/just by allowing them to share in God's righteousness/justice.

THE VOCABULARY OF RIGHTEOUSNESS, JUSTICE, AND JUSTIFICATION

Already in this commentary, we have seen the words righteousness and justice presented together as righteousness/justice. As noted in the introduction and briefly again here in the commentary on 1:16–17, there is a reason for this.

---

15. To be precise, Paul uses the more common word *sōtēria* for the LXX word *sōtērion*.

16. The connections of Ps 98 to Rom 1:16–17 are clearer in the Greek (LXX) than in the Hebrew text. Douglas Harink suggests that Romans can be considered as a commentary on these verses from Ps 98. See his *Resurrecting Justice: Reading Romans for the Life of the World* (Downers Grove, IL: IVP Academic, 2020), 28.

One Greek word-family, *dik-*, has been translated into English with two different word-families: "right-" and "just-."

In Greek, the *dik-* family of words runs throughout Romans to express God's righteousness or justice (*dikaiosynē*), God's just requirement (*dikaiōma*), our unrighteousness or injustice (*adikia*), righteous/just/justified persons (*dikaios*), justification (*dikaioō, dikaiōsis*), our righteous or just behavior in Christ and the Spirit *(dikaiosynē)*, and more. But as we can immediately see, English does in fact use two different word-families to express this single Greek word-family.

Moreover, translators and others often use both word-families, even in the same context, resulting in a separation of words—and thus of theological realities—that Paul keeps together. My own preference is for "just-" language, primarily because I think "justice" language, carefully used, comes closer to what Paul's intentions are than does "righteousness" language. In addition, all of the relevant Greek words *can* be rendered with that English word-family, which is harder to do with the "right-" family. Just, justice, and justification are common English words, but righteous and righteousness do not have the related words "righteousify" or "righteousification." ("Rectify" and "rectification" come close and are used by some interpreters of Paul, but although they convey the "setting things right" aspect of God's justice, they do not express the full sense of justice.)

It is also important to note that the members of each English word-family often have varying denotations and connotations. "Justice" has many different dictionary definitions and popular uses. If it is used in interpreting Romans, it must be carefully distinguished from Roman justice, American justice, justice as retribution, justice as a political ideology, and so on. "Righteousness," on the other hand, must be distinguished from "self-righteousness" and from a sense of purely inward purity or personal morality.

Whichever set of English words we use, we must try very hard to see and articulate the interrelationship among all of Paul's words in the *dik*-family, or we will fail to see the message of Romans clearly.

Note: For examples of how this linguistic challenge is handled in various Bible translations, see the introduction to the commentary, pp. 43–45.

Before writing Romans, Paul had made this point in 2 Corinthians: "For our sake he [God] made him [Christ] to be sin who knew no sin, so that in him [Christ] we would become the righteousness [or "justice"] of God" (2 Cor 5:21 NRSV alt.).[17] The gospel is "the power of God for salvation" because its announcement reveals and makes effective the faithful, saving, justice-creating power of God manifested in Jesus' death and resurrection, inviting us to participate in it. We will not be far off the mark if we understand "the righteousness of God" as God's faithful, saving, restorative justice, or simply God's saving justice. This is not Roman or American retributive justice but a justice that makes things right.

Faith/Faithfulness

The Greek word *pistis* can mean either "faith" or "faithfulness." It is therefore quite possible that the very important but compact, cryptic words in 1:17a—"the righteousness of God is revealed through faith for faith" (NRSV)—should be translated as including a reference to *divine* as well as human faith(fulness): the righteousness of God is revealed from [God's] faithfulness for [human] faithfulness.

What makes this interpretation possible? The Greek text has two different prepositions, one to indicate a starting point (source or agency) and the other a goal: *ek* [from] . . . *eis* [for, to, toward]. Consequently, the CEB translates the phrase as "from faithfulness for faith." N. T. Wright's rendering in his Kingdom New Testament is similar: "This is because God's covenant justice is unveiled in it, from faithfulness to faithfulness."

It is even quite possible that the first mention of faithfulness refers not to God generally (i.e., God the Father) but to Christ specifically. (We will interpret 3:21, 26 as references to Christ's faithfulness, so this option is not just speculative.) If this is correct, we could interpret the first half of 1:17 as follows: *For in the gospel, God's faithful, saving, restorative justice is revealed through Christ's faithfulness in order to generate faithfulness among those who hear it.*

These observations suggest that in Romans, Paul is presenting a gospel that involves three forms of faithfulness: God's, Christ's, and humanity's. We will see these three together more explicitly in Paul's restatement of his thesis in 3:21–26: God's faithfulness and justice are revealed in Christ's death, and are to be met by our faithful response that leads to justification. The initiative,

---

17. The NRSV and most translations actually have "might become," but Paul intends to speak of God's purpose and its realization, rather than simply a possibility, as "might" could imply.

of course, is God's, not ours, for it is only and always by grace that anyone is justified or saved.

The central reality of faith continues also in the second half of 1:17, where Paul quotes a version of Hab 2:4. This verse mentions key elements of Paul's theme that will be unpacked in the letter: righteousness/justice, faith/faithfulness, and life. It is not certain, however, exactly what Paul intends to say. Among the possibilities are the following:

1. the one who is righteous/just by faith will live (see NAB, NET, NJB);
2. the one who is righteous/just will live by faith (see NIV, NRSV);
3. the one who is righteous/just by the faithfulness of God (or Christ) will live; or
4. the Righteous One (Christ) will live by faithfulness.

Although Paul probably affirms interpretation (3) in 1:17a, and (4) is an interesting possibility, his focus in 1:17b is most likely on human faith: interpretations (1) or (2), or both. These are really two sides of the same coin. Faith, understood as complete trust and obedience, is both the means to and the ongoing manifestation of righteousness and life.

When Paul speaks of justification later in Romans, it is these realities of faithfulness, justice, and life that he has in mind. When people respond in faithfulness to the justice of God manifested in Christ's faithful death on the cross, they become righteous or just: they are justified, and they begin a new life that is life indeed. To be justified is to join the community of the just that is being created by the gospel of God's justice. It is not to enter a legal fiction, as some understand justification—being counted righteous even though one is not.[18] Rather, to be justified is to be powerfully, effectively moved into right covenant relationship with God (which will also entail right relations with others) and to take on that divine attribute of righteousness/justice; it is transformative. To be justified is to begin a new life of living faithfully and covenantally "to God" (cf. 6:11; Gal 2:19).

This sort of transformation is clearly what happened to Paul himself, and it is what he will later call "newness of life" (6:4), the final result of which is "eternal life" (5:21; 6:22–23). Indeed, Romans may appropriately be given the

---

18. The phrase "legal fiction" refers to certain understandings of justification claiming that God fictitiously pronounces as righteous those who trust in Christ, even though they are actually unrighteous. Theologically speaking, we should stress that Paul's God, the biblical God, is a God of fact, not fiction; of good news, not fake news; of transformative power, not pretense.

subtitle *l'chaim*—Hebrew for "to life!" The gospel it proclaims is power. It effects transformation and engenders life. In Greek, the last word in Rom 1:16–17 is *zēsetai*, meaning "will live." The rest of Romans unpacks the gospel and its life-giving effects that are so succinctly and tantalizingly summarized in 1:1–4 and 1:16–17.

REFLECTIONS AND QUESTIONS FOR 1:1–17

Pastoral, Spiritual, and Theological Reflections

1. The **gospel** is not first of all about us or me; it is **about God**, and specifically about God's Messiah, the crucified and resurrected Lord. The gospel is an apocalypse, a revelation, about what God has done in Christ and is continuing to do by the Spirit. The gospel reveals God's power as the power of life made possible by God's saving justice, God's faithfulness and mercy. The gospel reveals God's love, God's kind of justice and peace, God's dream for the world. To be a beneficiary of this gospel is to be caught up into the story, the mission, and the life of God.

2. On "the **obedience of faith**," Dietrich Bonhoeffer offered these two basic claims: "*only the believers obey*, and *only the obedient believe*."[19] Faith is a many-sided reality for Paul, including assent, trust, and allegiance/obedience. Many Christians, including many interpreters of Romans, overemphasize either trust or assent and underemphasize allegiance/obedience.

3. If **ministry** was a **two-way street** for Paul, it is imperative that ministers of the gospel today balance their leadership role and their role as a brother or sister in Christ—for the health of both the minister and the congregation. Anyone in Christian ministry would do well to adopt Paul's perspective, which requires a certain humility; in fact, many in ministry have said they learn or gain more from those to whom they minister than they themselves have given.

4. The **righteousness of God**—God's saving justice—is a fundamental divine trait and activity with huge implications that many Christians are unaware of. It is such a critical dimension of Romans that we need to try to get it right from the beginning and keep at it throughout our engagement with the letter. Unfortunately, as we have seen, the English language itself does not help the situation, nor sometimes does common usage of words such as justice and righteousness.

19. Dietrich Bonhoeffer, *Discipleship*, trans. Barbara Green and Reinhard Krauss, Dietrich Bonhoeffer Works 4 (Minneapolis: Fortress, 2001), 63.

5. Similarly, **"salvation"** is a word and (more importantly) a reality that is too narrowly defined by many Christians. Paul in general, and Romans in particular, provides us with a holistic, comprehensive understanding of the many dimensions of salvation. This understanding is rooted in the Scriptures of Israel but of course takes on new significance in the light of Christ.

Questions for Those Who Read, Teach, and Preach

1. What insights about the gospel have you gained from this section of Romans?
2. How do the perspectives on key gospel terms like *grace, peace, obedience, faith, justification,* and *the righteousness of God* offered here differ from what you, or those in your Christian community, have previously thought?
3. What is the significance of understanding the gospel as divine power, as a performative utterance?
4. What does it mean today to evangelize, or gospelize, those who are already Christian believers? To evangelize those who are not?
5. Identify some of the contemporary groups or movements offering salvation (in some sense—perhaps offering purpose or destiny) and community that some people see as alternatives to the Christian gospel and church. That is, what are some of the most significant ways in which contemporary men and women express their search for God, rebirth/renewal, peace and justice, and immortality? How might the answers to these questions affect the way the church interprets the Christian gospel to others?
6. What are some reasons people may feel some shame about their Christian faith (or *the* Christian faith) in their families, neighborhoods, workplaces, social gatherings, and so on? How can such shame be addressed, whether in the West (where opposition to Christianity is generally mild) or in places of real social, economic, or physical threat?

For Further Reading

Barclay, John M. G. *Paul and the Gift.* Grand Rapids: Eerdmans, 2015.
———. *Paul and the Power of Grace.* Grand Rapids: Eerdmans, 2020.
———. *Paul and the Subversive Power of Grace.* Cambridge: Grove Books, 2016.
Bates, Matthew. *Gospel Allegiance: What Faith in Jesus Misses for Salvation in Christ.* Grand Rapids: Brazos, 2019.
Bonhoeffer, Dietrich. *Discipleship.* Translated by Barbara Green and Reinhard Krauss. Dietrich Bonhoeffer Works 4. Minneapolis: Fortress, 2001. Previously

published as *The Cost of Discipleship*. Rev. ed. Translated by R. H. Fuller. New York: Macmillan, 1959.

Brueggemann, Walter. *Biblical Perspectives on Evangelism: Living in a Three-Storied Universe*. Nashville: Abingdon, 1993.

Harink, Douglas. *Resurrecting Justice: Reading Romans for the Life of the World*. Downers Grove, IL: IVP Academic, 2020.

McKnight, Scot. *The King Jesus Gospel: The Original Good News Revisited*. Grand Rapids: Zondervan, 2011.

Middleton, J. Richard, and Michael J. Gorman. "Salvation." Pages 45–61 in *The New Interpreter's Dictionary of the Bible*. Edited by Katherine Doob Sakenfeld. Vol. 5. Nashville: Abingdon, 2009.

Thompson, James W. *Pastoral Ministry according to Paul: A Biblical Vision*. Grand Rapids: Baker Academic, 2006.

Witherup, Ronald D. *Saint Paul and the New Evangelization*. Collegeville, MN: Liturgical, 2013.

Wright, N. T. *Simply Christian: Why Christianity Makes Sense*. San Francisco: HarperSanFrancisco, 2006.

Wu, Jackson. *Reading Romans with Eastern Eyes: Honor and Shame in Paul's Message and Mission*. Downers Grove, IL: IVP Academic, 2019.

1:18–4:25
GOD'S FAITHFUL, MERCIFUL, AND JUST RESPONSE
TO HUMAN SIN

If, according to 1:16–17, the gospel reveals God's covenant faithfulness to establish justice and save both Jews and gentiles, then there obviously must be something—in Jewish terms, some enemy—from which all people need to be rescued. Furthermore, this human predicament must be characterized by unrighteousness, or injustice, which this enemy fosters. According to Paul, by God's fidelity and grace in the Messiah Jesus—and the human response of faith, or believing obedience—people can in fact be rescued and made righteous/just. They can be given a new lease on life, individually and corporately. Romans 1:18–4:25 deals with this human situation and divine solution.

The enemy, it turns out, is a power both within and over people that Paul calls "sin," and which we will spell "Sin." He personifies Sin as a cosmic, or apocalyptic, power. Sin universally manifests its grip on humanity in all kinds of evils, or violations of our covenant obligations (what we call "sins"), for which we are all accountable (1:18–3:20). The early Greek manuscripts of Paul's letters do not begin the word "Sin" (singular; Gk. *hamartia*) with a special letter form, since, among other reasons, the entire texts are in uppercase letters. But this way of designating Sin the power, with an initial uppercase "S," has become fairly common among English-speaking scholars. Accordingly, from now on we will use "Sin" instead of "sin" when referring to Sin the power and when quoting biblical texts where Paul appears to refer to Sin the power.

It is the event of Christ's death and resurrection, which embodies God's saving faithfulness, mercy, and justice,[1] that deals with both sins and Sin (3:21–26). This saving event provides what humans need: justification and life through the forgiveness of sins and deliverance from Sin.

Paul sees the human condition as he does only retrospectively—that is, looking back, in light of the gospel. He views humanity's dire straits and God's gracious solution through the lens of the crucified and resurrected Messiah. This does not mean that everything Paul says is unique to him; quite the contrary, in fact. He draws on Jewish perspectives and texts to show, in part, that his assessment of human need and divine mercy is not his own invention; it is rooted in Scripture and tradition.

---

1. On the connection among these divine attributes/activities in Second Temple Judaism and New Testament theology, see, e.g., Luke 1:68–75.

But why would Paul need to inform believers—the already converted—at length about this? He is gospelizing in absentia. His goal is pastoral; the recognition of universal (i.e., Jewish and gentile) sin, judgment, and mercy places Jewish and gentile believers on the same footing. They are equally in debt to God's mercy and equally children of Abraham, who is the paradigm of receiving justification and life by means of grace through faith (4:1–25). There is therefore no room for arrogance or judgmentalism in the church (3:27–31). Paul's theology of sin/Sin and grace has a pastoral aim.

1:18–3:20
Divine Impartiality and Human Accountability

We have a tendency to read one Bible verse, or maybe one paragraph, at a time. But Rom 1:18–3:20 should be read as a sustained, if complex, unit of thought. This whole section of the letter moves toward the cluster of conclusions in 3:9–20 that are critical to understanding Paul's perspective on the human condition and thus on the divine solution to that condition. Paul claims that all people, gentiles and Jews alike, are "under the power of Sin" (3:9); that none is righteous but all are sinful (3:10–18); that "the whole world" is accountable to God (3:19); and that works of the law cannot be the means of justification—of establishing right covenant relations with God and becoming righteous/just (3:20).

Paul structures the argument of 1:18–3:20 toward that conclusion in ABA' (chiastic) form:[2]

A (1:18–32) The gentile predicament
   B (2:1–16) God's impartial judgment according to deeds
A' (2:17–3:8) The Jewish predicament

It is true that Paul does not label 1:18–32 "the gentile predicament." Yet the structure of his argument throughout the letter—naming Jew and gentile again and again—strongly suggests that if 2:17–3:8 clearly refers to Jews (as I think it does), then 1:18–32 refers, or at least primarily refers, to gentiles. In the middle lies something that applies to both groups: God's criterion for judgment.

Paul's charge, or indictment, in these chapters is that all human beings are what we may call *covenantally dysfunctional*; they are unwilling and unable to live in proper covenant relationship with God and others—and they have no excuse. Humanity's inexcusable behavior means that we have forfeited both

---

2. "Chiastic" means chi- (or X-) shaped, referring to the form of the Greek letter chi.

the righteousness and the glory (Gk. *dikaiosynē* and *doxa*) in which we were created to live (cf. 3:23).[3] As theologian Khaled Anatolios puts it, reflecting especially on the golden calf incident (Exod 32), sin is "*an interruption of the communication of divine glory.*"[4]

According to Romans, *the purpose of God is, in effect, to interrupt the interruption through the work of Christ and the Spirit.* But that part of the story is down the road quite a bit, after 1:18–3:20.

Romans 1:18–3:20 is a creative rereading of Gen 3, Wis 11–19 (esp. chs. 12–14), Exod 32, Ps 89 and several other psalms, plus additional texts, through the prism of salvation, righteousness, and glory in Christ. Of particular interest is Paul's use of the Wisdom of Solomon, a popular Jewish document written just before the apostle's time. Paul agrees with Wisdom that gentiles are sinful and God is faithful, but he disagrees with its claim that Jews are preserved from divine judgment. Paul's perspective resembles that of the biblical prophets, who regularly called their own people to account right after pronouncing judgment on the nations.

Underlying this entire negative portrayal of gentiles and Jews alike *apart from* Christ, with its stress on God's impartial judgment, is Paul's pastoral concern about the behavior of gentiles and Jews *in* Christ. Implicit in the text is a warning against inhospitable arrogance within the churches at Rome and a reminder that believers, too, are accountable to God's judgment (14:10–12).

1:18–32
The Gentile Predicament

The entirety of 1:18–32 bears some resemblance to ancient (and perhaps modern) stories of the decline of civilization. Paul's take on this decline is thoroughly theological and scriptural: God's eschatological wrath, or judgment, is being revealed already, now (1:18), in the very existence of the unholy and unhealthy realities Paul describes in this passage.[5]

---

3. Douglas A. Campbell (esp. in *The Deliverance of God: An Apocalyptic Rereading of Justification* [Grand Rapids: Eerdmans, 2009]) has argued that parts of this section of Romans do not represent Paul's views but are rather the views of a teacher or teachers in Rome whom Paul opposes, or perhaps a parody of Paul's actual beliefs. This view has not been widely accepted, in part because the solution Paul finds in Christ does in fact correspond to, and undo, the human condition described in these early chapters.

4. Khaled Anatolios, *Deification through the Cross: An Eastern Christian Theology of Salvation* (Grand Rapids: Eerdmans, 2020), 106; cf. 288, 297–302.

5. Some interpreters understand this passage to be referring, at least primarily, to the

78

Paul begins the body of the letter to the Romans with the bad news, so to speak: what appears in 1:18–32 is both the cause and the manifestation of God's wrath, the righteous response of the holy God of the covenant to human sin. "Wrath" (Gk. *orgē*) in this context is not merely God's emotional response, though it includes the dimension of divine feeling: God is distressed, disappointed, and displeased. But the main point is divine judgment; human decisions and actions have consequences, both immediate and long-term. Unless we think of God as apathetic about human beings, who bear the divine image and therefore in some fundamental way represent God, we should not be surprised at the reality of God's judgment. It is part of the biblical story from Genesis to Revelation.

This way of beginning the body of the letter does not, however, indicate Paul's actual theological starting point, which is (as we have just seen in 1:1–17) the *good* news. He begins here narratively to stress the critical point that the gospel is for the truly unworthy and helpless, thus leveling the playing field, so to speak, among his addressees, who are *believers*.

That is, Paul is not necessarily offering a model for evangelizing nonbelievers that would say, "You must first be told how bad you are." (Sometimes it is Christians, more than non-Christians, who need a reminder of how bad the human predicament is—and sometimes even how bad *we* are.) At the same time, Paul means what he says; his description of the human condition is not simply for rhetorical purposes or merely to trap the self-righteous who might think these words apply only to others (see further below). Paul is deadly serious.

However, 1:18–32 is one of the most challenging Pauline texts to interpret, especially in times of confusion and disagreement about human sexuality. (Is that not a description of all times in human history?) Yet despite the importance of Paul's words about same-gender sexual relations in this passage, *Romans 1:18–32 is not primarily about sexuality, and focusing only on sexuality may cause us to miss Paul's main point.*

1:18. Ungodliness/Godlessness and Injustice

Paul begins the first main section of Romans with a word about the revelation of God's *wrath*, ironically but appropriately echoing his statement about the

---

documented idolatries and immoralities of various Roman emperors. If Paul knows about and alludes to such accounts (which is not certain), he does not limit his description here to rulers but is describing a much wider swath of humanity.

revelation of God's *justice* in the previous verse (1:17). This divine judgment is here now, Paul says, directed not against human beings but against their sins.[6] The subsequent description of the human predicament in 1:19–32 is in large measure the substance of this revelation of divine wrath. To go our own way is simultaneously to experience God's judgment, as we will see in more detail as this chapter unfolds.

In 1:18, Paul uses two general terms for sin: the Greek words *asebeia* and *adikia*. Like many of the words for sins in this passage, they begin with the Greek equivalent of the English prefix "un-" (the Greek letter alpha, *a*).[7] That is, the focus is on what humans lack. There are several possible translations for each of these words, but they represent human failure to be in right relations with God and with others—covenantal dysfunctionality, both vertically (toward God) and horizontally (toward others).

Asebeia can be rendered as "impiety" (NAB; = "un" + "piety"), "godlessness" (NIV), or "ungodliness" (NRSV, NET, NJB, NASB, ESV, KNT). We will primarily use "ungodliness" to preserve the "un-" prefix, but this does not mean generic bad behavior (CEB has "ungodly behavior"). It means living without appropriate reference to and relationship with God—an "un-godded" existence. Thus, when we use the word "godlessness," we will spell it "Godlessness" (initial uppercase "g") to indicate we mean living apart from the one true God. Idolatry, therefore, is a form of Godlessness.

The best translation for *adikia* is "unrighteousness" (NET, NAB, ESV) or "injustice" (CEB, NJB, KNT). The latter rendering is preferable in order to show the connection between it and God's justice, justification, just people, and human justice, all terms that translate various members of the *dik-* family of Greek words (*dikaiosynē*, etc.). This is a theological link that is critical to the entire letter, beginning already in 1:17. The preference for "wickedness" in some of the most-used translations (NRSV, NIV, NAB) unfortunately masks this important linguistic and theological relationship.

Together, the two terms *asebeia* and *adikia* express the reality of people's violation of the basic Jewish understanding of the covenant's two great commandments: love of God and love of neighbor. Forms of the words *asebeia* and *adikia* appear in the opening chapters of the Greek text of the prophet

---

6. The NLT makes two major mistakes in this verse by using the word "anger" and wrongly indicating people, rather than acts, as the target of divine wrath: "But God shows his anger from heaven against all sinful, wicked people."

7. Its use in this way is known as the alpha privative. There are sixteen alpha-privative words referring to human beings in 1:18–32.

Jeremiah, when he indicts the people of God both for their idolatry/spiritual unfaithfulness and for their injustices, and calls for their repentance.[8]

The Jewish philosopher Philo, roughly Paul's contemporary, wrote, "there are, as we may say, two most especially important heads of all the innumerable particular lessons and doctrines; the regulating of one's conduct towards God by the rules of piety and holiness, and of one's conduct towards [people] by the rules of humanity and justice."[9] These two great commandments, which Jesus himself affirmed (Matt 22:34–40; Mark 12:28–34; Luke 10:25–28), summarize the two tables or tablets of the law given to Moses.

It is fascinating that Paul thinks in terms of the double commandment of the Jewish covenant even when describing (or describing primarily) gentiles.[10] Paul the Jew cannot articulate the human condition without recourse to this fundamental Jewish, covenantal understanding of human existence. Honoring God and caring for one's neighbors is not merely what it means to be *Jewish*; it is what it means to be *human*.

It was commonplace in much Jewish thought and literature (e.g., Wis 13–14) to charge gentiles (all non-Jews) with idolatry and unrighteousness, especially sexual immorality.[11] That is, in large measure, what Paul is doing here and in the rest of chapter 1. Paul echoes the common Jewish conviction that the basic gentile/human problem is idolatry, and that immoralities and injustices of various kinds flow from that basic error. "Do not learn the [idolatrous] way of the nations," warns Jeremiah (Jer 10:1), while Wisdom of Solomon claims, "The very notion of idols was the beginning of immoral sexual activity" (Wis 14:12 CEB).

But because Paul does not specify gentiles, he may implicitly include Jews (and thus all humanity) in his indictment. Although a Jewish-Christian audience would instantly recognize gentiles in 1:18 and the following verses, they might not—at least not before engaging chapter 2—see themselves or other Jews here. Astute Jews, however, might hear echoes of various scriptural texts, including the golden calf incident (Exod 32; see also Ps 106:16–23), where the

8. Jer 2:22–23; 3:13.

9. Philo, *Special Laws* 2.63, in C. D. Yonge, ed., *The Works of Philo: Complete and Unabridged*, new updated ed. (Peabody, MA: Hendrickson, 1993).

10. Paul does not seem to know about the tradition within Second Temple Judaism, and then later rabbinic Judaism, of seven (or more) special Noahide or Noahic (related to the time of Noah) commandments for gentiles, though his perspective has some similarities to that tradition.

11. Wisdom of Solomon is a Jewish writing in Greek from the late first century BC or early first century AD. It is part of the Roman Catholic and the Orthodox Old Testament.

people of God engaged in idolatry and immorality, and prophetic texts (like Jer 2) that indict God's people for breaking the double commandment.

To be is to be in covenant—and, sadly, to break covenant. People lack piety and justice, right relations with God and with others. This is what human dysfunction—covenantal dysfunction—looks like, and Paul summarizes it in two words: *asebeia* and *adikia*. Paul deals first with *asebeia* in 1:19–23 and then with *adikia*. We will learn in 5:5–8 that Christ died precisely for people guilty of these two fundamental sins.

1:19–23. UNGODLINESS/GODLESSNESS AND IDOLATRY

Paul begins his charge of ungodliness, or Godlessness, and idolatry in 1:19–20 with a kind of natural theology, or (better said) a theology of general revelation available to all: the claim that God's invisible "eternal power and divine nature" (1:20) are disclosed in the creation and can be known apart from a special revelation. The apostle shares the perspective of the psalmist: "The heavens are telling the glory of God; and the firmament proclaims his handiwork" (Ps 19:1).

Consequently, those who did not (and do not) acknowledge God "are without excuse" (1:20). Even though they knew God, they foolishly did not honor or thank God, which led to their mental darkening (1:21–22, 25, 28). Paul's language refers both to intellectual capacity and to the "heart" (1:21; Gk. *kardia*).[12] In Scripture, the heart is not merely the place of deep emotion; it is the center of who we are—the place of feeling, willing, and relating to God and others. As we will see later in Romans, it is therefore the human heart that most fundamentally and radically needs repair (2:5, 29), and it is the heart that is central to the experience of grace and salvation (5:5; 6:17; 10:9–10).

Nature abhors a vacuum, so desertion of the one true God led to blatant idolatry (1:23, 25) in an act of exchange (1:23, 25; see also 1:26). Godlessness, or being un-godded, is impossible for humans, and so it inevitably devolves into idolatry. This idolatry led in turn to various immoralities (1:24, 26–27, 28b–31; cf. Eph 4:17–19). As John Calvin observed, "Surely, just as waters boil up from a vast, full spring, so does an immense crowd of gods flow from the human mind, while each one, in wandering about with too much license, wrongly

---

12. The end of 1:21 in the NRSV says "their senseless minds were darkened," but the NIV and CEB have "their foolish hearts were darkened" (similarly, the NET: "senseless hearts").

invents this or that about God himself."[13] In fact, Calvin adds, human nature is "a perpetual factory of idols."[14]

For Paul, the notion of exchange or replacement is crucial to his understanding of both idolatry and immorality. Humans have "exchanged the glory of the immortal God for images" of humans or animals (1:23; cf. Deut 4:15–18), and they have "exchanged the truth about God for a lie" (1:25). That is, they "worshiped and served the creature rather than the Creator" (1:25). This is an echo of the psalmist lamenting the golden calf incident: God's people "exchanged the glory of God for the image of an ox that eats grass" (Ps 106:20). Jeremiah uses similar words about his own day: "Has a nation changed its gods, even though they are no gods? But my people have changed their glory for something that does not profit" (Jer 2:11).

The references to exchanging or changing God's "glory" in both the prophets and Paul may have a twofold sense. First of all, people have fashioned substitutes for God's glory—a word signifying God's resplendent, powerful presence, and thus ultimately God, in Israel's Scriptures.[15] Second, they have given glory (honor, worship) to those idols rather than to God. The result is that they—we—lack the presence and power of God in our lives. We were created to live with, before, and in God's presence, glorifying and honoring God as the most glorious and honorable human activity. But we have chosen both to abandon God and to ask God to leave us alone—and thus, essentially, to leave us. We now lack the glory of God (see 3:23).[16]

Worship of the creator becomes worship of the creature, Paul argues, whether in idolatry per se, in immorality, or in both, as at the time of the golden calf. This we may call the snowball effect of covenant breaking; it is like being wrapped further and further inside a situation from which there seems to be no escape.

When we abandon and dismiss God, someone or something happily moves in and becomes our god. It may be that I become my own god, devoted fully and only to myself and my desires, or it may be that another person, an entity

13. John Calvin, *Institutes of the Christian Religion* 1.5.12, in John T. McNeill, ed., *Calvin: Institutes of the Christian Religion*, vol. 1, trans. Ford Lewis Battles (Philadelphia: Westminster, 1960), 65.

14. *Institutes of the Christian Religion* 1.11.8, in McNeill, *Calvin: Institutes*, vol. 1, 108.

15. God's glory/presence is revealed for Israel especially in the creation, at Sinai, in the tabernacle, and in the temple. It is also associated with the eschatological transformation to come.

16. I am particularly indebted to Daniel Jackson for his interpretation of this topic in Romans.

(such as a country), a cause, or an "-ism" (capitalism, nationalism, communism, etc.) takes the place of the one true God as the focus of my—or our—total devotion and allegiance. Such misguided devotion, whether individual or corporate, is both delusional and dangerous.

Stephen Fowl, in his book *Idolatry*, argues that a basic meaning of idolatry is pledging allegiance to something that is not God. This does not happen overnight, however. We don't wake up and say, "Today I will become an idolater!" Rather, Fowl maintains, idolatry is a process of small decisions and compromises that create dispositions, habits, and practices that eventually become idolatry. The result, says Paul, is behavior that is appropriate to the resulting misplaced devotion and allegiance. But such behavior is a misguided replacement for the sort of behavior appropriate to a covenantal relationship of love and obedience to God.

1:24–27. THE CONSEQUENCES OF IDOLATRY AND HUMAN SEXUALITY

Breaking the first fundamental commandment inevitably leads to breaking the second. (It should be noted, however, that this sequence can be reversed; people who practice injustice and immorality often suppress the truth about God—see the end of 1:18.) Three times Paul describes the transition from idolatry to immorality as "God gave them up" (1:24, 26, 28; NAB, "handed them over"; Gk. *paredōken*).[17] God handed them over to "impurity" (1:24), "degrading passions" (1:26), and "a debased mind" (1:28).

The apostle is echoing the scriptural theme of God's exasperation with the people's willful disobedience, so the Lord hands them over to their enemies—or to their own folly:

> So the anger of the Lord was kindled against Israel, and he gave them over [LXX *paredōken*] to plunderers who plundered them, and he sold them into the power of their enemies all around, so that they could no longer withstand their enemies. (Judg 2:14)

> Then the anger of the Lord was kindled against his people, and he abhorred his heritage; he gave them (LXX *paredōken*) into the hand of the nations, so that those who hated them ruled over them. (Ps 106:40–41 = LXX 105:40–41)

---

17. According to 1 Cor 5:5, the immoral Corinthian man is to be handed over (*paradounai*—the same verb) to Satan.

But my people did not listen to my voice; Israel would not submit to me.
So I gave them over to their stubborn hearts, to follow their own counsels.
(Ps 81:11–12)

In return for their senseless and wicked thoughts through which they were
led astray to worship irrational reptiles and worthless vermin, you sent on
them a multitude of irrational creatures to take vengeance in order that they
might learn that *a person is punished by the very things by which the person sins.*
(Wis 11:15–16 NETS; emphasis added)

Paul is not placing the blame on God for human sin but is maintaining that,
when we insist on our own way, God allows human folly to run its natural
course without preventing its inevitable consequences. In fact, God gives us
what we explicitly or implicitly desire: freedom from God. But such freedom
from the true Lord means being governed by another lord, either ourselves
or some third party. All of this is part of what Paul means when he speaks of
the revelation of the wrath of God (1:18, 32).

This description of consequences as divine wrath does not contain words
we want to hear, because we want God to save us from ourselves and from the
enemies we invite into our lives. But God does not compel us to be devoted
to him or good to our neighbor, and when we are not, the unhappy results
eventually follow.

The exchange of truth about God (1:23, 25), Paul continues, led (and leads)
to the exchange of truth about God's creatures, including fellow humans (1:26).
Out-of-control sexual activity is a form of both idolatry (1:25) and injustice/
unrighteousness in which the whole person participates: heart, mind, and
body (1:24, 28). It is this comprehensive human predicament, symbolized
by—but not restricted to—human sexual sin that the gospel is intended to
repair, replacing misguided worship with true worship offered by the whole
person (12:1–2).

One specific result of the idolatry of sexual passion was that "natural intercourse" was replaced with "unnatural" (1:26–27). The word "unnatural" in 1:26
translates a Stoic idiom Paul uses (Gk. *para physin*; lit. "against nature") that
is better rendered as "contrary to nature" (ESV). This idiom meant "contrary
to the structure of created reality." For Paul, echoing the sentiments of other
Jews and foreshadowing that of subsequent Christians, "contrary to nature"
meant contrary to the truth revealed in creation (cf. 1:18). Specifically, it sig-
nified being contrary to the pattern of male and female relations described in

Gen 1.[18] Paul is not speaking about behavior that is somehow contrary to one's own nature (e.g., sexual orientation), as some have argued.

Disapproval of same-gender sexual relations is thoroughly and typically Jewish, rooted in Leviticus (Lev 18:22; 20:13) as part of Israel's call to sexual holiness. Homosexual activity was part of the stock catalog of vices that Jews (and even some gentile moralists) accused gentiles of practicing.

These verses in Romans have been understood by recent interpreters in several ways that attempt to limit what seems to be their broad, firm disapproval of homosexual relations, both male-male and female-female. Some of these interpretations include claims that Paul was referring only or primarily to

- people with a heterosexual orientation who engage in homosexual relations (and, by extension, heterosexual acts performed by persons attracted to the same gender);[19]
- exploitative homosexual acts, such as pederasty (sexual activity involving a man and a boy) or forced sex with slaves, not those of consenting adults;
- male prostitution;
- males acting passively, like females, in the homosexual relationship;
- casual homosexual activity rather than committed, covenantal relationships;
- same-gender sexual relations expressing uncontrolled passion—lustful rather than loving activity;
- homosexual activity in pagan temples or other settings of idolatry;
- a select group of elites within the Roman imperial structure, not gentiles or humanity as a whole.

In addition, some interpreters claim that

- Paul's language is only rhetorical, intending to create a sense of self-righteousness in his audience before including them among the unrighteous (beginning in 2:1); or
- Paul is merely describing what his audience thinks in order to show he is one of them and thereby gain their approval; or
- Paul did not say these things but is quoting a fire-and-brimstone teacher (or teachers) who does not (or did not) understand the Christian gospel as he does.

18. Paul uses the terms for male and female found in the Greek version of Gen 1:27.
19. This is the interpretation mentioned at the top of this page.

It is obvious that there is a huge debate about what Paul actually says here and why he says it. But it is highly unlikely that Paul intended any of the things noted in the bulleted lists. While these sorts of controversial biblical texts certainly require ongoing analysis and interpretation, sometimes the restriction of Paul's apparent blanket disapproval of same-gender sexual relations to one form or another reflects a general unease with such views in Western culture, as well as a corollary scholarly endeavor to reinterpret the texts in support of certain contemporary views.

Some have said that Paul was unfamiliar with long-term same-sex relationships, but people in the Greco-Roman world did, in fact, engage in various sorts of relationships (consensual, exploitative, short-term, long-term, etc.).[20] Others have said that Paul simply did not possess the knowledge and perspectives that come from contemporary science and social science. It is also highly unlikely, however, that Paul would have had a different perspective if he had known about modern and postmodern views of human sexuality. This is because human sexuality is, at least in part, a human construct that is fueled and formed by a worldview, or "social imaginary" (the term of philosopher Charles Taylor). Paul's social imaginary is framed by that of Genesis and Jesus: "a man leaves his father and his mother and clings to his wife, and they become one flesh" (Gen 2:24; Matt 19:5; Mark 10:7).

The most convincing analysis of Rom 1:24–27 comes from scholars who are sufficiently objective to allow Paul to speak *even when they disagree with him.* Here are some words from one such prominent scholar, E. P. Sanders: Romans 1 contains "a completely unambiguous condemnation of all homosexual activity"; this is because "Paul was a first-century Jew, and on ethical questions he ordinarily followed Jewish views precisely; more particularly he was a Diaspora [non-Palestinian] Jew, and therefore likely to be even more rigid on sexual ethics" as such Jews "made sexual immorality and especially homosexual activity a major distinction between themselves and gentiles."[21]

---

20. For a survey of ancient attitudes and practices, see (among others), E. P. Sanders, *Paul: The Apostle's Life, Letters, and Thought* (Minneapolis: Fortress, 2015), 727–47.

21. Sanders, *Paul*, 373. Sanders himself takes what he calls "the liberal attitude toward homosexuals in much of contemporary Christianity" (370). He does not feel that the Christian church should highlight one of the vices in the New Testament when it ignores others, such as allowing deceitful and boastful people full status in the church, including ordination (372–73). For a similar approach, see William Loader, "Paul on Same-Sex Relations in Romans 1," *Interpretation* 74 (2020): 242–52. Loader refuses to allow for special pleading in the interpretation of Rom 1. His main difference from Paul is that he believes there are faithful, practicing gay Christians.

For Paul, then, same-gender sex is inherently a dishonorable use of the human body, contributes to a person's (and humanity's) ongoing spiral away from the glory and honor the creator intended, and is inappropriate for the set-apart, holy people of God.

It often surprises people, and sometimes angers them, that Paul identifies same-gender sexual activity as sinful and that in Rom 1 he focuses more on this sin than on any other except idolatry. As noted above, the connection between idolatry and sexual immorality appears elsewhere in Jewish literature of the time. Becoming a Christ-follower, Paul proclaims from his earliest letter (see 1 Thess 1:9–10; 4:1–8), involves leaving both idolatry and sexual immorality behind; they must thereafter be completely avoided. It is both expected and significant, therefore, that in 1 Corinthians Paul tells the believers in Corinth to run away from two things: idolatry and sexual immorality (*porneia*):

Flee from sexual immorality! (1 Cor 6:18 MJG)

Flee from idolatry, my beloved! (1 Cor 10:14 MJG)[22]

These are matters of critical importance to faithful Jews and Christians. (See below for further reflections, especially about the need for humility and charity.) And yet, sex is not the be-all and end-all of Christian concern about the human condition. In fact, *Paul's attention to sexual sin, though the most extended description of human depravity, is neither the main nor the last point in his description of our predicament.*

1:28–32. FURTHER CONSEQUENCES OF IDOLATRY

The third and final mention of God's handing people over occurs in 1:28: to a "debased mind," an echo of 1:21. The result of failure to acknowledge God as God is now clearly much more than sexual impropriety.

This third occurrence of "handed over" breaks open the dam and unleashes a flood of evils. In 1:29–31, Paul lists some twenty additional sins that follow from failure to love God first and above all, and he twice says that people are full of such things (1:29). Paul characterizes these sins, echoing 1:18, as "every kind of" *adikia* (1:29; NRSV, NIV, NAB: "wickedness"; NET, ESV: "unrighteousness"; CEB, NJB: "injustice"). But he does not pause to analyze every

---

22. Similar translations for both of these texts can be found in the NIV, NET, NASB, and ESV.

aspect of these evils, though he could have done so. Together they outweigh in significance the one kind of sin that has received extended treatment. The apostle's main concern is the overall predicament, not the particular transgressions of individuals.

In a dramatic, almost poetic flourish (not fully translatable as such into English), Paul concludes his list with five words that begin with the Greek *a-*, the alpha privative, as in *adikia*: "**un**obedient to parents, **un**sound, **un**trustworthy, **un**caring, **un**merciful" (1:30b–31 MJG). Although he does not specifically use the language of "exchange" in this long list, that is certainly what Paul implies. Good has been exchanged for evil, peace for strife, honesty for deceit, wisdom for foolishness, faithfulness for faithlessness, and so on. Exchange, then, is at the heart of the human condition, and conflict—with God and with others—is the resulting order of the day.

Humans are as good at inventing evil ("contrivers of all sorts of evil"; 1:30 NET) as we are at creating idols. The wide variety of sins is symptomatic of a metastasized cancer that has affected not only the body (1:24) but also the mind (1:21, 28) and heart (1:24); every dimension of the human person and of the human community needs restoration to health.

In this situation of moral chaos—of people willfully discarding God, suffering the consequences, and all the while applauding (NRSV) or approving of (NAB, NIV) one another (1:32)—the wrath of God is experienced now, in advance, before the actual coming day of judgment and wrath (2:5; cf. 1 Thess 1:9–10). Paul may be reflecting on his own experience; according to Acts, he approved of the stoning of Stephen (Acts 8:1; 22:20). *Evil becomes normal and eventually normative when people (shamefully) endorse it by rewarding or imitating those who practice it.*

SUMMARY OF 1:18–32

What we have, then, according to 1:18–32, is a situation of *asebeia* and *adikia*, of Godlessness and idolatry, of injustice and immorality. It is a predicament that leads to death (1:32; cf. 6:23a)—both a sort of living death now and an eternal death to come. This is clearly not the glory, righteousness, and life for which humans were created (cf. 2:7–10). In such a situation, people do not merely need forgiveness and encouragement to start afresh. Nor do they need a legal fiction.

Rather, human beings need a powerful means of undoing the exchange, a potent means of experiencing the glory and goodness of God that God intended. *People need someone to rescue them from themselves.* Thankfully, although God handed people over (*paredōken*) to their own dishonorable passions and debased minds, God has also handed over (*paredōken*) his Son for their rescue—for our rescue (8:32). We shall come to that part of the story in due course.

REFLECTIONS AND QUESTIONS FOR 1:18–32

Pastoral, Spiritual, and Theological Reflections

1. C. S. **Lewis** has some lovely and wise words about **nature**:

   You must go a little way back from her, and then turn round, and look back. Then at last the true landscape will become visible. . . . To treat [Nature] as God, or as Everything, is to lose the whole pith and pleasure of her. Come out, look back, and then you will see . . . this astonishing cataract of bears, babies, and bananas: this immoderate deluge of atoms, orchids, oranges, cancers, canaries, fleas, gases, tornadoes and toads. How could you ever have thought that this was the ultimate reality? How could you ever have thought that it was merely a stage-set for the moral drama of men and women? She is herself. Offer her neither worship nor contempt. Meet and know her.[23]

2. Similarly, the great Jewish spiritual writer **Abraham Joshua Heschel** often wrote about **awe**, wonder, and radical amazement. Here are some of his most poignant lines:

   The surest way to suppress our ability to understand the meaning of God and the importance of worship is *to take things for granted*. Indifference to the sublime wonder of living is the root of sin. . . . Wonder or radical amazement is the chief characteristic of the religious [person's] attitude toward history and nature. . . . To the prophets wonder is *a form of thinking*. . . . [Humanity] will not perish for want of information; but only for want of appreciation. . . . *Radical amazement* has a wider scope than any other [human] act. . . . Since there is a need for daily wonder, there is a need for daily worship. . . . The sense for the "miracles which are daily with us," the sense for the "continual marvels" [phrases from an oft-recited Jewish prayer], is the source of prayer. There is no worship, no music, no love, if we take for granted the blessings or defeats of living. . . . This is one of the goals of the Jewish way of living: to experience commonplace deeds as spiritual adventures, to feel the hidden love and wisdom in all things.[24]

23. C. S. Lewis, *Miracles: A Preliminary Study*, at the end of ch. 9, "A Chapter Not Strictly Necessary," available in various editions.
24. Fritz A. Rothschild, ed., *Between God and Man: An Interpretation of Judaism; From the Writings of Abraham J. Heschel* (New York: Free Press, 1959), 41–43.

3. Theologically speaking, the atheist or **un-godded person does not truly exist**; the person who has left behind the true God is better characterized as *re-godded*. As Bob Dylan famously sang, "You're gonna have to serve somebody / Well, it may be the devil or it may be the Lord / But you're gonna have to serve somebody." Paul will make a similar point in Rom 6; everyone is enslaved to someone or something.

4. **Idolatry takes many forms and has many consequences.** Exploring these forms and consequences in each particular cultural (and ecclesial!) situation is an important part of Christian discipleship and pastoral ministry. The question of allegiance is a particularly important one. Many theologians and church leaders across the globe are especially concerned that nationalism and tribalism have become significant forms of contemporary idolatry.

5. Everyone should acknowledge that **human sexuality is a complex and confusing aspect of human existence**. If the analysis of 1:24–27 offered above is accepted, there are still multiple ways to interpret Paul's perspective on same-gender sexual relations for today. Some (not all of them) are these:

   a. One can affirm Paul's views because they are part of inspired Scripture and consistent with the explicit and implicit teaching of other parts of Scripture. (This is the perspective of the present commentator, though I try to hold that view with humility and respect for those who differ.)

   b. One can argue that a larger biblical theme (such as liberation or inclusion or love) sometimes takes precedence over a particular teaching.

   c. One can argue that when we consider *all* the main sources of theology—Scripture as a whole, reason, tradition, and experience—this particular Pauline perspective is not binding today.

   d. One can disagree with Paul's views because they are deemed to reflect, not the authoritative teaching of Scripture, but the limited worldview and knowledge of the human author.

   e. One can reject Paul's stance because it is simply deemed erroneous.

   Whatever one's views, they should be thought through carefully in conversation with others from a variety of perspectives, and they should be held with humility and with charity toward those who disagree. Our best interpretive efforts are never infallible. At the very least, all interpreters should be able to agree that unbridled sexual activity, or a fixation on sex, in which sex itself becomes an idol or a way of pleasing self by using others, or both, is a part of the human predicament that reveals covenantal dysfunctionality.

6. The **main point of 1:18–32** is not to condemn certain individuals or certain practices, sexual or otherwise. This passage ultimately describes *us* and *our* predicament, not *them* and *their* evil lives.

7. The **great irony of this passage** in the context of the entire letter is that the people described here are precisely the kind of people whom God loves and for whom Christ died. We who call ourselves Christians can do no less than fixate on that truth and imitate that love.

Questions for Those Who Read, Teach, and Preach

1. What are the gods and goddesses of our own day, and where are their temples? Which virtues or values or even vices have become deities, and how are their respective cults marked and celebrated?

2. The psalmist says, "Those who make them [idols] are like them; so are all who trust in them" (Ps 115:8). G. K. Beale (in *We Become What We Worship: A Biblical Theology of Idolatry*) argues that this is the central characteristic of idolatry in the Bible. What does it mean to become "like" our idols?[25]

3. Where does the connection between idolatry and immorality or injustice manifest itself today?

4. How might *focusing exclusively* on the issue of human sexuality distort our understanding of this passage and cause us to misinterpret its overall significance? How might *neglecting* the issue of human sexuality distort our understanding of this passage and cause us to misinterpret its overall significance?

5. How should individuals and churches that agree with the interpretation of Paul presented here speak about their understanding of sexuality without communicating condemnation and rejection to those not living by this ethic? How should individuals and churches that disagree with the interpretation of Paul presented here speak about their understanding of sexuality without communicating uncritical support for all forms of sexual practices?

6. If you were to single out certain of the evils listed at the very end of Rom 1 that are especially prevalent in your culture today, what would they be? Which new, culturally specific evils that Paul does not identify are part of the human landscape today?

FOR FURTHER READING

Beale, G. K. *We Become What We Worship: A Biblical Theology of Idolatry*. Downers Grove, IL: InterVarsity, 2008.

Belousek, Darrin W. Snyder. *Marriage, Scripture, and the Church: Theological*

---

25. G. K. Beale, *We Become What We Worship: A Biblical Theology of Idolatry* (Downers Grove, IL: InterVarsity, 2008).

Discernment on the Question of Same-Sex Union. Grand Rapids: Baker Academic, 2021.

Fowl, Stephen E. *Idolatry*. Waco: Baylor University Press, 2019.

Hill, Wesley. *Washed and Waiting: Reflections on Christian Faithfulness and Homosexuality*. Updated and expanded ed. Grand Rapids: Zondervan, 2016.

Laytham, D. Brent, ed. *God Is Not . . . Religious, Nice, "One of Us," An American, A Capitalist*. Grand Rapids: Brazos, 2004.

Lewis, C. S. *Miracles: A Preliminary Study*. New York: Macmillan, 1978 (orig. 1947).

Otto, Tim. *Oriented to Faith: Transforming the Conflict over Gay Relationships*. Eugene, OR: Cascade, 2014.

Prime, Derek. *Created to Praise*. Fearn: Christian Focus, 2013.

Rothschild, Fritz A., ed. *Between God and Man: An Interpretation of Judaism; From the Writings of Abraham J. Heschel*. New York: Free Press, 1959.

Sprinkle, Preston, ed. *Two Views on Homosexuality, the Bible, and the Church*. Grand Rapids: Zondervan, 2016.

Wright, Christopher J. H. *"Here Are Your Gods": Faithful Discipleship in Idolatrous Times*. Downers Grove, IL: IVP Academic, 2020.

Wright, N. T. *For All God's Worth: True Worship and the Calling of the Church*. Grand Rapids: Eerdmans, 1997.

2:1–16
God's Impartial Judgment according to Deeds

In 1:18–32, Paul is constantly speaking about people—they did this, they are this, and so on: words about others. In a sense, both the letter's original addressees and we are kept at a safe distance. Chapter 2, by contrast, begins with a direct address: "you have no excuse," and the "you" is grammatically singular in Greek, not plural. We are each confronted with a forceful, unavoidable call to self-examination.

This shift to direct, singular address (maintained through v. 5) indicates Paul's adoption of the rhetorical strategy of dialogue called the diatribe. In antiquity, the diatribe was often used by teachers, including a near-contemporary of Paul named Epictetus, in his lengthy *Discourses*, to advocate for the Stoic way of life. The diatribe did not consist primarily of a lengthy rebuke or attack (as we might understand the word today), but of a creative dialogical mode of instruction and exhortation. It employed rhetorical devices such as the following:

- imaginary conversation partners (interlocutors)—who represent and express actual or plausible points of view

- rhetorical questions
- exaggeration
- hypothetical objections
- erroneous conclusions

In an ancient diatribe, the real speaker refutes the imaginary interlocutor's errors (sometimes beginning with the phrase, "May it never be!"), using them as a springboard for teaching. Examples of the diatribal mode may be found not only in Rom 2 but also later in the letter (especially ch. 6).[26]

There has been considerable debate about the identity of the interlocutor in this diatribe. It is clear that, beginning at 2:17, Paul is addressing those who call themselves Jews (also, however, with the singular "you"). But is that the same "you" we find in 2:1? Or is the person addressed in 2:1 more generic, a sort of everyman, or at least every hypocrite? Or does 2:1 address the hypocritical *gentile*, continuing from 1:18–32?

The interlocutor's identity may not really matter, however. An imaginary conversation partner is precisely that: imaginary. "Whoever you are" (2:1, 3) means any and every judgmental person who happens to be hearing or reading these words. That is the power of the diatribe; it draws us in, allowing us to be addressed and, possibly, taught as we find ourselves as both the person questioned and the respondent. Moreover, in this particular passage, the diatribe is helping to make a specific case. The force of the argument in 2:1–16 is to establish one basic scriptural principle: *God judges impartially on the basis of deeds* (summarized in 2:6, 11, 13):

- "[God] will repay according to each one's deeds" (2:6);
- "God shows no partiality" (2:11); and
- "It is not the hearers of the law who are righteous in God's sight, but the doers of the law who will be justified" (2:13).

The emphasis on doing throughout the entire passage should not surprise us, given the focus on doing or practicing we saw in 1:18–32. In fact, there are numerous echoes of 1:18–32 in the opening verses of chapter 2: lacking an

---

26. "May it never be!" translates the Greek phrase *mē genoito*. Other translations include "By no means!"; "Of course not!"; "Absolutely not!"; etc. Paul uses it ten times in this letter; see Rom 3:4, 6 (plus a similar phrase in 3:9), 31; 6:2, 15; 7:7, 13; 9:14; 11:1, 11; also 1 Cor 6:15; Gal 2:17; 3:21; 6:14. We find the diatribe style also in Gal 2–3, and perhaps elsewhere in Paul.

excuse for what is done (1:20; 2:1), ignoring or mishandling the truth (1:18; 2:2), divine wrath (1:18; 2:5, 8), and unrighteousness/injustice (*adikia*, 1:18, 29; 2:8; NRSV "wickedness").

The principle of justification for "doers of the law" (2:13) does not undermine Paul's convictions about justification by God's grace that we find later in the letter. Rather, this principle is the necessary foundation for grace, because all have sinned and need a power to enable the doing of God's will (8:3-4). Our final judgment and justification can be on the basis of performance—on our keeping covenant with God or not—because God makes a way when God makes a demand.

Thus, Paul is hardly engaging in mere rhetoric here—catching the hypocrite after setting a trap for such a person in 1:18-32, as some have suggested, even contending that Paul did not mean what he said in 1:18-32. But much, much more than springing a trap set for hypocrites is happening in 2:1-16. Paul is establishing some fundamental principles about God, about the human condition, and about salvation.

2:1-5. HYPOCRITICAL HUMANITY

Paul begins chapter 2 in diatribe mode with a stinging critique of hypocrites who erroneously presume on God's patience and mercy (2:1-5). Such people have no more excuse than blatant sinners (no excuse in both 1:20 and 2:1).

Hypocrites' own actions condemn them before God with the very judgments they utter against others (2:1-2). The jarring shift in grammar and tone from 1:18-32 requires that each of us ask ourselves, "Am I being addressed? Is God speaking to me? Am I part of hypocritical humanity?" Though not a specific individual or kind of person, *the imaginary addressee/interlocutor is really not so imaginary.*

A set of rhetorical questions (2:3-4) reminds the interlocutor, and us, that God's patience does not indicate God's apathy about human sin. Rather, God's kindness and patience (2:4) are a call to repentance that, if unheeded, will result in God's wrath on the judgment day (2:3, 5; see also 2:8, 16; 5:9; 14:10). (It is interesting that kindness is one of the things people lack, according to 3:12; to be unkind is partly what it means to be ungodlike.)

It becomes clear here that hypocrisy and presumption are as serious as any evil listed in 1:18-32, for what is at stake is the interlocutor's future justification—here meaning acquittal at the eschatological divine court on judgment day (2:5, 13, 16) and reception of life eternal (2:7). It also becomes clear in this passage, as in 1:18-32, that the entire person being described is out of sync with God: body/deeds, mind/imagination (2:3), and heart (2:5). We will see later in the chapter (2:25–29) that the heart is the heart of the problem.

The language of a "hard and impenitent heart" (2:5) is scriptural idiom, used not only of evil gentiles like Pharaoh and the Egyptians (Exod 7–14) but also of God's own people ("heart of stone"; Ezek 11:19; 36:26). *A hard heart is a standard part of the hypocrite's anatomy,* and Paul will make the heart the focus of his prescription for the human patient (2:25–29). But—and this is critical—the heart is revealed in actions, what we do (see 2:1–3, echoing 1:20).

2:6–16. Divine Impartiality and Human Deeds

Paul's critique of hypocritical humanity leads to the main emphasis of 2:1–16: God's impartial judging of gentiles *and* Jews. To make this point, Paul reverts to the "they" language of 1:18–32. In 2:6, he quotes the biblical refrain that God "repay[s] according to each one's deeds" (see Pss 28:4; 62:12; Prov 24:12). We see that principle present in Jesus' teaching too (e.g., Matt 3:7–10; 25:31–46). In 2:11, Paul invokes the corollary scriptural principle that God so judges without partiality (see Deut 10:17; 2 Chr 19:7).

This necessarily means that God rewards and justifies only "doers of the law" (2:13). Those who do good, whether in accordance with the written Jewish law or the divine law inscribed on their hearts (2:12, 14–15), will be rewarded with glory, honor, peace, and immortality (2:7, 10), the proper ends (goals) of human life. Evildoers—practitioners of *adikia* (2:8, as in 1:18, 29), or unrighteousness/injustice—will experience "wrath and fury," "anguish and distress" (2:8–9).[27] Human *adikia*, which has now been named four times in this letter, is clearly at the very core of the human predicament.

Paul, that is, wants to establish an absolute connection between fulfilling covenant obligations (the law) now and final justification (leading to eternal life; 2:7) later. The question is whether a person obeys and follows the truth or obeys and follows injustice/unrighteousness (2:8).[28] Paul's notion of truth is thoroughly biblical; it has to do with behavior, not merely factual knowledge. This eliminates any prerogative when it comes to just possessing the law of Moses. The principle of judgment according to deeds applies to *all* people, "the Jew first and also the Greek" (2:9–10). (We have heard this Jew-Greek refrain already in 1:16.) Since the gospel is one gospel for all because there is

---

27. NRSV, again unfortunately, has "wickedness" for *adikia* in 2:8.

28. Later, Paul will say that people are summoned to obey the gospel (10:16) and, in Christ, to become slaves of righteousness/justice rather than of Sin (6:16–17).

but one God (see 3:29–30), the criterion for judgment must be the same for all. As many interpreters have said, commenting on 2:13, *it is performance, not possession, of the law that matters.*[29]

This conclusion becomes a fundamental Pauline principle with wide application in Romans: simply *possessing* the law is irrelevant for justification. A people's distinctive spiritual feature, such as possessing the Ten Commandments, or circumcision, or the Beatitudes, essentially becomes a nonfeature if that people fails to live differently from those who do not possess that spiritual marker. At the same time, *lacking* the written law, Paul declares, is no excuse for practicing impiety and injustice, for God has gifted all of humanity with creation and an internal law to guide people to honor God and treat others well.

At least two questions emerge from this passage. First, does all of this mean that Paul subscribes to some sort of theory of anonymous believers who have no written law (or gospel) but nevertheless keep God's covenant (2:14–16)?[30] Does he really believe there are gentiles who, by instinct (NRSV, CEB, NASB; lit. "by nature," 2:14), fully please God and achieve eternal salvation by virtue of following an internal law, one "written on their hearts" (2:15)?

The answer is almost certainly no. Theoretically, such law-keeping gentiles could exist and, if they did, would be rewarded with glory and immortality. But the point of this passage is to establish divine impartiality, not human success in God's court. In the end, *all* are sinners, as even 2:12 implies. Since Paul believes that *no one* is righteous/just (3:10), that *no one* seeks God (3:11), that *all* have turned aside (3:12), that *all* are under the power of Sin (3:9–20), and that *all* have sinned and lack the glory of God (3:23), the existence of anonymous gentile law-keepers, people who essentially lead the sort of life expected of God's covenant people, is a hypothetical situation that never occurs. (This does not mean, however, that nonbelievers do no good at all.) Judgment day, apart from God's grace, would mean that those with an internal, unwritten law are accused, not excused (2:15–16).

Some interpreters, however, think this interpretation (or one, alternatively, that proposes the actual existence of such gentile law-keepers) wrongly understands our text to be about non-Christian righteous gentiles. Therefore,

29. Readers who are concerned that this might imply works righteousness, or earning one's salvation, should recall the words of Jesus: "Not everyone who says to me, 'Lord, Lord,' will enter the kingdom of heaven, but only the one who does the will of my Father in heaven" (Matt 7:21).

30. The twentieth-century Roman Catholic theologian Karl Rahner coined the term "anonymous Christian."

they contend, this interpretation asks the wrong question, which is basically, "What about the unevangelized righteous gentile?" These interpreters suggest, rather, that the phrase "written on their hearts" in 2:15—which echoes Jeremiah's promise of the new covenant (Jer 31:31–34)—means that Paul is speaking of gentile *Christians* in these verses. Despite the allusion to Jeremiah, however, the logic and flow of the passage as a whole suggest that it is gentile *nonbelievers* (i.e., non-Christians) who are being described. The similarity to Jeremiah's promise simply tells us that God is the source of the internal law.

The second question is this: Does Paul, known as the apostle of justification by faith, contradict himself by asserting justification on the basis of deeds? Romans 3:20 borrows from Ps 143:2 (LXX 143:2) to forcefully state that "'no human being will be justified in [God's] sight' by deeds prescribed by the law, for through the law comes the knowledge of sin." Once again, as briefly noted earlier, the answer to the question is no—definitively no. Why? Because Paul is a Jew, a covenant theologian, and as such Paul believes the covenant must be and can be fulfilled. His solution, taken essentially from the prophets in light of what God has recently accomplished to fulfill their vision, will not be to reject the necessity of covenant keeping but to offer the means for doing so—the gift of Christ and the Spirit. To repeat, for emphasis: *the final judgment can be what it is because God always provides the means to do what God requires.*

In summary: just as the divine gospel is for Jew and gentile alike, so also is the divine criterion of judgment: performance, not possession, of God's law. The situation is not better now than it was at the end of 1:18–32. *God, however, is a God of mercy and grace who wants to bring about transformation, not condemnation.*

REFLECTIONS AND QUESTIONS FOR 2:1–16

Spiritual, Pastoral, and Theological Reflections

1. **Hypocrisy is so common in the human experience** that it is almost worthy of being called one of our fundamental character traits as a species, or at least part and parcel of our condition as sinners. And yet most of us find hypocrisy, at least in others, to be particularly repulsive. Hannah Arendt famously said, "Only crime and the criminal, it is true, confront us with the perplexity of radical evil; but only the hypocrite is really rotten to the core."[31] For example, Christians too often speak out about sexual immorality while ignoring, condoning, or outright practicing sexual immorality and sexual abuse. In

---

31. Hannah Arendt, *On Revolution* (New York: Viking, 1963), 94.

addition, we say the gospel is for all, even sending missionaries throughout the world, but we have practiced segregation and even racism in the church.

2.   Even if Paul does not believe in the existence of righteous gentiles, it is critical that Christians not presume to know what that means about the **final salvation of those who have not heard the gospel**, or even of those who have heard the gospel but not responded positively to it. We should not presume to know the mind of God in such situations.

   What we *can* know and say, according to the witness of Scripture, is that all need to hear the good news, all who believe in the good news are part of God's new community and new creation, all will stand before the judgment seat of God, and one day all will confess that Jesus Christ is Lord (Phil 2:9–11). (When and how that will happen, Paul does not say.) Because Christians, who have experienced the mercy of God, believe in a God of mercy, we can hope that because Christ died for all, there will be mercy for all. The Christian witness is to God's mercy and grace in Christ. Moreover, there is no room in the Christian faith for any sense of moral or spiritual superiority toward any person or group. The only legitimate form of Christian witness is one of empathy with the human condition in all of its forms and particularities because we are part of, and contributors to, that predicament.

3.   Many Christians, especially those who are part of Protestantism (broadly understood) are uncomfortable with the claim—the biblical teaching—that **God judges on the basis of deeds**. It will be important as Romans unfolds to see how and why this does not contradict Paul's emphasis on grace.

Questions for Those Who Read, Teach, and Preach

1.   What are some of the manifestations of hypocrisy in the church? In the culture?

2.   How might Paul respond to the oft-heard sentiment about not joining a church because churches are full of hypocrites?

3.   Many Christians hope there are people who are anonymous Christians or unevangelized righteous gentiles. If Paul is not suggesting that there are such people, how might we think and talk about the legitimate concern for the many people in the world who have not had the opportunity to respond to the Christian gospel?

FOR FURTHER READING

Bates, Matthew. *Salvation by Allegiance Alone: Rethinking Faith, Works, and the Gospel of Jesus the King*. Grand Rapids: Baker Academic, 2017.

Byrne, Brendan. *Paul and the Economy of Salvation: Reading from the Perspective of the Last Judgment.* Grand Rapids: Baker Academic, 2021.

King, Martin Luther, Jr. "Letter from a Birmingham Jail." The Martin Luther King Jr. Research and Education Institute. https://kinginstitute.stanford.edu/king-papers/documents/letter-birmingham-jail. A poignant unveiling of hypocrisy in the White American church; also available in other resources.

2:17–3:8
The Jewish Predicament

The stinging diatribe begun in 2:1–5 had lapsed into a third-person description in 2:6–16, but the diatribe returns with a vengeance in 2:17–24. In these verses, Paul applies the principles of 2:1–16 directly to an interlocutor who self-describes as a Jew. He then moves on both to essentially redefine the term "Jew" (2:25–29) and yet to reassert the value of being an ethnic Jew (3:1–8).

Like the prophet Amos, Paul has surprisingly turned the focus of divine judgment from the nations/gentiles to God's chosen people, from "them" to "you"—and perhaps also from them to us. Amos pronounces divine judgment on Israel's enemies (e.g., Tyre, Edom, Moab) in Amos 1:2–2:3 before briefly castigating Judah (2:4–5). He then launches into page after page of judgments against Israel—his own people—through the end of the book, until a brief but powerful glimmer of hope appears (9:11–15). Paul has taken on this sort of prophetic role.

Failing to recognize Paul's adoption of this common prophetic function—Amos is hardly alone in pronouncing divine judgment against God's people—can lead interpreters of Romans to call Paul anti-Jewish here. Although some interpreters understand "you call yourself a Jew" in 2:17 as a reference to a gentile Christian trying to take on a Jewish identity and Jewish practices,[32] most interpreters see this section as Paul's address to his fellow ethnic Jews. The language is strong, perhaps hyperbolic (in line with many prophets), but Paul's prophetic point is clear: his own people have not fulfilled their divinely given vocation.[33]

32. See, among others, Rafael Rodriguez, *If You Call Yourself a Jew: Reappraising Paul's Letter to the Romans* (Eugene, OR: Cascade, 2014).

33. Paul, writes Beverly Roberts Gaventa, "is not criticizing Judaism per se, but he is asserting that even the significant privileges of being a Jew, a member of God's household, do not separate Jews from wrongdoing" (*When in Romans: An Invitation to Linger with the Gospel according to Paul* [Grand Rapids: Baker Academic, 2016], 32).

2:17–24. Condemning Jewish Pride and Hypocrisy

In 2:17–24, Paul uses three groupings of five to (1) describe Jewish identity (five phrases in 2:17–18) and (2) define the Jewish mission (five phrases in 2:19–20) before (3) posing rhetorical, accusatory questions (five queries in 2:21–23). The five questions function to indict his representative Jewish interlocutor for two significant presenting sins: pride (2:17, 23) and hypocrisy (2:21–23).

The pride of which Paul speaks is in having the Jewish identity and mission to the nations. This involves possessing the name "Jew" (2:17), having knowledge of the divine law and will (2:17–18, 20, 23), and being certain about having a mission to instruct the gentiles—who are, according to many Jews, blind and in the dark (2:19–21). The hypocrisy Paul identifies is the existence of serious violations of the very law that defines Jewish identity and of the precepts that the Jewish people teach others (2:21–24). As Paul has just argued in 2:1–16, it is performance of the law, not possession of it, that matters.

The mission of God's people to which Paul refers in 2:19–20, and which he affirms as of profound significance, is expressed in texts such as these from Isaiah:

> I am the Lord, I have called you in righteousness, I have taken you by the hand and kept you; I have given you as a covenant to the people, a light to the nations, to open the eyes that are blind, to bring out the prisoners from the dungeon, from the prison those who sit in darkness. (Isa 42:6–7)

> [The Lord] says, "It is too light a thing that you should be my servant to raise up the tribes of Jacob and to restore the survivors of Israel; I will give you as a light to the nations, that my salvation may reach to the end of the earth." (Isa 49:6)

In spite of having this mission, claims Paul in his series of five sharp questions (2:21–23), his fellow Jews have broken the two tables of the law, failing in both aspects of the covenant, such as committing idolatry and adultery (2:22). This is obviously a case of hypocrisy. We hear similar rhetorical questions in the prophets:

> Will you steal, murder, commit adultery, swear falsely, make offerings to Baal, and go after other gods that you have not known, and then come and stand before me in this house, which is called by my name, and say, "We are safe!"—only to go on doing all these abominations? Has this house, which is called by my name, become a den of robbers in your sight? You know, I too am watching, says the Lord. (Jer 7:9–11)

In the rhetorical questions he poses, Paul is claiming that his fellow Jews are essentially no different from the gentiles he has criticized in the previous chapter. But even the words "pride" and "hypocrisy" do not capture the gravity of the problem. The real tragedy, from Paul's perspective, is that in their failure to keep covenant, those called to be God's light to the world have instead sullied God's reputation, God's honor (2:23–24). They have maintained certain distinctive practices, such as circumcision (see 2:25), while failing to maintain the holy life expressed in and required by the commandments.

From Paul's perspective, therefore, his fellow Jews have become God's embarrassment—a source of blasphemy, or defamation of character—among the gentiles (2:24, citing part of the Greek text of Isa 52:5):[34] "It is your fault that the name of God is held in contempt among the nations" (2:24 NJB). Paul the prophet finds it incredible that God's own people are as guilty of idolatry and all kinds of unrighteousness as are the gentiles (2:21–23). No doubt this was a painful conclusion for him to reach, even if it did echo the prophets.[35] Theologian Khaled Anatolios characterizes sin fundamentally as misrepresenting God, and Paul would agree.[36] Paul, like the prophets, would also describe sin as disappointing God: the Lord "expected justice, but saw bloodshed; righteousness [Heb. *sedaqah*; Gk. *dikaiosynē*], but heard a cry!" (Isa 5:7b).

Such prophetic speech from Paul in no way gives Christians a right to condemn Jews in a similar way. (Indeed, were Paul to use or condone such prophetic language today, he would undoubtedly say similar things about his fellow *Christians*. In fact, he was likely speaking *to* fellow Jewish Christians as well as speaking *about* non-Christian Jews.) Paul is speaking as an insider to and about his fellow Jews, not to condone Christian anti-Judaism but to contribute to his major point in 1:18–3:20: Jews as well as gentiles stand in need of God's grace. Moreover, as 1:1–17 has promised and the rest of the letter from 3:21 on will unpack, God has not permanently abandoned either us or them (whoever we or they may be) to our own devices and sins. This especially means that God has not abandoned the Jewish people—God's own people (chs. 9–11)—in spite of their failings.

34. "This is what the Lord says, Because of you, my name is continually blasphemed among the nations" (Isa 52:5b NETS). See also, e.g., Ezek 36:16–24, which includes these words: "I had concern for my holy name, which the house of Israel had profaned among the nations to which they came" (Ezek 36:21). See also passages such as Isa 1:10–20.

35. And also other Jewish writers; Paul is not the only ancient critic of fellow Jews.

36. Khaled Anatolios, *Deification through the Cross: An Eastern Christian Theology of Salvation* (Grand Rapids: Eerdmans, 2020), 285–312.

2:25–29. PROPHETICALLY REDEFINING "JEW" AND CIRCUMCISION OF THE HEART

This situation with respect to Paul's fellow Jews leads Paul, in 2:25–29, to take the claims of divine impartiality and judgment by deeds one step further: he redefines, in a sense, the word "Jew." In doing so, Paul also articulates, in Jewish terminology applicable to all people, the heart of the problem—which turns out to be the human heart—and hints at the solution.

What it meant to be Jewish was a contested question in Paul's day, but circumcision was the essential mark of the covenant. For Paul, however, a Jew is not someone who is physically circumcised but inwardly and spiritually circumcised: "circumcision is a matter of the heart" (2:29).[37] Here Paul is drawing directly from the books of Deuteronomy and Jeremiah, which some other contemporary Jews also similarly appropriated.

In Deut 10:12–22, Israel is called to return to her covenant obligations to God and others. God's people must "circumcise, then, the foreskin of your heart, and do not be stubborn any longer" (v. 16), because there is no partiality with God (v. 17). Likewise, Jeremiah calls the people to "circumcise yourselves to the LORD, remove the foreskin of your hearts" in order to avoid judgment (Jer 4:4). And Jeremiah promises a new covenant when God will write "my [God's] law" on the people's hearts (Jer 31:31–34; see also Ezek 36:26–27). Similarly, Deut 30:6 announces that God will perform the required heart-circumcision, while Jer 9:25–26 suggests that both the physically uncircumcised and the physically circumcised are in the same predicament of lacking heart-circumcision. That is also Paul's view.

These scriptural texts all claim that covenantal dysfunctionality can be overcome only by a radical form of participation: the gift of God's own self and mindset, by his Spirit and law, into human hearts. To please God by being like God—"you shall be holy, for I am holy"[38]—requires God's personal presence. Paul is preparing the way for his emphasis on the gift of the Spirit into human hearts (5:5; cf. 7:6; ch. 8), which is the mark of participation in the new covenant inaugurated by Jesus' death and resurrection. Physical circumcision, or lack thereof, is thus of no relevance in itself to one's covenant relationship with God, or membership in the people of God. Paul makes the same point elsewhere:

---

37. The word "real" in the NRSV, RSV, and NJB translations of 2:29 ("real circumcision is . . .") does not occur in the Greek text. Nor does Paul say that "a true Jew is one whose heart is right with God" (NLT).

38. See, e.g., Lev 11:45; 19:2; 20:26; Num 15:40; cf. 1 Pet 1:16.

In Christ Jesus neither circumcision nor uncircumcision counts for anything; the only thing that counts is faith working through love. (Gal 5:6)

Neither circumcision nor uncircumcision is anything; but a new creation is everything! (Gal 6:15)

In that renewal there is no longer Greek and Jew, circumcised and uncircumcised, barbarian, Scythian, slave and free; but Christ is all and in all! (Col 3:11)

The ethnic Jew who fails to keep covenant has, metaphorically and spiritually, become uncircumcised (2:25). Paul is again borrowing prophetic imagery: "all the house of Israel is uncircumcised in heart" (Jer 9:26).[39] The *ritual* boundary marker of circumcision neither guarantees nor prevents the keeping of the law, which is the *spiritual-ethical* boundary marker—and this latter marker is the only thing that matters to God (Rom 2:25–27).

As in 2:1–16, Paul is not suggesting in 2:26 that there are countless non-Jews who keep the law and are therefore inwardly circumcised Jews. What matters here is the principle, which Paul can (and will) use to define all who believe the gospel as true members of the new covenant, whether physically circumcised or not. In that sense—and in that sense alone—gentiles can and should become like Jews. *Heart-circumcision is available to all, and it is needed by all. The heart is the heart of the human problem.* Humanity requires cardiac surgery by the divine surgeon.

Paul concludes this section with his redefinition:

A person is a Jew who is one inwardly, and circumcision is circumcision by the Spirit, not by the letter. (Rom 2:29a MJG)[40]

Actually, however, Paul is not technically redefining what it means to be a Jew. He is, rather, borrowing the prophetic understanding of a renewed people of God, updating it in the light of Christ. He could also say that an uncircumcised gentile whose heart is circumcised by the Spirit is equally part of that same renewed people of God. (He comes close to this in 2:26, and it is completely in sync with

---

39. For Ezekiel, a "foreigner" is one who is "uncircumcised in heart and flesh" (Ezek 44:7, 9).

40. See also Col 2:11–13, which has similarities to both this passage and Rom 6: "In him also you were circumcised with a spiritual circumcision, by putting off the body of the flesh in the circumcision of Christ; when you were buried with him in baptism, you were also raised with him through faith in the power of God, who raised him from the dead. And when you were dead in trespasses and the uncircumcision of your flesh, God made you alive together with him."

the argument from the story of Abraham in ch. 4.) The renewed people of God consists of all, Jews and gentiles alike, who have received the life-giving Spirit. This is how heart-circumcision, heart-transformation, life-transformation takes place. But we must wait until chapter 5 to hear more about the gift of the Spirit.

3:1–8. THE JEWISH PEOPLE'S ADVANTAGES

Objections from Paul's interlocutor to this prophetic understanding of circumcision and Jewishness jump immediately from the page, beginning at 3:1, and Paul has answers ready. Most interpreters see in these verses a question-and-response dialogue, though different interpreters assign Paul and the interlocutor differing words. The following arrangement makes good sense of the dialogue, with certain important Greek words noted in parentheses:

THE INTERLOCUTOR	PAUL
¹Then what advantage has the Jew? Or what is the value of circumcision?	
	²Much, in every way. For in the first place the Jews were entrusted [*episteuthēsan*] with the oracles of God.
³What if some were unfaithful [*ēpistēsan*]? Will their faithlessness [*apistia*] nullify the faithfulness [*pistin*] of God?	
	⁴By no means! Although everyone is a liar, let God be proved true, as it is written, "So that you may be justified [*dikaiōthēs*] in your words, and prevail in your judging."
⁵But if our injustice [*adikia*] serves to confirm the justice [*dikaiosynēn*] of God, what should we say? That God is unjust [*adikos*] to inflict wrath on us? (I speak in a human way.)	
	⁶By no means! For then how could God judge the world?
⁷But if through my falsehood God's truthfulness abounds to his glory, why am I still being condemned as a sinner?	
	⁸And why not say (as some people slander us by saying that we say), "Let us do evil so that good may come"? Their condemnation is deserved!

As the table reveals, the language in this dialogue revolves around two key Greek word-families, *pist-* ("faith-") and *dik-* ("just-"/"right-").[41] Furthermore, these two word-families give voice to the fundamental theological issues at stake here: human faithlessness and unrighteousness/injustice, on the one hand, and divine faithfulness and righteousness/justice, on the other.

The interlocutor wants to know whether there is any advantage to being Jewish, to being part of the people marked by circumcision. Paul suggests there is an advantage—being entrusted with the divine oracles. (He returns to and expands this answer in 9:4–5.) Ah yes, but Israel, as Paul has just asserted in 2:17–24, has proven untrustworthy. Does this "nullify the faithfulness of God" (3:3)? To this question, Paul offers his first of ten "No way!" rejoinders in Romans (3:4a),[42] and he cites Ps 51:4 to support his exclamation (3:4b). Paul here skillfully uses his interlocutor to raise one of the central theological issues of Romans: divine faithfulness. He will give his most sustained attention to this issue in chapters 9–11.

In the meantime, the interlocutor's final questions serve to dismiss two other false conclusions from Paul's argument thus far. First, even if Israel's injustice and falsehood *confirm* (rather than nullify) God's justice and truthfulness, and even if they somehow magnify God by showing God's greatness vis-à-vis Israel's sinfulness, God's wrath and condemnation are not unjust, for God judges righteously and impartially (3:5–7; recall 2:1–16). Second, even if some good eventually comes out of injustice, this does not mean—as some, engaging in slander, accuse Paul of implying—that anyone should intentionally do evil.[43] Paul's proclamation of the gospel in no way implies the conclusion, "Let us do evil so that good may come" (3:8). He will later address this specific misinterpretation head-on (see 5:20; 6:1–2, 15). Unfortunately, this is a misinterpretation of the gospel Paul proclaims that has haunted the apostle and the church to this day.

In this brief passage, it feels like the God of Israel, who is of course the God of Paul and of all Christians, is on trial. There are hints, too, that Paul feels himself on trial. His self-defense is but a brief hint of things to come. His defense

41. Very closely related to the notions of faithfulness and faithlessness in this passage are the notions of truth and falsehood. In fact, God's faithfulness (3:3) and truthfulness (3:4, 7) are nearly synonymous, and they overlap with God's righteousness/justice (3:5). Paul's usage of these terms is consistent with his Scriptures.

42. NRSV has "By no means!"; lit., "May it never be!" See also 3:6.

43. In 3:8, Paul uses the same verb for slander (*blasphēmeō*) that appears in the text of Isa 52:5, cited in 2:24. Just as Paul shares in the suffering of Christ, he shares in the defamation of God.

of God is longer but still short, though forceful, with (again) more to come later in the letter. For now, the takeaway is this: *the most important advantage to being Jewish is, or ought to be, knowing that human faithlessness does not compromise divine faithfulness, and that the latter does not excuse the former.*

REFLECTIONS AND QUESTIONS FOR 2:17–3:8

Spiritual, Pastoral, and Theological Reflections

1. Despite the challenges of this passage, it makes some important theological claims that remain critical for Christians today. Among these are the following:

   › As God of all, God is impartial, merciful, and faithful.
   › God's judgment is based on "works"; what matters is *performance* of God's expectations, not merely *possession* or knowledge of them.
   › The proper end of humanity is glory, honor, peace, and immortality.
   › Judgmentalism and hypocrisy are two sins of presumption (the fruit of pride) that render people incapable of rightly perceiving others, themselves, and God.
   › The fundamental human problem vis-à-vis God is an interior dysfunction, a problem of the heart.
   › Salvation—in all its fullness—requires an empowering interior transformation that will enable the performance of God's essential requirements of humans; this interior transformation together with its resulting performance is the mark of God's people.
   › As God's chosen people, the Jews have advantages over non-Jews, but these advantages do not permit presumption about their relationship with God.

2. For Christians in ancient Rome, and anywhere today, this passage is in part a reminder that **failure to embody the gospel** in a missional vocation has serious consequences, not only for the church itself, but especially for the reputation of the God that Christians are called to represent. Theologian Khaled Anatolios argues that because we are made in God's image, we always represent God, either well or poorly. As noted above, he maintains that sin is essentially the misrepresentation of God.[44]

   There are of course many examples of this failure, but I cannot avoid mentioning one that occurred as I was completing the text of this commentary: the January 6, 2021 assault on the US Capitol by a mob—some (many?) of whom

44. Anatolios, *Deification through the* Cross, 285–312.

self-identified as Christians. Some engaged in White-supremacist "prayer" in the name of Jesus inside the US Senate chamber. That attack desecrated the Feast of Epiphany, the Holy Bible some cited in support of their threats and violence, and the name above all names that Christians confess. In response to defamation of all things holy, we can only ask, in the spirit of Rom 2:17, "But if you call yourself a Christian . . . ?" At the same time, we must always also direct such questions to ourselves and our own communities of faith.

3. Prophets sometimes (often?) overstate their case when they speak truth to power. **Hyperbole**, however, has a necessary place **in prophetic work**. Flannery O'Connor, when asked why she created such bizarre characters in her stories, replied that for the near-blind you have to draw very large, simple creatures.[45]

Questions for Those Who Read, Teach, and Preach

1. What safeguards must be in place so that this text is not read, taught, or preached in an anti-Jewish way?
2. How do Christians sometimes defame the character of God and disappoint God? What is needed to prevent, or respond to, such blasphemy and divine disappointment?
3. In what specific ways have Christians maintained certain distinctive practices while failing to maintain the holy life expressed in and required by the gospel?
4. How can Christians talk about the real danger and reality of sin without exhibiting arrogance or judgmentalism? What practices or safeguards could ground such discussion in humility and kindness?

FOR FURTHER READING

Du Mez, Kristin Kobes. *Jesus and John Wayne: How White Evangelicals Corrupted a Faith and Fractured a Nation*. New York: Norton, 2020.
Jones, Robert P. *White Too Long: The Legacy of White Supremacy in American Christianity*. New York: Simon & Schuster, 2020.
King, Martin Luther, Jr. "Paul's Letter to American Christians." The Martin Luther King Jr. Research and Education Institute. https://kinginstitute.stanford.edu/king-papers/publications/knock-midnight-inspiration-great-sermons-reverend-martin-luther-king-jr-1.

45. Cited in Eugene H. Peterson, *Reversed Thunder: The Revelation of John and the Praying Imagination* (New York: HarperCollins, 1988), 145–46.

3:9–20
Humanity under the Power of Sin

Leaving misguided objections to his particular proclamation of the gospel behind for now (recall 3:8), in 3:9–20 Paul returns to the main train of his argument in order to sum it up: *the human race is in serious trouble.* Sinning against both God and other people is the norm. As we consider this bold conclusion, we must remember Paul's overarching pastoral purpose: to remind his *Christian* audience of both Jews and gentiles that all of us were, and still would be, in the same predicament if it were not for God's amazing grace—which Paul will announce in 3:21–26.

3:9A. THE (CONFUSING) QUESTIONS

At the start of this passage, Paul continues in the diatribe style, with two quick questions (which are really one two-part question) and an answer, following up on 2:17–3:8. The translation and meaning of the principal question and its answer have been debated:

- Does Paul ask, "Are we [Jews] any better off?" (NRSV) or "Are we at any disadvantage?" (NRSV mg.).
- Does Paul answer the question with "No, not at all" (NRSV and most translations) or "Not entirely" (NAB) or something else?

Because the question in 3:9a is a follow-up to the similar question in 3:1 ("Then what advantage has the Jew?") and the subsequent conversation in 3:1–8, we might conclude that the most likely solution is: So, are we Jews at a *dis*advantage? Not at all! But this is not certain. The NRSV may be correct: "Are we [Jews] any better off? No, not at all." Unfortunately, this is one of those texts in Romans that (like 1:17) defies a definite interpretation. On balance, I lean toward the "disadvantage?/not at all" interpretation.

The claims of the rest of 3:9–20 are, however, crystal clear. Paul's language is that of Scripture and the law court as he offers a "jackhammer indictment of human sinfulness."[46] In fact, Paul is once again taking up the prophetic mantle as he engages in a sort of lawsuit (Hebrew *rib*) against all of humanity. The playing field, so to speak, is level; or, to use another sporting image: advantage, no one. We can consider the charge, the evidence, and the verdict found in this passage.

---

46. Richard B. Hays, *Echoes of Scripture in the Letters of Paul* (New Haven: Yale University Press, 1989), 50.

3:9B. THE CHARGE

All human beings—gentiles and Jews alike—are "under the power of Sin."

The conclusion that sinning, against both God and others, is universal has been the thrust of the letter since 1:18. But now Paul says that the problem for Jews and Greeks alike is being "under Sin" (NET, NASB, ESV), that is, under Sin's "power" (NRSV, NIV), "domination" (NAB), or "dominion" (NJB). In other words, Sin is a power, an active force in the world (which is why we are capitalizing the word). Sin is humanity's slave master and evil ruler.

As briefly noted earlier, this is one of Paul's most distinctive perspectives: that human beings are enslaved to a power that is so real that he can call it "Sin" (singular) and so personified by him that we should spell it with an initial uppercase "S." "Sin" (singular and uppercase) is both different from and bigger than sins, or transgressions. One French translation appropriately renders the phrase in 3:9 as "the empire of Sin."[47] Paul himself later speaks of Sin's exercise of "dominion" (5:21) in conjunction with a corollary dominion of Death (5:17).[48] He asserts that he has "already charged" that all of humanity is under the domination of Sin. But he has not specifically made this exact allegation before 3:9. What is going on?

The status of humanity as living under the domination of Sin-the-power is not self-evident. In the flow of Romans, it appears here as the culmination of Paul's claims since 1:18. But theologically speaking, Paul knows the human condition only retrospectively, in light of God's revelation in Christ. That is, he knows the problem fully only in light of the solution—God's liberating, transforming work in the Messiah's death and resurrection, about which we have heard a bit in 1:1–17 and will soon hear much more.

Romans 3:9, then, can come as a bit of a surprise if we follow Paul's argument beginning only at 1:18. Yet Paul has in fact already hinted that he is moving beyond sins to Sin as a power. In 1:24, he says that God handed people over to "impurity" (Gk. *akatharsia*). In 6:19, he will say that believers "once presented [their] members as slaves to impurity and to greater and greater iniquity," and in 6:20 he equates this with being "slaves of Sin." In other words, devotion to sexual impurity and other forms of sin is evidence of being enslaved—enslaved to Sin the power.

Ultimately, God's handing humans over to themselves and their desire for

---

47. TOB, Traduction Oecuménique de la Bible (Ecumenical Translation of the Bible).

48. When death is presented as a personified power, like Sin, we will use the uppercase form of it too: Death.

self-rule means captivity to the power of Sin. Similarly, those who do not practice what they preach are in bondage to hypocrisy and pride, and thus also captive to Sin. Apart from the reign of God, there is, in Paul's estimation, only the rule of Sin and Self (see 2 Cor 5:15; cf. Rom 14:7–9).

Using medical terminology, we might say that sins are the presenting symptoms that manifest a deeper problem, the illness itself. In contemporary idiom, we might also speak of an addiction, with Sin gripping the sinner as a drug enslaves the addict; the addict's behaviors demonstrate the reality and power of the underlying illness. The phrase "already charged" in 3:9 suggests that Paul thinks the universal evidence for human evil presented so far indicates something more sinister and fundamental than sins (plural) at work among human beings. Perhaps he should have said, "I explain all this more fully later," in chapter 6. But he now returns to the evidence itself.

3:10–18. THE EVIDENCE

None is righteous, but all engage in various evil practices,
as Scripture testifies.

So far in Romans, the evidence for human sins—various sorts of idolatry and injustice—has consisted of Paul's own observations and analysis, though these have certainly been rooted in scriptural texts. In 3:10–18, however, he pulls out all the stops by producing a string—a catena (chain)—of scriptural texts, mostly from the Psalms (but also Ecclesiastes, Proverbs, and Isaiah), to demonstrate that *his* indictment is really *God's* indictment. "I am not making this stuff up," Paul effectively declares. Here is, simultaneously, the list of charges and the scriptural evidence for the veracity of these charges:

THE SCRIPTURAL EVIDENCE OF PAUL'S CHARGES

VERSE	TEXT	SOURCE
10	There is no one who is righteous [or "just"; *dikaios*], not even one	Eccl 7:20
11–12	There is no one who has understanding	Pss 14:1–3; 53:1–3
	There is no one who seeks God	
	All have turned aside	
	Together they have become worthless	
	There is no one who shows kindness, there is not even one	
13	Their throats are opened graves	Ps 5:9
	They use their tongues to deceive	

VERSE	TEXT	SOURCE
13	The venom of vipers is under their lips	Ps 140:3
14	Their mouths are full of cursing and bitterness	Ps 10:7
15	Their feet are swift to shed blood	Isa 59:7; Prov 1:16
16	Ruin and misery are in their paths	Isa 59:7–8
17	And the way of peace they have not known	
18	There is no fear of God before their eyes	Ps 36:1

One scholar has said this passage can be seen as a "hymn" to *adikia* (injustice/unrighteousness, as in 1:18),[49] and this is partially true. But it is also a hymn to Godlessness and idolatry (*asebeia*, as also in 1:18). Most of these scriptural texts originally referred to evildoers, not to all of God's people (though Isa 57 refers to Israel as a whole). Paul, however, turns the spotlight of the texts on the gentiles, his contemporary fellow Jews, and all of us. These texts are inspired evidence for a pandemic of sins and Sin.

Human beings fail to seek or fear God (3:11, 18), which is the root of all other problems, according to 1:18–32. Thus, people fail to treat other humans with kindness; they are not righteous or just (*dikaios*, 3:10). That is, we are not in right covenant relationship with God or, consequently, with one another. The two failures go hand in hand. Ironically, most of Paul's scriptural evidence comes from the Psalms, the book of the praises of Israel, but his citations point to the very antithesis of praise: speech and deeds that dishonor, rather than honor, God.

Two other aspects of this text are of special note. First, Paul says that our speech and actions are violent rather than full of God's peace, or shalom (3:13–17). This aspect of the indictment and evidence takes up more than half the scriptural citations. Second, the evils we commit involve our minds (3:11) as well as all parts of our bodies (3:13–18), with the result that we humans can be characterized as sinful from head to toe (see also Prov 6:12–19; Isa 1:5–6). These symptoms point to the disease, the addiction, the root problem—bondage to Sin.

Taken together, the evidence and the charge we see in 3:9–18 suggest that whatever solution Paul proposes will have to deal both with sins (i.e., forgiveness for the misdeeds) and with Sin (i.e., redemption or liberation from the power). Of particular importance is the need for transformation, especially from ways of violence to the way of peace. The result of the power of Sin is a culture of violence and death, rather than a culture of peace and life (see also 5:12–21).

49. Beverly Roberts Gaventa, "Paul's Apocalyptic Epistemology" (lecture presented at the annual meeting of the SBL, San Diego, 23 November 2014).

Paul has already announced that the powerful gospel brings life (1:16–17), but the ramifications of that announcement can be appreciated only by those who know that there is death in the very air we breathe. Sins and Sin, death and Death, are as much cultural and corporate, even systemic, as they are personal and individual.

3:19. THE VERDICT

"The whole world" stands accountable to God.

Since the verdict Paul announces in 3:19 is based on Scripture, it includes Jews (those "under the law"), not merely gentiles, and thus everyone. Everyone is silenced, without excuse or defense. This is the *Nein*, the "No," of God to humanity's folly. By grace alone, God's "Yes" will come through loudly and clearly. But all of us, even (no, especially) Christians, must not forget that we are guilty before, and accountable to, the living God.

3:20. THE LOGICAL COROLLARY

The "deeds prescribed by the law" cannot be the means of justification.

In 3:20, Paul borrows from Ps 143:2 (LXX 143:2) to make his concluding point: "For 'no human being will be justified in his sight' by deeds prescribed by the law, for through the law comes the knowledge of sin" (see also Gal 2:16). As in 3:19, "the law" here means Scripture as a whole. There is, however, significant scholarly debate about the identity of the "deeds" (lit. "works of [the] law"). Are they good works, or what some scholars have called spiritual-ethical boundary markers (i.e., moral deeds and worship practices)? Or are they ritual boundary markers (i.e., circumcision, calendar observance, diet, etc.)?[50] In the end, this may be a false dichotomy, since Paul clearly believes the following:

1. possession of ritual markers does *not* ultimately matter;
2. performance of the spiritual-ethical markers *does* ultimately matter; and yet
3. even those who possess the former (ritual markers) are not performing the latter (spiritual-ethical markers).[51]

---

50. The latter option, ritual boundary markers, is generally associated with the new perspective on Paul.
51. As we will see more explicitly later, this is because the law, weakened by "the flesh," cannot empower people to observe its spiritual-ethical requirements.

Paul's point is that neither the actual possession of the law nor the failed attempt at its performance is going to be the source of anyone's right relationship with God now, or acquittal on the day of judgment. The law (or Scripture) can reveal the reality of sin, as it has just done in 3:10–18, but it cannot make people right or righteous. It cannot, in other words, give life.[52]

SUMMARY OF 3:9–20

What we have, then, is a "no-exit" situation, as the late J. Christiaan Beker used to call Paul's assessment of humanity. Or to repeat a term we have already used, humanity is in a state of covenantal dysfunctionality. *God's dream for humanity has been replaced by a nightmare.* Although the summary in 3:9–20 is largely a description of people apart from Christ, Paul is equally concerned that the believers at Rome—whom he will soon describe as no longer "enslaved to Sin" but rather "dead to" it (6:6, 11)—not fall back under Sin's power through boasting and its associated evils, or through any other sinful errors. The apostle has made it clear where humanity is apart from Christ so that we who are in Christ will recall the quicksand from which we—each of us and all of us, no matter our ethnicity, our skin color, our gender, or our socioeconomic status—have been rescued. There is no partiality with God, or with Sin.

Humanity in a no-exit predicament requires an intervention—a benevolent, divine intervention. Paul wants his audience then and now to recall how they and we have been set free and set right with God. That is the subject of 3:21–26.

THE BIG PICTURE OF THE HUMAN PREDICAMENT AND NEED IN 1:18–3:20

Here is a summary of what Rom 1:18–3:20 has told us:

1. Humanity is covenantally dysfunctional, committing sins against God and others.
2. Humans have lost and lack *doxa* and *dikaiosynē*, the Greek words for glory and righteousness/justice.
3. Humanity is in a condition of *asebeia* and *adikia*, the Greek words for ungodliness/Godlessness and unrighteousness/in-

---

52. See Gal 3:21b: "For if a law had been given that could make alive, then righteousness would indeed come through the law."

justice; this basic condition is expressed in an amazing variety of specific ways.

4. Among the most common human evils are various forms of violence.

5. The totality of humanity and of each human is involved and affected: mind, heart, body (from head to toe).

6. This is a no-exit situation, like a person trapped in quicksand.

7. The reality of sins (plural) points to Sin (singular), a cosmic power, as in addiction. The effects are both personal and corporate, even systemic.

8. The irony: without a transforming revelation, people do not and cannot see their own predicament.

The solution, therefore, will need to be a powerful act of God that involves:

1. Forgiveness of sins and deliverance from Sin

2. Healing of mind, heart, and body

3. Repair of relationships with God and with others
   a. Removal of *asebeia* and *adikia*
   b. Restoration of *doxa* and *dikaiosynē*

4. Renewal of both individual and corporate life.

REFLECTIONS AND QUESTIONS FOR 3:9–20

Spiritual, Pastoral, and Theological Reflections

1. The human condition of being **under the domination of Sin** in the empire of Sin can be usefully compared to being **enslaved to an addicting power.** This must be done cautiously, however, so as not to cause harm to those suffering from addiction. A number of spiritual and theological writers have also suggested that release from Sin and sins can be usefully compared to the twelve-step process.

2. In general, most Christians have paid **insufficient attention to the gospel's focus on violence**—verbal and physical, emotional and spiritual, individual and corporate, privately executed and state sanctioned—as a fundamental dimension of the human predicament that God in Christ came to heal. The result has been a corresponding lack of attention to the gospel's peace witness

GOD'S RESPONSE TO HUMAN SIN   · 1:18–4:25

apart from private peace with God and harmony in the church and home. These aspects of shalom are all important, but they do not comprise the entirety of God's peace plan. It is only when we take humanity's penchant for violence seriously, and when we see its many manifestations, that we will see with Paul the breadth and depth of the charge that "the way of peace" we have not known.

Humans are as creative in inventing forms of violence as they are at manufacturing idols. If, anatomically, we are sinful from head to toe, chronologically we are violent from womb to tomb: abortion and infanticide; child abuse and spousal/partner abuse; verbal and emotional abuse; sexual abuse, rape, and trafficking; gun violence and mass shootings; riots and insurrections; persecution and oppression; torture and disappearances; the death penalty and war; elder abuse and euthanasia. Even a politically divided country or humanity manifests a certain unity in utilizing violence to (allegedly) solve human conflict and to exercise power. *Kyrie eleison.*

Paul, no doubt, had his own pretransformation violent tendencies in mind as he wrote these words. He would also have known firsthand the violence of religious persecution, the violence of the empire, and the everyday violence of criminals (2 Cor 11:22–30). In a sense, these all coalesced not only in his own experience of the world but also, ironically, in his understanding of the event of salvation, the Lord's death (1 Cor 2:8). Still today, the gospel challenges all forms of violence: political, religious, and personal.

3.   As we will see, just as **all aspects of the human person** (mind, heart, body) and of human life are affected by the reality of Sin and sins, so also the gospel of God addresses and can heal each and every one of those dimensions of the human condition. Moreover, if Sin has both personal and systemic effects, the gospel creates both new people and new communities.

Questions for Those Who Read, Teach, and Preach

1.   In 1973, psychiatrist Karl Menninger wrote a book entitled *Whatever Became of Sin?*[53] What is the status of sin/Sin—as deeds or as a power—in the culture today? In the church?

2.   What manifestations of the dominion of *Sin* as a culture of *Death* are evident in the world today, including any that may not have existed in Paul's day?

3.   In what ways do people today make the ways of Sin and Death into idols?

4.   In the last quarter of the twentieth century, many Christians began to develop a "consistent pro-life ethic" that rejected violence in all its forms, often ap-

53. Karl Menninger, *Whatever Became of Sin?* (New York: Hawthorn, 1973).

pealing to the ethos and practices of the early church. For many cultural and other reasons, this has not become the contemporary Christian norm. What would such an ethic and lifestyle look like today, and what would it take to achieve them?

For Further Reading

Biddle, Mark E. *Missing the Mark: Sin and Its Consequences in Biblical Theology.* Nashville: Abingdon, 2005.

Gupta, Nijay K., and John K. Goodrich. *Sin and Its Remedy in Paul.* Eugene, OR: Cascade, 2020. (more technical)

Hauerwas, Stanley. *The Peaceable Kingdom: A Primer in Christian Ethics.* Notre Dame, IN: University of Notre Dame Press, 1983.

Menninger, Karl. *Whatever Became of Sin?* New York: Hawthorn, 1973.

Pope John Paul II. *Evangelium Vitae (The Gospel of Life).* 1995. http://www.vatican .va/content/john-paul-ii/en/encyclicals/documents/hf_jp-ii_enc_25031995 _evangelium-vitae.html.

Sprinkle, Preston, with Andrew Rillera. *Fight: A Christian Case for Nonviolence.* Colorado Springs: David C. Cook, 2013.

3:21–31
God's Faithfulness, Mercy, and Justice in Christ

The words "But now" in 3:21 mark a major turning point, not only in Paul's letter but also in the entire story of God as the apostle presents it. Human beings have proven to be unfaithful and unjust, full of *asebeia* (ungodliness, Godlessness) and *adikia* (unrighteousness, injustice). But Paul is about to narrate the revelation of God's righteousness, or saving justice, that is manifested in Christ's death and made available to all through the gospel he proclaims in word and deed.

As we peruse Paul's succinct but powerful account of this saving event, we should be struck by the word-family that permeates the passage: "right-/just-" (Gk. *dik*-): *dikaiosynē* (righteousness/justice) and its linguistic siblings. This group of words appears seven times in 3:21–26. The same word-family occurs two more times in 3:27–31.[54] How best to translate these words is part of the challenge of this passage.

Back to "But now." The astounding event of God's saving justice has inau-

---

54. The noun *dikaiosynē* occurs four times, the verb *dikaioō* twice, and the adjective *dikaios* once in 3:21–26. The verb *dikaioō* occurs twice in 3:27–31.

gurated a new age (see 2 Cor 5:17; Gal 1:4; 6:15), the age of grace (5:20–21) "in which we [now] stand" (5:2) by virtue of being "justified"—restored to a right covenant relationship with the righteous/just God and included in the righteous/just people of God. Thus, 3:21–26 unpacks the succinct claims of 1:16–17 and leads to the logical conclusion of 3:27–31: the exclusion of any form of human pride vis-à-vis our relationship with God, and therefore also vis-à-vis our relationships with other people.

3:21–26. JUSTIFICATION BY FAITH: GOD'S, CHRIST'S, BELIEVERS'

Romans 3:21–26 is among the most complex and challenging in the Pauline letters. We can only do our best to get at some of Paul's main points. The bold proclamation of God's righteousness/justice (*dikaiosynē*) and faithfulness in these verses stands over against the dismal portrayal of humanity's unrighteousness/injustice and faithlessness in 1:18–3:20. It appears that Paul is drawing on fragments of early Christian liturgical (worship) texts, some of which are quite challenging to translate. However, he makes them decisively his own, revealing a distinctively Pauline presentation of the gospel that is, as 1:17 announced, from faith for faith, or from faithfulness for faithfulness.

As we hinted in the discussion of 1:16–17, there are two aspects of the interpretation of 3:21–26 that most translations miss. First, we should understand God's righteousness/justice as God's saving covenant faithfulness, God's saving restorative justice—an attribute that issues in action. The phrase "of God" means "belonging to God" rather than "coming from God."

Second, we should render two phrases normally translated "faith in Christ" as "the faith [or "the faithfulness"] of Christ" (3:22, 26; see sidebar, p. 119). Thus, the faith(fulness) of God, Christ, and those who respond are all named in this passage. This appears most succinctly in 3:22—"the righteousness of God through the faith of Jesus Christ for all who have faith" or "the faithful justice of God through the faithfulness of Jesus the Messiah for all who respond with faithfulness" (my translations). This verse reveals the following:

> *What* is manifested: God's righteousness (= God's saving covenant faithfulness/ restorative justice)
>
> *Where* or *how* it is manifested: in Christ's act of faith/faithfulness (his death)
>
> *For whom* it is manifested: all who respond in faith, or faithfulness (believing allegiance)—the "obedience of faith" (1:5)

We will look at each of these aspects of the passage as a whole.

THE FAITH OF JESUS CHRIST/JESUS THE MESSIAH

There are several reasons for translating the phrases in Rom 3:22 and 3:26 as "the faith of Jesus Christ" or, even better, "the faithfulness of Jesus the Messiah." (Similar translations are also appropriate in parallel phrases elsewhere in Paul's letters: Gal 2:16 [twice], 20; 3:22; Phil 3:9.) Here are some reasons for this translation:

- The Greek word *pistis*, often translated "faith," can also mean "faithfulness."
- The most natural translation of the Greek phrase in question (and similar phrases) is as a reference to Jesus as the subject, not the object, of *pistis*.*
- This translation is parallel in form and content to the similar phrase "the faith/faithfulness of Abraham," which appears twice in the context (Rom 4:11, 16) and is never translated as "faith in Abraham."
- This translation makes God the consistent object of faith for Paul, rather than both God and Christ.
- This translation makes Christ's faithfulness (referring especially to his death) the consistent *means* of justification according to Paul, to which humans respond and in which they share; human faith/faithfulness is the *mode* of appropriating and expressing their justification.
- This translation ensures that we understand justification as God- and Christ-centered, not human-centered, while still making our response to God's grace significant and necessary. That is, justification is on the basis of divine initiative followed by human response rather than human initiative followed by divine response.
- In no way, then, does the interpretation "the faith of Christ" cancel or minimize the significance of our response of faith.

Among the scholars who also advocate for this view are N. T. Wright and Richard Hays.

*In Greek grammar, the construction in question is referred to as either a subjective or an objective genitive.

What Is Manifested

Paul says several things about God's saving righteousness (restorative justice), or saving covenant faithfulness.

1. First, it is "apart from [the] law" (3:21a), or distinct from the ethnically specific manifestation of covenant that the law of Moses constitutes. For Paul, the law cannot bring about life (Gal 3:21), but if it could effect justification and life, then Christ's death would be pointless (Gal 2:21). Yet the law and prophets (the Scriptures) attest to God's way of justification and giving life (3:21), a claim that Paul defends especially in chapter 4.

2. Second, it is "through the faithfulness of Jesus the Messiah" (3:22, 26), meaning his faithfulness to God manifested in his death. As noted above, although most translations have the phrase "faith in Jesus [Christ]" in 3:22 and 3:26, the Greek phrase is better rendered as "the faith[fulness] of Jesus."[55]

   Paul's melding of faith and obedience in 1:5 has prepared the reader to understand Jesus' death as an act of faith as well as obedience (for obedience, see 5:19). His death demonstrates that God's righteousness (justice) means neither ultimately ignoring sins (see 3:25) nor allowing Sin permanently to disturb the relationship between humanity and God. Rather, God's righteousness/justice leads to God justifying those who have faith (3:22)—which means sharing in "the faith of Jesus" (3:26).[56] (The meaning of sharing in the faith of Jesus is discussed below.)

3. Third, then, God's saving, restorative righteousness/justice means God's gracious activity of justifying sinners. The justice of God is not the opposite of compassion but the very expression of compassion. It is at once the manifestation of God's *faithfulness*, because it is God's character to rescue and restore, and of God's *grace and mercy*, because salvation is not what humans deserve.

As already noted, the Greek verb for "justify" (*dikaioō*) that appears in verses 24 and 26 (echoing 3:20 and anticipating 3:28, 30) is from the same fam-

---

55. This interpretation is still debated but, in my opinion, makes the best sense of this text and parallel texts elsewhere in Paul. See the sidebar. The NRSV margin offers "faith of Jesus [Christ]" as an alternative in both verses. The NET has "the faithfulness of Jesus Christ" in 3:22 and "Jesus' faithfulness" in 3:26. The CEB has "the faithfulness of Jesus Christ" in 3:22 but "faith in Jesus" in 3:26.

56. The Greek construction in 3:26 is parallel to that of 4:16, which speaks of "being of the" (i.e., sharing or having) the faith of Abraham.

ily of words as "righteousness/justice" (*dikaiosynē*), "righteous/just" (*dikaios*), "unrighteousness/injustice" (*adikia*), and so on. What then is justification?

A long-standing debate exists among interpreters of Paul: does justification mean (1) that God *considers* or *counts* or *declares* sinners righteous/just, or (2) that God *makes* sinners righteous/just? The former view understands justification as a legal, or forensic, concept, borrowed from the courtroom. The latter view understands justification—in Paul's experience and theology—as transformative because it involves sharing in the death and resurrection of Jesus (see further below).[57]

As noted above, the position taken in this commentary is that justification is transformative: sinners are not just *counted* righteous/just, we are *made* righteous/just. In justification, *dikaiosynē* (righteousness/justice) is restored to humans who have been characterized by *adikia* (unrighteousness/injustice). Although there may be a legal, or forensic, dimension to justification in the sense that God makes a declaration of acquittal, the result is decidedly not a legal fiction, as some have contended. This is because when God speaks, God acts; something happens, as in creation (Gen 1). For that reason, the either-or situation just described (declaring versus making righteous/just) is actually another false dichotomy. God declares, and that which is spoken happens. There is transformation.

Justification, God's Glory, and the Spirit

It is important, therefore, to stress the transformative and restorative substance of what God does, for justification is even more than a powerful legal pronouncement or act of pardon. Romans 3:24 implies that justification solves the problem of humans missing out on the divine glory (3:23). Justification means, in part, restoration to the glory we once possessed—to true humanity that renders glory to God as the essence of true humanity, experiencing the presence of God individually and in community. Justification is the beginning of a new reality that will reach its ultimate goal in eternal life and final glorification (5:2; 8:18).

Yet another key phrase in Rom 3:23 has been understood in several different ways. Does Paul say we "fall short of the glory of God" (NRSV, NIV, NET,

---

57. Paul's own experience of conversion from persecutor of the church to proclaimer of the gospel lies behind his understanding of justification. He explicitly narrates this transformation in Gal 1:10–24 and Phil 3:3–14, and also implicitly in Gal 2:15–21, a key text on justification that was written before Romans. (Gal 2:15–21 is simultaneously autobiographical and representative, or inclusive.)

RSV, NASB, ESV) or we "lack God's glory" (NJB; cf. NAB "are deprived of")? Despite the answer expressed in multiple translations, it is best to understand this verse in the second sense. That is, we are (or were, prior to justification) lacking God's glory. The basic meaning of glory (Gk. *doxa*) here seems to be divine presence, as in the glory of the Lord that filled the tabernacle and the temple.

Lacking that glory is one way, then, of describing the fundamental human predicament of life apart from God, when we have turned our backs on God and become un-godded. At the same time, then, what humans *need*, is precisely the glory of God. In justification, *doxa* is restored to humans who have been characterized by lacking *doxa*. This is likely what Paul means in 8:30 when he says believers have been "glorified" by God.[58]

Paul asserts that divine glory was one of the blessings God gave to Israel (9:4). We see this glory especially in the experience of Moses and the children of Israel at Sinai and in the wilderness, particularly at the tabernacle, or tent of meeting (e.g., Exod 29:43–46; 40:34–35), and later in association with the temple (e.g., 1 Kgs 8:10–11; 2 Chron 7:1–2). As a Jew, Paul of course also believes that not only his fellow Jews, but all human beings, were created in the image of God and given the breath of life from God (Gen 1:27; 2:7). As such, they were both to give glory (honor and praise) to God and also to be—individually and corporately—an ongoing representation of God and God's presence on earth.[59] God's glory is to be displayed in God's people (Isa 49:3).

We see this clearly when Paul designates both the church (1 Cor 3:16) and individual believers (1 Cor 6:19) as the temple of the Holy Spirit. When he speaks of lacking God's glory, he may once again have in mind the prophet Ezekiel. Ezekiel spoke of God's glory leaving the temple and God's people (e.g., Ezek 10:18–19; 11:23), but he also promised that God's glory would return (Ezek 43:4–7) to dwell, by the Spirit, in the people (Ezek 36:25–28) and also in a rebuilt temple (Ezek 40–48).

---

58. At the same time, it must be remembered that full and final glory is in the future (5:2), and that whatever glory believers experience now by virtue of the presence of the Spirit is stamped with the pattern of the cross (see esp. 5:3; 8:17). We can refer to the present experience of the Spirit as *cruciform* glory and as resurrection-infused, or resurrectional, cruciformity.

59. Paul would also affirm with the Scriptures that the whole earth is full of God's glory (e.g., Isa 6:3) and that salvation consists of seeing and experiencing that glory—which is something for "all flesh" (Isa 40:1–5).

Justification: Vertical and Horizontal

This aspect of justification as involving becoming God's temple, individually and corporately, also helps us settle another debate about justification that has been important especially in recent years. Is justification (1) about how an individual is restored to right relationship with God (a "vertical" understanding of justification) or (2) about who, and how, all people—especially gentiles—are included in the people of God (a "horizontal" understanding of justification)?

The answer to this question is "Yes." Once again, we are faced with a false either-or. Justification is about both the individual and the community; when we are justified, we are transferred into Christ, into the people of God, into the community of the just/righteous. In Christ, by the power of the Spirit, the justified share in the holiness, faithfulness, and righteousness/justice of God (2 Cor 5:21).

The idea that God's saving act of justifying sinful human beings includes remaking them into the temple of the Holy Spirit, individually and corporately, is not an aspect of justification that has received sufficient attention. Paul only hints at this truth here, when he implies that those *lacking* God's glory will now *possess* that divine glory. This sharing in God's glory will be only partial in the present, but full in the eschatological future. The apostle refers to this glorious future reality more explicitly in 5:2–5 and then puts all of its significance on display in chapter 8. We were made to be temples of God's glory, indwelt and transformed by God's Spirit, serving God in service to the world. That is why justification is inseparably connected to justice/righteousness—to holiness in living. Human *adikia* is being undone. Sin is being interrupted and replaced with the divine presence. Christ's death makes all of this possible (see also Gal 3:1–5).

Where/How It Is Manifested

For Paul, Christ's death is the manifestation (3:21) of God's saving justice. It is both *God's* faithful, righteous, and merciful gift (3:24, 25) and *Christ's* faithful act (3:22, 26), his display of justice/righteousness and obedience (5:18–19). Indeed, God has acted *through* Christ: "through the faithfulness of Jesus the Messiah" (3:22 MJG); "through the redemption that is in Christ Jesus" (3:24). Christ's death accomplishes two things with respect to sin: forgiveness of sins (plural) and redemption from Sin (singular). Both are part of what justification means.

First, Christ's death deals with sins (plural). According to 3:25, God "put forward" Christ as "a sacrifice of atonement" (NRSV, NIV), referring to the Jewish system of sacrifices for sins. The Greek word used here (*hilastērion*) may also be translated as a reference to the "mercy seat" (NET; cf. CEB) in the holy of holies (see Lev 16:12–16), and many recent scholars prefer this interpretation.[60] In either case, the emphasis is on sins (plural) and on grace, not on wrath or punishment. People who have committed the kinds of offenses against God and others listed in 1:18–3:20 clearly need forgiveness. *Most remarkably, it is a person—the Son of God!—rather than an animal or an object that is the manifestation and means of God's great mercy.*

Second, Christ's death deals with Sin (singular—the power named in 3:9). Christ's death was also an act of "redemption" (3:24) or liberation—the language of deliverance from bondage to Egypt or any other slave master (see also 6:7, 18, 22). People who are under the sway of a power, even if they are not aware of it, need release, liberation, freedom.

In other words, Christ's death deals with both sins (the deeds) and Sin (the power)—*just as Paul's analysis of the human predicament in 1:18–3:20 requires.* It is this twin reality of forgiveness and liberation that begins humanity's restoration to the experience of God's righteousness and glory for which it was created. This two-dimensional act of God in Christ's death constitutes the manifestation of God's faithful justice and the justification of humans. Paul is clear that this is God's free act of sheer grace, a point to which he will return in chapters 4 and 5.

For Whom It Is Manifested

The word "all" is critical to Paul's understanding of sin and salvation: "all, both Jews and Greeks, are under the power of sin" (3:9); "*all* have turned aside" (3:12); "*all* have sinned" (3:23). "*All* we like sheep have gone astray; we have all turned to our own way, and the Lord has laid on him the iniquity of us *all*," wrote Isaiah (Isa 53:6).[61] The benefits of Christ's death are available to Jews and gentiles, for universal sin—universal failure to keep covenant with God and enjoy God's glory, God's splendor and presence—yields a universal divine response (3:22–23).

But this is not automatic; Paul writes to and about "all who believe" or "trust" or "respond in faith/faithfulness" (3:22; cf. 1:16–17), whether Jew or gentile (cf. 2:10–11; 10:11–13). God's faithfulness in Christ's faithful death—

60. There are additional possible interpretations of *hilastērion*, including expiation, propitiation, and purification sacrifice.
61. Emphasis added to these biblical texts.

often called "the finished work of Christ"—is in some very real sense incomplete when it is not met with human faith. This does not mean the work was deficient, only that its goal was and is precisely to generate the human response. We could put it this way: God's gracious faithfulness, manifested in Christ's death, is the *means* of justification (the objective, divine act), while faith is the *mode* of justification (the subjective, human response). We should therefore not speak of justification by *faith*, but of justification by *grace* through faith.

When the faith of Christ is met with people's faith, as in the various house churches at Rome, those who respond are justified (3:24, 26). They are put into right covenant relationship with God, forgiven, freed from Sin for covenant living, assured of acquittal at the judgment, restored to participation in God's glory, and made righteous/just—part of the righteous/just people of God. The restoration to glory that has begun will mean the reversal of humanity's headlong descent into death, a return to glorifying the creator, a new experience of God's blessed presence (rather than God's wrath), and a new life of honoring others. Chapters 8 and 12–15 will spell all this out in detail. This is Paul's good news of God's impartial, universal, magnificent, transformative grace.

The phrase "for all who believe" in 3:22 is amplified by the phrase that says God "justifies the one who shares the faith of Jesus" (3:26 MJG). What does sharing in the faithfulness of Jesus, embodied on the cross, mean?

It means, first of all, to fully identify with Jesus' death as the means of our justification so that we are, Paul says, crucified with him and also raised to a new life (see 6:1–11; Gal 2:19–21). Our old way of life ends, and a new life begins; death leads to resurrection, just as it did for Jesus. (Paul will interpret justification as resurrection more fully and explicitly in chapter 4.) Furthermore, sharing in the faith of Jesus means that in identifying with Christ crucified, we respond to God in a way that is like Christ's: in total self-abandonment and trust, committing ourselves to live for God and God alone. *The human response to God's grace is both to receive the gift and to pledge allegiance to the Giver.*

Sharing in Jesus' faithfulness unto death also means beginning a life that reflects the character of Christ's death on the cross, which was simultaneously an act of obedience, or faithfulness, to God (e.g., Rom 5:19; Phil 2:8) and an act of love for others (e.g., Rom 8:35; 2 Cor 5:14; Gal 2:20; Eph 5:2). Christ's death, then, was the quintessential act of fulfilling the fundamental covenant obligations to God and others. When we share in that faithful and loving death, we are raised to a new life of similar self-giving faithfulness to God and love for others.

The justified, then, are those who have begun the process of replacing *asebeia* (ungodliness) with *pistis* (faith) and replacing *adikia* (unrighteousness/injustice) with *agapē* (love) and *dikaiosynē* (righteousness/justice) by the power of the Spirit, thus fulfilling the two tables of the law. Although Paul does not say so explicitly, we should conclude that justification therefore entails heart-circumcision by the Spirit, as mentioned in 2:29. (In 5:1–11, Paul will explicitly connect the gift of the Spirit into our hearts with justification. Similarly, in Gal 2:15–3:5 and Gal 3:11–14 Paul understands justification in terms of the indwelling of Christ and the gift of the Spirit.)

All of this is possible because the faithful God of the covenant has demonstrated that divine faithfulness in the death of Jesus the Messiah, God's Son, generates faithfulness on the part of gentiles and Jews alike. And this is taking place "now" (3:21), "at the present time" (3:26).

Summary of 3:21–26

To summarize Paul's amazingly robust understanding of justification expressed in or implied by this passage, we may name the following:

- forgiveness of sins
- liberation from Sin
- participation in the faithfulness of Jesus in his death
- circumcision of the heart and reception of the Spirit
- becoming the Spirit's temple
- restoration of the glory of God/the beginning of glorification
- incorporation into the covenant people of God
- not only benefiting from God's righteousness/justice but also beginning the process of embodying that righteousness/justice
- beginning a new life of faithfulness and love instead of Godlessness/idolatry and unrighteousness/injustice

Some interpreters will say that many of these are *consequences* of justification rather than aspects of justification itself. But Paul thinks and says otherwise. The remainder of the letter unpacks this text's succinct but comprehensive understanding of what God has done for us in Christ, and how that impacts life in the Christian community and in the wider world. Justification—and the letter to the Romans—is about transformation and life.

3:27–31. THE EXCLUSION OF PRIDE

In 3:27–31, Paul returns to the diatribe style of 3:1–8, using a question-and-answer format to name a critical consequence of the gospel narrative presented in 3:21–26. It takes no great leap of logic to arrive at Paul's practical conclusion: there is absolutely no grounds for boasting if justification is by means of what God has graciously done through Christ's faithful death and is available for all on the basis of the same "law," or principle, of faith (3:27).[62]

Boasting about oneself or one's misdeeds is a sign of both gentile (1:22, 30) and Jewish (2:17) sin. So Paul reminds his audience that the "law" (principle) of faith correlates with the "law" of divine impartiality in judgment (3:27–30; cf. 2:1–16). This principle, in turn, is grounded in the oneness of God (3:29–30a), the most basic Jewish theological conviction, expressed in the Shema (Deut 6:4). According to 3:28 and 3:30, therefore, those who have or do "works prescribed by the law" (3:28)—that is, Jews—are justified no differently than are gentiles. In the words of Leander Keck, "*The one God provides the one solution to the one human dilemma.*"[63]

Martin Luther read 3:28 to mean "faith *alone*": "For we hold that a person is justified by faith [alone—so Luther] apart from works prescribed by the law." Paul would not disagree with Luther's maxim, as long as he was permitted to define the key terms. Certainly Paul does not think anyone ever could (or ever did) earn right standing with God, either by doing certain acts or by possessing certain identity markers such as circumcision.

The problem with introducing "alone" is not that Paul believes something other than faith is needed, but rather that common definitions of faith are often so narrow when compared to Paul's. "Faith alone" does not mean "intellectual assent alone"—either for Paul or for Luther. For Paul, faith is clearly a comprehensive response: trust, absolute surrender, obedience, and commitment. It includes faithfulness. The gospel offers grace and demands obedient faith, and thereby opens covenant membership to all on the same terms; that is the point of these verses. Moreover, Paul asserts (3:31), probably in response to actual or anticipated criticism, this claim does not "overthrow" but "uphold[s]" the law (the Scriptures). This will lead him in chapter 4 to two biblical figures, Abraham and David, to prove his claim—and to say much more about justification.

---

62. There is, therefore, an appropriate form of boasting for Christians: in what God has done and will do (5:2–3).

63. Leander E. Keck, *Romans*, Abingdon New Testament Commentaries (Nashville: Abingdon, 2005), 116 (emphasis added).

REFLECTIONS AND QUESTIONS FOR 3:21–31

Spiritual, Pastoral, and Theological Reflections

1. Theologian **Peter J. Leithart** has coined the term "**deliverdict**" to express an understanding of justification as both a divine declaration, or verdict, and a divine act of deliverance.[64] It captures in one word the point just made in the discussion of 3:21–26. It is not necessary to choose between justification as declaration and justification as transformation.

2. A **definition of justification** that comes from the preceding discussion would be this:

    > the establishment of right covenant relations with God, including fidelity to God and love for neighbor, and incorporation into the covenant community of the just/righteous inhabited by the Holy Spirit, the presence of God, by fully identifying with (and thus participating in) the liberating death and resurrection of Jesus.

    When we do embrace Christ's death and resurrection, the saving event that overcomes Sin and Death and delivers us from their sway, we are in fact liberated, freed for service to God—and that is both liberation and justification. As we will see in later chapters of Romans, this reality also possesses many present dimensions as well as the certain hope of acquittal on the day of judgment, followed by final glorification.

3. Despite Paul's indictment of humanity's violence in 3:9–20, certain criticisms of Christian faith have **accused Christianity itself of being violent** at its core because it centers on a crucified Messiah. Some have even described God as a child-abuser for allegedly killing his own Son. It is therefore important to recognize two things about Christ's death on the cross. First, Jesus' death, though an act of faithfulness and obedience to his Father, was—paradoxically, perhaps—freely chosen (Phil 2:6–8) and was an act of love for us. Second, the atonement was not a divine act, from a heavenly distance, of punishing Jesus with death; rather, it was an event of God's compassionate self-involvement—God's faithfulness—in and through Jesus' death: "God was in Christ reconciling the world to himself" (2 Cor 5:19 MJG). Paul will develop this theme in Rom 5:1–11.

    Moreover, if we keep in mind that the atonement is a multifaceted reality (as we see even in 3:21–26), we will not fixate on the "blood" and sacrifice

---

64. See especially his book *Delivered from the Elements of the World: Atonement, Justification, Mission* (Downers Grove, IL: InterVarsity, 2016).

language as if that is the only way Paul, or the Christian tradition, understands Jesus' death. Indeed, Paul's view is that the *violence* of the cross is to be attributed to human, political powers (1 Cor 2:6–8) and not to God. At the heart of the cross is not divine punishment or vengeance or violence, but divine self-giving, sacrificial love (Rom 8:39).

4. The **justice of God** depicted in these verses is fundamentally **at odds with many, if not most, human practices of justice**, whether those of Rome or of modern superpowers. Christians who have any influence, small or large, in the execution of justice, as it is normally understood and practiced, are called to be agents of transformation and restoration.

5. In the Christian tradition, **pride is one of the seven deadly sins.** As we will see later in Romans, it is a sin that can lead not only to inappropriate judgmentalism but also to severe self-injury. While there may be certain kinds of appropriate pride, pride always remains something that can become a spiritual danger.

Questions for Those Who Read, Teach, and Preach

1. What sorts of understanding, if any, do you and the people with whom you read Romans understand the term "justification"? How might that understanding be refined or expanded? Why is such refinement or expansion spiritually and pastorally significant?

2. What is the significance of understanding justification as being rooted in three expressions of faith, or faithfulness (God's, Christ's, and ours)?

3. Why is it important, spiritually and pastorally, to understand the death of Jesus as an act of divine love rather than one of punishment, violence, or vengeance? How might that understanding impact Christian approaches to various social issues, such as incarceration and capital punishment?

4. In what ways do Christians today manifest inappropriate pride in their relationships with other Christians, with people of other faiths, and with people in general? How does, or how could, the gospel address and correct such forms of pride?

FOR FURTHER READING

Baker, Mark D., and Joel B. Green. *Recovering the Scandal of the Cross: Atonement in New Testament and Contemporary Contexts.* 2nd ed. Downers Grove, IL: InterVarsity, 2011.

Bates, Matthew W. *Gospel Allegiance: What Faith in Jesus Misses for Salvation in Christ.* Grand Rapids: Baker Academic, 2019.

———. *Salvation by Allegiance Alone: Rethinking Faith, Works, and the Gospel of Jesus the King.* Grand Rapids: Baker Academic, 2017.

Bird, Michael F., and Preston M. Sprinkle, eds. *The Faith of Jesus Christ: Exegetical, Biblical, and Theological Studies.* Peabody, MA: Hendrickson, 2009. (more technical)

Bonhoeffer, Dietrich. *Meditations on the Cross.* Edited by Manfred Weber. Translated by Douglas W. Stott. Louisville: Westminster John Knox, 1998.

Gorman, Michael J. *The Death of the Messiah and the Birth of the New Covenant: A (Not So) New Model of the Atonement.* Eugene, OR: Cascade, 2014.

Gupta, Nijay K. *Paul and the Language of Faith.* Grand Rapids: Eerdmans, 2020.

Jackson, W. Daniel. "The Logic of Divine Presence in Romans 3:23." *Catholic Biblical Quarterly* 80 (2018): 293–305. (more technical)

Johnson, Andy. "Navigating Justification: Conversing with Paul." *Catalyst.* November 1, 2010. http://www.catalystresources.org/navigating-justification-con versing-with-paul.

"Joint Declaration on the Doctrine of Justification, 20th Anniversary Edition." Lutheran World Federation. 2019. https://www.lutheranworld.org/content/re source-joint-declaration-doctrine-justification-20th-anniversary-edition.

Leithart, Peter J. *Delivered from the Elements of the World: Atonement, Justification, Mission.* Downers Grove, IL: InterVarsity, 2016.

Macchia, Frank D. *Justification in the Spirit: Creation, Redemption, and the Triune God.* Grand Rapids: Eerdmans, 2010. (more technical)

Senior, Donald. *Why the Cross? Reframing New Testament Theology.* Nashville: Abingdon, 2014.

Stegman, Thomas D. "The Faith of Christ." *Bible Odyssey.* http://www.bibleodyssey .org/en/people/related-articles/faith-of-christ.

Stephenson, Bryan. *Just Mercy: A Story of Justice and Redemption.* New York: Spiegel & Grau, 2014.

4:1–25
The Witness of Scripture in the Story of Abraham

In the drama that is Rom 4, we come to the towering figure of Abraham, with a supporting cast of David and Sarah. Abraham, especially as portrayed in this chapter and in Galatians 3, is highly significant for any interpretation of justification. What Paul does with Abraham here is quite fascinating.

For Jews in Paul's day, Abraham filled a variety of roles:

- founder of monotheism who abandoned polytheism/idolatry
- paradigmatic convert to Judaism
- exemplar of virtue, righteousness, fidelity, and meritorious obedience, especially in his offering of Isaac (Gen 22, known to Jews today as the Akedah ["binding"] but not discussed by Paul here)
- biological father (forefather/ancestor) of all Jews: the first to be circumcised and thus the first member of the covenant people

Ancient Jews embraced Abraham and especially stressed their father's obedience. Some believed he obeyed the law even before Moses gave it. And clearly some saw him not only as the father of the Jewish people but also as the model proselyte (convert), a former gentile/pagan. A Jewish argument about who and what a Jew actually is (recall 2:28–29) needs Abraham to be convincing.

For Paul, Abraham is a hybrid; he wears many hats in Rom 4. He is still, perhaps (see below), "our [Jewish] ancestor according to the flesh" (4:1), but he is clearly not restricted to that role. Paul claims that Abraham is "the father of all of us" (4:16), meaning both Jewish and gentile believers in Christ. Abraham is a paradigmatic justified *gentile* (like a proselyte) inasmuch as he was justified by faith without having either the law or circumcision. But he is also a paradigmatic justified *Jew* inasmuch as he was justified not by the law (or circumcision) but by faith (4:9–17a). Paul even implies that Abraham was ungodly, since God justifies the ungodly (4:5; cf. 1:18; 5:6). Thus, Paul reads Abraham's story as the story of a sinner, a gentile, a Jew, and a Christian—a justified, forgiven believer brought from death to life. *Abraham is Paul's everyman.*

That said, we can summarize the role of Abraham in Rom 4 with two words: *proof* and *paradigm*. Abraham is not only the proof but also the paradigm of justifying faith. In this chapter, Paul reveals much about his unique understanding of justification and faith. He does so with two methods. First, he again employs the diatribe form, with questions that invoke the audience's careful consideration. Additionally, he uses the Jewish approach to scriptural interpretation called midrash, and specifically the form of midrash that involves the careful rereading of a biblical story for its contemporary significance. Here Paul rereads the story of Abraham in Gen 15–17, with special emphasis on Gen 15:6 and 17:5.

But Paul is also tacitly rereading and challenging another biblical story, that of Phinehas, grandson of Aaron (Exod 6:25). Although Paul never names Phinehas, it is likely that he was one of the inspirations for Paul's preconversion zeal in trying to destroy the church (Gal 1:13–14, 23; Phil 3:6; cf. Acts

8:1–3; 9:1–5). According to Num 25, Phinehas was so zealous that he killed an Israelite man and his Midianite consort in order to purify the people of God from their idolatry and immorality. The text says that the Lord rewarded Phinehas with a perpetual priesthood for his zeal and for turning away God's wrath from the people, which was an act of atonement for their sins. Psalm 106 declares that Phinehas' violent act was "reckoned to him as righteousness" (Ps 106:30–31).

In all of Israel's Scriptures, only two figures are said to have had something "reckoned to him as righteousness": Abraham and Phinehas. It is now clear to Paul that Abraham, not Phinehas, is the model of justification—that faith, not violence, is the way to right relationship with God. In addition, Paul now knows and affirms in this chapter (4:23–25), and on either side of this chapter (3:21–26; 5:1–11), that God's way of atonement, God's way of dealing with people's idolatry and immorality, is not by inflicting violence, but by absorbing it.

A final introductory note about Rom 4: there are two common mistakes in reading Rom 4 that we need to avoid. First, interpreters often pay attention primarily to the first part of the chapter (vv. 1–15) and underestimate the significance of the second part (vv. 16–25). The two parts offer different but complementary views of Abraham's faith and of justification; we must be sure not to neglect the second part of the story.

Second, interpreters frequently forget that although Abraham is clearly the subject of this chapter, the story's actual protagonist—the hero (so to speak)—is not Abraham, but God. It is not Abraham's *faith*, but Abraham's *God*, that makes him righteous. The chapter has many passive verbs—"was reckoned/credited," "was written," "are forgiven," "was handed over," "was raised," and so on. In all of the phrases with these passive verbs, the actor is God. *Ultimately, then, this chapter is about God.*

4:1–15. Abraham's Justification by Faith without Circumcision or the Law

The first part of the chapter (4:1–15) focuses on Abraham's justification by faith according to Gen 15:6—supported by Ps 31 and a dose of economic commonsense and rabbinic logic. Paul pays tribute to the Jewish principle of "two or three witnesses" (e.g., Deut 17:6; 19:15), drawing on Abraham, undergirded by David, in support of several critical claims about justification from 3:21–31. Justification as Paul has just presented it is

1. the work of God
2. for the ungodly/sinners
3. by grace through faith
4. irrespective of circumcision and the law
5. exclusive of pride
6. supported by Scripture

4:1–8. Abraham Justified by Grace through Faith

Chapter 4 begins with a conundrum: how to translate the first verse. There are several viable interpretations:

1. What then shall we say to have found about Abraham, our forefather according to the flesh? (see RSV)
2. What then shall we say that Abraham, our forefather according to the flesh, found/gained [concerning this matter]? (see NRSV, NAB, NIV, NET, NASB)
3. What then shall we say? That we have found Abraham to be our forefather according to the flesh? (see CEB)
4. What then shall we say Abraham, our forefather, found according to the flesh [i.e., by means of the flesh]? (proposed by several scholars but not currently in translations)

My own preference is for number 2 or 3, but no matter how we interpret 4:1, what follows is quite clear. (Recall a similar situation at 3:9–20.) In 4:1–8, Paul argues that Abraham was justified by grace through faith, rather than by human effort. Interestingly, Paul dismisses the propriety of boasting before God even if justification were by works (4:2). But his main concern is the thesis that Abraham's faith was "reckoned to him as righteousness" (4:3, citing Gen 15:6; cf. Gal 3:6–9).[65] The passive verb "reckoned" ("credited" in many translations) tells us that God is the source, the initiator, the reckoner, for God is the justifier of the ungodly (4:5; cf. 3:26).[66]

The verb "reckon" (or "credit") appears eleven times in Rom 4.[67] Most

---

65. See also Jas 2:21–24. Paul and James use the word "faith" in different ways, but they agree that belief and action are inseparable.

66. This is actually a claim that some of Paul's peers might challenge, since Israel's Scriptures sometimes suggest that God does not do so (Exod 23:7; 34:7).

67. Rom 4:3, 4, 5, 6, 8, 9, 10, 11, 22, 23, 24.

translations say that Paul's faith was reckoned "as" righteousness, as if the act of faith itself was inherently righteous. But the sense of the Greek wording is more precisely that his faith was reckoned "for" or "toward" righteousness, meaning that the faith resulted in (God's gift of) righteousness/justification.

In 4:4–5, Paul uses an accounting analogy from common labor practice: those who work earn wages and are due those wages, but those who do not work can receive only an unearned gift: *charis* (4:4), which is also the word for grace. This analogy provides an initial witness about reckoning that illustrates what David in Ps 32:1–2 also says (4:6–8), using the same language of reckoning found in Gen 15:6. Paul interprets the blessing that the psalm celebrates to mean that God's reckoning righteousness means *not* reckoning sin, and thus forgiving it. Somewhat surprisingly, as noted above, Paul implies that Abraham had been one of the "ungodly" whom God justifies (4:5; recall 1:18), and for whom Christ died (5:6).

Justification, then, is God's free gift that

- is given to the ungodly/sinners (analogous to the one who does not work)
- is received in faith and trust
- brings about a state of blessedness due to the forgiveness of sins

Thus, justification is clearly an act of grace that includes forgiveness and that can be described metaphorically with accounting terminology. But that metaphor does not mean justification is a legal fiction, as some have asserted (and we have previously rejected). Justification is not a matter of *un*reality but of a *new* reality. Furthermore, the accounting metaphor hardly *exhausts* the significance of justification, as we will see in 4:16–25.

4:9–15. Abraham Justified Apart from Circumcision and the Law

The next section of the first half of the chapter (4:9–15) establishes Abraham's justification prior to his circumcision (vv. 9–12) and apart from the law of Moses (vv. 13–15). Abraham's circumcision is narrated in Gen 17:9–14, which is obviously an event that postdates his justification by faith recounted in Gen 15:6. Circumcision, then, was not a prerequisite for Abraham's justification but a sequel to it, serving as a seal (4:10–11). The implication, of course, is that still in Paul's day, circumcision is not necessary for the blessings of forgiveness, justification, and membership in God's family (cf. 3:30), and, in fact, circumcision is insufficient to make one a descendant of Abraham. He is the "ancestor" (lit.

"father") of the uncircumcised who believe (4:11b) and of the circumcised who believe in the way Abraham did before his circumcision (4:12a).[68]

The promise to Abraham, that he would "inherit the world" (4:13), came, moreover, before God gave Moses the law. This promise most likely refers to the promise of Gen 17:5, which Paul will cite twice in 4:17–18, that Abraham would be the "father of many nations." The law cannot deliver what the promise, received in faith, can (4:14–15). (Paul will later explain, in chapter 7, that he does not mean the law is bad; it is simply powerless to bring life.)[69]

All of this means, Paul claims, that Abraham was intended all along to be the father of both Jewish and gentile believers (4:11, 13; cf. Gal 3:7–9). That is, Paul again stresses, neither circumcision nor uncircumcision matters for justification (cf. Gal 5:6). What does matter is following in the "footsteps" (NIV, NET) of the uncircumcised Abraham's faith (4:12)—that is, sharing his faith, as Paul will put it in 4:16.

4:16–25. ABRAHAM'S JUSTIFICATION AS RESURRECTION FROM THE DEAD

The second main part of the chapter (4:16–25) does two things. First, it reinforces the claim that God's gracious gift of justification is for all who share Abraham's faith. Second, it portrays the extraordinary circumstances and nature of Abraham's paradigmatic faith, and thus also the extraordinary nature of *justification as a resurrection from the dead*. That is, Abraham is the prototype of justification as resurrection, as benefiting from and participating not only in Jesus' death but also in his resurrection (4:24–25).

4:16–18. Abraham's Faith and Hope in the God Who Gives Life to the Dead

Paul begins with a rather cryptic, verbless phrase in Greek, something like, "Therefore, from faith, so that by grace" (4:16). The NRSV renders it, "For

68. As Paul has made clear in 2:28–29, his ultimate concern about physical circumcision is that it does not affect the heart and thus does not bring about transformation—life out of death. What is needed for such a resurrectional transformation is heart-circumcision by the Spirit. Although Paul does not make that explicit point in this chapter, it lies behind the discussion here, as evidenced by the language of resurrection in 4:16–25.

69. See also Gal 3, esp. v. 21: "Is the law then opposed to the promises of God? Certainly not! For if a law had been given that could make alive, then righteousness would indeed come through the law."

this reason it depends on faith, in order that the promise may rest on grace." This phrase is an apt summary of 4:1–15 and its emphasis on God's grace and human faith; it is repeated in connection with Abraham at the end of 4:16. But the phrase "from faith" here is also an echo of the same Greek phrase in 1:17 and 3:26, which means that Paul may also be stressing that this human faith is made possible by the faithfulness of God or of Christ. The story of Abraham, like the reality of justification, is all about grace (4:16, echoing 4:4).

The divine promise to Abraham and his descendants (lit. his "seed") is for all believers, all who are his descendants (lit. "for the entire seed") by virtue of sharing his faith, Jews and gentiles alike. This is because God's promise was graciously extended to Abraham for all nations (4:16–17), as the Genesis story makes clear to Paul, who quotes Gen 17:5 in both 4:17 and 4:18: "'I have made you the father of many nations.'" A brief quotation from Gen 15:5 reiterates this promise (4:18b). In fact, the standard translations of part of 4:16, such as the NRSV—"not only to the adherents of the law but also to those who share the faith of Abraham"—may hide what Paul actually means: "not to those who adhere to the law alone but *rather* to those who share the faith of Abraham" (MJG).[70] The language of "the faith of Abraham" is the same language and grammatical construction Paul used of Christ's faith in 3:21 and 3:26.

We learn in these verses that for Paul, looking to Abraham and also, implicitly, to Christ, faith includes fidelity; to trust in God and the promises of God is to be faithful. The object of Abraham's trust and fidelity is the God who "gives life to the dead and calls into existence the things that do not exist" (4:17b). This is an extremely important description of God. The God who creates life out of nothing is also the God who raises the dead (cf. Ps 71:20); they are similar divine activities. Moreover, Paul has just described God as the one who "justifies the ungodly" (4:5). *The creating God who is the resurrecting God is also the justifying God; this implies that justification is an act of new creation and resurrection.* The story of Abraham will soon confirm this implication.

Faith, therefore, is forward-looking—centered on resurrection and new creation—and therefore virtually synonymous with hope: "Hoping against hope, he [Abraham] believed" (4:18a), meaning he demonstrated unwavering trust and fidelity. Hope, then, is future-oriented, even eschatological (focused on

---

70. More literally, "the one who is of the faith of Abraham." The phrase "of the" is normally understood to mean to "have" (NIV, NET) or to "share" (RSV, NRSV, ESV) Abraham's faith, though some understand it to mean "follow" (NAB) or "rely on" (NJB) that faith.

the age to come)—but also focused on the realization of God's promises in this age, especially the promise of life out of death. Such was Abraham's focus.

4:19–22. Abraham's Fidelity in the Face of Death

In 4:19–22, Paul describes the bleak situation in which Abraham and Sarah found themselves: a state of death. English translations often fail to convey the severe stench of death arising from Paul's words. Abraham did not consider his body to be "as good as dead" (NRSV, NIV, CEB); it was, to him, literally "*already dead*" (4:19 MJG). Furthermore, he recognized the "deadness" (NET; cf. NIV, CEB) of Sarah's womb; Paul uses a Greek word indicating the condition of a corpse (*nekrōsis*), obviously a much stronger image than simply "barrenness" (NRSV). For Jews of Paul's day, a barren womb and the lack of children were a living death. *Abraham and Sarah needed a resurrection from the dead.*

This dire situation did not cause Abraham to waver, but to trust more fully and deeply in God and, unlike un-godded humanity (1:21–23), he glorified God (4:20). Abraham's trust and worship were grounded in his conviction that God can and will do what God has promised (4:21). It was this sort of robust faith—fidelity—that resulted in Abraham's justification (4:22, again citing Gen 15:6), and it is this sort of justification—a resurrection from the dead—that the trustworthy God of Abraham provides.[71]

Accordingly, although justification can be described as reckoning (cf. 4:3, 9, 22), it is not a mere accounting (or, by extension, juridical) event. The creator God has promised to turn death into life. Abraham's story is not one of generic trust or hope but of a specific hope: for new life, for resurrection, for eternal life.

If barrenness was the equivalent of death for ancient Jews, birth and progeny were essentially resurrection and an afterlife. Because Abraham himself was functionally dead (4:19a)—as was his wife's womb (4:19b)—his faith was that God could bring life out of *his* death, could transform *their* deadness into life. In other words, Abraham's faith was completely self-involving and participatory, truly a matter of life and death.[72]

The birth of Isaac (Gen 21:1–8)—and thus also of many descendants—therefore meant resurrection from the dead, the deadness of both Abraham

---

71. Abraham's faithfulness is not a meritorious "work," but it clearly indicates that Paul attributes to Abraham a thick rather than a thin form of faith.

72. Several other ancient Jewish texts from around the time of Paul associate resurrection and eternal life with Abraham.

and Sarah. For Paul, however, this story is not only about Abraham and Sarah but also about God. The birth of Isaac in spite of the deadness of Abraham's body and Sarah's womb emphasizes God's resurrection power.

4:23–25. Abraham as the Prototype of Justification as Resurrection

The whole scriptural story of Abraham and Sarah, summarized in the words "reckoned to him for righteousness" (MJG), is told, Paul says, "for our sakes" (4:24). It is a foreshadowing of the kind of faith of which Paul speaks—faith in God's handing over the Son to death (cf. 8:32) and in God's raising him from the dead (4:24–25).[73] The God "who gives life to the dead" (4:17) is, more specifically, the God who "raised Jesus our Lord from the dead" (4:24).[74] Paul makes it clear that both the death and the resurrection of Christ are essential for restoration to right relations with God, which includes both forgiveness of trespasses and liberation from Sin for resurrection to new life (4:25).[75]

Ultimately, then, Abraham bears witness not only to the nature of faith as trust, hope, and fidelity but also to the nature of justification—receiving both the forgiving mercy of God and the new, resurrection life of God. That is, the *means* of justification is faith, but the *meaning* (content) of justification includes resurrection from the dead (cf. 6:4) as well as forgiveness—and (as we saw in 3:21–26) even more. Abraham has a kind of proto-Christian faith; he is the prototype of justification as resurrection to new life, a topic Paul will discuss at length in chapter 6, in connection with baptism as participation in Christ's death and resurrection. Even in 5:18, however, he will summarize justification as consisting of life.

What Abraham found (NRSV, "gained," 4:1), then, was in essence the reality revealed in the gospel Paul proclaimed: grace, faith, justification, and life apart from circumcision and law. These are the gifts of the God of grace and life who forgives sins, raises the dead, and creates new life. Without ever de-

---

73. The Greek verb for "hand over" (*paradidōmi*) used in Rom 4:25 and 8:32 is found in two verses of the famous poem about the suffering servant, Isa 53:6, 12 (LXX). It is the same verb, used for a dramatically different purpose, for God's handing people over to their passions, etc. (1:24, 26, 28).

74. See also 6:4; 8:11; 10:9; Gal 1:1; 1 Thess 1:10; Eph 1:20; Col 2:12. In the oft-quoted words of Lutheran theologian Robert W. Jenson, "God is whoever raised Jesus from the dead, having before raised Israel from Egypt" (*Systematic Theology*, vol. 1, *The Triune God* [New York: Oxford University Press, 1997], 63).

75. On the necessity of both Christ's death and his resurrection, see 6:4; 8:34; 1 Cor 15:4; 1 Thess 4:14.

nying Abraham's Jewishness, Paul universalizes him. That is why the justified are defined as those who "share the faith of Abraham" (4:16). But Paul claims that this universalizing is not original to him: according to Genesis, he reminds us, the covenant with Abraham was for him to be the "father of many nations" (4:17, from Gen 17:1-8). Paul sees that covenant faithfully fulfilled in the taking of the gospel to the nations, which he articulates in Rom 10 and practices in his own ministry (see 15:14-33).

SUMMARY OF 4:1-25: ABRAHAM AND JUSTIFICATION

So what does Abraham teach us about justification? The first part of chapter 4 employs the story of Abraham to stress the *necessity and function of faith*, leading to forgiveness, while the second part of the chapter uses the story of Abraham and Sarah to emphasize the *nature and content of faith*, leading to transformation and life: a self-involving experience of death and resurrection.

These are essentially the two main elements of justification we found in 3:21-26. To be justified is to receive, experience, and embody the promise of life, because in that act, God turns sinners like Abraham—and sinners like you and me—into new people. The ungodly and unjust are both forgiven and transformed into the godly and just. In other words, *Abraham's experience also teaches us that justification involves liberation from both sin/Sin and death/Death*—which is in many ways the main concern of the next major section of Romans, chapters 5-8. The story of Abraham in chapter 4 is a bridge between the succinct retelling of the letter's thesis contained in 3:21-26 and the detailed unpacking of that thesis beginning in chapter 5.

That Abraham was justified by faith does not mean God fictitiously considered him righteous, but that God graciously gifted him with life out of death. Now that the Messiah has come, Abraham's story points us to new life through our participation in Christ's death and resurrection. This is good news indeed for Jews and gentiles, people of worldly status and those of no status, whether in the first century or the twenty-first. It is good news to treasure, and to share.

ABRAHAM AS THE PROTOTYPE OF JUSTIFICATION

From Abraham, we learn that justification is

- an act of God's grace and forgiveness for ungodly sinners who have a faith like Abraham's, apart from works (the mode);

- for all, both the uncircumcised and the circumcised (the scope);
- appropriated through unwavering trust in the God who brings life out of death (the means);
- a participatory experience of resurrection from death (the substance); and
- the start of a new life of devotion to God and righteousness/justice (the result).

In a word, justification means *life*.

REFLECTIONS AND QUESTIONS FOR 4:1–25

Theological, Spiritual, and Pastoral Reflections

1. We learn much about theology proper (i.e., the **doctrine of God**) in this text, which continues and supplements what we have learned in previous parts of the letter, most especially in 3:21–31. It is God who handed Jesus over to death for our sins and then raised him to life. God is the one who creates, resurrects, forgives sins, and justifies the ungodly. All of these actions are manifestations of God's "eternal power and divine nature" (1:20) and of God's righteousness/justice (1:17; 3:21–22).

2. As we saw in 3:21–26, Paul offers a much **more robust understanding of justification** than many interpreters of Paul have recognized. We now see that all the dimensions of justification can be summarized in the phrase "resurrection from death to life," or "participation in the death and resurrection of Jesus." This means that the understanding of salvation in Eph 2:1–10 ("even when we were dead through our trespasses, [God] made us alive together with Christ," Eph 2:5a) is very much in line with the understanding of justification present in Rom 4.

3. **Justification** is, or ought to be, a **great unifying doctrine and reality**, as it was for Paul here and in Galatians—or at least how Paul wanted it to be. As it turns out, however, justification has been divisive throughout at least five hundred years of Christian history. The tide has turned in many quarters, and some divisions have been healed, but there is still a need for greater understanding and unity.

4. Christians need to embrace **Abraham and Sarah** more fully as our **spiritual parents**.

Questions for Those Who Read, Teach, and Preach

1. How might Paul's understanding of Abraham and his faith shape Christians today?
2. What difference might Paul's understanding of justification in this chapter make in the daily life of individual Christians and Christian communities?
3. What experiences have you witnessed in your personal life, the church, or the world that have demonstrated or affirmed God as the one who brings life from death?

For Further Reading

Boakye, Andrew K. *Death and Life: Resurrection, Restoration, and Rectification in Paul's Letter to the Galatians*. Eugene, OR: Pickwick, 2017. (more technical)

Gupta, Nijay K. *Paul and the Language of Faith*. Grand Rapids: Eerdmans, 2020.

"Joint Declaration on the Doctrine of Justification, 20th Anniversary Edition." Lutheran World Federation. 2019. https://www.lutheranworld.org/content/resource-joint-declaration-doctrine-justification-20th-anniversary-edition.

Levenson, Jon D. *Inheriting Abraham: The Legacy of the Patriarch in Judaism, Christianity, and Islam*. Princeton: Princeton University Press, 2012.

Madigan, Kevin J., and Jon D. Levenson. *Resurrection: The Power of God for Christians and Jews*. New Haven: Yale University Press, 2008.

Martini, Carlo Maria. *Abraham: Our Father in Faith*. Melbourne: Coventry, 2020.

Wilson, Marvin R. *Our Father Abraham: Jewish Roots of the Christian Faith*. 2nd ed. Grand Rapids: Eerdmans, 2021.

SUMMARY OF ROMANS 1–4

In the opening chapters of Romans, Paul makes the following central claims about the gospel as God's response to the human predicament:

- The gospel is the power of God to save anyone and everyone, both Jews and gentiles.
- Both gentiles and Jews have failed to live in proper covenant relationship with God, each group having its distinctive ways

of failing to obey God (ungodliness, idolatry) and love others (immorality/injustice); they are covenantally dysfunctional.

- Human beings are judged impartially by God according to their deeds; performance, not possession, of the law is what matters and what is required for right relations with God.

- The various kinds of sins people commit, and to which the Scriptures attest, are manifestations of the power of Sin, to which humans are enslaved.

- In Christ's faithful, obedient death, God's gracious, saving covenant faithfulness and restorative justice are revealed as God extends both forgiveness from sins and redemption/liberation from Sin.

- Both gentiles and Jews who believe the gospel are justified, but they have no grounds for boasting. They have had their hearts circumcised and are therefore members of God's covenant people.

- Abraham is the paradigm and prototype of such justifying faith, which he had apart from circumcision and the law; he is Paul's everyman, the example for both Jews and gentiles, demonstrating justification to be both the forgiveness of sins and the resurrection of the dead to new life.

The Character of Justification by Faith: Righteousness and Reconciliation; Liberation and Life

It would be difficult to imagine any part of a work with more theological depth than Rom 5–8. For some interpreters, it is not only the richest passage in Paul's letters, it is almost all we need to comprehend Paul. (Not true, but perhaps understandable.) This section of Romans contains some of Paul's most significant teaching on the salvation and new life that come through Christ's death and resurrection. The focus throughout is what God has done "through" or "in" the Lord Jesus Christ, which constitutes a sort of refrain that appears especially at the end of various sections of chapters 5–8 (5:1, 11, 17, 21; 6:23; 7:25; 8:39). But what is the purpose of these chapters in the letter?

Some have argued that Paul here spells out the normal progress of Christian growth, from justification (ch. 5) to sanctification (ch. 6), and then from despair at one's ongoing sin (ch. 7) to freedom in the Spirit (ch. 8). Although these chapters may describe some development,[1] that is not their main thrust. Paul is not presenting a sequential outline of phases in the Christian life. Rather, he looks at the new life in Christ that comes in justification from a variety of angles. John Barclay describes Rom 5:12–8:39, along with 12:1–15:13, as Paul's construction of a Christian *habitus*—a set of dispositions, values, and practices that reflect God's gracious gift of Christ.[2] The general outline of this *habitus* appears in chapters 5–8, while more concrete practices of the new life are discussed in 12:1–15:13.

Principally, then, Rom 5–8 functions to spell out the multifaceted meaning and character of justification.[3] In other words, Rom 5–8 cannot be severed from what precedes. The language of resurrection and life in chapters 5–8 is not in contrast to, or in conflict with, the justification language of the first part of Romans. (In fact, there are twenty occurrences of the *dik-*, or "right-/just-," family of words in Rom 5–8, following twenty-nine in Rom 1–4.)[4] On the

---

1. For example, the narrative of Israel's exodus, from slavery to freedom, as suggested especially by N. T. Wright in various publications.

2. John M. G. Barclay, *Paul and the Gift* (Grand Rapids: Eerdmans, 2015), 493–519; *Paul and the Power of Grace* (Grand Rapids: Eerdmans, 2020), 88–100.

3. N. T. Wright also interprets Rom 5–8 as continuing the discussion of justification: *Paul and the Faithfulness of God* (Minneapolis: Fortress, 2013), 1024.

4. There are also occurrences of the most important member of this word-family in Romans, *dikaiosynē* (righteousness, justice) in chs. 9–11 (eleven times) and in 14:17.

contrary, this sort of language is in continuity with the idiom of justification, as Paul builds on his discussion of Abraham and continues to expound on the meaning of justification as the gift of new life. In fact, Rom 5–8 tells us about the fundamental reconstruction of our entire life, our very being, into the life of God. This happens in Christ, by the Spirit.[5]

With Rom 3:21–4:25 as his foundation, Paul now constructs an extended explanation of justification as new life through a series of antithetical (opposing) narratives that echo the "but now" of 3:21. After a preliminary exposition of the significance of justification in 5:1–11, he sets out the story of those who, through God's saving act of righteousness/justice in Christ and the transformation it affords, have moved from outside Christ into Christ. He tells this story—for Paul's original audience in Rome and for us—from three narrative perspectives, focusing on three sets of antitheses that highlight three distinct yet interrelated themes, with each set following from and building on the preceding passage.

In each narrative, as well as in the initial overview, the death of Jesus highlighted in 3:21–26 figures centrally. The following table summarizes these chapters:

SUMMARY OF ROMANS 5–8

TEXT	NARRATIVE PERSPECTIVE	DEATH-LIFE ANTITHESIS	THEMES (A) JUSTIFICATION AS ... (B) NEW LIFE AS ...	CHRIST'S DEATH AND RESURRECTION
5:1–11	overview	being God's enemies vs. being God's reconciled friends	(a) inclusive of reconciliation (b) the experience of peace, love, and hope	Christ's death as God's love
5:12–21	cosmic, apocalyptic, and salvation historical	Adam = death vs. Christ = life	(a) the gifts of acquittal, righteousness, and life (b) being free from Sin, under grace (anticipating ch. 6)	Christ's death as his obedience

5. Douglas Campbell uses the term "ontological reconstitution" to describe the substance of justification and the content of Rom 5–8. See Douglas A. Campbell, *The Deliverance of God: An Apocalyptic Rereading of Justification in Paul* (Grand Rapids: Eerdmans, 2009), 185.

TEXT	NARRATIVE PERSPEC- TIVE	DEATH-LIFE ANTITHESIS	THEMES (A) JUSTIFICATION AS . . . (B) NEW LIFE AS . . .	CHRIST'S DEATH AND RESURREC- TION
6:1–7:6	participation- ist: baptismal	slavery to Sin = death vs. slavery to righ- teousness = life	(a) liberation from Sin, and as a death and resurrection (b) being liberated from, and dead to, Sin; being enslaved to, and alive to, God	believers' co- crucifixion and co-resurrection with Christ[6]
7:7–8:39	participation- ist: existential (practical)	flesh = death vs. the Spirit = life	(a) inhabitation by the Spirit and fulfilling the just requirement of the law (b) living in the Spirit, not in the flesh	believers' death to the old life and new life in the Spirit, co-suffering with Christ in antici- pation of full and final glory

In these three sets of narrative antitheses, we find that, in Christ, the human story circumscribed by wrath, sin/Sin, the law, and death/Death (1:18–3:20) is transformed into one of freedom from all these powers and negative aspects of human existence. Following the overview in 5:1–11, the antitheses (opposites) can be summarized in two words: death → life. This is about a transformation that means life!

This part of Romans, then, is not about the *effects* or *results* of justification (as some set of separable and perhaps optional consequences) but about the very *meaning* of it. *Justification means to experience the fullness of the life of the triune God.* Just as all who have sinned stand accountable before God, all who are justified live in grace, free to be members of the covenant community that lives under the sign of the cross—those reconciled with God through the death and resurrection of the Messiah and empowered by the Spirit.

All this lays the foundation for the rest of the letter: for the anguish Paul feels about fellow Jews missing out on the joy of justification, as well as his

6. From this point forward in Romans, we will find numerous occurrences of words that, in Greek, begin with the prefix *syn*, meaning "co-" or "with." These words manifest the importance of participation in, and solidarity with, Christ as well as solidarity with others. We will indicate them in this sort of hyphenated form.

hope for them (chs. 9–11); and for Paul's more explicit covenantal stipulations for life in Christ in the new reign of grace (chs. 12–15), whether then or now.

5:1–11
Justification and Reconciliation through the Cross

As noted above, in 5:1–11 we find an overview, a preliminary exposition of the significance of justification (5:1–11). It is a multidimensional and carefully constructed text, functioning as a bridge between the first four chapters of Romans and the next four. Paul summarizes the past, present, and future aspects of the new, resurrection-life of reconciliation and righteousness.

The passage contains many key Pauline words and themes, some of which reappear in the following chapters, especially in chapter 8. Some of its principal motifs appear also in other masterful summaries of the gospel, such as 2 Cor 5:14–21 and Eph 1:3–14. In fact, Rom 5:1–11 is really an amplification of Paul's claim in 2 Cor 5:19: "God was in Christ reconciling the world to himself" (MJG). Furthermore, the saving activity of God, Christ, and the Spirit described in 5:1–11 anticipates the Christian doctrine of the Trinity (see also 8:9–11; 15:17–19, 30).

This passage of Romans is artfully composed in chiastic form—shaped like the Greek letter chi (X)—as follows:

A (vv. 1–2a) **Justification** means peace through Christ
   B (vv. 2b–5) **Hope** for future glory
      C (vv. 6–8) **Christ's death as God's love**
   B' (vv. 9–10) **Hope** for future salvation
A' (v. 11) **Reconciliation** through Christ

Noticing this arrangement of the text enables us to make several key observations.

First, the way the passage begins and ends in parallel form (a rhetorical technique called *inclusio,* or literary bookends) suggests that justification (5:1) includes the present experience of reconciliation with God (5:11), or "peace with God" (5:1). Reconciliation is not something separate from justification; "justified" and "reconciled" are used in the same breath, almost interchangeably, also in 5:9–10.[7] In a nutshell, Christians are those who now stand in grace (5:2), reconciled with God.

---

7. These two ways of referring to God's saving work in Christ are also joined in 2 Cor 5:18–21. Some interpreters call justification a legal term and reconciliation a personal or relational term. Paul refuses to make such a sharp distinction, for the God of the covenant is always personal and relational.

Second, the center or fulcrum of this text (5:6–8) indicates that the focal point of God's justifying and reconciling work is Christ's death, which specifies the meaning of "through our Lord Jesus Christ" (5:1, 11). The passage as a whole contains four explicit (5:6, 8, 9, 10) and two implicit (5:1, 11) references to Christ's death; "through our Lord Jesus Christ" means "through the death of his [God's] Son" (5:10), echoing 3:21–26. As we will see below, however, and as indicated in 4:24–25, this focus on Christ's death does not leave out the resurrection.

Third, the Christian experience of God's grace has not only past and present aspects but also a future dimension, as the parallel sections B and B' between the bookends and the fulcrum demonstrate (5:2b–5, 9–10). Paul speaks of this future dimension in two ways. First he notes our hope for God's glory (5:2b), which probably includes our "sharing" that glory (so NRSV).[8] Then Paul uses the language of salvation ("much more surely . . . will we be saved," stated twice in 5:9–10). The future tense verbs in 5:9–10 are critical. Paul's concept of salvation is oriented toward the future (cf. 13:11) and entails the fullness of participation in God's glory. Even when he speaks of salvation in the past tense, Paul qualifies it: "in hope we were saved" (8:24).[9]

In this passage, then, Paul understands justification as including reconciliation with God in the present, together with certain hope of salvation and glory in the future, based on the death of Christ in the past, and this is all known through the gift of the Spirit (5:5). This understanding is borne out by both the structure and the actual content of 5:1–11, and it both coheres with and amplifies other texts on justification.

What is especially noteworthy is the Trinitarian character—involving Father, Son, and Spirit—of both the justifying, reconciling, saving act and our experience of that gracious work of God. As in Rom 4, God's gracious initiative is sometimes expressed in the passive voice—*we are justified/have been justified, we were reconciled/having been reconciled, we have now received*. The point in such verbs is this: God justified, God reconciled, God gave. We are the unworthy recipients.

5:1–5. Justification, Peace with God, and the Gift of the Spirit

In 5:1–5, Paul depicts a close relationship between believers' past, present, and future experience. The phrase "since we are justified" (NRSV) is better

8. The hope of God's glory being widely revealed and known is prominent in the latter parts of Isaiah; see, e.g., Isa 40:1–5; 60:1–2; 66:18–19.

9. And, paradoxically, he also speaks of our glorification not only as future but also as an accomplished reality (8:30).

rendered "since we have been justified" (NAB, NIV) or even—in light of our comments on 3:21–31 and chapter 4—"since we have been made righteous" (CEB; cf. 5:19).[10] Justification began in the past (with the response of faith in the gospel) but has an ongoing, permanent effect. To be justified is to be, like Abraham, in a state of blessedness (cf. 4:6–9); it means having peace with God and standing in grace (5:1–2), and it means experiencing God's love by means of the presence of the Holy Spirit (5:5).

5:1–2. Justification, Peace, and the Hope of Glory

The means of justification, as in the previous chapter, is faith (5:1). This is normally understood as referring to *our* faith, but it is possibly (once again) referring to God's or Christ's faithfulness (so CEB).[11] However, if we understand 5:1 to be a reference to human faith (as most interpreters do), it is still critical to see that Paul stresses that God has taken the initiative and faith is the human response. So it is better to say, as noted in the discussion of 3:21–26, that God's grace, manifested in Christ's death, is the *means* of justification (the objective, divine act) and faith is the *mode* of justification (the subjective, human response): "justification by grace [the means] through faith [the mode]."

As in chapters 3 and 4, the human response of faith Paul refers to is not mere assent but is robust: a sharing in the faithfulness of Jesus (3:26) and of Abraham (4:16). This is the sort of faith that results, by God's grace, in moving from death to life. It is an unqualified act of trust that is therefore simultaneously an unqualified pledge of allegiance.

Peace with God accompanies justification (5:1b). Centuries before Paul, the prophet Isaiah had said that peace, shalom, would be the fruit of a divine act of righteousness, prefiguring what God has now done in Christ:

> Then justice will dwell in the wilderness, and righteousness abide in the fruitful field. The effect of righteousness will be peace, and the result of righteousness, quietness and trust forever. My people will abide in a peaceful habitation, in secure dwellings, and in quiet resting places. (Isa 32:16–18)

---

10. Some important Greek manuscripts say "*let us* have peace with God" (emphasis added). The difference in Greek between it and "we have peace with God" is just one letter, and the two letters in question (omicron and omega) are both "o" sounds. Although Paul *might* have meant "let us have peace," the overall argument he is making about what God has done favors "we have peace."

11. CEB: "since we have been made righteous through his faithfulness."

We see here that peace is both personal and public, even political.

Later in Isaiah, we hear another announcement of God's peace initiative:

> I will appoint Peace as your overseer and Righteousness [or Justice] as your taskmaster. Violence shall no more be heard in your land, devastation or destruction within your borders; you shall call your walls Salvation, and your gates Praise. (Isa 60:17b–18)

Similarly, the psalmist speaks beautifully of God's saving activity as righteousness and shalom kissing, or embracing (Ps 85:10).

By alluding to Isaiah and the psalmist, Paul is declaring that the cause and effects of the human predicament narrated in 3:9–20, which depicts violence and the antithesis of shalom, are being undone. It was also Isaiah, quoted by Paul in 3:17, who declared that untransformed people do not know the way of peace (Isa 59:8). But now, transformation is occurring; life and peace are springing forth. For victims of domestic or political violence in ancient Rome, such as slaves, the promise that the church would be a safe space of shalom was no doubt part of its appeal.

The Hebrew concept of shalom entails right relations with God, others, and the entire creation. The focus here is on believers and God because the broken God-human relationship is the source of other broken relationships, as we learned in 1:18–32. But peace/shalom with others will become an important theme in chapters 12–15, while the hope of glory includes the hope for shalom and salvation for all creation (8:18–25). *The peace-gift of Rom 5 becomes the peace-mandate and the peace-hope of later chapters.* To be justified—made just—means that all of our relationships have been, and must continue to be, transformed into peaceful ones.

Paul's understanding of peace is in continuity with the biblical prophets' vision of shalom but in stark opposition to the claims of Rome and its supporters. The first-century ex-slave and Stoic teacher Epictetus wrote, "Caesar has obtained for us a profound peace. There are neither wars nor battles, nor great robberies nor piracies, but we may travel at all hours, and sail from east to west."[12]

This claim is perhaps partly true (although Paul had a different experience! [2 Cor 11:25–27]), but what Epictetus fails to note here is that the *pax Romana*, like most imperial versions of peace, was the consequence of oppression and death. Rome's peace and God's peace are antithetical realities, as we will see

---

12. Epictetus, *Discourses* 3.13.9 (Loeb).

more fully in 5:6–8. In fact, Rome had made *Pax*, along with *Iustitia* and *Fides* (justice and fidelity), as well as other Roman values, into deities in what is called the "cult of the virtues." Paul would tell us that such deities are idols; the true God effects peace and justice through absorbing violence, not inflicting it. The true God desires fidelity to a savior who conquers only by love.

5:3–5. Suffering, the Spirit, and Hope

Believers' experience also has a future dimension, the hope of participating in the glory of God that sinful humanity lacks (3:23) apart from Christ and the Spirit. In fact, Paul believes that this glorification has already in some sense begun (see 8:30; 2 Cor 3:18). Yet it is the sure hope of future, full participation in God's glory that is the new basis of legitimate boasting—in God, not self (5:2–3; cf. 3:27; 5:11).

The road to glory, however, is bumpy and has a cruciform shape: it includes, or will include, suffering (5:3), as Paul well knew. Although ultimately Paul connects the suffering of believers to Christ's cross (e.g., 8:17; Phil 3:10–11), here he stresses not its basis but its educative role (a role frequently acknowledged in antiquity) and its final goal (5:3–4). Suffering begins a chain reaction leading to character, endurance, and hope. This is not a cross-your-fingers kind of hope but one that, like Abraham's, is grounded in God's promise. Thus, it "does not disappoint" (either now or on the last day)—or better translated, "put us to shame" (NIV, CEB, ESV).

Christians do not need to be ashamed of their experience of suffering on behalf of the gospel, in solidarity with others, or for any other reason. Nor do they need to be ashamed of the hope for eternal life with God when that suffering has ended. Why? Because the present experience of the Holy Spirit ensures believers of God's love (5:5), of God's being "for us" (cf. 8:31–39), both now and at the hour of death, and beyond.

This attitude of joyful confidence is grounded in the experience of God's love and the Spirit that have been "poured out" (5:5 NAB, NIV) into believers' hearts. For the biblical writers, the heart is the core of our humanity and the seat of our will. It is therefore the first place or space in need of transformation. The experience of the Spirit in human hearts fulfills the prophetic promises that God will pour out the Spirit in the last days.[13] In fact, the prophet Ezekiel promised that God would place his Spirit in the hearts of God's people

---

13. See, e.g., Isa 32:15; 44:3; Ezek 39:29; Joel 2:28–29; cf. Acts 2:17–18.

to inaugurate a new covenant and new life.[14] This is the Spirit-caused heart-circumcision Paul noted in 2:29.

Some would say this outpouring is a reference to baptism, while others think it refers to the moment of justification. Both are likely correct. Paul associates the Spirit with justification, when people respond in faith to the gospel (Gal 3:1–5). He also connects it with baptism (1 Cor 12:13). Paul expected all who responded to the gospel and were justified to be baptized, and his descriptions of justification and baptism can be remarkably similar (compare Gal 2:15–21 with Rom 6). But the emphasis in this passage is on the gift of the Spirit as part of justification (which would then be followed by baptism). That is, all people who respond in faith to the gospel receive the Spirit, the gift of God's presence.

In these verses, then, Paul speaks briefly of a unified experience of the Spirit, suffering, love, and hope that he will develop in chapter 8. He says that Christians can and should "boast" (some translations say "rejoice" or "celebrate").[15] They should do so both in their hope of divine glory (5:2)—the fullness of God's presence and conformity to Christ's resurrected body—and in their sufferings (5:3). This is Paul's redirecting of pride, or honor, away from the self (3:27–28; 4:2) and onto God. It is based ultimately in the story of Christ, whose own suffering led to glory, and in whose sufferings and glory Christians are graced to participate (see 8:17).[16]

5:6–11. God's Reconciling Love of Enemies in Christ's Death

In 5:6–11 Paul celebrates the past love of God demonstrated in Christ's death and then restates both the future and the present consequences of this great, life-transforming, world-altering event. Implicit in all of this is a call for those who are beneficiaries of God's enemy-love and reconciliation to practice such Godlike, Christlike love by the power of the Spirit.

---

14. Ezek 11:19–20; 36:25–28.

15. The Greek verb used in vv. 2, 3, 11 (*kauchaomai*) is sometimes translated as "boast" or something similar (e.g., CEB, NAB, NIV, NRSV), and sometimes as "rejoice" or something similar (e.g., ESV, NET, RSV). The KNT by N. T. Wright says "celebrate." "Boast," however, is probably the best translation, reflecting Paul's location in an honor-shame culture.

16. On glory/glorification, see also, e.g., 1 Cor 15:35–57; 2 Cor 3:7—4:18; Phil 3:17–21; Col 1:24–29; 1 Thess 2:11–12.

5:6–8. God's Love Manifested in Christ's Death

The mention of God's love in 5:5 leads Paul, in the central section of this passage (5:6–8), to the ultimate source and manifestation of that love in Christ's death (cf. 8:32). This was an act of grace (5:2): a counterintuitive, sacrificial death ("for us," 5:8; cf. "by his blood," 5:9), a description echoing 3:25. Like 4:25 and 5:19, it also echoes the poem of the suffering servant in Isa 53, especially in the phrase "for us":

> He was wounded for our transgressions, **crushed for our iniquities**; upon him was the punishment that made us whole, and by his bruises we are healed. All we like sheep have gone astray; we have all turned to our own way, and **the Lord has laid on him the iniquity of us all.** . . . The righteous one, my servant, shall make many righteous, and **he shall bear their iniquities.** Therefore I will allot him a portion with the great, and he shall divide the spoil with the strong; because he poured out himself to death, and was numbered with the transgressors; yet **he bore the sin of many**, and made intercession for the transgressors. (Isa 53:5–6, 11b–12)[17]

Christ has died for our benefit, a benefit we could not manufacture for ourselves: life. Paradoxically, death (Christ's) yielded life (ours). That is the unusual divine economy of the scriptural sacrificial system: forgiveness, purification, sanctification; in a word, life. This is grace indeed, a counterintuitive response to human rebellion from a counterintuitive God, a God who breaks with the ancient (and often the modern) convention of waiting for the offending party to start the reconciliation process.

The Messiah's life-giving death was not for righteous/just or good people (5:7). On the contrary, Paul offers a quartet of images to describe those for whom Christ died:

- weak/powerless (5:6)
- ungodly/godless (5:6; cf. 1:18; 4:5)
- sinners (5:8)
- enemies of God (5:10; cf. "God-haters" in 1:30).

God's intervention came "at just the right time" (5:6 NIV) indeed.

Christ's act of self-giving love for us means there has been a cessation of

---

17. The "for us" character of Christ's death is noted also in 14:15; 1 Cor 8:11; 15:3; 2 Cor 5:14–15; 1 Thess 5:10.

hostilities, the transformation of God's enemies into friends. It is possible that Paul was aware of the words of Jesus forgiving enemies from the cross (Luke 23:34). Those who were outside grace—outside the covenant—are now inside it, headed ultimately for Paradise.

This is divine grace, or benefaction, of the most extraordinary kind: reaching out to those who are in no way deserving, whether Jew or gentile. It is an act of divine love, not of divine punishment. In antiquity, an action like this would be seen as the ultimate kind of grace or gift, because it is such a magnanimous display of the giver's benevolence to recipients who are totally unworthy of the gift. When someone, especially a social superior, was offended, the offending party was expected to initiate the reconciliation. Not so with the God of love revealed in the crucified Messiah Jesus. We, the offending party, were both unable to rescue ourselves and undeserving of assistance.

John Barclay refers to this situation as the "incongruity" of grace. Our response of faith does not mean we contribute to our rescue.[18] Faith, Barclay writes, does not create merit but is "a declaration of bankruptcy, a radical and shattering recognition that the only capital in God's economy is the gift of Christ crucified and risen."[19] At the same time, Barclay contends, God's grace is *unconditioned* but not *unconditional*; it requires an initial and ongoing appropriate response. The gift represents the start of a new relationship.

Paul's use of the first-person plural ("we"/"us") throughout this passage is important because of its inclusiveness—the death was for him and all other Jews, as well as gentiles, as well as the author and readers of this commentary. It was for each and for all. It is grace offered irrespective of ancient or modern status, or other claims to significance or insignificance.

In light of 3:21–26, we know that Paul sees this gracious gift also as the display of God's righteousness/justice and covenant faithfulness. This divine faithfulness will allow Paul to be confident in the future—boasting in God (5:11).

5:9–11. The Certain Hope of Future Salvation

As Paul concludes 5:1–11, he borrows an ancient technique of interpretation: using a greater-to-lesser argument. This appears in the twice-used phrase "much more surely" (5:9, 10). That is, Paul moves on to the logical and easier corollary to justification/reconciliation, which is salvation, meaning rescue from "the [future, divine] wrath" (5:9–10; cf. 1 Thess 1:10). Two more refer-

---

18. Hence, as noted earlier, the importance of saying "justification by grace through faith," rather than "justification by faith."

19. John M. G. Barclay, *Paul and the Gift* (Grand Rapids: Eerdmans, 2015), 383–84.

ences to Christ's death in these verses lead to the conclusion that God's saving love shown in the cross and experienced in the present will, for the justified, remain consistent in the future. God has already done the difficult work, so to speak, and the rest is but follow-up.

The attribution of future salvation to Christ's life at the end of 5:10 is a reference to the resurrection as the guarantor of hope and salvation (cf. 4:25), as well as to the current intercessory work of the Son before the Father (8:34). God's past action to make enemies into friends gives us assurance that we will be saved from the coming divine wrath.

This talk of hope once again returns Paul to the theme of the passage, the present ("now" in 5:11) experience of justification/reconciliation through Christ. For him, this is an equal, if not greater, reason to "boast" in God than the future hope (5:11).

SUMMARY OF 5:1–11

The three temporal aspects of salvation depicted in 5:1–11 may be summarized in the following table:

PAST	PRESENT[20]	FUTURE
justified (vv. 1, 9)	justified (vv. 1, 9)	saved from God's wrath (v. 9)
	peace with God (v. 1)	(lit., "the wrath")
	access to grace (v. 2)	
reconciled (vv. 10, 11)	reconciled (vv. 10, 11)	saved by Christ's life (v. 10)
Christ died for us as the demonstration of God's love (vv. 6–8)	experience of God's love (v. 8)	
	boast/rejoice in the hope of God's glory (v. 2)	God's glory (v. 2)
	boast/rejoice in sufferings (v. 3)	
	hope (vv. 2, 4)	
God's love poured into our hearts by the Holy Spirit given to us (v. 5)	experience of God's love by the presence of the Holy Spirit (v. 5)	
	boast/rejoice in God through Christ (v. 11)	

20. "Justified" and "reconciled" appear in the "Present" column as well as the "Past" because they are past events that create realities that continue in the present.

What unites past, present, and future is the love of God in Christ through the Spirit. And that triadic saving activity of God narrated by Paul (cf. 8:9–11; 15:17–19, 30) anticipates the later, full-blown doctrine of the Trinity.[21] In addition, we see in this passage another triad at work: faith (5:1), hope (5:2, 4, 5), and love (5:5, 8)—which Christian tradition has called the theological virtues. Paul seems to have coined this triad. It can be found in many of his letters, including the earliest, 1 Thessalonians.[22] The presence of these three significant triads in 5:1–11 may be described as follows:

- the soteriological, or salvific triad: past, present, future;
- the theological triad: God the Father, the Son, the Spirit; and
- the ethical triad: faith, hope, love.

Paul will return to many of the themes from 5:1–11 in Rom 8.

REFLECTIONS AND QUESTIONS FOR 5:1–11

Spiritual, Pastoral, and Theological Reflections

1. Any **fully formed theology of the atonement** must depict the cross not only as a sacrifice for sins but also as the expression of God's enemy-love and reconciliation.

2. The well-known hymn **"Amazing Grace"** celebrates in pure poetry, and music, what Paul beautifully celebrates in poetic prose in 5:1–11. Paul is often misunderstood, however, to be advocating a sort of "cheap grace," to borrow Dietrich Bonhoeffer's distinctive idiom. No one can read Rom 5 properly without going on to Rom 6. To do so would be to repeat a common misreading of Ephesians, which rightly stresses Eph 2:8–9 but wrongly leaves out 2:10:

    > [8]For by grace you have been saved through faith, and this is not your own doing; it is the gift of God— [9]not the result of works, so that no one may boast. [10]For we are what he has made us, created in Christ Jesus for good works, which God prepared beforehand to be our way of life. (Eph 2:8–10)

3. **Suffering is not the sort of education any of us seeks**, but we all experience it. The theme of suffering's educative or formative role in life was well known

---

21. That is, Trinitarian language is once again used here in recognition that although Paul does not have a fully developed theology of the Trinity, such language is nonetheless appropriate.

22. For example, 1 Thess 1:3; 5:8; Gal 5:5–6; 1 Cor 13:13.

in antiquity. Christians can, and should, connect suffering to Christ's suffering and subsequent glorification (see 8:17)—what Paul calls the fellowship (*koinōnia*) of Christ's suffering in anticipation of resurrection (Phil 3:10–11). In addition, as Paul also says in Romans, such suffering needs to be connected as well to the suffering of all creation (8:18–25) and of other people (12:12–15).

4. Some contemporary readers of Romans may hesitate to acknowledge the presence of **Trinitarian theology** in Paul's writings. To be sure, Paul does not use the language of later Christians, but the Trinity—in terms of both inner relations and activity in the world—is present in robust, if not fully developed, ways.

5. There are many contemporary examples of **turning cultural values into idols** that parallel the Roman practice of deifying their values. Violence, for instance, can be understood as sacred in a variety of ways and circumstances. It is often idolized along with Freedom, Choice, Patriotism, Family, and other values that may have a proper place but should never become ultimate values. The cross of Christ as the way of God's liberation and love, God's way of peace and justice, challenges the idolatries of the twenty-first century too.

Questions for Those Who Read, Teach, and Preach

1. What is the significance of thinking about Christian life in terms of its past, present, and future dimensions?

2. How can Christians today preach, teach, and embody the message of the cross as one of enemy-love and reconciliation?

3. Is cheap grace still an issue today? How can it be addressed? What other kinds of mistaken notions about grace are present in the church today? How can they be addressed?

4. Why is it important for the church to have a robust theology of justification that includes reconciliation with God and, by implication and extension, reconciliation as essential to Christian life and ministry?

FOR FURTHER READING

Baker, Mark D., and Joel B. Green. *Recovering the Scandal of the Cross: Atonement in New Testament and Contemporary Contexts*. 2nd ed. Downers Grove, IL: InterVarsity, 2011.

Barclay, John M. G. *Paul and the Gift*. Grand Rapids: Eerdmans, 2015. (more technical)

———. *Paul and the Power of Grace*. Grand Rapids: Eerdmans, 2020.

———. *Paul and the Subversive Power of Grace.* Cambridge: Grove Books, 2016.

Bonhoeffer, Dietrich. *Discipleship.* Translated by Barbara Green and Reinhard Krauss. Dietrich Bonhoeffer Works 4. Minneapolis: Fortress, 2001. Previously published as *The Cost of Discipleship.* Rev. ed. Translated by R. H. Fuller. New York: Macmillan, 1959.

Hill, Wesley. *Paul and the Trinity: Persons, Relations, and the Pauline Letters.* Grand Rapids: Eerdmans, 2015.

Jervis, L. Ann. *At the Heart of the Gospel: Suffering in the Earliest Christian Message.* Grand Rapids: Eerdmans, 2007.

Katongole, Emmanuel, and Chris Rice. *Reconciling All Things: A Christian Vision for Justice, Peace and Healing.* Downers Grove, IL: InterVarsity, 2008.

Senior, Donald. *Why the Cross? Reframing New Testament Theology.* Nashville: Abingdon, 2014.

5:12–21
Free from Sin, under Grace

Paul has just provided a succinct overview of God's gracious transformation of sinners and enemies into people who are justified and reconciled by means of Christ's death. He now engages in the first of the three analyses of the contrast between death (existence outside Christ) and life (being in Christ). Romans 5:12–21 is actually full of contrasts. The principal contrast is between Adam and Christ, and specifically the antithetical nature of the deed and its consequences associated with each. This is ultimately a contrast between the reign of Sin and the reign of Grace, between death/Death and life; the key word "life" occurs three times in this passage (5:17, 18, 21).[23]

The transformation humans experience as a result of Christ's death is because that death was an act of grace, obedience, and righteousness/justice (Gk. *dikaiōmatos*; 5:18) that leads to righteousness/justification (*dikaiōsin*; 5:18) for us.[24] The result is life indeed (5:18), as God transforms sinners into righteous, or just, persons (*dikaioi*; 5:19), undoing the predicament described in 1:18–3:20. Paul does not explicitly use the language of being "in Christ" versus being "in Adam" in this passage, as he does in 1 Cor 15:22, but that is essentially what he depicts. To be in Christ is to benefit, by grace, from his

---

23. I continue to capitalize Sin and Death when they appear to be personified as a power, and will do so also with Grace.

24. The NRSV and many other translations here have "justification" rather than "righteousness" for *dikaiōsin*, while some others have "acquittal."

act of justice/righteousness and to become a people characterized by similar justice/righteousness. In Rom 5:1–11, God's grace is *amazing*; in 5:12–21, it is *abundant*, indeed *super*-abundant.[25]

5:12–14. ADAM, HUMANITY, AND CHRIST

Before Paul presents in detail the contrast between Adam and Christ—specifically between the consequences of each one's singular act—he describes the human condition of Sin and Death that exists because of Adam's deed. This deed, though it had cosmic consequences in itself, is also reaffirmed by Adam's successors.

5:12. *The Appearance of Sin and Death via Adam*

Paul first begins, but then halts, his contrast between Adam and Christ with the words "therefore, just as" at the beginning of 5:12. He was apparently about to finish the verse with something like, "so also righteousness came into the world through one man and so grace spread to all." Paul gets momentarily sidetracked, however, in a defense of the existence of sin/Sin (i.e., both the act and the power) before and without the law of Moses (5:13–14). He probably felt compelled to do this because his most recent words about the law claimed, in part, that "where there is no law, neither is there violation" (4:15). The absence of law surely does not mean the absence of sin! (Paul will return to and complete the incomplete sentence at 5:18.)

But back to 5:12. Paul asserts that the action of one representative person (Adam) brought sin or, more likely, Sin (the power) and thus death/Death into the world (Gen 2:15–17; 3:1–5, 19). Death is depicted here as a power (like Sin) that, in fact, spread to all people "because all have sinned" (5:12; cf. 3:23). Thus, Sin and Death exercise dominion over the human race. They are our masters and our enemies, but God in Christ has been and will be victorious over them (cf. 1 Cor 15:51–57) by the power of Grace.

The centuries-long debate about original sin has been in part an interpretation of 5:12. The debate seems to have begun when Augustine (d. 430) unfortunately followed the Latin translation of the Greek New Testament (because he did not know Greek). The Latin translation, called the Vulgate, incorrectly

25. See 5:15, 17, 20 for the abundance of grace. At the end of 5:20, Paul intensifies his description of this grace by using a verb with the Greek prefix *hyper-*, or "super": "super-abounded."

rendered the final Greek words of 5:12, resulting in a Latin phrase that means "in whom [i.e., in Adam] all sinned." Using the original Greek, not a Latin translation, contemporary versions generally translate this phrase as "because all" (NRSV, NIV; cf. CEB) or "inasmuch as all" (NAB) have sinned. Paul's point is not really to blame Adam, and much less to suggest that original sin is passed on biologically (i.e., through sexual intercourse), but to affirm the universality of sin.

Paul contends that we confirmed and continue to confirm the sin of Adam, acting like little Adams ourselves. We cannot blame our first parents, or anyone else, for our predicament. The ancient Jewish document called 2 Baruch says this: "Adam is, therefore, not the cause, except only for himself, but each of us has become our own Adam" (2 Bar 54.19). Paul would be sympathetic, especially to the second part of this quotation. Both ancient Judaism in general and Paul in particular perceived Adam's act to have corporate consequences while also believing that individuals are accountable for their own individual acts. *We are in this mess together, but we cannot pass the buck.*

5:13–14. The Dominion of Death

Although 5:13–14 constitutes a digression from where 5:12 was originally headed, these verses are not insignificant. For Paul, Adam is a "type" (5:14)— an antithetical foreshadowing or prefiguring—of Christ. By extension, sinners are types of the justified. Paul's main point in these two verses, however, is that Sin existed and that Death "exercised dominion" (NRSV) or "reigned" (NIV, NAB, NET, ESV) over humanity even before the law of Moses entered the scene and allowed for violations to be reckoned as such.

Overall, however, Paul is more concerned about the *reality* of sins and Sin than about their *origin*. The nefarious reign of Sin needed, and needs, to be replaced by a benevolent reign.

5:15–21. CHRIST VERSUS ADAM

According to the rest of chapter 5, that necessary benevolent reign has arrived in Christ—the reign of superabundant, overwhelming grace (5:20–21) that overturns the consequences of Adam's error. Paul announces the arrival of that reign by continuing the Adam-Christ contrast in 5:15–19. Paul here makes one main point in a variety of images and terms: Adam's deed means Sin and Death, while Christ's means justification/righteousness and *life* (5:18). This remarkable divine intervention to overturn the forces of Sin and Death can be summed up in the word "grace" (*charis*; 5:15 [twice], 17, 20, 21) or "free gift" (*charisma* and synonyms; 5:15, 16, 17; cf. 6:23). Paul says that this grace/Grace did not come like a trickle but as a mighty stream: it "abounded" (5:15; cf. 5:17, 20).

5:15–19. Contrasting Deeds and Consequences

As in other places in Romans, there is debate among scholars about how to translate the Greek *dik-* (just-/right-) family of words found throughout this passage. However they are rendered, the two most important aspects of these verses are crystal clear: (1) the stark contrast between Adam's deed and Christ's; and (2) the antithetical results of their contrasting acts. Moreover, however one nuances the various *dik-*family words, justification means righteousness and life.

Paul may be echoing chapters 3 and especially 4 by referring to both forgiveness, or acquittal (possibly in 5:16, 5:18, or both), and transformation (5:19) as two critical dimensions of justification. Taken all together, however, these verses culminate in 5:19 with *transformation*: "many were made sinners," but now "many will be made righteous." This verse is an allusion to the suffering-servant poem in Isa 53: "The righteous one, my servant, shall make many righteous, and he shall bear their iniquities" (Isa 53:11b).

This verse should not be understood as a temporal, future reference indicating that at some future time believers will be made righteous. (This interpretation is sometimes connected to the claim that believers are only *counted* as righteous in the present.) This sort of interpretation both sells short the gospel's power and misunderstands the overall argument of Romans (and indeed every Pauline letter). Rather, the future tense of 5:19 is a logical future—an expression of certainty about the effects of Christ's obedience (the suffering servant's death) on people here and now. The power of the gospel (1:16–17) has indeed transformed, and will continue to transform, many people in Rome and beyond, as Paul knew well. And it is a power that continues effectively today.

The following table, drawing on the language of the NRSV, NAB, and NIV in 5:15–19, shows the contrasting parallels between Adam and Christ with respect to the nature and consequences of their individual acts.[26] The table also demonstrates some of the differing interpretations of the *dik-*family:

26. Such a comparison was known in ancient rhetoric as *synkrisis*.

CHRIST VS. ADAM

	Adam's Deed	Consequences	Christ's Deed	Consequences
15	trespass	many died	(free/gracious) gift, grace	the grace of God and the free gift abounded/overflow/have overflown for the many
16	sin/sinning, one trespass	many trespasses, judgment, condemnation	(free) gift	justification/acquittal
17	trespass/ transgression	Death exercised dominion/came to reign/reigned	abundance/abundant provision of grace, free gift of righteousness/ justification	exercise dominion in life/ (come to) reign in life
18	trespass	condemnation for all	act of righteousness	righteousness/justification/ acquittal and life for all[27]
19	disobedience	many were made sinners	obedience[28]	many will be made righteous

As the table indicates, in 5:15–19 Paul sings the same brief tune in several keys to emphasize one thing: Christ has solved the Adam problem—which is our problem. The news with respect to Adam was grim; his misdeed set in motion a string of terrible consequences: people were made sinners and subjected to sin, condemnation, death, and the reign of Death. But this is only the case—as we saw in 5:12–14—because all others have followed Adam as well.

The Christ-gift, on the other hand, is God's grace incarnate: it means people are acquitted, made righteous or just, and filled with life now and in the future. There are many words for grace in this passage, but they all indicate one source of that grace, God the Father, and one manifestation of that grace, Christ the Son. Grace has arrived and prevailed.

27. The translation of 5:18 is challenging. The last two words of the Greek text might best be rendered as something like "the righteousness/justification that is in fact life itself" or "that consists of life" or "that is full of life." Whatever the precise translation, Paul makes a powerful connection between justification and life. As elsewhere in Romans, he probably has Deuteronomy 30 in mind, which promises life (Deut 30:19–20).

28. See also Phil 2:8.

5:20–21. *The Reign of Grace*

The reign of Grace has begun! The coming of the law had done nothing to help the situation of either Jews or gentiles but only compounded the problem—it led to more trespasses (5:20a).[29] It could not and did not, Paul implies, stop the spread of Sin and Death, overturn the condemnation, or provide righteousness and life. However, in a grand summary, Paul says that where Sin increased, or intensified, Grace *super*-abounded, or overflowed, all the more (5:20b). The result was the new reign of Grace that is characterized by righteousness/justice and leads to "eternal life" (5:21; cf. 6:23). Paul will have to deal with the possible misinterpretation of this reality in chapter 6. The formula, so to speak—"an increase in sin yielded an increase in grace"—does not justify continuing to sin!

A more powerful force—a superpower called Grace—has "come to reign" (5:17 NAB) through the death of Christ Jesus, a force that liberates believers from the triumvirate of Sin, Death, and the law (which is good in itself but has been co-opted by Sin; see 7:7–12). Paul clearly means that this life is not merely in the future (everlasting life) but already here: life abundant and full as people are "alive to God in Christ Jesus" (6:11).

As one scholar has put it, Grace is the power of God for the fullness of life.[30] Thus, *while justification is a many-sided term and reality for Paul, it can never be fully understood or described without recognizing that justification is a death-defeating, life-giving, transformative reality—as we had already been told in chapter 4.*

SUMMARY OF 5:12–21

According to 5:12–21, the death of Christ was a divine incursion to overthrow the empire of Sin and Death—the potent powers opposed to God, people, and, indeed, all of creation. It was also Christ's act of righteousness/justice and obedience. One gracious act of obedience and righteousness, of faith and faithfulness (cf. 3:21–26), has changed everything. Those who benefit from that death share in Christ's obedience—"the obedience of faith" (1:5; 16:26)—and in his righteousness/justice (see especially ch. 6).

---

29. The NRSV translation of 5:20a, "But law came in, *with the result* that the trespass multiplied" (emphasis added) is preferable to the NIV's "*so that* the trespass might increase" (emphasis added; similarly NET, CEB, NASB, ESV, NAB, NJB).

30. This phrase comes from Jane Patterson in a presentation at the annual meeting of the Society of Biblical Literature in November 2020.

Just as all, in effect, shared in Adam's act of disobedient sin and became sinners, so also all who share in Christ's obedient act of righteousness on the cross are justified—forgiven and made just. The righteousness needed for life (2:1–16) could not be attained by humans enslaved to sin (3:9–20). That righteousness is now found in, and communicated to us through, Christ's death (see also 3:21–26; 8:3–4).

As noted above, Paul does not here use the explicit language of being "in Adam" versus being "in Christ," as he does in 1 Cor 15:22: "as all die in Adam, so all will be made alive in Christ." But that sort of participation is what he implies. The participatory dimension of this world-altering event will be the subject of the next two sections of the letter (6:1–7:6 and 7:7–8:39), in which the contrast between life outside and life in Christ is explored from new angles.

REFLECTIONS AND QUESTIONS FOR 5:12–21

Spiritual, Pastoral, and Theological Reflections

1. We do not need to debate about **the historicity of Adam** and the Genesis accounts to understand and accept Paul's perspective on the nature of Sin and Death. He is interpreting a foundational Jewish and Christian narrative in a way that reveals something of the nature of each (Sin, Death) as well as the inevitable connections between them. Together they constitute a powerful force that only a more powerful—and thus obviously a suprahuman—force can overcome.

2. Each of us and all of us must own up to **our own complicity in the human problem**. Sin creates a network, a web, so that we are complicit even when we are not the main (individual) sinful actor. There is a corporate character both to sins and to Sin, and there is a reciprocal relationship between individual sin and corporate sin. For example, individuals may be guilty of Whiteness—of thinking White people are better, more human, more civilized, or more religious (even more Christian!) than non-Whites. But where do such attitudes come from? They are likely inherited or adopted, intentionally or (quite often) unintentionally, from one's family or culture, or both. And yet the family and culture depend on individuals to maintain and advance the racist agenda.

    Similarly, a culture that is dedicated to a completely unfettered display of personal freedom (especially with respect to rights, whichever rights are cherished) will help create individuals who embody that notion of freedom. In addition, those individuals (some, of course, more than others) will defend and advocate for their individual understanding of freedom as a social good, and the circle starts all over again. Such a circular relationship is often, if not always, toxic for both the individuals and the corporate body.

3. It is especially important, in the face of evil, to realize that **Grace is in fact a power**. Of course, Grace is not an independent entity or force. Grace is only a power that reigns in the sense that it is the manifestation of God's powerful presence, God's Spirit, in the world. But when we are faced with our own sin, or even with unspeakable evil, we can be both comforted and challenged— challenged to pray, to act—because we know that something and someone much greater than sin and evil is at work in the world, and will have both the final word and the final victory.

Questions for Those Who Read, Teach, and Preach

1. What kinds of mistaken notions about Adam and sin/Sin are present in the church today? How can they be addressed?
2. What are some contemporary examples of the way sin leads to death, either literally (physically) or metaphorically (spiritually, emotionally, etc.)?
3. What is the significance of thinking of grace as Grace—a power?

FOR FURTHER READING

Barclay, John M. G. *Paul and the Gift.* Grand Rapids: Eerdmans, 2015. (more technical)

———. *Paul and the Power of Grace.* Grand Rapids: Eerdmans, 2020.

———. *Paul and the Subversive Power of Grace.* Cambridge: Grove Books, 2016.

Biddle, Mark E. *Missing the Mark: Sin and Its Consequences in Biblical Theology.* Nashville: Abingdon, 2005.

Gupta, Nijay K., and John K. Goodrich. *Sin and Its Remedy in Paul.* Eugene, OR: Cascade, 2020. (more technical)

Haarsma, Loren. *When Did Sin Begin? Human Evolution and the Doctrine of Original Sin.* Grand Rapids: Baker Academic, 2021.

6:1–7:6
Dead to Sin, Alive to God

In 5:12–21, Paul does not explicitly spell out *how* believers have moved from outside Christ to inside Christ, from the reign of Sin to the reign of Grace, from death to life. That he must now do, amplifying his references to faith in earlier chapters. But he must also dig himself out of a bit of a hole. If more sin/Sin resulted in more grace/Grace (5:20b), perhaps more sin is in order—as some seem to have thought Paul believed (see 3:8).

Chapter 6 exposes the fallacy of this argument while describing how believers participate in the messianic event that has inaugurated the reign of Grace. Through Christ's death and resurrection (recall 4:24–25), we escape from the reign of Sin and Death (6:1–23) and even the law (7:1–6). But connecting the law with Sin and Death will force Paul to dig himself out of yet another hole in 7:7–25.

In 6:1–7:6, Paul presents us with the second death-life, outside Christ–inside Christ antithesis found in chapters 5–8. He continues his diatribal, or at least dialogical, style, with another set of questions and answers. We, on the other hand, will return to another device—tables—to show graphically some of the most important aspects of this rich section of Romans.

THEMES AND STRUCTURE

Before we consider 6:1–7:6 section by section, we can use tables to assist us in simultaneously seeing both key themes in this passage and its structure. First, we will look at Paul's understanding of the relationship between baptism and justification. Second, we will note his presentation of baptism and new life as both "slavery" and "marriage" to God.

Baptism and Justification

Many interpreters of the letter's theologically and rhetorically powerful chapter 6 think Paul has left the subject of justification behind and is now describing the process of sanctification, of becoming more and more holy, or Christlike. Although we do find the language of holiness or sanctification in this passage (6:19, 22), it is a mistake to separate sanctification from justification.

Paul, in fact, has not left justification in the dust but is further explaining its significance by once again stressing the transition from death to life that has occurred for believers. To do this, he draws on his discussion of justification from the letter to the Galatians. Paul depicts justification in Galatians and baptism in Romans within the same framework: participation in the death and resurrection of Christ. (The connection of baptism to death probably derives from Jesus' interpretation of his death as a baptism in which his disciples would share; Mark 10:38–39.) The following table shows the similarities between justification according to Galatians and baptism according to Romans:[31]

31. This table is adapted from my book *Inhabiting the Cruciform God: Kenosis, Justifica-*

SIMILARITIES BETWEEN GALATIANS 2:15–21 (JUSTIFICATION) AND ROMANS 6:1–7:6 (BAPTISM)

FEATURES	GALATIANS 2:15–21 JUSTIFICATION	ROMANS 6:1–7:6 BAPTISM
Transfer into Christ	"we have come to believe in [Gk. *eis*; "into"] Christ Jesus" (2:16); "justified in Christ" (2:17); cf. Gal 3:27	"baptized into [Gk. *eis*] Christ Jesus" (6:3); "alive to God in Christ Jesus" (6:11); "eternal life in Christ Jesus our Lord" (6:23)
Death to the law/ law and Sin	"through the law I died to the law" (2:19)	"you have died to the law through the body of Christ" (7:4); cf. "died to Sin" (6:2); "so that the body of Sin would be destroyed, and we would no longer be enslaved to Sin" (6:6); "dead to Sin" (6:11)
Co-crucifixion (expressed in the passive voice), death of self	"I have been crucified with Christ; and it is no longer I who live" (2:19–20)	"baptized into [*eis*] his death" (6:3); "buried with him by baptism into death" (6:4); "united with him in a death like his" (6:5); "our old self was crucified with him" (6:6); "we have died with Christ" (6:8)
Resurrection to new life	"so that I might live to God. . . . And the life I now live in the flesh" (2:19–20)	"just as Christ was raised from the dead by the glory of the Father,[32] so we too might walk in newness of life" (6:4); "alive to God in Christ Jesus" (6:11); "those who have been brought from death to life" (6:13); "died to the law . . . the new life of the Spirit" (7:4, 6)
Present and future dimensions	*Present*: see 2:19–20 *Future*: "no one will be justified" (2:16)	*Present*: throughout *Future*: "we will certainly be united with him in a resurrection like his" (6:5b); "eternal life" (6:22, 23)
Participation with Christ and "to" God	"so that I might live to God . . . it is Christ who lives in me" (2:19–20)	"alive to God in Christ Jesus" (6:11); "so that you may belong to another, to him who has been raised from the dead in order that we may bear fruit for God" (7:4)

---

tion, and Theosis in Paul's Narrative Soteriology (Grand Rapids: Eerdmans, 2009), 76–77. I have generally quoted the NRSV but changed "sin" to "Sin."

32. "By the glory of the Father" is likely a reference to the power and presence of God expressed in the Holy Spirit. See also 8:11 for a reference to the Spirit in close connection to the resurrection.

FEATURES	GALATIANS 2:15–21 JUSTIFICATION	ROMANS 6:1–7:6 BAPTISM
Faith and love (Christ's and ours); that is, proper covenantal relations with God and others	"faith of Jesus Christ . . . faith of Christ" (2:16); "we have come to believe in [*eis*; "into"] Christ Jesus" (2:16); "I live by the faith of the Son of God, who loved me by giving himself for me" (2:20 MJG). Cf. Gal 5:6 for believers' faith and love explicitly.	"No longer present your members to Sin as instruments of wickedness, but present yourselves to God as those who have been brought from death to life, and present your members to God as instruments of righteousness [/justice]" (6:13); "you . . . have become slaves of righteousness [/justice]" (6:18; cf. 6:19b); "the advantage you get is sanctification" (6:22) Cf. Rom 5:19; 8:34–35 for Christ's faith/obedience and love explicitly.

In 6:1–7:6, then, Paul is depicting the same sort of reality he describes in Gal 2:15–21: namely, a participatory experience of co-crucifixion and co-resurrection with Christ.[33] Justification is like baptism, and vice versa. More precisely, *justification and baptism are two sides of the one coin of entrance into Christ and his body through dying and rising with him.* Both faith and baptism involve transferal *into* Christ by means of dying and rising *with* Christ. The result is life: being "alive to God" now (6:11) and one day having "eternal life" (6:22–23). And this means that *in* Christ, we are meant to become *like* Christ.

Baptism and New Life as "Slavery" and "Marriage" to God

Many interpreters of Rom 6 (or 6:1–7:6) understandably believe that it presents Paul's theology of baptism. This is of course, to some extent, self-evidently true. But this section of Romans is not primarily about baptism as past event. To be baptized is to be *immersed*, to be *plunged* into something—or someone. Paul takes baptism as the common starting point—immersion into the Messiah and his people—for participation in the new covenant community, and he seeks to unpack that common experience.

But Paul's major focus is on the contrast between the pre- and postbaptismal life. He especially emphasizes believers' new life "to God" (6:10–11) as a continuation of our crucifixion and resurrection with Christ in justification/

---

33. The only two occurrences of the verb "co-crucify" in Paul's letters are in Gal 2:19 and Rom 6:6. Paul has apparently borrowed the word used in the gospel tradition referring to those literally crucified with Jesus (Matt 27:44; Mark 15:32; John 19:32).

baptism. There is, above all, in the chapter nothing that could be interpreted as giving the baptized/justified any reason for complacency. On the contrary, justification/baptism means the start of a new life, a new relationship. It is difficult to imagine a more appropriate image for thoroughgoing participation than the liquid metaphor of immersion. *To be baptized is to begin a life of being "all in."*

The substantive theme of Rom 6 as a whole is the assertion that life is a type of "slavery," either to Sin or to God. One or the other is the master to whom people "present," or offer, themselves and their bodies (6:13, 16, 19; cf. 12:1). Baptism means a change of masters.

Rom 6 divides rather neatly into two parallel parts, each structured as follows:

THE PARALLEL STRUCTURE OF 6:1–14 AND 6:15–23

FEATURE	6:1–14	6:15–23
Rhetorical question: Should we/shall we . . . ?	6:1b	6:15a
Emphatic negation: "By no means!" (NAB: "Of course not!")	6:2a	6:15b
"Do you not know?": introducing a major claim	6:3	6:16
Detailed exposition of the claim, with corollary practical consequences and exhortations	6:4–14	6:17–22
Conclusion	6:15	6:23

The two rhetorical questions in 6:1b and 6:15a are normally translated quite similarly as "Should [or Shall] we [continue/persist in] sin?" But the entire context suggests a more nuanced interpretation:[34]

1. *Should* we remain in Sin that grace may abound? (6:1b, as the allegedly logical consequence of 5:20);

and

2. *May* we sin because we are not under law but under Grace? (6:15a, as the supposedly logical sequel to the conclusion of 6:14).

The first question is about obligation (6:1–14), the second about permission (6:15–23). The first question almost sounds perverse. But it serves to generate

34. Depending on context, the Greek grammatical feature used in these questions (the deliberative subjunctive) can imply possibility, obligation, or permission.

a necessary response to misinterpretations of Paul both ancient and modern. It simultaneously provides Paul the opportunity for deep theological teaching about baptism into Christ as sharing in his death and resurrection. The second question follows from the negative answer to the first, allowing Paul to continue his teaching with a focus on the new life in Christ as liberation from Sin, and slavery to God.

The beginning of chapter 7 (7:1–6) is actually a continuation of chapter 6, illustrating the nature of the new life with an additional metaphor, not slavery but marriage.

6:1–14. BAPTISM, GRACE, AND SIN

Question 1: Should *we, the justified, remain in Sin and continue to sin in order to increase the flow of grace/Grace?*

As the table above indicates, Paul addresses this question systematically: rhetorical question, emphatic negation, "Do you not know?" question, exposition, and conclusion.

6:1–2. *The Question and the Answer*

The formula we observed in 5:20—"where sin increased, grace abounded all the more"—could be misinterpreted; hence the question in 6:1: *Should* we sin? After all, who would not wish to see grace increase?

"Of course not! Are you out of your mind?" answers Paul (6:2a, paraphrased). It is impossible to be "in Christ" and to remain "in Sin." That is, there is absolutely no place for cheap grace in the Christian life. In baptism believers have relocated. They have died to the power called Sin (6:2b–11); they have terminated their bondage and allegiance to it. Therefore, we now present our bodies to God, not to Sin (6:12–14).

6:3–11. *Co-Crucifixion and Co-Resurrection with Christ*

As the table above indicates, it is important to see how closely connected baptism and justifying faith are for Paul. People believe "into" (Gk. *eis*) Christ (Gal 2:16) and are baptized "into" (Gk. *eis*) Christ (6:3; Gal 3:27). By faith and baptism, people are transferred into the realm of the Messiah. This involves both an inner conviction and a public confession (cf. Rom 10:5–13), a commitment no doubt made at the moment of baptism.

What Paul says of faith in Galatians can also therefore be predicated of baptism: it involves a kind of death-and-resurrection experience, a co-crucifixion with Christ that results in new life in a new community: the local and global assembly of Christ-followers. The description of "faith into Christ," or justification through faith, is also a description of baptism into Christ. Paul's main point is that entry into Christ is an experience of death and resurrection, as already suggested by the story of Abraham in chapter 4. It is also a change of locations and lords—a movement out of the reign of Adam and Sin and into the reign of Christ and Grace.

The apostle therefore clearly thinks his audience should know the answer to the question he poses in 6:1 and understand the meaning of their baptism ("Do you not know?" [6:3a]). Drawing on already established beliefs, basic logic, and an early Christian creed preserved in 1 Cor 15:3–11, in 6:3–11 Paul outlines several parallels between Christ's death and resurrection and that of believers. Those who believe that Christ died, was buried (demonstrating the reality of the death), was raised, and appeared (demonstrating the reality of the resurrection) participate in his story and in the realities that story narrates:

BELIEVERS' PARTICIPATION IN THE STORY/REALITY OF THE MESSIAH

DRAMATIC ACT	THE STORY OF MESSIAH JESUS (1 COR 15 MJG)	THE STORY OF BELIEVERS (ROM 6 MJG)
Death	The Messiah died for our sins in accordance with the Scriptures (15:3)	We . . . died with respect to Sin . . . all of us who have been baptized into the Messiah Jesus, into his death were baptized (6:2–3); we have been co-joined with him [*symphytoi gegonamen*] in the likeness of his death (6:5); our old self was co-crucified with him [*synestaurōthē*] (6:6); we have died with the Messiah [*syn Christō*] (6:8); dead with respect to Sin (6:11)
Burial	he was buried (15:4a)	we have been co-buried with him [*synetaphēmen*] by baptism into his death (6:4)
Resurrection	he was raised on the third day in accordance with the Scriptures (15:4b)	*Present (resurrection to new life):* just as the Messiah was raised [by God] from the dead . . . so we too might walk in newness of life (6:4); alive in relation to God in the Messiah Jesus [*en Christō Iēsou*] (6:11; cf. 6:13) *Future (bodily resurrection):* we will certainly also be [co-joined with him] in [the likeness of] his resurrection (6:5); we will also co-live with [*syzēsomen*] him (6:8; cf. "eternal life" in 6:22–23)

DRAMATIC ACT	THE STORY OF MESSIAH JESUS (1 COR 15 MJG)	THE STORY OF BELIEVERS (ROM 6 MJG)
Appear-ance	he appeared to Cephas, then to the twelve [. . . others] (15:5–9)	present yourselves to God as those who have been brought from death to life, and present your members to God as weapons of justice (6:13)[35]

The whole process—death, burial, resurrection, and (implicitly) appear-ances—is summarized in 6:3–4. The resurrection following death and burial in baptism is in order to "walk in newness of life" (6:4)—to appear publicly, so to speak, as part of the new creation. Here, as in Gal 2:15–21, we see the thor-oughly participatory and transformative character of Paul's spirituality. Paul repeatedly uses the language of sharing in Christ by using the Greek words for "into," "in," and especially "with."[36] To believe the creed is not merely to assent to its truthfulness but to enter it, even, in a sense, to become it. *Creeds have consequences.* Christ's story becomes our story, and our story is folded into his.

In other words, Paul's spirituality is also a *narrative* spirituality. Life in Christ is inaugurated by participating in the story of Christ. But it also con-tinues as a story, both individually and corporately—an ongoing story of both death and resurrection.

This first part of Rom 6 clearly speaks of a *present* resurrection: "newness of life" (6:4), being "alive to God" (6:11), and having been brought from death to life (6:13). This is not the resurrection *of* the body, but it is a resurrection *in* the body. This language may sound, then, like a metaphorical rather than a literal resurrection, perhaps better termed a revivification. But Paul cer-tainly sees the transformation that occurs in baptism as more than a metaphor. Some interpreters, however, fear that talk of present resurrection smacks of triumphalism—an overconfidence in having arrived spiritually—or of failing to recognize that the kingdom of God is not yet fully present.

What keeps Paul from going down that sort of road, however, is his under-standing of "newness of life" as an ongoing state of being dead to Sin (6:11). Paradoxically, because baptism into Christ is baptism into his death, the new-ness of life is cross-shaped, or cruciform (see also ch. 8 and, in more detail, chs.

35. Interestingly, Luke has similar language about Jesus' own appearances in Acts 1:3, using the same Greek verb (*paristēmi*) that is translated in Rom 6:13, 16, 19 as "present." Most translations of Acts 1:3 say "he appeared," but NET has a better rendering of the Greek: "he presented himself alive."

36. In Greek, a form of the word "with" or "co-" (*syn*), as either prefix or preposition, appears five times in 6:4–8.

12–15). We may refer to this resurrection-infused, cross-shaped life as *resurrectional cruciformity*. This shape is not static but dynamic, constant yet never the same. It is faithful but creative, having the form of a story, not a single page; of a movie, not a snapshot.

Moreover, there is a connection between 6:5–11 and Paul's discussion of the end of the reign of Sin and Death in 5:12–21: through participation in Christ's death and resurrection, believers experience for themselves the defeat of Sin now and will experience the defeat of Death later. The story continues into the future. (See also 1 Cor 15:51–57 on the defeat of Death.) In these verses, then, Paul affirms the fundamental Christ-pattern of death → resurrection, applying it to believers in two senses: new life in the body now (6:4, 11, 13), and bodily resurrection and eternal life later (6:5, 8; cf. 6:22–23). *This story is a story of life at the heart of the epistle of life.*

Again paradoxically, however, believers currently experience *both a death and a resurrection.* According to 6:6–7, being crucified with Christ means liberation from Sin as slave master (cf. 3:9, 24). In fact, Paul uses a form of the verb "justify" in 6:7—literally "justified from Sin"—that is variously translated as "freed" (NRSV, CEB, NET), "set free" (NIV, ESV), or "absolved" (NAB). The use of justification language, however, confirms the connection between baptism and justification, and it further demonstrates the transformative, liberating character of justification. Similar phrases using the word "freed" or "free" from Sin appear in 6:18, 22. It is likely that Paul has the exodus in mind; God's people are being delivered, through water, into a new life, "set free from the power of sin" (6:7 NLT).

Co-crucifixion also means the death of the "old self," meaning the destruction of the "body of Sin"—that is, the body ruled by Sin the power (6:6). This is a present, permanent, irreversible situation, just as Christ died "once for all" (6:10a). We cannot go back to Egypt (remain in Sin)—even if at times we want to do so. Although a once-for-all death to Sin occurs in baptism, this death must be constantly reactualized.

Paul summarizes his conclusions for the first part of chapter 6 with the words "so" (6:11) and "therefore" (6:12). The justified should look at themselves as those raised from the dead (6:11), like Abraham (4:16–25). The death that occurs in baptism also means resurrection into a state of being "dead to Sin and alive to God" *in* Christ (6:11) and *like* Christ (6:10a).[37] In continuity with this reality, believers are also guaranteed a future resurrection and life

---

37. That is, dead with respect to Sin and alive with respect to God.

with Christ (6:8)—"eternal life" (6:23).[38] As with Christ, this will mean total freedom from Death as slave master and evil ruler (6:9). Thus, believers experience Christ's death now, as death to Sin (like his), and they experience his resurrection in two stages, as being alive *to* God now (6:11) and as experiencing freedom from death/Death by being *with* Christ in the future (6:8).

6:12–14. *The Fundamental Character of Life under Grace*

The present character of resurrection is reaffirmed in 6:12–14, where Paul draws the ethical consequences of what he has said so far in the chapter. Liberated from Sin (6:14; cf. 6:7), believers are not to allow it to regain its reign over their bodies (6:12) by presenting their "members" to their old slave master/ruler (6:13). To do so would be to reenter the prebaptismal, prefaith sphere of Adam and thereby to live an anachronism—to live in the wrong historical period. But such a mistaken regression *is* a possibility and must therefore be actively avoided. To continue being subject to "passions" or misdirected desires (6:12, echoing 1:24) and to "injustice/unrighteousness" (*adikias*; 6:13, echoing 1:18, 29; 2:8; 3:5) would be to continue in the ways that lead to death described in 1:18–3:20.

Rather, the justified are to be just! The "righteoused" are to be righteous! They are to present their members to God as "weapons" (CEB, NAB; not merely "instruments" as in NRSV, NIV) in God's righteous army, since they have been brought from death to life (6:13).[39] Their weaponry, therefore, is Christlike Godlikeness: love and hospitality, peace and nonretaliation, and other marks of Christian discipleship described especially in chapters 12–15. Paul in no way intends to suggest that Christians are, or can use, literal weapons.

As in 1 Cor 6:12–20 and Rom 12:1–2, but in contrast to Rom 1:18–32, the body is now the place of service to God, at God's disposal for the glory of God and for participation in God's mission of rescuing humanity from the powers of Sin and Death. Christians are called to offer themselves and every aspect of their bodily existence to God for God's mission in the world *accomplished in God's way.*

---

38. Romans 6:5 is usually understood as referring to the future bodily resurrection, but the parallel to v. 4 suggests that the future tense verb may be logical, not chronological (or temporal).

39. As in Eph 6:10–18, Pauline martial language is about combat not with human forces but with spiritual ones.

Paul's call for righteousness, then, is not an exhortation to a narrow form of personal holiness. It is an appeal for a radical identification with God's purposes in the world over against powers and forces that oppose God's purposes and God's ways, revealed in the Messiah, at every turn. In other words, both the ends (the goal) and the means of Christian mission must be Godlike, which means Christlike, which means cross-shaped: cruciform. Being a weapon in God's hands is essentially the same as putting on the armor of God (Eph 6:10–18), which Paul says later in Romans means putting on Jesus (13:12, 14).

Paul also characterizes this state of bodily self-giving to God as "under Grace" and not "under law" (6:14)—his own phrases, based on the end of chapter 5, for being part of the post-Christ powerful reign of Grace and not the pre-Christ reign of Sin, Death, and the law. *The empire of Sin (3:9) has been replaced by the empire of Grace*—the beneficent rule of Jesus the Messiah (cf. 14:9). But what does "not under law" actually mean?

6:15–23. BAPTISM, SIN, AND SLAVERY TO GOD

> Question 2: May *we, the justified/baptized, sin because we are not under law but under Grace?*

Paul now addresses this new question in a manner parallel to his strategy in 6:1–14: rhetorical question, emphatic negation, "Do you not know?" question, exposition, and conclusion.

6:15–19. Slavery to God and Righteousness/Justice

Despite the clear and forceful argument of 6:1–14, the phrase "not under law" in 6:14 prompts the next rhetorical question: If sin is not *required*, is it *permitted* (6:15)? *May* we sin? What is the nature of Grace? The justified have in some sense been liberated not only from Sin but also from the law (see further in 7:1–6). That clearly means freedom! Is Paul's law-free gospel antinomian—completely lacking any ethical implications and thus conducive to moral chaos?

This theoretical possibility (or explicit accusation; see 3:8) may have caused Jewish believers no little consternation and gentile believers either confusion or glee, depending on their inclinations. Paul once again responds to the absurd (to him) question with a forceful "no" and a "Do you not know?" (6:15b–16a). He explains his negative answer by returning to the slavery/rulership image with the assumption that everyone is an obedient slave to something, either to Sin or to righteousness/justice, meaning to God (6:16, 18, 20). Throughout this passage, Paul uses a common early Christian pattern of contrasting the old life with the new in terms of "once . . . now" (6:19).[40]

The justified, as Paul has already said (6:6–7), were liberated from their old master/ruler Sin when they obeyed the "teaching" (gospel) from their heart (6:17) and were re-enslaved to righteousness/God (6:18, 20, 22). Obedience (6:17–18) is not only a word from the sphere of the slave-master relationship. It comes as well from the reality that Christ's death was his act of obedience (5:19), and we have been baptized into that obedient death—called to share in it with an "obedience of faith" (1:5; 16:26), or Christlike believing allegiance.

The wording of 6:19a, in fact, suggests that Paul may be a bit uncomfortable with the slavery analogy, but it serves his rhetorical purposes well, and he uses it elsewhere (1 Cor 7:22; Gal 5:13). And, more importantly, he depicts both Christ (e.g., Phil 2:7) and himself (e.g., Rom 1:1; 1 Cor 9:19; 2 Cor 4:5; Phil 1:1) as slaves.

6:20–23. *The End Result: Life or Death*

Slavery to Sin meant freedom from righteousness (6:20) and growth in iniquity, but now slavery to righteousness (perhaps also worthy of recognition as a power and capitalized as Righteousness) means self-presentation to this new master/ruler and growth in the new, alter-cultural life of holiness, or "sanctification" (6:19b–20, 22). The results of the two forms of slavery and obedience are also antithetical: the "wage," which is death, or the free gift (*charisma*, an echo of 5:15–16), which is eternal life (6:21–23, echoing 6:16). In 6:21–22, Paul uses the image of "fruit" to express these consequences, though most translations miss the image (using words like "advantage," "benefit," or "consequence"). Paul returns to this image in 7:4–5.

Eternal life, then, is the ultimate conclusion of the new life begun in justification and baptism. It is the full experience of God's glory that is known in part in the present.

7:1–6. FREEDOM FROM THE LAW AND MARRIAGE TO GOD/CHRIST/ THE SPIRIT

Finally, Paul turns in 7:1–6 to yet a third topic related to 5:12–20, freedom from the law (7:1–6). Once again, he introduces the matter with "Do

---

40. See also 1 Cor 6:9–11; Gal 4:8–9; Eph 2:2–5; 5:8; Col 1:21–22; Titus 3:3–7; 1 Pet 2:10.

you not know?" (7:1). Although Paul does not see the law in any sense as evil (see 7:7, 12–14), it "aroused" humanity's "sinful passions" (7:5; cf. 1:24; 6:12) and is therefore part of the old regime that ended with Christ's death. Thus, believers have also "died to the law through the body of Christ [his death]" (7:4; cf. Gal 2:19) and are "discharged" from it (7:6), as they are also from Sin.

To make this point, Paul offers another image of freedom in Christ. Death ends a marriage relationship and frees a person to remarry. Similarly, Christ's death—and believers' sharing in it—has ended believers' connection to the Jewish law and liberated them to belong to Christ and God via the Spirit.

The legal metaphor Paul chooses to illustrate "death" to the law is a bit contorted but creative (7:1b–4). Marriage laws apply only when both spouses are alive. The principle Paul capitalizes on is that through death (the husband's), a wife is "discharged" or "freed" from the law that forbids living with another man; she can therefore honorably remarry (7:2–3).

Paul reads this metaphor as authorizing believers' freedom from the law based on a death—not of the former spouse but of the new one, Christ. This new freedom then permits liberated believers to "belong to another" (Christ) and "bear fruit for God" rather than "bear fruit for death" (returning to the "fruit" image of 6:21–22) through the "new life of the Spirit" (7:4–6).[41] Although the new marriage partner may, first of all, be Christ, it is clear that the marital relationship depicted here involves believers with the Father, the Son, and the Spirit.

This whole line of thinking will allow Paul once again to be charged with antinomianism. "Our sinful passions [were] aroused by the law" (7:5)—really, Paul?! "We are discharged from the law" (7:6)—really?! Whether Paul intends the "we" to refer only to himself and fellow Jews or to all Jews and gentiles in Christ, the stakes in such a claim are extraordinarily high. As we will see, Paul sees Sin and the law as partners (7:7–25), but Sin is the principal offender, the inherently evil and deadly power (7:11–12).

Paul's final word regarding these high-stakes claims and the possible charges that follow from them will be the contrast between life in the flesh and life in the Spirit. Paul alludes to that contrast here (7:5–6) and turns to it at length in 7:7–8:39. Ironically, but significantly, the law returns briefly in a positive way in that discussion, for "the just requirement of the law" is fulfilled in believers (8:3–4; cf. Gal 5:23b).

41. See 6:4 for "newness" and Gal 5:22–24 for the fruit of the Spirit.

SUMMARY OF 6:1–7:6

To briefly summarize 6:1–7:6: We died and were raised with Christ so that our bodies that had previously been governed by Sin and therefore embodied injustice/unrighteousness would henceforth be ruled by God and thus embody justice/righteousness. This is how believers, individually and corporately, are called to live to and for God in holiness and newness of life—and thus as participants in God's mission in the world.

REFLECTIONS AND QUESTIONS FOR 6:1–7:6

Spiritual, Pastoral, and Theological Reflections

1. Many **people like to believe they are autonomous**, subject to no one but themselves and claiming with the English poet William Ernest Henley (1849–1903), "I am the master of my fate: / I am the captain of my soul" (the conclusion to his famous poem "Invictus"). Paul sees the human person/soul, not as "unconquerable" (as in the first stanza of "Invictus"), but as inevitably subject to, and even enslaved by, powers and forces outside him- or herself, whether for ill or for good.

2. For understandable reasons, some people (especially, but not only, descendants of enslaved peoples) are **hesitant about using terms like "slave"** or even "servant" to describe our relationship with God. Although this image must be used with caution, its theological substance and significance should not be discarded. At the same time, we can perhaps use the language of allegiance to express much of the same reality. In faith and baptism, we change loyalties. Our previous allegiance to Sin and self is replaced with allegiance to God and righteousness.

3. Certain people within every Christian tradition have found both subtle and not-so-subtle ways of using their baptism, conversion date, reception of the Spirit, election, reception of the sacraments, and so on as **identity markers**, or status indicators, that allow them an **almost boundless freedom** to do as they please. They assume either that they are protected from divine disapproval by that identity marker/status, or that they will be almost automatically forgiven for whatever they do because of that identity marker/status. Paul's interpretation of baptism and its consequences deals the death blow to such faulty logic. His words are the foundation for Bonhoeffer's critique of cheap grace.

4. **Baptism** is not only an event of incorporation into Christ, for it also contains

the **shape of ongoing life** in Christ. Although a once-for-all death to sin and resurrection occur in baptism, as Christ died only once and was raised, this death and resurrection must be constantly reactualized in daily newness of life. Baptism/justification liberates us from the hostile powers that rule human existence and brings us into the powerful sphere of Christ's benevolent lordship and community. But the offering of the self must occur daily, hourly, minute by minute.

5. In ways large and small, with images (like liberation and slavery and marriage) and specific words (like "passions" and "righteousness/justice" and "unrighteousness/injustice"), Paul has begun to describe **the undoing of the human condition** depicted in Rom 1:18–3:20 that has been made possible by Christ's death and resurrection. Participation in that saving event, named especially by Roman Catholics as the paschal mystery, unleashes its resurrection power—its cruciform resurrection power—into the lives of individuals and communities, transforming them from head to toe (metaphorically speaking; recall 3:9–20).

6. **Creeds have consequences.** To be more specific, Paul encourages his original audience and us to become a living exegesis of the story of Christ. The shape of this living exegesis will appear more definitively later in the letter (chs. 12–15). Whatever creeds or theological statements we write, recite, or otherwise affirm, they must always be embodied individually and corporately. How that happens will not always be the same from person to person or community to community, but there must always be a correspondence between belief and behavior.

7. **"Resurrectional cruciformity"** is a term meant to convey two inseparable truths:

   a. that the resurrection-infused and Spirit-empowered life in Christ is always cross-shaped, or cruciform; and

   b. that the cruciform life is always infused with the power of the resurrection and is therefore life-giving, in terms of both spirituality and ministry.

   To try to have one without the other—the resurrected Christ without the crucified Christ, or vice versa—is to divide Christ into two different "portions" that neither Paul nor the rest of the New Testament will permit. When we wrongly divide Christ in such a way, we will be prone to excesses of either some form of self-flagellation or some form of self-centered or oppressive power.

8. **Christians have often thought that sanctification, or holiness, is a private matter** about very personal dimensions of the spiritual life. This makes holiness less comprehensive and Christlike than Paul intends. Romans 6 makes

it clear that holiness includes being part of God's mission in the world, which in turn includes practicing righteousness/justice in that world as God's weapons—not with literal violent arms but as godly instruments of peace and reconciliation.

9. **Eternal life**, in the sense of **the resurrection of the body and life after death**, is not something to be dismissed or considered to be of minimal importance in the Christian faith. Although it is true that some people overemphasize this as if it were the full meaning of salvation and thus the only goal of life on earth, overreacting to that misunderstanding is neither appropriate nor necessary. We all face the reality of our suffering and mortality, and immortality is a central component of their reversal, that is, of our glorification. As Paul says to the Corinthians, "If the dead are not raised, 'Let us eat and drink, for tomorrow we die'" (1 Cor 15:32).

Questions for Those Who Read, Teach, and Preach

1. In what ways does your tradition or church understand baptism and teach about its consequences? How does, or how could, Paul's discussion enrich that understanding?
2. Does your tradition or church, or people within it, inadvertently misinterpret baptism (or conversion, etc.) in ways that allow for cheap rather than costly grace? How might this be diagnosed and addressed?
3. When and how do Christians justify sin in the name of grace or freedom?
4. In many Christian traditions, baptism includes questions such as this: "Do you renounce the spiritual forces of wickedness, reject the evil powers of this world, and repent of your sin?" What is the church's appropriate Christian response to a person who obviously reneges on the promises contained in an affirmative response to that sort of question?
5. What does the term *cruciformity*, or *resurrectional cruciformity*, say to you in your particular ecclesial and cultural context?

FOR FURTHER READING

Bonhoeffer, Dietrich. *Discipleship*. Translated by Barbara Green and Reinhard Krauss. Dietrich Bonhoeffer Works 4. Minneapolis: Fortress, 2001. Previously published as *The Cost of Discipleship*. Rev. ed. Translated by R. H. Fuller. New York: Macmillan, 1959.

Colwell, John E. *Living the Christian Story: The Distinctiveness of Christian Ethics*. New York: T&T Clark, 2001.

Gorman, Michael J. *Cruciformity: Paul's Narrative Spirituality of the Cross.* 20th anniversary ed. Grand Rapids: Eerdmans, 2021 (orig. 2001).

———. *Participating in Christ: Explorations in Paul's Theology and Spirituality.* Grand Rapids: Baker Academic, 2019. (more technical)

———. *Participation: Paul's Vision of Life in Christ.* Cambridge: Grove Books, 2018.

Harink, Douglas. *Resurrecting Justice: Reading Romans for the Life of the World.* Downers Grove, IL: IVP Academic, 2020.

Hogan, Laura Reece. *I Live, No Longer I: Paul's Spirituality of Suffering, Transformation, and Joy.* Eugene, OR: Wipf & Stock, 2017.

Johnson, Andy. *Holiness and the* Missio Dei. Eugene, OR: Cascade, 2016.

Macaskill, Grant R. *Living in Union with Christ: Paul's Gospel and Christian Moral Identity.* Grand Rapids: Baker Academic, 2019.

Rankin, Wilbourne, and Brian Gregor. *The Cross before Me: Reimagining the Way to the Good Life.* Colorado Springs: David C. Cook, 2019.

7:7–8:39
In the Spirit, Not in the Flesh

We have now seen two of Paul's three sets of antitheses, or opposites, regarding the move from death to life that has occurred for us by means of the gift of justification in Christ. The first, in 5:12–21, contrasted Adam and Christ. The second, in 6:1–7:6, contrasted slavery to Sin and, following liberation from Sin, the new slavery to God/righteousness.

Paul's third antithesis essentially covers two full chapters, 7:7–8:39. This lengthy passage unpacks justification in terms of the contrast between life in the flesh (a phrase to be defined below) and life in the Spirit. As noted earlier, although 7:7–25 and 8:1–39 should be read together as descriptions of two different ways of life, they should *not* be read as a sequential account of the normal Christian life.[42] This popular understanding of the two chapters views chapter 7 as a description of the defeated Christian life and chapter 8 as a description of the victorious Christian life.

Rather, we should see 7:7–8:39 as giving us contrasting depictions of life *before* and life *after* justification—that is, life outside Christ and life in Christ—as in 5:12–21 and 6:1–7:6. Paul's focus on the life of the justified as one of participation continues in this section. Now he depicts concrete daily existence as one of *mutual indwelling*: living within and being inhabited by a power, a lord.

---

42. See, e.g., Watchman Nee, *The Normal Christian Life* (Carol Stream, IL: Tyndale House, 1977 [orig. 1957]).

For believers, this is the reality of the prophetically promised new covenant: God's Spirit inhabits and empowers the people of God.

But mutual indwelling is not simply the dynamic of *Christian* existence; it characterizes all human life. Just as Paul believes that living means being a slave to a powerful lord (either Sin or God/Christ/righteousness), so also he believes that living in relationship with that lord means existing under both its external power and its internal presence. Paul is on to something critical that we understand from daily life: the air that sustains us both *surrounds* us and *inhabits* us. We and it are in a relationship of mutual indwelling, or reciprocal residence: we inhabit the air, and the air inhabits us (our lungs).

Being in a relationship of mutual indwelling vis-à-vis Sin—being under Sin and having Sin within—is what Paul means by life in the flesh as opposed to life in Christ. "The flesh" in Rom 7 does not refer merely to the body, as if the body were the problem. Nor does "the flesh" mean "sinful nature."[43] *Life in the flesh means bodily existence apart from the enlivening and empowering Spirit of God.* This life in the flesh and under Sin is, from Paul's reconfigured Jewish perspective, also life under the law (6:14–15; 7:6). The law makes demands that people cannot fulfill and thus functions like an unreasonable taskmaster because the deeper problem is enslavement to Sin and self-centered desire.

For those in Christ, however, as chapter 8 proclaims, the slavemaster Sin is replaced by the Spirit as the internal power and external influence that guides and enables human action. The Spirit enables believers to do the righteousness that the law demands but does not empower people to perform. According to chapter 8, the slavery to righteousness portrayed in 6:1–7:6 is made existentially real, and realizable, by the indwelling Spirit, as Paul had already hinted in 7:6.

7:7–25
Life in the Flesh

Romans 7:7–25 is one of the most difficult and diversely interpreted texts in Romans. For this reason, we must take a careful look at the forest before examining the trees. Interpreters agree on some key details but radically disagree on the main point and function of the text. Agreements include the following:

1. Paul pronounces the law good and holy.
2. Paul depicts Sin as a force or power that makes use of—even hijacks—the good law.

43. This is the translation of, e.g., the NLT throughout Rom 7 and 8 (except "old nature" in 7:5).

3. Sin enslaves and indwells people.

4. The use of "I" is significant, although the identity of this "I" is hotly debated.

5. The "I" of the text experiences a divided self, indeed a mastered or dominated self, and a resulting moral frustration.

6. The shift of verb tenses associated with the "I" and with "Sin," from past tense (7:7–13) to present tense (7:14–25), is significant.

7. Paul presents Christ and the Spirit as the solution to the existential dilemma felt by the "I."

8. Life in the Spirit (ch. 8) is the alternative to the life depicted in chapter 7.

THE IDENTITY OF THE "I"

The rather substantial agreements just listed also hint at the major interpretive issue concerning 7:7–25: the identity of the "I" who is speaking, and the life-situation(s) to which this "I" is referring:

- Is Paul using the "I" to speak autobiographically, representatively for a group, or imaginatively for others (sometimes called speech in character)?
- If he is speaking autobiographically, is he speaking about his own Jewish experience outside Christ, or his own experience in Christ?
- If he is speaking representatively or imaginatively, is he speaking instead (or also) about all Jews or even all human beings outside Christ, or about all believers in Christ?
- Or does Paul somehow engage in rhetorical multitasking? Does the "I" represent some or even all of the categories of people listed here?

Furthermore, is Paul's main goal to depict some existential plight? Or is it to defend either the law itself or his view of the law? Or, again, does the answer include some or all of the above? The questions are complex.

Historically, most readers of Rom 7 have understood Paul to be narrating his own personal story, seeing the "I" as an autobiographical reference to himself. They think he is either describing his existence before being converted to Christ or his life as a believer. Both interpretations seem plausible, for it is difficult (simply as a human being, or specifically as a Christian) not to identify with the inner struggle the "I" (in this interpretation, Paul) depicts in such texts as 7:19 and 7:21–23. Who has never had this thought: "For I do not do the good I want, but the evil I do not want is what I do" (Rom 7:19)?

This sort of interpretation is certainly possible. Nevertheless, the majority of scholars today do not believe Paul is narrating his own preconversion Jewish experience, since elsewhere he indicates no sense of a preconversion struggle with the law, but only success and pride in doing it (Gal 1:14; Phil 3:4–6).

Neither, however, is it likely that Paul is narrating his current experience as a believer. Despite the appeal of this interpretation because we resonate with certain sentiments expressed in the chapter, many interpreters today maintain that Paul's "I" is not the Christian believer. There is no reference to the Spirit in these verses. Rather, the description of the "I" as "sold into slavery under Sin" (7:14; cf. 7:23b, 25b) and indwelt by it (7:17, 20, 23b) is clearly a reference to the person who is "under the power of Sin" (3:9) and a slave to Sin (6:6, 16, 20, etc.). It does not refer to someone redeemed from Sin, dead to it but alive to God as God's slave (3:24; 6:6, 11, 18, 22, etc.), enjoying "the new life of the Spirit" (7:6).

According to this view, Paul does not—indeed, *cannot*—portray Christians as slaves of Sin without engaging in radical self-contradiction. Does this mean believers are automatically and permanently exempt from Sin's sway? No! Believers still must struggle not to allow Sin to regain mastery (6:12; cf. 8:13), but they do so on the assumption of their liberation from Sin, not their slavery to it.

According to many contemporary interpreters, therefore, Paul is using the "I" to speak imaginatively but appropriately, as a believer, about the experience of nonbelievers: either fellow Jews or people in general who are outside the Messiah. The apostle is offering his perspective on unredeemed humanity seen through the prism of his redemption in Christ. Paul is following the ancient convention of speech in character (which is occasionally still used today). This involves using "I" to speak about someone other than oneself—a person, group, or humanity in general—for some rhetorical purpose. We see something similar in 1 Cor 13 (the love chapter), in which the "I" is more than Paul.

More specifically, we may say that Paul's "I" in Rom 7 is Adam, in the sense of everyone living in Adam and thereby under the reign of Sin, Death, and (after Moses) the law (cf. 5:12–14; 1 Cor 15:22). Paul even alludes to Gen 2–3 to tell the story of sin's entry into the human race (past tense, 7:7–13) and the ongoing consequences of its reign (present tense, 7:14–25). This condition of being in Adam and enslaved to Sin is also described as being "of the flesh" or in my/the flesh (7:14, 18; 8:8–9). Its antithesis—and its antidote—is being "in Christ" and therefore "in the Spirit" (8:1, 9–11).

THE SENSE OF THE TEXT

The significance of this view for understanding Paul's spirituality should not be underestimated. Although Paul clearly expects believers to grow in "sanctification" (6:19, 22), or Christlikeness, he does not believe that the experience he narrates in chapter 7 is the standard experience of believers as they (allegedly) constantly lose the existential battle between good and evil. Rather, Paul sees the normal life of believers as one in which they are liberated from Sin and empowered by the Spirit to fulfill "the just requirement of the law" (8:4) as they "put to death the deeds of the body" (8:13).

Nonetheless (to repeat for emphasis), even though Rom 7:7–25 describes life in Adam and not life in Christ, those who are in Christ and liberated from Sin must guard against slipping back into this sort of spiritual predicament, as Paul had warned in 6:12: "Therefore, do not let sin exercise dominion in your mortal bodies, to make you obey their passions." Freedom from Sin and the law does not mean freedom from obedience to God, and re-enslavement to the old master is a possibility.

But why does Paul even discuss the connection between the law and Sin, risking a serious misunderstanding? His discussion in 7:7–25 begins with a rhetorical question about the possibility of equating the law with sin (7:7). The structure of verse 7 is similar to 6:1–2a and 6:15: a rhetorical question leads to a strong negation ("By no means!") that initiates an exposition of the subject at hand: Is the law Sin? The rhetorical question in 7:7a arises because Paul has said that believers have died both to Sin (6:2) and to the law (7:4, 6); they have been "discharged" from the law that "held us captive" (7:6). The law seems to be at odds with life in Christ and the Spirit, and thus at odds with God and God's will. These would be problematic conclusions for any Jew—and indeed for any Christian.

What follows from Paul is in part a defense of the goodness of the law, but it is even more a description of the frustrated human (and especially Jewish) condition apart from Christ in spite of the law. *The law is not the culprit; Sin is.* But at the same time, the law cannot bring life (cf. Gal 3:21) in the face of such a death-dealing power. Moreover, *the law cannot empower its own fulfillment.*

With this important overview of the issues and an overall approach to the passage, we turn to the text itself. Paul writes as a Jew: a Jew in Christ.

7:7–13. The Entrance of Sin and Its Co-opting of the Law

Repeating his rhetorical question-and-answer approach from 6:1–2 and 6:15, Paul begins these verses with a swift denial—"By no means!"—of the possibility that the law *is* Sin because the law *reveals sin/Sin* (7:7). In the rest of 7:7–13, Paul shows how Sin "deceived" and "killed" the human race by "seizing an opportunity in the commandment" (7:11), a commandment that "promised life" (7:10).[44] He will conclude with another strong "By no means!" denial, this time renouncing the erroneous inference that the law had "become" Death for him (7:13 NAB, NIV, NET), echoing the place he began. The law is not the cause of Sin and therefore not the cause of Death.

This section of Rom 7 is Paul's retelling of what Christians call the fall, from the opening chapters of Genesis, mixed with echoes of the giving of the law in Exod 20. The allusions to the Genesis account (Gen 2:15-17; 3:1-24) of God's life-giving commandment (Gen 2:16; 3:2-3), the serpent's death-inflicting deception of Eve (Gen 3:1-5, 13), and the first couple's covetousness (Gen 3:6) are unmistakable and explain the many past-tense verbs Paul uses in 7:7-13. In fact, the Greek verb for "deceived" in 7:11 echoes the Greek version of Gen 3:13, and the same verb appears in 2 Cor 11:3 and 1 Tim 2:14 in explicit reference to the Genesis account.[45]

In Paul's retelling of the Genesis story, the deceiver is not a serpent but a power, Sin. "Seizing an opportunity" (Rom 7:8, 11)—that is, the issuing of God's good, life-giving commandment—Sin provoked covetousness, which led (implicitly, through disobedience; cf. 5:12-21) to death. The law is "holy," and the commandment against covetousness was, and is, "holy and just and good" (7:12). The law is "spiritual," or inspired by God's Spirit, as Paul will soon claim (7:14). The good law given by God functioned, in part, to reveal what sin is (7:7; cf. 3:20b). But the divine mandate was, and is, also used by Sin the power to increase sinning in the world (7:13; cf. 5:20). That which should have led to life (see, e.g., Lev 18:5) yielded death.

Paul's version of the Genesis narrative interprets the first couple's misplaced desire and disobedience as a violation of the commandment from the decalogue that begins simply, "You shall not covet" (Exod 20:17 and Deut 5:21, cited in 7:7). In 7:8, Paul claims that Sin as a power relied on the emergence of this commandment against covetousness to activate "all kinds of covetousness." This could be read to mean Sin, not people, are responsible for their predicament, and as we see in 7:11 and 7:13 (and will see further in 7:14-25), there is some truth to this conclusion.

But that is not the whole story. In exonerating the law and shifting the blame to Sin, Paul is not excusing Adam or himself or us. Paul has already told us in 7:5 that our own "sinful passions" were "aroused by the law," passions

---

44. The correlation between keeping God's commandments and life is especially strong in Deuteronomy (e.g., 4:1, 40; 5:33; 8:1; 30:16).

45. Paul also uses the same verb in 16:18 of people who deceive the Christian community.

that get expressed through the body's "members" (7:5; cf. 6:19; 7:23). That the law is an igniter of passions is also essentially the main claim of 7:7–10, unpacking 7:5. Inappropriate, or disordered, desire is at the root of the human predicament, as we have seen in Romans since 1:18–32.

For Paul, the law generates new opportunities for us to exercise our creative abilities to manufacture new forms of evil. The prohibition of what is obviously an evil can begin to make that evil look like a good. (Think of the common sermon illustration: what does a toddler do when you instruct her not to touch the stove?) That is why Paul speaks of Sin deceiving us (7:11)—even more so as adults. (See Gen 3:1–13 for the serpent's similar deceit.)

Simultaneously, then, Sin enables us, individually and collectively, to carry that evil out, thinking that it is good for me or for humanity, with the result that Sin becomes "sinful beyond measure" (7:13). There is no end to the possibilities of human ingenuity with respect to sins when Sin is allowed full sway. The end result, Paul says, is that the very thing that was supposed to bring about life led, instead, to death (7:9–10), as in Gen 2:17; 3:17–19.

It is clear, however, that the law is not Sin, or sinful, or evil, or the cause of our death-situation. In 7:13a, Paul echoes in form and content—like part of a set of bookends—the rhetorical question of 7:7a: "By no means!" The "good" law did not become the cause of our deadly predicament (lit. "become death for me," NAB; "to me," NIV, NET). But it is, Paul would add, an indicator that what we need is *life*.

7:14–25. The Ongoing Effects of Sin as Indwelling Power

The brief shift to the present tense in 7:12 to describe God's commandment/law has prepared us for Paul's repeated use of the present tense in 7:14–25. He has transitioned from the past, and the beginning of Sin's exploitation of the law, to the present, and the ongoing effects of this sinister arrangement. What Paul finds in human beings is a confused (7:15), divided self, with two laws, or principles, at war within. "I," he says, "do not do what I want, but [what] . . . I hate" (7:15b, 19). Despite having a delight in the law and a desire to do good (7:21–22, 25), "I cannot do it" (7:18b). These are words of personal lament. Paul, speaking in character, is attributing this moral frustration and grief, not to himself, but to persons outside Christ—those without the Spirit.

The repetitious character of these verses is deliberate; in 7:14–20, Paul describes the situation twice in careful, parallel form:

OUR PREDICAMENT ACCORDING TO ROMANS 7:14–20

FEATURE	7:14–17	7:18–20
Acknowledgment of the reality	*We know*	*I know*
Status of the law	spiritual (v. 14a) good (v. 16b)	[not repeated]
Human condition	of the flesh (v. 14b) sold into slavery (v. 14b) under Sin (v. 14b)	nothing good in me/my flesh (v. 18a)
Moral frustration	lack of self-understanding (v. 15a) doing what I hate/don't want (vv. 15b, 16a)	I can will but not do right (v. 18b) I don't do the good I want but I do the evil I don't want (vv. 19, 20a)
Conclusion	no longer I but indwelling Sin (v. 17)	no longer I but indwelling Sin (v. 20b)

One small but perhaps important difference between 7:14–17 and 7:18–20 is the absence of a reference to the law in 7:18–20. Perhaps Paul is once again reflecting the letter's theme of Jew (7:14–17) and gentile (7:18–20).

In similar parallel fashion, in 7:21–25 Paul states his main conclusion three times for emphasis (7:21, 7:22–23, 7:25): "I am"—that is, each person outside Christ is—a slave to indwelling Sin that impacts my bodily life in this world. Even when I want to do good, there is another power at work: "evil lies close at hand" (7:21b).

This sentiment is perhaps reminiscent of the Lord's words to Cain in Gen 4:7: "sin is lurking at the door; its desire is for you, but you must master it."[46] But, Paul believes, such mastery is impossible for humans in their natural, normal state. The only means of rescue from this predicament that drives the speaker ("I") in the text to despair (7:24a)—and the only sign of hope in all of 7:7–25—is the saving work of God in Christ mentioned in a brief interjection (7:25a). This momentary outburst of spiritual relief and gratitude points ahead to chapter 8, where it explodes with power.

It is important to note the moral frustration Paul powerfully portrays in 7:14–20. He does not suggest here that humanity is so morally bankrupt that

46. The Greek text in the LXX is slightly different, so we cannot be certain of the connection to Gen 4:7.

we are unable ever to conceive of the good. This assertion might seem at first blush to stand in tension with Paul's description of the human condition in 1:18–32 (esp. 1:21). But Paul's focus here has shifted. He is building on the claims made in chapter 1 that our minds and bodies are both impaired; even when we know and desire the good (which is more or less the case from person to person), we cannot perform it. The main problem (not unlike the situation depicted in Rom 2) is not *possession* but *performance*: putting knowledge into action. But of course, since Paul knows that the human mind and heart have been corrupted, human beings do not always *know* the good either.

Paul's diagnosis of our human predicament, as already described in 3:9 and chapter 6, is humanity's enslavement to Sin, which he mentions at both the beginning and the end of this passage (7:14, 23b, 25b). Particularly vivid is the image Paul uses in 7:23b: being "captive to" or a "prisoner" (NIV, CEB) of Sin is the unusual language of being taken captive in war, ultimately to become a slave.

What is new in this part of chapter 7, however, is the idea that Sin the tyrant *indwells* people (7:17, 20) and actually does the evil that humans wish they would not do (7:20). Sin is not merely an external force or master *over* the human race but also an internal power *within* each person. Paul calls this bleak situation the "law," or principle, of Sin (7:23, 25; cf. 8:2). The human mind cannot control the human body, in part because both the mind and the body have been affected by Sin (recall 1:18–32). This is life without the mutual indwelling of God's Spirit and human beings, or life in the "flesh": life determined solely by Adam and not Christ.

The apostle's repeated negative use of the word "flesh" does not mean that "the body" is inherently evil. "The flesh" refers to human, bodily life in that natural, normal state just noted: without God's Spirit to inspire and enable. The manifestation of Sin in the body's "members" (7:23) has made the self into a "body of Death" (7:24), similar to the phrase "body of Sin" (6:6). That is, Paul says, we are characterized by, and plagued by, the realities of Sin and Death. Of course, this situation can be altered (cf. 6:12–23 and ch. 8), but not by human effort.

We must be careful in speaking of indwelling Sin not to restrict it to individual persons and their behavior. The "I know" of 7:18 is preceded by the "We know" of 7:14; Sin inhabits us not just individually but also corporately. The "I" of Rom 7 represents each of us and all of us together. This also means that living in, or according to, the flesh refers to something more than yielding to one's own personal desires and passions. If the flesh is that which ignores and even opposes God, then living in the flesh, empowered by indwelling Sin, essentially means living in accord with the values and powers of this age (cf. Rom 12:1–2). It therefore means being formed by cultural, social, and political values and powers, whether ancient or modern. These powers of malformation include, of course, all sorts of imperial ideologies and systems.

The result is a mindset and its corollary practices (see 8:5–8) that devalue the vulnerable, pursue personal and national glory at any cost, and embody in multiple ways the antithesis of Jesus' life, teaching, and death. Humans, often unknowingly, are caught in a fleshly spider's web of Sin, the power that determines the practices of this age, while simultaneously being energized by that same power from within. This predicament of oppressive mutual indwelling—Sin in people and people in Sin—and its deadly consequences means that humanity is not *what* it was created to be because it is not *where* it was created to be.

Yet Paul's theology of enslaving and indwelling Sin does not mean that human beings are exonerated. This is not a case of "the devil made me do it" or, perhaps worse, "I am simply being myself." We have gotten ourselves into this predicament and have no excuse (1:18–3:20), but now (apart from Christ) we are powerless, covenantally dysfunctional. We cannot choose life or death, as Deut 30:15–20 had called for.

A heart-wrenching emotional outburst follows this conclusion: "Wretched" or "miserable" (NAB, CEB) person that I am (7:24)—a sentiment found in other ancient meditations on humanity's moral frailty. The only solution to the crisis is what God has done through Christ (7:25a) to provide the Spirit, to which Paul turns in chapter 8.

Paul, then, has once again leveled the playing field. Christian readers must recognize where we have come from—all of us. And Christian readers must understand the character of Sin in order both to avoid it and to participate, with compassion and understanding, in the divine rescue mission. This passage of Romans teaches us that Sin, like life, is complicated.

REFLECTIONS AND QUESTIONS FOR 7:7–25

Spiritual, Pastoral, and Theological Reflections

1. Paul offers us a **robust theology of Sin** here, further explaining some of his claims about Sin earlier in the letter. Sin as a power is a force with uncanny strength and nearly unlimited effect. It dominates and it inhabits; it hijacks good things and uses them for nefarious purposes; it deceives, and it influences behavior. While some moderns, even some Christians, are uncomfortable with such an understanding of Sin because it might appear to excuse individual sinful behavior and evil more generally, it actually does just the

opposite, especially when it is firmly tethered to the reality of misplaced, disordered desire that is at the heart of human responsibility for sin and evil.

2.   Covetousness is not arbitrarily chosen by Paul as his sample sin. Unlike many sins, **covetousness is hidden,** safely ensconced in the human heart—until it manifests itself in action in any one of a thousand ways. To borrow from another Pauline letter, covetousness is the root of all sorts of evil (cf. 1 Tim 6:10).

3.   If Rom 6 reminds us that we are all **subject to external powers and forces,** Rom 7 reminds us that such powers and forces also live deep within us. If we are tempted to judge others about their moral or other personal failures, Rom 7 instructs us to turn the mirror on ourselves and to look within our own hearts and souls, where Sin has also dwelt. Grace, and grace alone, is what makes any difference.

4.   Paul's theology of the **mutual indwelling of Sin and people** does not mean that we have no **responsibility for our sins.** Rather, as Paul himself says, we have made decisions and choices that put us into the predicament we are in apart from God's grace. Sinning is what we do. At the same time, Paul's understanding of Sin the power helps us understand two things: (1) how bodies of people (from cliques to mobs to communities to political parties to entire nation-states) become complicit in evil without giving it any thought or while defending it; and (2) how individuals can generally want to avoid evil but cannot always do so, *and* at times even desire to do what they know is wrong.

5.   Paul's theology of Sin is not simply about Sin and me. Rather, it is (once again) also about **Sin and us.** If the "I" of Rom 7 is representative, even corporate, then we must deal pastorally not only with the power of personal addictions but also with the power of systemic evils in the form of racism, nationalism, and the like.

Questions for Those Who Read, Teach, and Preach

1.   Can you think of ways in which deceit functions to encourage and equip people to do evil in the name of good, or even in the name of God?

2.   How might Paul's theology of Sin as a ruling and indwelling power help us to understand something like systemic racism or an individual's chronic pathological behavior? How does this perspective on the human predicament not excuse such behavior?

3.   If Rom 7 does not, from Paul's perspective, describe the normal Christian experience, how do we explain the fact that Christians resonate with much of the chapter? Are there ways to make sense of Christian identification with

the sentiments expressed in this chapter while still maintaining that they are intended to describe existence outside of Christ?

4. How might awareness of the power of Sin and Death make us more compassionate toward others in their struggles?

5. What is the significance of understanding life in the flesh to include both disordered personal passions (such as the unbridled pursuit of sex, power, or wealth) and accommodation to disordered cultural and political values and practices?

6. How can the message of this text serve, not to make people feel helpless and wretched, but to give them (us) hope?

For Further Reading

Bringle, Mary Louise. *Envy: Exposing a Secret Sin*. Louisville: Westminster John Knox, 2016.

Croasmun, Matthew. *The Emergence of Sin: The Cosmic Tyrant in Romans*. New York: Oxford University Press, 2017. (more technical)

Eastman, Susan Grove. *Paul and the Person: Reframing Paul's Anthropology*. Grand Rapids, Eerdmans, 2017. (more technical)

Snodgrass, Klyne R. *Who God Says You Are: A Christian Understanding of Identity*. Grand Rapids: Eerdmans, 2018.

Wilder, Terry L., ed. *Perspectives on Our Struggle with Sin: Three Views of Romans 7*. Nashville: Broadman & Holman, 2011.

8:1–39
Life in the Spirit: Resurrectional Cruciformity

Anyone who has heard or read Rom 7 is more than ready for Rom 8. We have already received brief but promising hints, first in 5:1–11 and just now in 7:25a, of what is to come. But those hints now explode.

Chapter 8 is in many ways the climax of the section of Romans that begins at 5:1, and also the climax of the letter—*thus far*—as a whole. In this chapter, Paul presents a very full discussion of participating in the life of the triune God: being in Christ as God's children who live in the Spirit (Gk. *pneuma*), a life that is the antithesis of life in the flesh. This is the life of the new covenant, even though Paul does not use that term explicitly. But it is clear that the Spirit has been poured into human hearts so that the Spirit-inhabited people can keep the covenant of love for God and for others: "the just requirement of the law" (8:4). This is the reversal of human *asebeia* and *adikia* (ungodliness and unrighteousness/injustice; 1:18). People who were covenantally dysfunctional are now able to function properly before God and others.[47]

Although the chapter's focus is life in the Spirit—the word *pneuma* appears twenty-one times in this chapter[48]—it is clear from beginning to end that salvation is the work of the triune God. It is equally clear that the experience of believers—those who have responded to the gospel in trust, allegiance, and baptism—is, in fact, an experience of that triune God: Father, Son, and Spirit.

We find in this chapter at least five main elements of the Christian life:

- the mutual indwelling of Christ and the Spirit with believers, and thus the profound solidarity between Christ/the Spirit and Christians, individually and corporately;
- believers' adoption as God's children;
- the Christ-shaped pattern of suffering followed by glory;
- the hope of redemption, not only for human beings but also for the entire creation; and
- the certainty of God's presence and love in the midst of suffering.

However little or much the Roman believers had been previously taught about such subjects, Paul's presentation undoubtedly enriched and expanded their vision of the Christian life, of who they were and what they had received, as it has done throughout the centuries.

For God's children in Christ, the Spirit replaces Sin as the indwelling power that determines a person's, or a community's, direction and behavior. Perhaps Paul learned a valuable lesson from his encounters with the Corinthians, who had a robust but distorted view of the Spirit as enabling practices of power and honor, resulting in a divided community rather than a community of self-giving love. *In Rom 8, the Spirit is clearly set out as the Spirit of cruciformity—cross-shaped participation in Christ.* Since we have repeatedly seen that Romans is about God's gift of life (and that will be strongly affirmed in ch. 8), we know that such Spirit-enabled cruciformity is, paradoxically, life-giving. Life in the Spirit is a life of *joyful, resurrection-infused cruciformity.*[49]

47. Paul's understanding of the new covenant blends the theology of Jeremiah (esp. 31:31–34) and Ezekiel (esp. 11:17–20; 36:23–28; 37:21–28); see also Deut 30:1–6, 8.

48. All but four of these are in vv. 1–17. Some translations see certain occurrences as references to the human spirit.

49. The word "joy" or "rejoice" does not appear in the chapter, but its substance is nonetheless present.

The effect of the Spirit's presence is resurrectionally cruciform in two major ways: (1) putting to death the deeds of the body, or dying to the flesh in order to truly live (8:13); and (2) suffering with Christ as the prelude to glory (8:17). These two dimensions of the Spirit-filled life are discussed in 8:1–17 and 8:18–39, respectively, and they constitute both the proof of the Spirit's presence and the guarantee of abundant and eternal life. When Paul arrives at the ultimate pastoral goal of his letter in chapters 12–15, he will explain what a Spirit-filled, cruciform community of the resurrection should look like in the nitty-gritty of daily life together, though there are certainly plenty of hints in this chapter.

This new life Paul describes is one of intimacy with God, not merely individually but especially corporately. The introspective, frustrated "I" of Rom 7 has become the liberated, united "we" and "you [plural]" of Rom 8. We relate to God as God's adopted children, as family, even calling God "Abba! Father!" as co-heirs with Christ, assured of our status by the Spirit.

Paul expresses the intimacy of believers' participation in and identification with Christ and the Spirit in two especially significant ways.[50] First, there is a series of short phrases beginning with the Greek preposition *en*, which is generally translated as "in" but can also mean "among":

- those who are in Christ Jesus (8:1)
- the law of the Spirit of life in Christ Jesus (8:2)
- you are in the Spirit (8:9; versus in the flesh: 8:8–9)
- the Spirit of God dwells in/among you (8:9)
- if [since] Christ is in/among you (8:10)
- if [since] the Spirit of him who raised Jesus from the dead dwells in/among you (8:11)
- his Spirit that dwells in/among you (8:11)

Second, we also find a series of words that begin with the prefix "co-" (Gk. *syg-*, *sym-*, *syn-*, *sys-*; often rendered as "with"):

- *symmartyrei* = "bearing witness with"; lit. "co-witness" (8:16)
- *synklēronomoi* = "joint heirs"; lit. "co-heirs" (8:17)
- *sympaschomen* = "suffer with"; lit. "co-suffer" (8:17)
- *syndoxasthōmen* = "be glorified with"; lit. "be co-glorified" (8:17)

50. These two ways ("in" and "with" language) were also noted in the introduction to the commentary.

- *systenazei . . . synōdinei* = "groans and suffers together" (NET); lit. "co-groans . . . co-agonizes" (8:22)[51]
- *synantilambanetai* = "helps us"; lit. "co-takes hold of" (8:26)
- *synergei* = "work[s] together"; lit. "co-work[s]" (8:28)
- *symmorphous* = "conformed to"; lit. "co-formed" (8:29; cf. Phil 3:10, 21)

In addition, there is the phrase "with him [Christ]" (*syn autō*) in 8:32.

Together these two groups of phrases and words—the "in" group dominating the first half of the chapter and the "with" group dominating the second half—exhibit Paul's profound spirituality of participation. They echo and further develop the "in/into" and "with" language associated with baptism and new life in Christ in 6:1–7:6. This life is not a spiritual free-for-all, however. To live in and with Christ and the Spirit is to live *according to*, or *in sync with* (Gk. *kata*), the Spirit rather than the flesh (8:4, 5, 12, 13). And this means also in sync with (*kata*) the will of the Father (8:27–28) and in sync with (*kata*) Christ (15:5). In other words, the Spirit enables the children of God to resemble their Father by resembling his Son, who is their elder brother.[52] Living *in* Christ means living *according to* Christ.

The language of life is, therefore, also abundant in Rom 8. The "life" word-group appears in 8:2, 6, 10, 11, 12, 13 (twice), and 38—echoing and amplifying that theme from chapters 5 and 6.[53] A key claim of this theme in the entire chapter is paradoxical: death, whether Christ's or ours, whether figurative or literal, and whether past or present or future, gives way to life (8:2–4, 13). Thus, co-suffering with Christ results finally in co-glorification with him (8:17). In anticipation of that full and final glory, the faithful have the indwelling and surrounding presence and love of Father, Son, and Spirit now, no matter what circumstances they may find themselves in. The glory lost (1:18–32; 3:23) is presently being restored (8:30; cf. 2 Cor 3:18) in anticipation of eschatological glory. And this loving, empowering presence means that life in the present is already life indeed.

8:1–17. Dying to the Flesh and Living in the Spirit

Paul's emphasis in the first half of chapter 8 is on the stark contrast between believers' situation in the Spirit and their previous situation in the flesh, domi-

---

51. Many translations miss the "together" dimension of one or both of these verbs.

52. It is these sorts of connections here in Rom 8, along with other texts noted below, that have led many Christian theologians, since the earliest days of the church, to speak of salvation in terms of theosis (deification) or Christosis (Christification), or both.

53. See 5:10, 17, 18, 21; 6:2, 4, 10 (twice), 11, 13, 22, 23.

nated and inhabited by Sin (esp. 7:7–25). They are now enabled to please God (8:1–13) and to live as God's adopted children (8:14–17). This section of chapter 8 is in large measure an expansion of Gal 4:4–7:

> But when the fullness of time had come, God sent his Son, born of a woman, born under the law, in order to redeem those who were under the law, so that we might receive adoption as children. And because you are children, God has sent the Spirit of his Son into our hearts, crying, "Abba! Father!" So you are no longer a slave but a child, and if a child then also an heir, through God.

8:1–8. *The Spirit and New Life in Christ*

Paul begins the chapter by stating a thesis of sorts, which is the undoing of chapter 7 as well as 5:12–21: there is no condemnation for those who are now "in Christ Jesus" (8:1),[54] those who have been baptized into him and thus into his death and resurrection (6:1–11). This declaration of "no condemnation" is in stark contrast to the predicament of humanity in Adam and in the flesh (cf. 5:16, 18; 7:24)

Why no condemnation? Because those in Christ have been liberated from the law (or principle) of "Sin and of Death" that Paul has described in 1:18–3:20 and, more immediately, in 7:7–25.[55] This liberation was brought about by the law (principle) of "the Spirit of life in Christ Jesus" (8:2). Just as Ezekiel had said God's people would be renewed in a resurrection, or revivification, effected by the Spirit (Ezek 37), Paul claims that this resurrection is happening now—and has been extended beyond Israel, to all who enter Christ.

In this new reality of resurrection life, the Spirit replaces Sin, and life replaces death/Death. When enslaved to Sin, people's present reality and final destination do not consist of life with God, but of death (cf. 3:23; 6:23), the natural outcome of their failure to keep covenant with God. This was a profound spiritual collapse that the law of Moses, good as it was, could not rectify.

In a highly significant text, which may incorporate an early Christian mini-confession of faith, Paul says in 8:3 that God's sending of the Son both dealt with Sin/sin and condemned it. This text refers succinctly to Jesus' coming, life, and death: what Christians call the Son's incarnation, his sinlessness, and his atoning death:

---

54. The KJV and related translations add "who walk not after the flesh, but after the Spirit" to 8:1, but this phrase is not in the best manuscripts.

55. As in 3:27–28 and 7:21–25, Paul is engaging in wordplay, using the Greek word *nomos* to mean both "law" (of Moses) and "principle."

- *Incarnation*: God did not send just any messenger or human savior but his Son—his *own* Son, his beloved Son (see also 8:32; John 3:16). The Son became a real human—the most truly human person there has ever been. The phrase "in the likeness of sinful flesh" does not mean that Jesus only *appeared* to be human.[56] That claim is the essence of the heresy called docetism—the belief system asserting that the Son only appeared to become a human and only appeared to die. No, Jesus was fully human except that he did not sin, unlike all other humans. The word "likeness" in 8:3 conveys both Jesus' similarity to and difference from the rest of us.

- *Sinlessness*: Paul affirms Jesus' sinlessness more explicitly in 2 Cor 5:21: Jesus "knew no sin." Jesus' sinless life as a real human demonstrated a way of being human that is not normal, so to speak: not dominated by Sin, not "according to" the flesh (words that appear in 8:4–5, 12–13).[57] In this sense, the incarnate son of God "condemned" sin/Sin, revealing its error. As John's Gospel also says, God's intervention in Jesus was not meant to condemn us—we took care of that ourselves by our rejection of God and our embrace of sin/Sin—but to deliver us from Sin and save us (see John 3, esp. 3:14–21). That deliverance occurred in the Messiah's atoning death.

- *Atonement*: Revealing the folly of sin/Sin while manifesting the alternative was not enough. Something had to be done to forgive sins and defeat the power of Sin. As with 3:21–26, 8:3 (a quick summary of that earlier passage) probably refers to Christ's death in two ways. First, the sinless one died as a sacrifice, a sin offering, for the sinful—"to deal with sin" (lit. "concerning sin").[58] This is an echo of the discussion of the day of atonement in Lev 16. Like the sacrifice of the slaughtered goat, Christ's death as a sin offering brings about forgiveness from sins and purification.

  Furthermore, in Christ's death, God also defeated and disabled Sin the power (a further aspect of the condemnation of Sin) so that those who are forgiven, purified, and empowered by the Spirit can fulfill the "just require-

---

56. A similar phrase, with the same word "likeness," in Phil 2:7 also refers to Jesus' incarnation and humanity.

57. "According to the flesh" can have a neutral or a negative sense. Paul uses it of Jesus in the neutral sense in 1:3 and 9:5. He uses it of humans more generally in 4:1 and 9:3. See also 7:7–25 for existence in, and dominated by, the "flesh," and 1:18–3:20 for normal sinful human existence more generally.

58. The Greek phrase that could be translated "concerning sin" appears in the Greek version (LXX) of Lev 16:6, 11 (twice), 15, 27 (twice). NRSV translates it consistently as "sin offering" in those Leviticus texts.

ment of the law," or faithfully keep the covenant in the manner of the Son. For the Spirit of *God* is the Spirit of *the Son* (8:9). The law itself could not deliver to morally disabled, covenantally dysfunctional human beings what it demanded, namely, life in covenant with God (cf. Gal 3:21).

The purpose of the Messiah's death, then, was not merely forgiveness but also empowerment and transformation (cf., again, 2 Cor 5:21), which is what the prophets Ezekiel and Jeremiah had promised for God's people. There has been restoration to life, a resurrection or revivification from the dead (cf. Eph 2:1–10), as prefigured by Abraham (ch. 4). The righteousness/justice that humanity failed to embody (e.g., 1:18–32; 3:9–20) can now be enacted—*is* now being enacted.

After reading texts like 8:3–4 in conjunction with 8:29–30, 2 Cor 5:21, and others, many Christians since at least the second century have articulated salvation in words like these: Christ became what we are so that we could become what he is. Terms for this process include theosis, or deification, and Christosis, or Christification.

Now, therefore, those in Christ/in the Spirit are finally able to please God (8:8); their covenantal dysfunctionality has been reversed by the action of God (8:3). Sin, the great interrupter, has been interrupted! Those in Christ, those who have the Spirit within them, have experienced the prophetic promises of a new heart and the indwelling divine spirit (e.g., Ezek 36:26–28; Jer 31:31–34). They therefore constitute the renewed covenant community as those circumcised in the heart (recall 2:25–29) who can now embody the heart, or fundamental substance, of the law—its "just" or righteous requirement (8:4).

Paul's language in 8:4 is carefully chosen. The "so that" at the beginning of 8:4 is critical, indicating the purpose of God's action in Christ. The gospel of God's righteousness/justice (1:16–17) is about more than the forgiveness of sins; it is about the transformation of people into righteous/just people. This transformation of people from being *unable* to keep the covenant into people who *can* and *do* keep the covenant is why Christ came, lived, died, and was raised. Paul puts it this way in 2 Cor 5:21: "For our sake he made him [Christ] to be sin who knew no sin, so that in him we would become the righteousness [justice] of God" (NRSV alt.). As in Rom 8:3–4, God's initiative, Christ's humanity and sinlessness, his death for our sake, and its purpose are again succinctly named.

In addition to "so that" in 8:4, Paul employs the verb "fulfill" in the passive voice: "so that the just requirement of the law *would be fulfilled* in us" (MJG;

emphasis added).[59] Paul includes himself as a co-participant in Christ with all his hearers and readers. The passive voice implies that we do not fulfill the law on our own. It indicates believers' reliance on the indwelling Spirit, both individually and corporately. The promise of Ezekiel has been realized—"I will put my spirit within you, and make you follow my statutes and be careful to observe my ordinances" (Ezek 36:27). It is the indwelling Spirit that makes life and holiness possible.

But Ezekiel's plural "statutes . . . and ordinances" have become the singular "just requirement," perhaps referring to what Paul elsewhere calls the "law [of love] of the Messiah" (Gal 6:2; MJG). The reappearance of the language of fulfillment in Rom 13:8–10 suggests that the just requirement is, broadly speaking, others-oriented love (cf. Gal 5:14), but that love is expressed in the fulfillment of concrete commandments.[60] As in Galatians and 1 Corinthians, it will include the cessation of divisions and judgmentalism in the church (14:1–15:12; cf. Gal 5:13–6:5; 1 Cor 3:1–4).

The meaning of fulfilling the just requirement of the law—or becoming the righteousness/justice of God (2 Cor 5:21)—will be unpacked in some detail in chapters 12–15. It is summarized in general terms, however, in the early part of this chapter, in phrases like the following:

- walking according to the Spirit rather than according to the flesh (8:4)[61]
- thinking according to the Spirit rather than according to the flesh (8:5)
- submitting to God's law rather than being hostile to it (8:7)
- pleasing God (8:8)[62]

Paul is here depicting the stark contrast between life *in* the flesh, which is life *guided by* the flesh (7:17–25) and life *in* the Spirit, which is life *guided by* the Spirit. A person focused on the flesh—one's own self-determined desires and passions as well as the distorted norms of a culture infected by Sin—simply cannot please God (8:7–8, as in 8:3; cf. 1:26; 7:5). Both thinking and acting (walking/living) are in play because both mind and body have been affected by Sin and need to be reoriented toward God (cf. 12:1–2).

59. The NRSV and most translations actually have "might be fulfilled," but Paul intends to speak of God's purpose and its realization rather than simply a possibility, as "might" could imply, even if its use follows the rules of English grammar.

60. As in 8:4, Paul uses the passive voice for fulfilling the law in 13:8 and in Gal 5:14.

61. Some translations of 8:4 have "live" rather than "walk," but the Greek says "walk," a common biblical image for life with God. Paul uses it also in 6:4; 13:13; 14:15.

62. See also, later, "putting to the death the deeds of the body" (8:13).

This stark either-or between flesh and Spirit, which will be continued in 8:9–13, is reminiscent of Deuteronomy: "I call heaven and earth to witness against you today that I have set before you life and death, blessings and curses. Choose life so that you and your descendants may live, loving the LORD your God, obeying him, and holding fast to him; for that means life to you and length of days" (Deut 30:19–20a). The Roman co-participants in Christ have made their most fundamental choice in baptism, having received the gift of the Spirit. They are now recipients of what humans long for and sometimes seek but can neither find nor achieve on their own: "life and peace" (8:6; see 2:7, 10). These blessings are now theirs as a gift, the fruit of justification and incorporation into Christ.

8:9–13. *The Spirit, Not the Flesh*

Paul now, therefore, addresses the Roman faithful directly with a plural "you" beginning in 8:9 and continuing to 8:15. According to 8:9–13, these believers are no longer "in the flesh" but are "in the Spirit," which means also that the Spirit lives in them (8:9a). This is, as in 7:13–17, the language of mutual indwelling, but now Sin has been replaced by the Spirit, who is referred to in three different ways in 8:9: the Spirit, the Spirit of God, and the Spirit of Christ. Because the Spirit of God is also the Spirit of Christ—see also Gal 4:6 and Phil 1:19—Paul speaks interchangeably of believers being in *Christ* and being in *the Spirit* (8:1, 9). He also speaks of *the Spirit* being within (or among) the faithful and *Christ* being in (or among) them (8:9–11).

In other words, the newness of life that comes from justification and baptism is animated and enabled by Christ's own power and presence, experienced as the Spirit of God and of Christ. The church as a body and all believers individually are constantly enveloped and possessed by Christ's Spirit, like the air around and within them. In faith and baptism, people are moved into Christ, into the sphere of his Spirit; simultaneously, those who move into Christ find that Christ has moved into them, so to speak, his Spirit having taken up residence there. There is no Christian, or Christian community, without the Spirit (8:9a; cf. 1 Cor 12:3), for Christian individuals and communities are temples of the Holy Spirit (1 Cor 3:16–17; 6:19).

Paul describes the present result of this divine indwelling in 8:10–11. He had already said in chapter 4, while relating the story of Abraham, Sarah, and Isaac, that God is the God who brings life out of death (esp. 4:17). In the same chapter, he said that Christ was raised for our justification, or righteousness (4:25). The consequence in the present for those in Christ is that the body deadened by Sin can be resurrected to live a Christ-filled, Spirit-empowered life (8:10). The indwelling Spirit is none other than the Spirit of the God who raised Jesus from the dead (8:11; cf. 4:24; 6:4; 10:9). Although the emphasis here is on the present experience of new life, freed from the power of Sin and thus from a death-like existence (recall 6:4, 6), the future tense verb in the phrase "will give life to your mortal bodies" (8:11) at least hints at future, bodily resurrection (as in 6:5, 8).

Life in the Spirit is not, however, automatic; it requires active participation by believers, who must now set their minds on (the things of) the Spirit (as Paul said in 8:5–6) and actively oppose the flesh (8:12–13; cf. 6:12–13; Gal 5:16–26). In other words, we cannot forget that the Spirit is the *Holy* Spirit (5:5; 9:1; 14:17; 15:13, 16), who makes people holy. There is the real, though totally anachronistic, possibility that some who are baptized will not make their death to Sin an existential reality. This would be a failure at paying our "debt," or obligation, to the one who has redeemed us (8:12; cf. the debt of love in 13:8).

For this reason, the fate of the baptized is conditional—dependent upon their ongoing cruciform mortification of the old way of life: "if . . . you put to death . . ." (8:13). For those who do live according to the Spirit, the end result is that which the law promised but could not deliver: resurrection and life (8:11, 13b). This conviction leads Paul to the metaphor of adoption, which is about the creation of heirs—those who are alive, not dead.

8:14–17. Adopted Children of God

Paul has stressed that the baptized are those who have received God's Spirit and are to live in sync with that Spirit. Such people—those "led" by the Spirit of God—are God's children (8:14; lit. "sons" in Greek, as in 8:19, though 8:16, 17, and 21 have "children" in Greek).[63] This is the case, Paul says, because of the nature of the Spirit: God's Spirit is not a Spirit (or perhaps spirit) that creates slaves and thus fear of a tyrannical, abusive master who is ready to condemn and punish. Rather, God's Spirit lovingly creates a family of adopted children,

---

63. In this passage, Paul uses the Greek words both for "children" and for "sons" to refer to Christians. Translations differ in how they render "sons," depending on their approach to translating gendered nouns that are clearly gender inclusive. For instance, the Greek word for "sons" in 8:19 is translated "sons" (NET, RSV, ESV, NASB), "children" (NRSV, NAB, NIV, NJB, ESV), and "sons and daughters" (CEB). The language of "sons" is significant and should not be completely erased; it is related to two other important words in this chapter. Jesus is called God's "own Son" (8:3), and the Greek word for adoption (*huiothesia*; 8:15, 23) has the Greek word "son" (*huios*) within it.

and it is that Spirit—and therefore that special status—the faithful enjoy. The Spirit marks them out as people liberated from slavery and fear, and as members of God's family by adoption (8:15).[64]

The Roman custom of adoption made the adopted children full heirs of the adoptive father's estate. In fact, an adopted son could sometimes be granted greater benefits and status than the biological children. In Jewish tradition, being God's son(s) or children meant intimacy with God and entitlement to the inheritance (cf. 9:4), first of the land and later of eschatological salvation. This eschatological salvation—the hope of glory (5:2)—is what gentiles and Jews alike, in Christ, will inherit as God's adopted children.

What is particularly amazing is that adoption, with its chief benefits of intimacy and inheritance, is available to all through Christ: male and female, slave and free, rich and poor. This sort of status would be understood by its recipients as an astounding gift. People of little to no importance in the eyes of the world (i.e., in the estimation of peers, family members, employers, masters, imperial authorities, and so on) are now suddenly, in Christ, children of God, individually and collectively inhabited by the Spirit. *Even nonpersons, slaves who are the property of others, can become children of God, co-equal with any and all whom the world deems their superior.* Indeed, it is a status that even the emperor, who often called himself (or was called) son of God, did not actually have. And it is a status that no human can grant—or remove.

The experiential proof (8:16) of believers' adoption is their address to God in the Aramaic language of Jesus—"Abba," meaning "Father" (8:15; see Mark 14:36).[65] That churches consisting largely of gentiles maintained this custom in prayer, perhaps beginning with their baptism (cf. Gal 4:6, following 3:27) and then in both gathered and private worship, attests the power of Jesus' exemplary relationship of both intimacy with and obedience toward God.

God's covenant with the people of God has always included a familial dimension in scriptural and later Jewish tradition. Now that aspect of the relationship receives new emphasis: "I am your God, and you are my people" means especially, for Paul, "I am your Father, and you are my children" (see also 2 Cor 6:16–18). Here, moreover, Paul focuses on the familial privilege the faithful share with Christ: as God's children, they are "joint heirs" or co-heirs with Christ the (elder and unique) Son (8:17a; cf. 1:3–4). That is, they will share in the inheritance of resurrection and life (8:11), of glory (8:17–18, 21).

---

64. In ch. 4, we learned that all believers are children of the one father Abraham with a shared inheritance (4:13; see also 9:7–8). The images are clearly related but stress different aspects of believers' status.

65. "Abba" does not mean "Daddy."

However, once again—as in 8:13—Paul attaches a responsibility, even a condition: "if, in fact, we suffer with him [lit. co-suffer] so that we may also be glorified with him [lit. co-glorified]" (8:17b). Sharing the glory of God is humanity's original state (1:23) and final goal,[66] but to be co-heirs with Christ in future glory requires co-suffering with Christ now. This is not a statement about suffering as meriting glory but a claim about the nature of full participation in the messianic story. Christ's story is a narrative of suffering before full and final glory, of death before resurrection, of being humbled before being exalted. And that story, Paul says, is now our story.

This sort of narrative pattern can be found in various parts of Scripture, for two fundamental biblical principles are (1) that God exalts the humble; and (2) that God vindicates his suffering, oppressed people.[67] Paul tells the story of Jesus in such terms in the Christ-poem found in Philippians:

> Though he [Christ] was in the form of God, [he] did not regard equality with God as something to be exploited, but emptied himself, taking the form of a slave, being born in human likeness. And being found in human form, he humbled himself and became obedient to the point of death—even death on a cross. Therefore God also highly exalted him and gave him the name that is above every name. (Phil 2:6–9)

These poetic lines are, in turn, reminiscent of Isaiah's fourth suffering servant hymn (Isa 52:13–53:12):

> See, my servant shall prosper; he shall be exalted and lifted up, and shall be very high. Just as there were many who were astonished at him—so marred was his appearance, beyond human semblance, and his form beyond that of mortals—so he shall startle many nations. . . . Out of his anguish he shall see light; he shall find satisfaction through his knowledge. The righteous one, my servant, shall make many righteous, and he shall bear their iniquities. Therefore I will allot him a portion with the great, and he shall divide the spoil with the strong; because he poured out himself to death, and was numbered with the transgressors; yet he bore the sin of many, and made intercession for the transgressors. (Isa 52:13–15a; 53:11b–12)

66. Prior to ch. 8, see 2:7, 10; 3:23; 5:2; see also 9:23.
67. For the exaltation of the humble, see, e.g., Job 22:29; Ps 18:27; Prov 29:23; Matt 23:12; Luke 14:11; 18:14; Jas 4:10. For the vindication of God's people, see, e.g., Deut 32:36; Ps 22; 35; 43:1–5; 54.

As we saw in chapter 6, those who are baptized into Christ are baptized into his story of death and resurrection. Dying to an old way of life (to Sin, to the flesh) and living in the Spirit constitute one dimension of resurrectional cruciformity, which has been highlighted so far in chapter 8.

The other dimension of resurrectional cruciformity, first mentioned in 5:3–4 in anticipation of 8:17, and now to be developed in 8:18–39, is no less challenging, but also no less ultimately life-giving: suffering with and for Christ. This is a life that Paul knew well and expected the faithful in Rome and elsewhere also to experience.[68] His confidence was, and ours should be, in the God who raised and raises the dead (4:17; 2 Cor 1:9).

8:18–39. PRESENT SUFFERING AND FUTURE GLORY

The second half of Rom 8 is among the most moving parts of the Bible, culminating in 8:31–39, "one of the most stunning pieces of rhetorical art in the New Testament."[69] Paul puts the suffering of the faithful into the larger context of the suffering of the entire creation and the hope of future salvation. He portrays the story of the universe as a dramatic sequence:

- human sin
- creation's subjection and decay
- believers' present experience of the Spirit in the midst of suffering
- believers' final glorification and salvation
- the liberation and salvation of all creation

Paul contends that life in the Spirit—life in Christ, life as God's children—is indeed a life of suffering, but also that no suffering can destroy believers' hope of glory or separate them from God's love in Christ.

8:18–27. *The Creation and Believers in Spirit-Filled Solidarity*

Paul begins the second half of the chapter by defining the present as an era of suffering but one that pales in comparison to the coming glory. The apostle seems to have adapted a common Jewish belief that the age of eschatological

---

68. See also, e.g., Rom 12:12; 1 Cor 12:26; 2 Cor 1:3–11; 11:22–12:10; Phil 1:27–30; 3:10–11; Col 1:24; 1 Thess 3:1–9.

69. Luke Timothy Johnson, *Reading Romans: A Literary and Theological Commentary* (Macon, GA: Smyth & Helwys, 2001 [orig. New York: Crossroad, 1997]), 143.

salvation would be preceded by a great time of suffering, or messianic woes. For Paul, such suffering is a constitutive part of life in Christ because Christ suffered prior to his glorification (8:17). Life in the Spirit, who is the Spirit of Christ (8:9), therefore means not the *absence* but the necessary *presence* of suffering before participating in eschatological glory. Paradoxically, however, even the present suffering, because it involves the presence of God the Holy Spirit and takes the shape of the crucified Messiah Jesus, is a form of glory—*cruciform* glory.

Paul characterizes the present age of suffering as creation's "labor pains" (8:22; cf. Mark 13:8), during which creation (8:19–22), the faithful (8:23–25), and even the Spirit of God (8:26–27) groan, even as suffering shapes believers into the image of Christ (8:28–30). Apocalyptic writers often used the imagery of labor pains—intense suffering just before intense joy—to indicate the run-up to the prophetically promised new creation (e.g., Isa 65:17–22). Paul is such a writer, but his views are shaped by his belief in a crucified and resurrected Messiah.[70]

8:18. Suffering in Relation to Glory

In 2 Corinthians, Paul—who suffered much—had already proclaimed that "this slight momentary affliction is preparing us for an eternal weight of glory beyond all measure" (2 Cor 4:17). The same sentiment appears in 8:18 at the start of this extended meditation on suffering. This glory is to be revealed not "in us" (NIV) but "for us" (NJB, NAB) or "to us" (NRSV, RSV, NET, NASB, CEB).

8:19–22. The Suffering of Creation, in Hope

Creation, personified as a sentient creature, or a community of sentient creatures, is first on Paul's list of the suffering. Scholars debate the exact referent of the word "creation" in 8:19–22. Is it limited to the nonhuman creation, or does it include humanity, at least nonbelievers (since believers are discussed specifically in 8:23–25)? Certainly non-Christians suffer, but Paul's focus here seems to be on the material world (see 8:39).[71] The good creation (recall Gen 1) is not something that God plans to discard but to liberate, to save (8:21).

---

70. Thus, in 2 Corinthians, as in Romans, Paul anticipates full and final glory but also rejoices in our present, if incomplete, renewal in Christ.

71. The use of the same word (*ktisis*, "creation" or "creature") in 1:25 suggests to some that Paul here (8:19–22) includes humanity as part of the creation. But *ktisis* in 1:20 and

The groaning (8:22) of creation is a community lament; Paul actually says that the entire creation co-groans and co-agonizes, like women experiencing labor together. This "co-" language in 8:22 fits in well with the other instances of "co-" words in chapter 8 (see the list above). Creation's communal pain is due to its being "subjected to futility," or (in some translations) "frustration" (8:20),[72] and its "bondage to decay" (8:21). There has been much debate about who or what caused the subjection of creation. (It was not creation itself.) It seems best to see 8:20–21 as another allusion to Genesis: an interpretation of the curse of the earth following the first act of disobedience (Gen 3:17b–19). The precise agent of creation's subjection (Adam? Adam and Eve? humanity? God?) is perhaps less important than the result. The nonhuman creation, like humanity itself, stands in need of liberation.

The key here, however, is the note of "hope" (8:20) that characterizes 8:19–21. Creation is not doomed; rather, it will share in the future liberty of God's children. The earth, indeed the entire cosmos, and humanity were created to be partners. Despite whatever present issues exist, they will one day be co-participants in God's glorious future. Paul's poetic image of "eager longing" (8:19) rhymes nicely with the hope depicted at the end of the canon, in Rev 21–22.

Although Paul does not use the word "peace" here, his vision is also one with the prophetic promise of shalom: the restoration of right relations between people and God, among humans, and between humans and the nonhuman creation. This means the end of all forms of violence and the permanent establishment of God's justice. Paul's hope is rooted in the theme of cosmic renewal, including animals and what we normally call nature, in the Scriptures of Israel (e.g., Isa 11:6–9; 55:12; Ezek 34:25–31).[73] It is a solid hope that is guaranteed by God, not the supposed golden age of salvation offered by Rome and other imperial powers, both ancient and modern.

It is nearly impossible to read this passage in Romans without thinking of the ways in which humans have continued to curse the earth by their actions,

---

8:39 seems to refer to the created order apart from humanity, and that is likely the case here too.

72. KJV: "vanity."

73. Particularly lovely and hopeful are the words of Isa 11:6–9: "The wolf shall live with the lamb, the leopard shall lie down with the kid, the calf and the lion and the fatling together, and a little child shall lead them. The cow and the bear shall graze, their young shall lie down together; and the lion shall eat straw like the ox. The nursing child shall play over the hole of the asp, and the weaned child shall put its hand on the adder's den. They will not hurt or destroy on all my holy mountain; for the earth will be full of the knowledge of the LORD as the waters cover the sea."

whether those of first-century Roman exploits or those of contemporary businesses and individuals who pollute the earth and otherwise wreak ecological havoc. Just as the earth suffers as a result of humanity's sinful violence and injustice, so also will it be liberated and will prosper with humanity's redemption, when God's children are identified, marking the time of final salvation (8:19, 21). Thus, the suffering creation is also "breathless with anticipation" (8:19 CEB).

For Paul, then, salvation is cosmic. Contemporary Christians often rightly find in this Pauline passage (as in Col 1:15–20) motivation for creation care, or environmental stewardship, in anticipation of the coming cosmic liberation. If nonviolence and harmony are where the story written by God is going, then Christians have the privilege and responsibility of foreshadowing that conclusion in the chapters of the story in which they participate.

8:23–27. The Suffering of Believers, in Hope

At the same time and along with the cosmos, Christians (according to 8:23–27) also participate in the birth pangs as they await the ultimate fulfillment of their adoption, the "redemption" of their bodies: bodily resurrection (8:23). Like the material world, human bodies are destined not for destruction but for salvation. Thus, believers' salvation is not yet complete but is experienced in hope, sharing the anticipation of the entire creation and requiring patient endurance (8:24–25; cf. 12:12). A form of the word "hope" occurs five times in 8:24–25, picking up on its occurrence in 8:20.

In fact, although Paul can speak of justification and reconciliation in the past tense (5:1–11), the phrase "in hope we were saved" (v. 24) emphasizes the truth that we have not yet arrived. The tension between the "now" and the "not yet" of Christian experience is summarized in the phrase "wait for adoption" (8:23); God's adopted children have not yet received their inheritance.

The faithful do already possess, however, the "first fruits" of their salvation, namely, the Spirit (8:23).[74] The agricultural image of a harvest suggests that we have a real and significant portion of God's gift of presence (glory) and salvation, but not its entirety. The image reinforces Paul's assurance in 5:1–5 that the Spirit is the presence of God's love and the guarantee that hope for future glory is not a pipe dream.

---

74. In a similar vein but with a financial image, Paul speaks of the Spirit as an *arrabōn*, variously translated as "first installment," "down payment," "pledge," "deposit," and "guarantee" (2 Cor 1:22; 5:5), and specifically as the first installment or guarantee "of our inheritance" (Eph 1:14).

Possessing the Spirit, however, is no protection against suffering; in fact, just the opposite is true. Having the Spirit connects us to the suffering creation and, by extension, to other people who suffer (cf. 1 Cor 12:26). For Paul, in fact, even the Spirit participates in this suffering; the Spirit groans while giving aid to, and interceding for, believers, who do not know how, or what (so NIV), to pray in the midst of suffering (8:26).[75] This remarkable assertion becomes all the more noteworthy in the corollary that God (the Father) and the Spirit of God are of one intercessory mind and will (8:27), thus implying not only fatherly concern but even participation in the children's groans. And we will hear in 8:34 that Jesus also intercedes for us. *Communication about the welfare of God's children is characteristic of the communion among the persons of the Trinity.*

8:28–30. Conformity to the Son: The Good Purpose of God

The thought of God's love and will leads to the famous claim of 8:28: "all things work together for good for those who love God," or perhaps "God works all things together for good" (CEB).[76] This means neither that God orders all the details of believers' lives into a rose-garden experience nor that God inflicts suffering. Rather, Paul proclaims that all things contribute to the final, or eschatological, good of glorification (8:30), of conformity to Jesus, the firstborn Son (8:29; cf. 8:17; 2 Cor 3:18; 4:4; Phil 3:10–11). This is the purpose for which Christians as a family of adopted children have been "called" and "predestined" (8:28, 29).

The language in these verses is that of Israel's election, now applied to the family of Jews and gentiles in Christ (cf. Eph 1–2). Paul's point is not to claim that certain individuals, rather than others, have been predestined to salvation, but to identify the scope, purpose, and dependability of God's call in Christ. God is creating a family of Christlike siblings who already partially share in God's righteousness and glory (Gk. *dikaiosynē* and *doxa*).

The past-tense verbs in 8:30 have sometimes been understood as a summary of the chronological sequence of salvation (Latin *ordo salutis*), or "golden chain" from predestination in eternity past to glorification in eternity future

---

75. NRSV's "sighs too deep for words" in 8:26 should be "groans"; the word echoes verbs for groaning in 8:22 and 8:23. Furthermore, one possible translation of the beginning of 8:23 is, "Not only the creation, but we ourselves—even though we have the firstfruits of the Spirit—groan within. . . ."

76. The meaning would be the same for Paul. See also Gen 50:20.

(predestination—call—justification—glorification). This interpretation is called into question, however, by the presence of the final verb, "glorify," in the past tense. Some understand this apparently past glorification as actually a future reality but one so certain that it can be described as a *fait accompli*.

It is better, however, to interpret this reference to glorification in connection with 2 Cor 3:18 and 4:4. In those texts, Paul says that "all of us, with unveiled faces, seeing the glory of the Lord as though reflected in a mirror, are being transformed into the same image from glory to glory; for this comes from the Lord, the Spirit" (2 Cor 3:18 NRSV alt.). Paul identifies Christ as that divine image (2 Cor 4:4). Christ is the second Adam (1 Cor 15:45–49), the perfect image of God (cf. Gen 1:26), the truly human one. In 2 Corinthians, Paul seems to have in mind a present, cruciform glory and Christlikeness that will eventually become an eschatological, fully resurrection-shaped glory.

In Romans, similarly, Paul can speak of glorification in the past tense because in Christ the process of restoring humanity into the image and glory of God—into Christlikeness—has begun. Paul may be alluding to Isa 55:5, where God, speaking through the prophet, says that God "has glorified you" (his people). In that chapter, the prophet correlates this glorification with covenant renewal, shalom, and hope.

For Paul, the onset of glory is due to the presence of God's Spirit. As in 2 Corinthians, present glory takes the form of power in weakness, life in death, glory in suffering; but it is nonetheless glory, nonetheless participation in the life and power of God in Christ by the Spirit. In chapter 6, we learned that the baptized experience resurrection *in* the body before they experience resurrection *of* the body. So too here in chapter 8, Paul says that conformity to Christ's *character* in the present precedes conformity to Christ's *body* in the future.[77] Conformity to Christ is both moral (present) and physical (future). Christoformity—to use the term of Scot McKnight and others—is fully realized only in the future. The final outcome of conformity to Christ is eschatological co-resurrection, co-glorification, and eternal presence with Christ.[78]

This goal of Christoformity, or co-formity (Gk. *symmorphous*) to "the image of his Son" (8:29), thus requires, as Paul has already explicitly said, co-suffering (*sympaschomen*, 8:17). This reality raises the question of theodicy. Does the necessity of suffering mean God and Christ somehow seek believers' harm?

---

77. On glory/glorification, see also, e.g., 1 Cor 15:35–57; 2 Cor 3:7–4:18; Phil 3:17–21; Col 1:24–29; 1 Thess 2:11–12.

78. See also Rom 6:8; 8:17; 2 Cor 4:14; Phil 1:23; 3:20–21; 1 Thess 4:17.

8:31–39. Deus Pro Nobis: *The Love and Certain Victory of God in Christ*

Paul's answer to that question appears in 8:31–39, which is the *peroratio* (rhetorical climax) of the chapter and of the first half of Romans: No! God is not against us but absolutely for us; in Latin, *pro nobis*. No matter what comes, God's love, Christ's love, is certain.

This passage is one of the most beautiful and eloquent texts in the Pauline letters. It is reminiscent of Isa 50, the third servant-poem in that book:

> I know that I shall not be put to shame; he who vindicates me is near. Who will contend with me? Let us stand up together. Who are my adversaries? Let them confront me. It is the LORD God who helps me; who will declare me guilty? (Isa 50:7b–9a).

8:31–36. *Questions about Suffering*

Paul formulates his answer to the fundamental question about suffering with such intensity and passion that only a flurry of emotionally charged rhetorical questions, borrowed from the courtroom, will suffice (8:31–35). It is possible that there are declarative sentences in the second half of 8:33 and 8:34, which refer to God as the one who justifies and Christ as the one who died, was raised, and now intercedes for us. But these sentences are also more likely rhetorical questions: "Is it *God the justifier* who brings charges . . . or Christ Jesus, *who died for us and prays for us*, who condemns?"

If this approach to the passage is correct, then 8:31–36 consists of eight successive rhetorical questions, the last one supported by a scriptural quotation. These questions are all answered only implicitly, but clearly—until the final answer is given in explicit, declarative form in 8:37–39.

Here are the questions and implicit or explicit answers (with some changes to the NRSV):

QUESTIONS AND RESPONSES IN ROMANS 8:31–39

QUESTION	EXPLICIT RESPONSE/[IMPLICIT RESPONSE]
What then are we to say about these things? (8:31a)	[Tell us, Paul!]
If God is for us, who is against us? (8:31b)	[Certainly not God, and so no one/nothing of any consequence]

QUESTION	EXPLICIT RESPONSE/[IMPLICIT RESPONSE]
He who did not withhold his own Son, but gave him up for all of us, will he not with him also give us everything else? (8:32)	[Of course!]
Who will bring any charge against God's elect? (8:33a)	[Certainly not God or the Son]
Is it God, who justifies? (8:33b)	[Of course not!]
Who is to condemn? (8:34a)	[Again, certainly not God, and so no one/nothing of any consequence]
Is it Christ Jesus, who died, yes, who was raised, who is at the right hand of God, who indeed intercedes for us? (8:34b)	[Of course not!]
Who will separate us from the love of Christ? Will hardship, or distress, or persecution, or famine, or nakedness, or peril, or sword? (8:35, reinforced by 8:36)	No, in all these things we are more than conquerors through him who loved us. . . . (8:37–39)

"These things" (or "this" in some translations) in 8:31 refers back to the experiences of co-suffering and groaning that the faithful in general face, ahead to the seven kinds of hardships Paul has especially experienced (8:35b–36),[79] and still further ahead to the ten general powers in the cosmos that oppose or might oppose humanity and separate them from God's love in Christ (8:38–39a). In 8:36, Paul quotes Ps 44:22 ("Because of you [God!] we are being killed all day long, and accounted as sheep for the slaughter"), but instead of blaming God for his suffering, he accepts it as the norm of apostolic existence. He implies as well that the "we" of Ps 44:22 includes all the faithful as co-sufferers with Paul and, more importantly, sufferers with and for Christ—even if this suffering is not to the point of martyrdom. To be in Christ means, in part, to suffer. But it does not end with suffering (see 8:17–18).

This present suffering does not mean that God stands against us like a sentencing judge, or that God will fail to bring us to glory. The God who did not *withhold* but *gave*, or handed over, his own Son (cf. 8:3; also 3:21–26; John 3:16),[80] the God who justified us (8:33b), will certainly complete the work

79. Moreover, the context suggests that, in some sense, Ps 44:22 is the norm for all believers (cf. 8:17; 2 Tim 3:12). For other lists and descriptions of the apostle's sufferings, see 1 Cor 4:8–13; 2 Cor 1:3–11; 4:7–12; 6:3–10; 11:23–33; 12:10; Phil 4:12.

80. An allusion to Abraham's offering of Isaac, recounted in Gen 22. Paul can also say that Christ gave himself/handed himself over for us (Gal 1:4; 2:20; Eph 5:2, 25; cf. Phil 2:6–8).

of salvation (8:32; "everything else" is literally "all things"; cf. the end of 8:30). This is the nature of grace: it is the expression of God's mercy and faithfulness. Glory will follow suffering: not might or might not, but *will*.

Nor does the present suffering mean that *Christ Jesus* opposes believers, for the love he embodied in his death persists in the present, after his resurrection and exaltation, as he intercedes for us at God's right hand (8:34–35a), thus making intercession a Trinitarian activity (cf. 8:26–27). There is no present (8:1) or future condemnation for those who belong to Christ.

8:37–39. *Nothing Can Separate Us from the Love of God!*

The series of questions in 8:31–36 finally brings Paul to his explicit answer, his thesis: "in all these things we are more than conquerors [Gk. *hypernikōmen*] through him who loved us" (8:37 NRSV, NIV, ESV). The Greek verb *hypernikōmen* is an unusual word, used only here in the New Testament. Other translations include "we conquer overwhelmingly" (NAB), "we come through all these things triumphantly victorious" (NJB), and "we win a sweeping victory" (CEB). It could be translated more colloquially as "we super-conquer" or "we are victorious to the max." This victory is the work of divine love.

The preceding paragraph suggests that the one who "loved us" is Christ (8:35), the past tense referring to his loving death for us (8:34). But 8:39 reminds us that Christ's love was and is God's love too: "the love of God in Christ Jesus our Lord." It is by means of this divine love, displayed in Christ's death for us while we were sinners and enemies (5:6–8), and poured into our hearts through the Holy Spirit (5:5), that we "conquer"—that is, that we are victorious in, through, and over suffering. Romans 8:31–39, then, is thoroughly God-oriented: we know God is with us and for us, even in times of suffering, because God in Christ has so fully and amazingly loved us.

A common Jewish attitude toward suffering was to endure it and, when possible, to resist it and overcome it; the Stoic attitude was to "conquer" (Gk. *nikaō*) it by recognizing its inability to affect the true, inner self. Paul's attitude was that those in Christ "hyper-conquer" (*hypernikōmen*) in the midst of suffering because they know God's love and they possess a sure hope as they suffer with Christ. Therefore, Paul is absolutely convinced that nothing in all creation (8:38–39)—not the vicissitudes of life and death or the uncertainties of present and future, not cosmic or political powers of any sort or in any location—can separate Christians from God's love and purpose in Christ the Lord for his adopted children. A statement of such conviction is credible because the one making it knows its truth from firsthand experience. *Paul is bearing witness in the courtroom of real life.*

These words undoubtedly brought immense comfort and hope to the suffering Christians of the Roman house churches. Some members probably suffered for lack of sufficient food. Others were likely victims of abuse from their masters. Still others may have endured economic reprisals for having abandoned pagan worship at their guilds and confessed Jesus as Lord, or emotional mistreatment from family members or fellow synagogue members for having confessed Jesus as Messiah. And more.

Still today, of course, Christians suffer like their Roman siblings in the faith and like all human beings, sometimes for reasons that relate directly to their allegiance to Jesus and sometimes just because they co-groan with the rest of humanity and all creation. No matter what or why we suffer, the apostle invites us to share the confidence and hope in the face of suffering and death that he offered—or rather that God provided—to the members of the first-century Roman house churches.

REFLECTIONS AND QUESTIONS FOR 8:1–39

Spiritual, Pastoral, and Theological Reflections

1. Paul's **Trinitarian theology and spirituality** in Rom 8 are remarkably rich and robust for someone who is often described as not having a fully developed Trinitarianism. We see in this chapter much about the nature of the relationships among the persons of the Trinity, their distinctive and shared roles in the triune act of salvation, and the nature of our relationship with the three persons of this triune God.

2. It is tempting to question, or even reject, **Paul's conditional terms**: *if* we put to death the deeds of the body (8:13) and *if* we suffer with Christ (8:17). This sounds like grace with strings attached. And in a sense, that is exactly what it is. Life in Christ, though full of joy, can never be separated from the crucified Messiah, for the resurrected Lord himself always remains the crucified one. To be in Christ is to be absorbed into a story not of our own making, a story whose plot always includes the cross.

3. Many, if not most, Christians have an understanding of **life in the Spirit** that has little or nothing to do with **the cross**. Perhaps, if pressed, they might agree that life in the Spirit includes dying to Sin, but co-suffering with Christ and with the creation? It sounds like a category mistake, a case of spiritually mixing apples and oranges. But the connection between life in the Spirit and cruciformity—*resurrectional* cruciformity—is a clear teaching of this passage.

4. **Adoption is perhaps the perfect image of grace**: an unconditional, transfor-

mative reality with present benefits in the form of new, intimate relationships with new corollary loyalties and obligations, as well as a future inheritance previously unimagined and unattainable.

5. It is no accident that Paul **interchanges "sons" and "children"** when referring to adoption into God's family. In a male-dominated society, the biological fathering and the adopting of male children will naturally be more highly valued than the fathering or adopting of female children. In a society in which the elites oppress the non-elites and the powerful own the powerless, it is the elites and powerful who receive honor. But God's grace in Christ breaks down these sorts of structures, whether in ancient Rome or in contemporary cultures where systems of oppression, caste, slavery, and racism still exist. Communities of Spirit-filled people in Christ who have the one true God as their Father are, or should be, signs of hope that there is another way of being human and of structuring relationships among people.

6. **Hope is itself cruciform**, a participation in the sufferings of Christ, of others, and of the creation. Cruciform hope means that the very thing (suffering) that makes us think glory is distant or even unattainable—if not altogether fictitious—is, in fact, the divine hint of its proximity.

7. Worthy of meditation is this passage from **C. S. Lewis**, in *Miracles*: "If we are immortal, and if she [**Nature**] is doomed (as the scientists tell us) to run down and die, we shall miss this half-shy and half-flamboyant creature, this ogress, this hoyden, this incorrigible fairy, this dumb witch. But the theologians tell us that she, like ourselves, is to be redeemed. The 'vanity' to which she was subjected was her disease, not her essence. She will be cured, but cured in character: not tamed (Heaven forbid) nor sterilised. We shall still be able to recognise our old enemy, friend, playfellow and foster-mother, so perfected as to be not less, but more, herself. And that will be a merry meeting."[81]

8. Following the April 2021 conviction of former police officer Derek Chauvin for murdering **George Floyd**, New Testament scholar **Dennis Edwards** penned these comments on **Paul's words about groaning** (Rom 8:22–23):[82] "We African Americans understand this inward groaning—the discomfort of waiting for the full redemption of our physical selves. Like all creation, our bodies await renewal because they have borne pain and loss for far too long." Edwards names reasons for Black and Brown groaning, from the actions of

---

81. This passage is from the conclusion to ch. 9, "A Chapter Not Strictly Necessary," of *Miracles: A Preliminary Study*; the book is available in multiple editions.

82. Dennis R. Edwards, "The Derek Chauvin Verdict Is Good. But I'm Still Groaning," *Christianity Today*, April 21, 2021, https://www.christianitytoday.com/ct/2021/april-web-only/derek-chauvin-george-floyd-good-verdict-still-groaning.html.

police officers and vigilantes to the realities of poorer health and lower life expectancy—and more. He continues:

> When I heard the verdict that Chauvin was found guilty, I wept in relief. But my inward groaning hasn't stopped. The apostle Paul writes that all creation groans, yet we know that some parts are in more agony than others. Of course, our hope is eschatological, which is to say that justice will reach a climactic fulfillment at the end of time when Jesus returns. However, in the meantime, we strive—in the words of an old hymn—for a "foretaste of glory divine."

Edwards concludes by rightly calling on the church to practice justice, challenge unjust systems, and work to reduce suffering in our world, all as a foretaste of that future glorious redemption.

9. Paul's "story of glory" (a term I borrow from Ben Blackwell) runs something like this:

> humans fail to glorify God → God's glory departs → humans lack God's glory → God gives the Spirit → God's glory is present and (cruciform) glory begins → humans glorify God → humans are fully glorified

10. One way the **Spirit intercedes** for us is through the prayers of those in whom that Spirit abides.

11. **Prayer in the context of suffering** is in some sense both the easiest thing and the hardest thing for Christians to practice. It is easy because we are so needy, so fragile, so cognizant of our weakness and our mortality. It is hard for the same reasons. But it is also hard because we often truly do not know how or what to pray. Should we pray for a cure or for permanent deliverance from pain? Should we pray for the strength to endure injustice that we cannot remove, or pray to be removed from the injustice we cannot endure? Paul's perspective does not offer trite advice on what to pray but guarantees us that we do not pray alone. The triune God of love is present in our suffering, the Spirit and the Son interceding, the Father lovingly willing nothing but good and grace.

12. It is also critical to remember, therefore, that **our suffering is never a sign of God's departure** and absence but is rather an occasion of God's presence and participation. This is not a generic assertion about God based on an undefined hope in a hopefully all-loving force in the universe. No, this knowledge comes from our recognition that God our heavenly, adoptive Father has already hyper-loved us through Christ and continues to do so through the Spirit. Such love cannot be conquered, for it is the ultimate form of victory in this life and for all eternity.

Questions for Those Who Read, Teach, and Preach

1. What are some of the advantages and possible disadvantages of a theology and spirituality that require suffering as a prerequisite of glory?
2. Can the following well-known quotation (wrongly attributed to Saint Augustine) help Christians think about hope in the face of the abuse of the creation or other evils? "Hope has two beautiful daughters; their names are Anger and Courage: Anger at the way things are, and Courage to see that they do not remain as they are."
3. How do contemporary Christians understand and perhaps misunderstand salvation—such realities as justification, sanctification, resurrection, redemption, and glorification? How should Paul's corporate and cosmic perspectives on these realities affect our Christian beliefs and practices today?
4. How can the necessity of Christians suffering be understood and communicated without sounding, or becoming, morbid or even sadistic?
5. What understandings and practices of pastoral ministry that embrace resurrectional cruciformity should emerge from a close reading of Rom 8:1–17, and of 8:18–39?
6. If the reading of Rom 5–8 presented in this commentary is correct, is Paul a believer in Christian perfection? Does he allow any room for mistakes, for sin(s)?

For Further Reading

Blackwell, Ben C. *Christosis: Engaging Paul's Soteriology with His Patristic Interpreters*. Grand Rapids: Eerdmans, 2016. (more technical)

Campbell, Constantine R. *Paul and the Hope of Glory: An Exegetical and Theological Study*. Grand Rapids: Zondervan, 2020. (more technical)

Davey, Wesley Thomas. *Suffering as Participation with Christ in the Pauline Corpus*. Lanham, MD: Lexington, 2019. (more technical)

Fee, Gordon D. *God's Empowering Presence: The Holy Spirit in the Letters of Paul*. Grand Rapids: Baker Academic, 2011 (orig. 1995).

Gorman, Michael J. *Cruciformity: Paul's Narrative Spirituality of the Cross*. 20th anniversary ed. Grand Rapids: Eerdmans, 2021 (orig. 2001).

———. *Participating in Christ: Explorations in Paul's Theology and Spirituality*. Grand Rapids: Baker Academic, 2019. (more technical)

———. *Participation: Paul's Vision of Life in Christ*. Cambridge, Eng.: Grove Books, 2018.

————. *Paul, the Spirit, and the People of God*. Grand Rapids: Baker Academic. 2011 (orig. 2001).

Hogan, Laura Reece. *I Live, No Longer I: Paul's Spirituality of Suffering, Transformation, and Joy*. Eugene, OR: Wipf & Stock, 2017.

Horrell, David, Cherryl Hunt, and Christopher Southgate. *Greening Paul: Rereading the Apostle in a Time of Ecological Crisis*. Waco: Baylor University Press, 2010.

Jervis, L. Ann. *At the Heart of the Gospel: Suffering in the Earliest Christian Message*. Grand Rapids: Eerdmans, 2007.

Moo, Jonathan A., and Robert S. White. *Let Creation Rejoice: Biblical Hope and Ecological Crisis*. Downers Grove, IL: InterVarsity, 2014.

Oakes, Peter. *Reading Romans in Pompeii: Paul's Letter at Ground Level*. Minneapolis: Fortress, 2009.

Snyder, Howard A., with Joel Scandrett. *Salvation Means Creation Healed: The Ecology of Sin and Grace*. Eugene, OR: Cascade, 2011.

Wright, N. T. *Surprised by Hope*. New York: HarperCollins, 2008.

Wu, Siu Fung. *Suffering in Romans*. Eugene, OR: Wipf & Stock, 2015.

————, ed. *Suffering in Paul: Perspectives and Implications*. Eugene, OR: Wipf & Stock, 2019.

SUMMARY OF ROMANS 5–8

- Chapters 5–8 spell out the multidimensional meaning of justification with an overview and then three sets of antithetical narratives.
- Justification includes reconciliation with God in the present, together with certain hope of salvation (acquittal and glory) in the future, based on the death of Christ in the past, and all known through the gift of the Spirit.
- Adam's one act of disobedience inaugurated the reign of Sin and Death, while Christ's one act of obedience on the cross inaugurated the reign of Grace and believers' participation in it (first antithesis).
- In baptism, believers have died to Sin and been raised to new life with Christ, liberated from the old self for service ("slavery") to God rather than to Sin, the end of which is future resurrection and eternal life (second antithesis).
- The justified are no longer indwelt by Sin and captive to the flesh but experience a mutual indwelling of Christ and the Spirit

(in Christ and the Spirit, Christ and the Spirit within) so that they may live in covenant relationship with God as adopted children (third antithesis).

- This Spirit-filled, resurrection-infused life has a cruciform shape in two main senses, dying to the flesh and suffering, and it culminates in glory: the bodily resurrection, completion of the process of being made into Christ's likeness, and sharing the splendor of God with the entire redeemed creation.

9:1–11:36

God's Faithfulness and Mercy and the Future of Israel

The gospel that Paul—often called the apostle to the gentiles—preached was first for Jews and "also" for Greeks, or gentiles (1:16). But Paul found that many of his fellow Jews, not unlike himself at one time, rejected the good news of God's saving work in Jesus the Jewish Messiah. At the same time, many gentiles were coming to faith, often because of the work of Paul and his associates.

This situation caused Paul immense agony; it was perhaps his greatest practical, spiritual, and theological challenge. After all, the Lord "is mindful of his covenant forever, of the word that he commanded, for a thousand generations" (Ps 105:8). Is God a promise-breaker? Has God been unfair? Unfaithful? Unjust? Does the gospel of the righteousness, or justice, of God proclaimed by Paul (1:17) ultimately reveal an *unrighteous* God, an *unjust* God?

These questions, briefly raised and addressed in 3:1–9, are now taken up in detail. Paul proposes more than twenty questions in chapters 9–11. He employs the techniques of midrash (scriptural interpretation) and diatribe (questions and answers). He draws on the bank of Scripture—which he quotes, sometimes with slight alterations, more than thirty times in these chapters—for his answers. Nearly half the citations come from Isaiah. But Paul is not simply quoting the prophets; he is fully in prophetic mode, speaking words of judgment and mercy/salvation.

As in chapters 1–8, then, God's judgment is not God's only, or final, word. Dealing with the past, present, and future of God's salvific activity, Paul asserts that God is faithful to Israel even if most Jews are not now confessing the gospel's central conviction: that the crucified and resurrected Jesus is the Jewish Messiah and universal Lord. The faithful God of Israel, and of all, is the God of mercy. A form of the Greek word for "mercy" occurs eight times in these chapters.[1]

Complicating Paul's situation is the apparent arrogance of at least some of the gentile believers in Rome. This arrogance may have arisen due to the earlier banishment of Jews, including Jewish Christ-followers, from Rome under the emperor Claudius (see the introduction to the commentary, pp. 23–25). It may also have been due to the small number of Jewish believers in the Roman assemblies of Christ-believers.

---

1. 9:15, 16, 18, 23; 11:30, 31 (twice), 32. The similar word-family "pity/compassion" also occurs twice in 9:15 and then in 12:1, where it is generally translated "mercies" or "mercy."

218

Both realities may have been interpreted by gentiles as a sign of divine disapproval and even rejection of the Jews. Paul's sustained theological argument in Romans focuses on God's great mercy (9:14–29; 11:30–32; cf. 12:1; 15:9) and thus God's faithfulness. But his argument has a very pastoral aim: (1) to prevent pride and (2) to engender unity and mutual respect. This purpose is later fleshed out in the specific admonitions to the community of gentile and Jewish believers in 14:1–15:13.

Romans 9–11 is, therefore, at once deeply theological and highly practical. It celebrates the mystery and magnificence of God's mercy. It provides the rationale for gentile gratitude and for gentile-Jewish unity in the Messiah. Moreover, it has ongoing significance for Christians and their understanding of Jews today. It is not, however, a text for the faint of heart; it can be confusing, with more than a few puzzling lines. For that reason, it may be best to begin where Paul ends: "O the depth of the riches and wisdom and knowledge of God! How unsearchable are his judgments and how inscrutable his ways!" (11:33).

9:1–29. JEWISH UNBELIEF, PAULINE ANGUISH, AND DIVINE FAITHFULNESS

Paul's extended discourse that we call chapters 9–11 begins with a passionate statement of his anguish over the unbelief in the gospel, by and large, of his fellow Jews (9:1–5). These words of lament are followed by a narrative defense of God's freedom, faithfulness, and mercy (9:6–29). The God of Rom 9 is the God who calls, and that calling is both unpredictable and irrevocable (11:29).[2]

9:1–5. Paul's Anguish over Jewish Unbelief

Paul's claim to have "great sorrow and unceasing anguish" (9:2), affirmed three times as a solemn oath (9:1), is one of the most emotional and self-revelatory remarks in his letters. In this prophetic, poetic lament, he is essentially willing to be cursed (made *anathema*)[3] and cut off from Christ—to forfeit his own salvation—for the sake of his fellow Jews/his siblings (9:3), who have failed to believe in the Messiah despite all their privileges (9:4–5; cf. 3:1–2).[4]

2. The Greek verb for "call" occurs in 9:7, 12, 24, 25, 26, but in 9:7 it is usually translated as a form of the verb "name," "reckon," or something similar.

3. Paul also uses the word (but not in reference to himself!) in 1 Cor 12:3; 16:22; Gal 1:8–9.

4. The translation of the verb in 9:3 is challenging; it might mean "I could wish" (NRSV, NAB, NIV, and others), "I could pray," or even "I used to pray." If the last of these

Paul's oath is more than simply a cry of anguish (echoing 8:22) and frustration from the depths of his heart—though it is clearly that. But it is also nothing less than an outburst of sacrificial, or cruciform, love (cf. 10:1), for he knows that Christ became a curse for others (Gal 3:13). It is also reminiscent of Moses' plea before God to punish him rather than the Israelites who had committed idolatry and immorality before the golden calf (Exod 32): "'But now, if you will only forgive their sin—but if not, blot me out of the book that you have written'" (Exod 32:32).

The privileges that have not assisted Jews ("Israelites"; 9:4) in coming to faith in the gospel of the Messiah include, ironically, the very realities that Paul's preaching affirms as fulfilled through the past, present, and future action of God in Jesus (9:4–5):

- adoption/sonship (see 8:14–24)
- glory (see 5:2; 8:17–18, 21, 30; 15:6–9)
- covenants (see 11:27)
- giving of the law (see 8:2–4; 10:4; 13:8–10)
- worship (see 1:9; 12:1)
- promises (1:2; 4:13–22; 15:8)
- patriarchs/fathers (see ch. 4; 11:28; 15:8)
- the Messiah according to the flesh (see 1:3–4)

Nevertheless, despite this sad irony, the thought of God's goodness to Israel leads Paul at the end of 9:5 into praise. The translation of these words is difficult and debated. Paul is either blessing God (i.e., God the Father; so NRSV, NAB), as a foretaste of 11:33–36, or he is affirming the deity of the Messiah and blessing Jesus (NET, NIV). Although Paul does not specifically call Jesus "God" elsewhere in the letters of undisputed authorship,[5] it is quite clear that he includes Jesus within the divine identity of Father, Son, and Spirit. And in various places and ways, Paul attributes to Jesus the name of God, declares him to be the ultimate referent of scriptural texts about God, and calls for worship of Jesus, so it is certainly possible that "God" in 9:5 means Jesus.[6]

---

is correct, it would likely mean that what Paul is about to tell us in chs. 9–11 has resolved his former profound concern.

5. But see Tit 2:13; this letter is one of the letters whose authorship is disputed.

6. See, e.g., Rom 10:11–17; 14:9; 1 Cor 8:6; Phil 2:6, 9–11. See also David B. Capes, *The Divine Christ: Paul, the Lord Jesus, and the Scriptures of Israel* (Grand Rapids: Baker Academic, 2018).

However we understand the reference to God here, the main point is that, in his lament, Paul begins chapters 9–11 as he will end them: with a spontaneous outburst of praise.[7]

9:6–29. God's Freedom, Faithfulness, and Mercy

In 9:6–29, lament is replaced with scripturally rooted theology. In these verses, Paul makes the central claim of chapters 9–11: despite appearances to the contrary, God is not unfaithful and unjust, but merciful.

9:6–18. God's Freedom Is Not Divine Failure or Injustice

The question lurking behind the lament of 9:1–5 is *Why?* Paul's initial response is that the failure of belief bemoaned in that lament cannot be the failure of God's performative word (9:6a). This assertion—God is not at fault—is the negative dimension of Paul's central thesis. The notion that God's word has failed is a theological nonstarter. The apostle offers an alternate starting point: "not all Israelites truly belong to Israel" (9:6b).[8]

This bold claim leads Paul into a narrative of God's salvific activity (extending to 9:29) that reveals a pattern: that which looks like capricious and unjust divine action is actually part of a larger plan in which God acts freely, faithfully, and mercifully. This admittedly difficult section of Romans must be read in context as offering precedents for God's surprisingly merciful activity in and through the gospel. If it is read—as it often is—as a theological treatise on predestination rather than as a testimony to God's mercy and faithfulness, then Paul's main concern in chapters 9–11, and perhaps beyond these chapters, will likely be missed.

Paul begins by recognizing a biblical distinction between descendants of the "flesh" and descendants of the "promise" (9:6b–9). This develops the important contention of 2:28–29 that not all physically circumcised people are actually Jews (cf. 9:6b) and places it in the framework of divine election and promise rather than human choice or merit. Paul says Abraham's true offspring, and thus God's real children, are not merely Abraham's physical descendants but "the children of the promise" made to Abraham and Sarah and fulfilled in the birth of Isaac (rather than Ishmael, 9:9; cf. Gen 21:8–14; Rom

---

7. See also 1:25 for another example of spontaneous praise in the letter.

8. A word for "truly" does not appear in the Greek text, but it helps capture the basic point.

4:13–25).[9] Ishmael, son of Abraham and Sarah's slave Hagar, was Abraham's firstborn but was the result of human planning rather than divine promise (Gen 16).

Somewhat similarly, according to 9:10–13, the story of Rebekah's love for her second-born twin son Jacob, rather than the firstborn Esau (Gen 25:19–28), demonstrates God's freedom in carrying out his purposes. God loved Jacob (= Israel, from whom the twelve tribes of Israel descended) but not Esau (from whom the people of Edom, rejected by God [Mal 1:3], came). This was due solely to God's call, not anything good or bad done by either of Isaac's sons (9:11–12).

A quotation from Mal 1:1–3 (referring to Israel and Edom) in 9:13 lends scriptural weight to Paul's claim: "I have loved Jacob, but I have hated Esau." The mention of hatred in this verse does not mean that God loves certain people and detests others. Paul's point is to emphasize the inexplicable mystery of God's preferring—in the sense of freely, sovereignly calling—Israel to be the people of God. The love-hate language is about a divine decision, not a divine emotion.

These two examples of God's election (Isaac not Ishmael; Jacob not Esau) at the foundation of Israel as a nation are confirmed for Paul as examples of divine freedom and mercy, not divine injustice (Gk. *adikia*; 9:14). Once again, the apostle uses the question-and-answer format in 9:14: Divine injustice? By no means! Impossible! And, once again, Paul calls on Scripture to make his point, offering a word about God's freely given mercy, spoken to Moses after the exodus (9:15–16; cf. Exod 33:19), and a word about God's freedom in extending his glory, spoken to Pharaoh during the exodus itself (9:17). The Lord, as God, is free to show mercy or not to any and all (9:18), but Paul's main point is that God is in fact the mercy-showing God (9:16). This God has been (and is) about the business of unexpected, undeserved mercy that will expand the worship of God "in all the earth" (9:17).

The reference to "all the earth" is clearly a hint about God's ultimate plan in all of these mysterious workings: that not only ethnic Israelites but also gentiles—and thus all people everywhere—will know the glory of God and will, in turn, give glory to God. (A further hint: this requires messengers to go into all the earth; see 10:18.) In 9:18, Paul's conclusion further emphasizes God's

---

9. For Paul, those who are in fact children of Abraham and children of God are those who share Abraham's faith by acknowledging Jesus as God's resurrected Son/Messiah (4:12–25; 8:12–17). This central conviction is assumed here in ch. 9 and reaffirmed in ch. 10. See also Gal 4:21–31.

freedom as he enunciates the principle of divine freedom to have mercy and to harden hearts. This is neither capriciousness nor injustice, because—as we will shortly see—it was through the temporary and partial hardening of Israel's heart (11:7) that salvation was opened to the gentiles (11:11). Paul's theology of mercy is ultimately tied to his theology of mission. *The merciful God is the missional God, and vice versa.*

9:19–29. *Scriptural Witness to God's Mercy toward Gentiles and Jews*

The principle of divine freedom is further affirmed in the scriptural illustration of the potter and the clay (9:20–24, alluding to Isa 29:16; 45:9; cf. Jer 18:1–12, esp. v. 6). Paul places a completely logical question in the mouth of his interlocutor: If God shows mercy to some and hardens the hearts of others, how can God possibly find fault with those who oppose God?—for they are simply doing God's will! (9:19; cf. 3:7).

At first glance, Paul seems to be defending the *capriciousness* of God, but his theological point is, rather, the Godness, or sovereignty, of God and the non-Godness of humans. Moreover, such a conclusion about God's caprice would fail to consider the larger purpose of Paul in chapters 9–11: to show how that which appears to be a divine whim is actually an expression of God's mercy and love to extend salvation *even to those who are recipients of divine judgment*—"objects of wrath" (9:22).

In other words, Paul is not articulating a doctrine of double predestination: the predestination of some individuals to salvation and others to damnation. Rather, he is proclaiming the freedom of God to surprise people with mercy and ultimately to glorify them (9:23; cf. 3:23; 5:2; 8:18, 30). Human beings have no right to challenge this divine prerogative, because the same freedom allows God to have mercy on the undeserving and unrighteous, whether Jews or gentiles (9:24). This is the meaning of grace for Paul.[10]

The mention of both Jews and gentiles in 9:24 is an echo of the thematic statement of 1:16–17 that has surfaced repeatedly in the letter. The pattern of God's merciful election is now occurring in the salvation of both gentiles (9:25–26) and Jews (9:27–29). Again, Paul appeals to Scripture. In 9:25–26, he applies Hosea's prophetic word spoken about disobedient *Israelites* (Hos 1:10b; 2:23) to *gentiles* contemporary with Paul. More hopeful words than these are

---

10. Because God as God is free, faithful, and merciful, God can and does justify the ungodly, even if Israel's wisdom tradition condemned such a practice on the part of humans (Prov 17:15; 24:24–25).

difficult to find in Scripture: "Those who were not my people I will call 'my people,' and her who was not beloved I will call 'beloved'" (9:25). Over the centuries, this text has caused many people to feel included in God's grace.

In 9:27–29, Paul applies texts from Isaiah to his fellow Jews. The salvation of "the children of Israel" is not always in large numbers—another surprising feature of God's mercy. In fact, Isaiah saw divine mercy in the saving of a small number, a "remnant" (9:27–28, citing Isa 10:20–23, which contains an echo of Hos 1:10a). Otherwise, Israel would have been destroyed like Sodom and Gomorrah (9:29, citing Isa 1:9). This past divine action becomes the paradigm for Paul's own time in his analysis of the Jewish response to the gospel (also a "remnant"; 11:1–5), for some Jews have in fact believed the gospel. But even this remnant theology will not be Paul's final word about Israel's salvation (see 11:26).

Summary of 9:6–29

In 9:6–29, then, Paul has affirmed God's free exercise of unexpected and undeserved mercy in the past and thus God's faithfulness to Israel and to his promises. This pattern of surprising mercy, according to Paul's reading of Israel's prophets, goes beyond the bounds of ethnic Israel to include even gentiles, while it simultaneously saves a remnant of Israel. This practice of gentile inclusion, paired with the formation of a Jewish remnant, is for Paul the paradigm of God's present activity through the proclamation of the gospel by Paul and others, as we will see in what follows.

9:30–10:21. REAFFIRMATION OF SALVATION FOR ALL THROUGH THE GOSPEL

In 9:6–29, Paul has narrated and defended the pattern of God's startling mercy for gentiles as well as Jews. He will now connect that pattern with its specific present manifestation in two events: (1) the arrival of the Messiah and (2) the spread of the gospel about the Messiah throughout the empire. Paul begins by noting the contrasting responses to the Messiah among gentiles and among Jews (9:30–33), and he restates his desire (now a prayer) for the salvation of his fellow Jews because the law they zealously embrace points to the Messiah (10:1–4). He then reaffirms the availability of the gospel to Jews and gentiles alike (10:5–13), and thus the necessity of its proclamation because God's merciful mission to both Jews and gentiles continues (10:14–21).

9:30–10:4. The Current Situation and Paul's Prayer

Romans 9:30–10:4 begins with a familiar question: "What then are we to say?" (cf. 3:5; 4:1; 6:1; 7:7; 8:31; 9:14). This question always introduces a significant theological discussion that builds on an immediately preceding theological discussion. In this instance, Paul applies the theological observations of 9:6–29 to his own context of significant gentile belief in the gospel and significant Jewish disbelief.

9:30–33. The Gentile versus the Jewish Situation

Paul answers the question that begins this discussion by noting that gentiles who were not even looking for righteousness have attained righteousness through, or on the basis of (Gk. *ek*), faith or faithfulness (9:30; cf. 10:20). This could refer to the human response of faith to the gospel, to the Messiah's faithfulness (if the translation of 3:22 and 3:26 offered in the commentary is correct), or to both. "Israel," on the other hand, although it pursued "the law of righteousness" (what Paul literally says), or "righteousness that is based on the law" (NRSV), did not attain, or fulfill, the "law" (9:31). Paul may be engaging in a play on words here, but his point is clear: although Israel had the law (unlike the gentiles), they failed to gain righteousness because they wrongly thought it was achieved by "works" rather than by faith/faithfulness (9:32).

Paul has already dismissed the idea that works of any kind—however we understand what he means by works—bring about righteousness or justification (3:19–20; 3:27–31; 4:1–15). He succinctly repeats that claim in 9:32, but what follows is both new and highly significant. Paul is not disparaging the law per se but identifying misguided zealous attempts to fulfill it apart from the Messiah, as he will say shortly, in 10:2–4 (cf. 8:3–4). God's chosen people have by and large missed the boat, so to speak, or in Paul's biblical metaphor (9:32b), "stumbled over the stumbling stone" *(petran skandalou)*—the Messiah (9:33), a stone that causes people to stumble. Paul even says the stone offends people (CEB), but those who believe in it/him will not be put to shame (9:33; cf. 10:11).

This stone has sometimes been mistakenly interpreted as the law or the gospel (the latter perhaps because of the reference to shame; recall 1:16–17). With many other early Christians, however, Paul associates Christ with this stone spoken of by Isaiah, whose words are cited in 9:33.[11] For Paul, at least,

---

11. Isa 28:16; cf. 8:14, and see also Matt 21:42; Acts 4:11; 1 Pet 2:6, 8. The words Paul

the cause of stumbling or scandal among his fellow Jews was specifically the death of the alleged Messiah by crucifixion (1 Cor 1:23; Gal 5:11). A crucified messiah was, for non-Jesus-following Jews, simply an oxymoron.

10:1–4. Paul's Prayer and the Messiah as the "End" of the Law

In 10:1–4, Paul reveals that his earlier lament is also a prayer. Though (most of) his fellow Jews have stumbled over the crucified Messiah, Paul repeats his deep, heartfelt desire for their salvation (10:1), echoing 9:1–5. (In 11:11, we learn that the stumbling is not "so as to fall.") He acts as a court witness, claiming—no doubt echoing his present perspective on his own past life of persecution (cf. Gal 1:13–14; Phil 3:6)—that they have a misguided "zeal" by which they attempt to establish right relations with God on their own terms rather than on God's (10:2–3).[12]

The means to God's righteousness is not the law, for the law points beyond itself to the Messiah, who is the "end" *(Gk. telos)* of the law (10:4; cf. Gal 3:24). The sense of "end" here has been hotly debated; does Paul mean "termination," "goal," or both? The context suggests that Paul means both but with an emphasis on goal. Paul means that the Messiah is the focal point of Scripture, the goal of the salvation history to which Scripture bears witness, and thus the God-given means of righteousness.

The arrival of the Messiah, then, means that the law ceases to be the means of righteousness, not because it is bad (see 7:7–25) or abrogated but because only the divine gift of the Messiah and his Spirit makes the fulfillment of the law, and thus righteousness, possible (see 8:3–4; 13:6–8). Righteousness is now available to "everyone who believes" (10:4)—that is, both Jews and gentiles, but also both slave and free, male and female, and so on.

10:5–21. The Ongoing Universality of the Gospel

To clarify what "righteousness for everyone who believes" means, in 10:5–21 Paul summarizes for the Roman faithful the content and availability of God's

---

attributes to Isaiah differ from the standard text of the LXX, which reads, "therefore thus says the Lord, See, I will lay for the foundations of Sion a precious, choice stone, a highly valued cornerstone for its foundations, and the one who believes in him will not be put to shame" (NETS).

12. The Greek of 10:2 is accurately conveyed by the NIV's description of the zeal as "not based on knowledge," rather than, e.g., NAB's "not discerning" or NRSV's "not enlightened."

gospel: salvation for all, gentiles and Jews alike, who believe that God raised the crucified Messiah Jesus and confess that he is Lord.

10:5–13. Salvation for All Who Confess Jesus as Lord

With a string of Scripture quotations, in 10:5–13 Paul provides a brief overview of key aspects of the gospel. The theological question implicitly behind this passage asks, What is the source of life with God—of justification and salvation? Moses had said that the law is the answer to that question (10:5, citing Lev 18:5), but in Deut 30, Moses tells the people they need covenant renewal through heart-circumcision. Paul has already implied that this heart-circumcision, establishing a new, or renewed, covenant, has come to pass through the Messiah Jesus (2:25–29). The law itself could not accomplish what it required of God's people (8:3–4); it could not "make alive" (Gal 3:21). Thus, life—justification and salvation—come through Jesus the resurrected Lord to all who confess him and call upon him.

The somewhat confusing scriptural citations in 10:5–8 are meant principally to affirm the proximity of this divine word of salvation and its character as God's means of covenant renewal, and thus righteousness, through Christ. As in Deut 30, which supplies the quotations and key words "mouth" and "heart" in 10:7–10 (esp. Deut 30:11–14), this invitation to covenant renewal and life with God is not something to be searched for hither and yon. It is present here and now, in the apostolic proclamation, not of the law but of the Messiah Jesus.

In 10:9–10, Paul recounts the essential gospel message and the need for both inner trust and public confession: "Jesus is Lord (Gk. *kyrios*)," the basic Pauline statement of faith (cf. 1 Cor 12:3; 2 Cor 4:5; Phil 2:11). Those who respond in faith, affirming with heart and mouth Jesus' lordship by virtue of God's resurrection of him from the dead, receive justification/righteousness. They are reconciled to God, made part of God's covenant people, and delivered from Sin and *adikia* (unrighteousness/injustice) to become God's just/righteous people. They also receive, or will receive, salvation, probably meaning future salvation.[13] A scriptural quotation from Isaiah already cited in

13. Many translations of 10:10 state that a believer "is justified" and "is saved." The Greek is not so clear; the CEB conveys the original sense: "Trusting with the heart leads to righteousness, and confessing with the mouth leads to salvation." The references to salvation in 10:9, 10, 13 could mean that those who confess Jesus will be immediately "saved." But they more likely refer to salvation at the parousia (second coming) and day of judgment, since salvation is, for Paul, primarily a future reality. In 10:13, the verb is

9:33 offers assurance (10:11; Isa 28:16). Although it is unwise to split hairs about the sequence of human and divine actions named in 10:10 (belief, confession, justification, salvation), it is important to note Paul's emphasis on both internal conviction and public affirmation.

Once again, Paul emphasizes that this good news is for all people, without distinction (cf. 3:22), for the Lord is Lord of all and "generous" (lit. "rich"—i.e., rich in mercy) to all who call on him (10:12). Because the covenant renewal of Deut 30 was to take place after exile (Deut 30:1–5), Paul apparently reads that passage in light of prophetic texts that speak of the postexilic salvation of the nations (gentiles) as well as Israel. The explicit theological grounding of the universal availability of the gospel, however, is the oneness of the Lord (10:12)—that is, Jesus.[14]

As the confession of faith "Jesus is Lord" in 10:9 makes clear, in 10:13 Paul again applies the word *kyrios* (lord), the Greek Bible's title for YHWH, to Jesus (citing Joel 2:32). The quotation of Joel is, for Paul, both a promise and an exhortation. Salvation is offered to all those, but only to those, who "call on" the Lord—on Jesus.[15] Paul knows no other way of salvation—of participation in the covenant and in the life of God—for Jews or for gentiles.

10:14–21. Participation in the Mission of God

If the gospel is for all, then it must be disbursed, even if it is "near" (10:6–8). In 10:14–15a, Paul poses a series of four rhetorical questions, each one carefully linked with a word to the previous question, to make this point with clear logic and subtle passion. God's offer of the gospel to all comes through human agents, such as Paul, but also others who are sent (10:15–16).

The four rhetorical questions in 10:14–15a and the partial quotation of Isa 52:7 in 10:15b—"How beautiful are the feet of those who bring good news!"—forcefully affirm Paul's personal commitment to the spread of the message about the Messiah (10:17), as well as the necessity of other evangelists. The word indeed must go out, and has gone out (10:17–18). But like Isaiah, the preachers of good news may encounter disbelief and disobedience.

It is significant that Paul speaks about the proper response to Christ and the gospel as both believing (10:14, 16–17) and obeying (10:16), for the two words

---

specifically "will be saved"—but the precise timing of the future (right after confessing Jesus? at the parousia?) is not clear. The shame referred to in 10:11 is probably primarily eschatological shame, as in 5:5, where the NRSV translates the same verb as "disappoint."

14. Cf. 3:29–30, where a similar affirmation about God (the Father) and justification is made.

15. See also Acts 2:21; 9:14, 21; 22:16; 1 Cor 1:2.

are essentially synonymous for Paul (see also 11:20, 31). His missional goal was to bring about "the obedience of faith" (1:5; 16:26), a phrase that likely echoes his understanding of Jesus' death as both his obedience (5:19) and his faith/faithfulness (3:22, 26).

In 10:16–21, Paul again wrestles with Jewish unbelief and gentile belief, citing Scripture to interpret the situation to both his audience and himself. In spite of people's disbelief/disobedience, Paul sees himself as part of the team of messengers embodying Isaiah's text about announcing good news of the Messiah to the ends of the earth (10:18; cf. Isa 52:7–10). The problem is not the message; "the word of Christ"—the gospel of God's Son (1:1–6)—is in fact the means by which people come to faith (10:17). The word of God has not failed (9:6a), for the gospel is the "power of God for salvation to everyone who has faith, to the Jew first and also to the Greek" (1:16b). But, of course, not everyone responds positively to this good news.

With the message having gone out, Paul wonders aloud whether perhaps Israel has not heard it, but they indeed have (10:18). He then wonders whether they have not understood it (10:19b) but does not explicitly respond. The answer, however, seems to be that, yes, they have understood, but they persist in disbelief and disobedience (see 10:21). Nevertheless, Paul finds in Scripture—specifically in the words of Moses (Deut 32:21) and Isaiah (Isa 65:1) warrant for the belief that God is making Israel jealous by finding (i.e., saving) those not looking for God (10:19b–20; cf. 9:25–26, 30). Paul's quotation of Isaiah in 10:20 ("I have been found by those who did not seek me; I have shown myself to those who did not ask for me") demonstrates his belief in *God's habit of demonstrating undeserved mercy in unexpected ways.*

The prophet's words in Isa 65:1 originally referred to a remnant in Israel, but Paul interprets them as a reference to the gentiles. This interpretive move offers Paul's audience then and now a profound characterization of the nature of Israel's God as the one who seeks nonseekers (like Paul himself!) and self-reveals to the spiritually apathetic. At the same time, Isaiah bears witness to Paul and his audience that God also extends open arms to Israel, ready to welcome back the "disobedient and contrary" covenant people (10:21, quoting from the very next verse in Isa 65, 65:2; cf. 9:31–33). God's mercy for some does not exclude mercy for others.

Summary of 9:30–10:21

Paul ends 9:30–10:21 where he had begun, reflecting on the troublesome phenomenon of gentile belief and Jewish unbelief, but also affirming the fidelity and mercy of God to Israel. The point of this section as a whole, then, is that justification and salvation remain available to all, Jew and gentile alike, who confess Jesus as the (crucified Messiah and) resurrected Lord. The gospel has gone out, and though many Jews have not yet obeyed it, God stands ready to take back his chosen but disobedient people. A sense of anticipation carries us to the doorstep of chapter 11.

11:1–36. The Mystery of Mercy

Paul has now, on several occasions in chapters 9–10, offered scriptural proof for the availability of God's grace and gospel for both Jews and gentiles, while seeking also to defend the freedom of God to offer that mercy in ways we humans may not understand. The situation on the ground is, for Paul, disturbing, with lots of belief to be found among gentiles, but mostly unbelief among his own people. But Paul does not give up hope, because he knows God will never give up. Although Paul does not quote Ps 130, he does share its sentiment: "O Israel, hope in the LORD! For with the LORD there is steadfast love, and with him is great power to redeem. It is he who will redeem Israel from all its iniquities" (Ps 130:7–8).

Moving toward his stirring doxological conclusion (11:33–36), in chapter 11 Paul firmly dismisses any thought of God's unfaithfulness or of God's rejecting Israel (11:1a). He first reaffirms the existence of a remnant that *does* believe the gospel (11:1–10) and concludes by announcing the salvation of "all Israel" (11:25–32). Between these pronouncements, he describes the role of gentile belief as, in part, a tool to make Israel jealous (11:11–16), and he uses the famous image of the olive tree (11:17–24) for three main reasons:

- to discourage gentile believers from pride;
- to urge them to faithfulness and kindness; and
- to remind them that nonbelieving Jews can still come to faith.

11:1–24. The Remnant and the Olive Tree

11:1–10. God's Rejection of Israel Denied: The Remnant

"Has God rejected his people?" asks Paul rhetorically at the start of this chapter. With another resounding "Of course not!" (11:1a NAB) and a firm declaration (11:2a), Paul answers the burning question of whether *Israel's* rejection of the gospel means *God's* rejection of Israel. Returning to the historical pattern of a "remnant" (11:5; cf. 9:27–29), Paul offers himself (11:1b)—and other Jewish

Christ-believers, implicitly—as tangible proof that once again, as in the time of Elijah (11:2b–4; see 1 Kings 19), God has preserved a remnant of faithful, obedient people, "chosen by grace" (11:5).

The situation was bleak in Elijah's day: murdered prophets, destroyed altars, and (so it seemed) no faithful Israelites (11:3). But no, there were actually seven thousand loyalists to YHWH (11:4). The situation may have seemed similarly grim to Paul (and others?), but now there is a parallel group of messianic loyalists (11:5). In both cases, Paul stresses, the presence of a faithful group is the result of God's grace, not human works (11:6).

How should we characterize the larger situation of Israel—the nonremnant? Unsurprisingly, Paul again appeals to Scripture, both alluding to and citing texts that claim divine involvement in Israel's hardened heart (11:7) and blind eyes (11:8, 10). They are spiritually "sluggish" and hard of (spiritual) hearing because God has seen fit to treat his own people in this way—for the moment. It must be stressed, however, that this situation is not the final word. Sometimes, in God's mysterious working, only a remnant, not the entire people (11:7), perceives what God is up to; the rest trip over a "stumbling block" (*skandalon* in 11:9, citing Ps 69:22 LXX).

That stumbling block is the Messiah Jesus (cf. 9:33), because, as we have already seen, he is a *crucified* Messiah: "we proclaim Christ crucified, a stumbling block to Jews and foolishness to Gentiles" (1 Cor 1:23). Yet there *is* a remnant, and there *is* hope for even more—many more.

11:11–16. The Gentiles and Israel in the Divine Economy

The current situation does indeed seem bleak, however, which prompts another rhetorical question and strong negation: "Have they stumbled so as to fall? By no means!" (11:11). The good news in all of this is that Israel's unbelief is neither a fatal fall nor a disaster without purpose in the divine economy. The metaphor of stumbling, rather than falling, suggests that this situation of unbelief/disobedience is only partial and temporary, as Paul will soon declare explicitly. Israel's stumbling (11:11a) over the Messiah (9:32–33; 11:9) has resulted in salvation for gentiles (11:11b), making Israel "jealous." (Of course, not every Jew would have shared Paul's perspective.)

If Israel's stumbling and "defeat" enriched the gentiles, Paul avers, Israel's "full inclusion" (NRSV, NIV, ESV), "full restoration" (NET), or "full number" (NAB)[16]—that is, their eventual salvation (11:26)—will bring even more

---

16. The Greek is *plērōma*, "fullness," as of the gentiles in 11:25.

blessings (11:12, 15). In the meantime, Paul hopes, through his ministry to the gentiles (11:13–16), to continue making Israel "jealous" and thus to bring "some" to faith and salvation (11:14). Already the gospel, in the context of Israel's unbelief, has brought about reconciliation in the world, so their belief will mean a resurrection from the dead (11:15)—like the dead bones of Ezek 37, but inclusive of both Israel and those outside Israel.

In 11:13, Paul addresses his gentile audience specifically and directly. He speaks to them as a body, using you-singular pronouns and verbs through 11:24. (He switches to the plural in 11:25.) *This should not be taken as an indication that the letter as a whole is aimed only at gentiles.* Rather, at this point in his argument, Paul is explaining to non-Jews what Jewish disbelief means—and does not mean.

The existence of a believing remnant within Israel, imaged in 11:16 as holy "dough" related to a large "batch" (see Num 15:17–21) and as a holy "root" related to multiple "branches," is a sign of the holiness of the entire batch and all the branches. That is, God's holy, set-apart people are still God's holy, set-apart people, and they always will be. God has not rejected them; the remnant is like a firstfruits offering (11:16), with more to come. So, what does the future hold? The reference to a "root" and "branches" leads Paul to begin answering this question with the well-known analogy of the natural and grafted branches of the olive tree and its root (11:17–24).

11:17–24. The Olive Tree and the Kindness of God

Once again, Paul is indebted to the prophets and psalmists for his theology and language. They often describe God's people as God's tree, vine, or vineyard.[17] Jeremiah says God called the people an olive tree (Jer 11:16; cf. Hos 14:6). As we just observed, it is important to note that Paul addresses his analogy, or allegory, of the olive tree directly to the gentiles (11:13; i.e., gentile believers as a body), using second-person-singular language through 11:24 and then second-person-plural language through 11:31. Paul is offering his fellow gentile participants in the messiah a word of instruction and warning.

In his use of this traditional image, Paul understands the olive tree not as ethnic Israel but more broadly as God's covenant people rooted in Israel. He says (11:17) that some natural branches of God's olive tree were broken off (= unbelieving Jews) and replaced by a wild olive shoot grafted on (= the contin-

---

17. For example, Isa 4:2; 5:1–7; 27:2–6; 60:21; 61:3; Jer 2:21; 11:16–17; Ezek 19:10–14; Hos 10:1; Pss 80:8–19; 92:12–14; cf. John 15:1–11.

gent of believing gentiles). The grafted-on branches (gentile believers) should not "boast over" (be arrogant toward) the broken-off branches, for they are supported by the tree's root (11:18).[18] (This root is probably Israel, but perhaps the patriarchs or Abraham.) Accordingly, they are even more liable to pruning than were the natural branches (11:18–21).

Gentile believers, then, must not be proud of their status (11:20 reinforces 11:18) or unmerciful toward the natural branches, not even toward those that have been broken off. For without "awe" at God's mercy,[19] as well as mercy in turn to others, gentile believers may themselves be cut off (11:20–22). The whole situation has nothing to do with the merits of individuals or of ethnicity but only with the kindness of God and the response of faith.

The fact that some original branches were broken off was, in God's providence, to make room for gentiles, but that divine action cannot be the basis of gentile presumption or pride. In fact, the unbelief or faithlessness of Israel is a reminder that God's grace, God's kindness, requires faithfully remaining in that grace: "Note then the kindness and the severity of God: severity toward those who have fallen, but God's kindness toward you, provided you continue in his kindness; otherwise you also will be cut off" (11:22). "Consider yourselves warned," declares Paul. "Don't underestimate the seriousness of this merciful God."

Moreover, Paul continues in 11:23–24, if God can perform the agriculturally abnormal feat of grafting unnatural branches onto a "cultivated olive tree" (11:24), God surely has the power to graft the broken-off natural branches back on again (11:23).[20] The only thing that must happen for God to do just that is for the broken-off branches—the unbelieving Jews—not to "persist in unbelief" (11:23).

Just as the gentiles who have been grafted on to the tree are there only by God's mercy and their faith (11:20, 22)—that is, their faith in the gospel of the Messiah—so also Jews need only God's mercy and that same faith in the gospel of the Messiah to be reconnected to God's covenant people. This is what Paul has already said repeatedly in chapter 10 and throughout the letter. It is imperative, in other words, to note that Paul does not here change the criterion for

18. Paul had already ruled out boasting about salvation in 3:27; 4:2.

19. So NRSV, NAB for Gk. *phobeomai*, rather than NIV's "tremble" or CEB's "be afraid."

20. Various interpreters have questioned some of the horticultural language and practices described in this image, but these questions should not deter us from grasping and engaging the image.

inclusion (i.e., for salvation). That criterion is, negatively, the end of unbelief and, positively, a faith-filled response to the gospel of Christ.

Such words spoken to gentiles seem stern but contextually appropriate. Such words spoken about the chosen people, however, could be interpreted to mean that God has essentially disinherited his own children and thus proven completely faithless. This sort of concern has led some interpreters of Romans to look for a different approach, not only to chapter 11, but also to the letter as a whole. They suggest that Paul must have another way in mind for his fellow Jews to remain in covenant relationship with God. (Hence the "two-ways" interpretation of salvation noted and ruled out in the introduction to the commentary, pp. 47–49.) Such concerns are both anticipated and answered by Paul, which takes us to 11:25–36 and Paul's remarkable conclusion(s) to this part of the letter.

11:25–36. The Logical and Doxological Conclusions

11:25–32. The Mystery of Mercy

Everything Paul has said so far in chapters 9–11 now comes to its logical (for him) conclusion in 11:25–32, but it is a conclusion that has puzzled interpreters for nearly two thousand years. Paul may have thought of this conclusion as a "mystery" (11:25) in the sense of clear revelation, but for his later readers it has been much more confusing than clear. The following paragraphs acknowledge other possible readings of the text but argue for a particular interpretation— with a few loose ends. Whatever Paul's precise conclusion, it was and is meant to lead to the praise of the one all-merciful God (11:33–36). For Paul, of course, the ultimate mystery and the ultimate revelation of mercy is Jesus Christ.

Paul's discourse is directed primarily to the gentile believers ("brothers and sisters"; 11:25), now addressed with the plural rather than the singular "you."[21] The tone of instruction and warning that began in 11:13 continues. The first claim Paul makes is relatively clear. Israel's current unbelief ("hardening") is only *partial* and *temporary* ("part of Israel . . . until . . ."; 11:25b). It will last only until "the full number [Gk. *plērōma*, as in 11:12 of the Jews] of the gentiles has come in" (11:25).

Some interpreters understand this as a fixed number or time period, as is common in apocalyptic thought, while others take it as a general reference to a widespread gentile response to the gospel. It may, however, in parallel

---

21. Paul does not specify gentiles in addressing his audience as "brothers and sisters" in 11:25, but this paragraph (11:25–32) clearly continues the "you-they" distinction of the previous verses.

with 11:12, mean *all* gentiles as opposed to some (cf. 11:15, "the reconciliation of the [gentile] world"); we cannot be sure. But when the gentiles (in one of these senses) have believed, then ("at that time") or, more likely, thus ("in the following way") "all Israel will be saved" (11:26).[22] Their sins will be forgiven, marking God's renewed covenant with them (11:27).

This second main claim—"all Israel will be saved"—is far less clear, eliciting three basic questions: *Who? How? When?* Many different answers to these questions have been suggested. We will start in the middle.

How? The basic *how* question seems self-evident: by abandoning unbelief and disobedience, and by believing and obeying the gospel. Both the immediate context (11:23) and the larger context (e.g., 10:5–17, not to mention the letter as a whole) require this answer, however much it might offend the modern or postmodern sensibilities of some. In other words, the *how* question must be answered with a firm christological response and not merely a theological one: belief in Christ, not a generic belief in God. For Paul, there is no way to salvation (e.g., via the law) except confession of Jesus as Messiah and Lord, as chapter 10 makes clear.

But part of the question *How?* involves identifying the agent of Israel's salvation through faith: Is it Paul through his preaching, a broader group of evangelists, or perhaps God acting in some as-yet-unknown future way? We shall return to this issue when considering *when*.

Who? As for the *who* question, it is tempting to import the idea of a spiritual Israel comprised of believing Jews and gentiles. In other words, this would mean all Christians will be saved. A few texts in Romans and elsewhere in Paul make this a possibility, for Paul does indeed distinguish between ethnic Israel and a heart-circumcised Israel (2:28–29; 9:6–7; cf. Gal 6:15; Phil 3:3). Once again, however, the whole context and flow of the argument in this part of Romans suggest a different answer.

Throughout chapters 9–11, Paul's burden is for his fellow Jews, ethnic Israel, the large number of broken-off branches. He has already expressed hope, if not confidence, that the fate of the "batch" and the "branches" will be that of the "dough" and the "root" (11:16). That is, Paul has already implied that God's nonrejection of Israel means more than that *some* nonbelieving Jews will change their minds. Otherwise, Paul's argument about a "remnant" of faithful Jews would have been sufficient to demonstrate the fullness of God's fidelity. But for Paul, the remnant proves God's fidelity yet also indicates that the story of that divine faithfulness is not over. It is difficult, therefore, to resist

---

22. For "in the following way" or something similar, see NIV, CEB, NJB, ESV. Some translations simply say "and so all Israel will be saved" (NRSV, RSV, NET).

the conclusion that "all Israel" means "all Jews" rather than "all gentiles and Jews who believe the gospel."[23]

The oft-quoted text "the gifts and the calling of God are irrevocable" (11:29) confirms this interpretation. This is a critical theological affirmation about God's integrity. Practically speaking, if Paul simply meant that Jews are not excluded from the gospel, he would be merely restating the obvious, for there is already a remnant of Jewish believers. But a remnant, however large, hardly seems like a long-term fulfillment of an irrevocable call; it is more a stopgap measure. It does not seem to qualify as undisputable evidence for a fundamental theological axiom about divine promise-keeping.

On the other hand, attempts to interpret the words in 11:29 as Paul's affirmation of the salvation of Jews apart from the Messiah Jesus, or by some other means, pay insufficient attention to the context and argument of chapters 9–11. Rather, Paul affirms that the stance of *all* Jews will one day be reversed from disobedience to obedience, just as gentile believers have received mercy and become obedient (11:30–32). The final statement in 11:25–32, "For God has imprisoned all in disobedience so that he may be merciful to all" (11:32), refers, in context, to all Jews and to all gentiles who believe the gospel.[24]

When? Remaining to be answered is the *when* question. The phrase "will be saved" of 11:26 is linked to two texts from Isaiah (Isa 27:9; 59:20–21) that, together, forecast the forgiveness of Jacob's (Israel's) sins, the removal of its ungodliness (Gk. *asebeia*; cf. 1:18), and the renewal of the covenant when "the Deliverer" comes "out of Zion [Jerusalem]" (11:26–27). Although Paul does not use the phrase "new covenant" here, he does seem to be alluding to texts like Jer 31:31–34 and Ezek 36:26–27. This Deliverer could be YHWH but is more likely YHWH's Messiah; the text refers, then, either to the first or, more likely, second advent (Gk. *parousia*) of the Messiah, Jesus.

The eschatological coming of Jesus the Deliverer will result in the salvation of all Jews through faith, that is, through the acknowledgment of Jesus' lordship. Specifically, Paul likely means that all his contemporary Jews who have so far disbelieved the gospel and thus been "broken off" from the olive tree (i.e., those alive during and after the time of Jesus' death and resurrection) will believe it, joining the ranks of all faithful Jews who preceded the advent of

23. There is still the question of whether that means all Jews of all time, Israel as a whole but not every individual Jew, all Jews of Paul's day, or all Jews alive at the parousia (second coming); see below.

24. If the "full number" of each (gentiles and Jews) means "all" in both instances (11:12, 25), then Paul here affirms that eventually all human beings will believe the gospel and be saved. But that interpretation of this passage as affirming universal salvation cannot be sustained, or denied, with certainty.

Jesus and all gentiles who have believed the gospel.[25] Although the phrase "all Israel" *can* mean Israel as a whole but not every individual, and *might* actually mean that if *plērōma* (fullness) is interpreted narrowly, there is more reason to think that Paul envisages all Jews.

Whatever we make of these challenging questions, the bottom line for Paul is this: God's mercy has been, is, and will be for all (11:30–32). "God has imprisoned all in disobedience so that he may be merciful to all" (11:32). Does this mean Paul is a universalist? Not necessarily. For one thing, the word "all" might be meant to emphasize people as a whole, both Jews and gentiles, rather than every individual. Furthermore, Paul's logic is also guided by passion, and his rhetoric expresses that passion. Is emotion here prevailing over previously articulated theology?

There are, in fact, texts in Paul's letters that clearly anticipate something other than universal salvation (e.g., 1 Cor 1:18; 2 Cor 2:15; 4:3; 2 Thess 1:9). Moreover, Paul himself, in chapter 10, has just made an argument for the church's ongoing work of spreading the gospel, which of course he himself is committed to doing. He has also made it clear, and we have emphasized, that salvation is dependent on confessing Jesus as Lord. For these and other reasons, I find the arguments for Paul as a universalist ultimately unconvincing.

At the same time, if this passage is Paul's final answer, so to speak, to the huge theological question, "Who will be saved?" then Pauline universalism cannot be definitively ruled out. If, however, one concludes that Paul is a universalist and grants that he is also a careful, coherent theologian (which Romans shows him to be), then one must also conclude that Paul's affirmation of universal salvation is accompanied by two other, more certain affirmations: (1) that the church's mission includes worldwide evangelization and (2) that people need to believe and obey the gospel of Jesus' lordship for salvation.

All of that said, it seems that the primary focus of 11:30–32 is both properly theological (i.e., about the nature of God) and pastoral. First, Paul is emphasizing the merciful character of God, who has graciously worked all things together for good (recall 8:28) in order to make salvation available to everyone. He is not primarily concerned about numbers or even about being precise with respect to the meaning of the word "all." Second, Paul's aim is pastoral in light

---

25. Given Paul's definition of unbelief (rejection of the gospel of Jesus as Messiah and Lord), it seems he either has no concern, or at least expresses none, about Jews who lived before the Messiah and "the end of the law" (10:4). It is also possible, however, that Paul means that at the parousia, when the dead are raised, there will be an acknowledgment of Jesus as Messiah and Lord by all Jews. In either case, it is quite possible that Paul believes that an appearance of Jesus, not unlike what Paul himself experienced, is what Jews as a whole will require to acknowledge the crucified Jesus as Messiah and Lord. (I owe this last observation to my late colleague Judy Ryan.)

of the situation in the Roman house churches. He wants all believers to realize their dependence on God's mercy, and to praise God for it—without a hint of pride or judgmentalism.

If we think that these various affirmations and concerns make sense together but also leave us with some remaining questions, face to face with a mystery, we are likely in good company—Paul's.

11:33–36. Concluding with a Doxology

The *logical* conclusion of chapter 11, of chapters 9–11 together, and indeed of the letter to this point found in 11:25–32 yields finally to a *doxological* conclusion in 11:33–36. Paul's confidence in God's mysterious, magnificent mercy engenders in him praise to God that is expressed in some of the most beautiful language of the New Testament: "O the depth of the riches and wisdom and knowledge of God! How unsearchable are his judgments and how inscrutable his ways!" (11:33). Paul employs biblical words, allusions to texts, and explicit scriptural citations (11:34–35 = Isa 40:13; Job 41:3). The Scripture texts are in the form of rhetorical questions, recalling the series of questions in 8:31–39. (Some of Paul's best theologizing takes the form of questions.)

Paul is convinced that all Israel will experience the glory (*doxa*) and justice/righteousness (*dikaiosynē*) that are God's gifts to the chosen people and to the entire world in the Messiah Jesus. Paul therefore shares in this glory, and invites us to do the same, by giving glory to the God of inscrutable, universal riches and mercy: "To him be the glory forever. Amen" (11:36b). This act of praise anticipates the description of gentiles and Jews united in Christ to glorify God that follows in chapters 12–15, culminating in another round of praise in 15:7–13 and again in 16:25–27, the last lines of the letter.

REFLECTIONS AND QUESTIONS FOR 9:1–11:36

Spiritual, Pastoral, and Theological Reflections

1. Many Christians cannot even consider the possibility that God exercises **wrath and judgment** toward humans. Yet it is impossible to describe the God of Scripture without reference to this reality. At the same time, as rabbi Abraham Joshua Heschel said about the biblical prophets (speaking for God), "Anger and mercy are not opposites but correlatives."[26] Heschel rightly says

---

26. Abraham Joshua Heschel, *The Prophets* (New York: HarperCollins, 2001 [orig. 1962]), 364.

that God's anger in the Bible is not about spite but is an act of "righteous indignation."[27] He refers us to the prayer of Habakkuk: "in wrath may you remember mercy" (Hab 3:2). As noted in the commentary proper, for Paul—as for the prophets—judgment is not God's only or final word; that word is *mercy*.

2. Romans 9–11 has prompted centuries of debates about predestination. One view expressed in those debates has been the claim that Rom 9–11 supports the belief that God predestines some people to salvation and others to non-salvation (death, hell, destruction, etc.). But if there is any sense of **double predestination** in Rom 9–11, it is double predestination of Jews and gentiles to mercy.

3. The **image of being "grafted in"** is clearly an image of grace and of indebtedness both to God and to the chosen people of God. But it is also an image of incorporation and participation in a story, in the divine mission to the world that is rooted in Israel, the people created to bring glory to God and to be a light to the nations. Being incorporated into God's people is not a matter of private salvation but a privileged participation in the story of God. It is a call to live into that mission in the community of all who call upon the name of the Lord and seek to have that name lifted up through praise and obedience.

4. Some Christians find the idea of **messianic Jews, Jewish Christians, or Christian Jews** to be self-contradictory. Even if "all Israel will [eventually] be saved," it is clear from Romans and the rest of the New Testament that the gospel is always for all people. The very earliest Christians were messianic Jews, as was Paul, and as were many of Paul's colleagues and some of his "converts."

5. Christianity is **deeply indebted to the Jewish people**. As the document "Nostra Aetate" from the Second Vatican Council of the Roman Catholic Church (section 5) puts it, "The Church . . . cannot forget that she received the revelation of the Old Testament through the people with whom God in His inexpressible mercy concluded the Ancient Covenant. Nor can she forget that she draws sustenance from the root of that well-cultivated olive tree onto which have been grafted the wild shoots, the Gentiles [referring to Rom 11:17–24]. Indeed, the Church believes that by His cross Christ, Our Peace, reconciled Jews and Gentiles, making both one in Himself [referring to Eph 2:14–16]."

6. "**What all Israel means** or what the fullness of the Gentiles will be only God knows along with his only begotten Son, and perhaps a few of his friends" (Origen, *Commentary on Romans*, in *Ancient Christian Commentary on Scripture*, vol. 6, 298).

7. There is simply no place whatsoever for **anti-Semitism or anti-Judaism** in Christianity.

27. Heschel, *Prophets*, 363.

Questions for Those Who Read, Teach, and Preach

1. Are there any gifts (broadly understood) that the Christian church has received but failed to appreciate or to use for the benefit of others?

2. What are some of the ways Christians understand their relationship to Jews? How should Rom 9–11, if the reading in this chapter is correct, influence us in that relationship? How can Christians express love and respect for Jews and the Jewish community, especially in light of the long history of Christian anti-Semitism?

3. In what ways do Christians today demonstrate inappropriate attitudes, such as arrogance or judgmentalism, toward Jews and others who do not accept the Christian gospel?

4. Is it appropriate for Christians to share the Christian gospel with their Jewish friends or other Jewish people? Why or why not?

   a. If yes, how should it be done? What would be an appropriate response to those who find such evangelism disrespectful and offensive?

   b. If no, what would be an appropriate response to those who engage in such evangelism? What should be said to Jews considering becoming followers of Jesus?

5. How should the fundamental theological claims of this chapter, which attest to God's integrity, faithfulness, and mercy, shape Christian thinking and living today?

6. What is the significance for Christian spirituality of understanding the ways of God as mystery?

For Further Reading

Capes, David B. *The Divine Christ: Paul, the Lord Jesus, and the Scriptures of Israel.* Grand Rapids: Baker Academic, 2018.

Dabru Emet [Speak Truth]: A Jewish Statement on Christians and Christianity. National Jewish Scholars Project, Institute for Christian and Jewish Studies, 2000. https://icjs.org/dabru-emet-text/.

Levenson, Jon D. *The Love of God: Divine Gift, Human Gratitude, and Mutual Faithfulness in Judaism.* Princeton: Princeton University Press, 2016.

Nostra Aetate [Declaration on the Relation of the Church to Non-Christian Religions]. http://www.vatican.va/archive/hist_councils/ii_vatican_council/documents/vat-ii_decl_19651028_nostra-aetate_en.html

Rudolph, David, and Joel Willitts, eds. *Introduction to Messianic Judaism: Its Ecclesial Context and Biblical Foundations.* Grand Rapids: Zondervan, 2013.

Soulen, R. Kendall. *The God of Israel and Christian Theology*. Minneapolis: Augsburg
    Fortress, 1995.

Spina, Frank Anthony. *The Faith of the Outsider: Exclusion and Inclusion in the Biblical
    Story*. Grand Rapids: Eerdmans, 2005.

Still, Todd D., ed. *God and Israel: Providence and Purpose in Romans 9–11*. Waco:
    Baylor University Press, 2017. (more technical)

Tucker, J. Brian. *Reading Romans after Supersessionism: The Continuation of Jewish
    Covenantal Identity*. Eugene, OR: Cascade, 2018.

Wilson, Marvin R. *Our Father Abraham: Jewish Roots of the Christian Faith*. 2nd ed.
    Grand Rapids: Eerdmans, 2021.

SUMMARY OF ROMANS 9–11

In these chapters, Paul addresses the problem of his fellow Jews' general unbelief in the gospel. He raises three key questions that all receive "By no means!" as their answer: "Is there injustice on God's part?" (9:14); "Has God rejected his people?" (11:1); and "Have they stumbled so as to fall?" (11:11).

- The situation of Jewish unbelief tears Paul's heart, not due to some sentimentality, but to its apparent challenge to his own gospel and especially to God's fidelity to Israel.
- This widespread unbelief is not due to the failure of God's word, and it is not an example of divine injustice, for God is both free and merciful.
- Israel's lack of faith is due to stumbling over the Messiah in a misguided zeal about the means to righteousness.
- Salvation is available for all those (and only for those) who believe God raised Jesus from the dead and who confess his lordship.
- Israel's unbelief is partial and temporary; a remnant exists, and after a time of the gentiles coming to faith, the remainder of Israel will also come to faith at the parousia, so that "all Israel will be saved."
- In the meantime, gentiles should humbly acknowledge their status as "branches" that have been "grafted in" to God's olive tree, and thus should not boast vis-à-vis the Jews.
- The appropriate response to the mystery of mercy is praise.

12:1–15:13
FAITHFUL LIVING BEFORE THE FAITHFUL GOD:
CRUCIFORM HOLINESS AND HOSPITALITY

Romans 1–11 ends with a declaration of God's mercy and a response of dumbfounded, awe-filled praise before the mystery of that mercy. The word "mercy" summarizes the good news of God's love in Christ, crucified and raised, to bring new life to both Jews and gentiles—to all. The appropriate response to this amazing grace must be more than an attitude of wonder and words of praise. The gospel requires, in light of God's mercy, what Paul calls the "obedience of faith" (1:5; 16:26), or believing allegiance.

Although the character of this believing allegiance has been explained in somewhat general terms in chapters 5–8, it is in 12:1–15:13 that Paul describes in more detail the shape this new life—this Christian *habitus*—should take.[1] Here we have a picture of the community of the new covenant, the covenantally functional (rather than dysfunctional) people who live in Christ as God's children, empowered by the Spirit. The various topics addressed in chapters 12 and 13 relate both to the community's internal life and its external relations, while 14:1–15:13 centers on the very specific need for mutual acceptance in the face of internal factions and judgmentalism.[2]

Those who live together in the Messiah Jesus are being restored to the life of righteousness (Gk. *dikaiosynē*) and glory (Gk. *doxa*) God intended for humanity. Accordingly, the question for the Roman Christians, and for us, is the following: What does it mean, on the ground, to be a community that participates in the life of the Father, Son, and Spirit whose saving activity has been narrated throughout the letter and extended explicitly to both Jews and gentiles? Fundamentally, Paul calls for holiness and hospitality that are rooted in the cross; it is cruciform. But this cruciform *habitus* is full of life; it is *resurrectional* cruciformity.

The late New Testament scholar Leander Keck labeled this entire section of the letter "Daybreak Ethos," a reference to 13:12—"the night is far gone, the day is near. Let us then lay aside the works of darkness and put on the armor

---

1. As noted in the introduction to 5:1–8:39, the notion of a Christian *habitus*—a set of dispositions, values, and practices that reflect the gift of Christ—comes especially from John M. G. Barclay, *Paul and the Gift* (Grand Rapids: Eerdmans, 2015), 493–519; *Paul and the Power of Grace* (Grand Rapids: Eerdmans, 2020), 88–100.

2. Some of what Paul says to the Romans in these chapters he has already said to the Corinthians (esp. 1 Cor 8–13), though it is adapted for new circumstances.

242

of light."[3] One might also say Paul is calling on his readers and hearers to "become" the gospel: to become a faithful, living embodiment of the good news in service to one another and in mission to others for the glory of God.

12:1–13:14
Holiness: A Community of Goodness and Love

Chapters 12 and 13 contain a fairly comprehensive overview of the new life that those who are in Christ are to practice together—a succinct guide to Christian discipleship that speaks as clearly today as it did in first-century Rome. This guide begins with a brief, general exhortation (12:1–2) that governs the entire discussion found in 12:1–15:13. We then find more specific words of apostolic counsel, with the themes of Christ-shaped, Spirit-enabled goodness and especially love emphasized. These exhortations concern the essentials of life together—the Christian nonnegotiables, so to speak. As a whole, these two chapters are like a Christian Holiness Code (see Lev 17–26). They are especially reminiscent of Lev 19:1–18, which focuses on love of neighbor (Lev 19:18).

12:1–2. EMBODIED HOLINESS: A LIVING SACRIFICE

Paul's appeal contained in 12:1–2 sets the tone and provides the framework for everything that follows through 15:13. These two verses begin with a clear link ("therefore") to all that Paul has said thus far, especially in chapters 9–11, for Paul's entire appeal is based on the "mercies of God" (12:1) that he has just narrated with passion (see also 15:8–9).

Although the word "cross" does not appear in the text of 12:1–2, Paul is clearly calling for a cruciform, alter-cultural (i.e., "holy"; 12:1) community that embodies the gospel and serves as both a contrast and a witness to the surrounding culture. The community address ("brothers and sisters") is important; Paul is not writing merely to individuals. The text's imperatives—"present your bodies as a living sacrifice" (12:1) and "do not be conformed to this world [lit. "age"], but be transformed by the renewing of your minds" (12:2)—use plural forms of the verbs to address the Roman believers collectively. (This will be true in most of 12:1–15:13.) The exhortation "be transformed" is a passive verb, implying that the process requires a power outside ourselves: the Spirit. This process has sometimes been described as one of unlearning and relearning.

---

3. Leander E. Keck, *Romans*, Abingdon New Testament Commentaries (Nashville: Abingdon, 2005), 289.

Together, the two imperatives also suggest *death* and *difference*. That is, being a living sacrifice means a constant process of *dying* yet living, or resurrectional cruciformity (cf. 6:1–7:6; 8:1–17). Being transformed as a result of this holy process, guided by the Holy Spirit, means becoming *different* from the environment that hosts the community. The verb Paul uses for transformation occurs only here and in 2 Cor 3:18, where he explicitly attributes this spiritual renovation to the Spirit. (We get the word "metamorphosis" from this verb.) This transformation dramatically affects both minds and bodies, such that believers, Paul implies, are conformed to Christ and take on *his* mind and *his* ways (cf. 8:29; Phil 2:1–11).

First, Christians are to adopt a new way of *perceiving* everything, a new worldview: they should follow Paul and "take every thought captive to obey Christ" (2 Cor 10:5). They will not continue thinking in the same ways that those unshaped by the Spirit of Christ think, as Paul has already said in chapter 8 (8:5–7). "Don't let the world around you squeeze you into its own mould, but let God re-make you so that your whole attitude of mind is changed" is how the J. B. Phillips paraphrase vividly interprets 12:2.[4] To think differently requires a clear understanding of how people of this world, or age, think, and such clarity can be achieved only by careful, critical analysis. Few people can undertake such analysis completely on their own; it requires both community and leadership by gifted individuals.

Furthermore, those who are in Christ are also to take on a new way of *doing* everything in and with our bodies, so that we actually do love God with all our heart, mind, soul, and strength. The result is, or can be, doing everything "in accordance with Christ Jesus" (15:5). The Rev. Dr. Martin Luther King Jr. referred to the Christian disciples described here as "transformed noncomformists," and he emphasized that such nonconformity in conformity to Jesus will mean cross-bearing.[5] In other words, resurrectional cruciformity.

As this transformation occurs, the darkening of minds and the degrading of bodies (1:18, 21, 24–25, 28) associated with life in Adam and Sin are gradually undone. Humanity's failure to worship God and our corollary misdirected, idolatrous worship of the creature (1:21–23, 25, 28, 30) are also being unraveled in Christ. The result of the transformation is that people experience the glory of God and the righteousness for which humanity was created.

The image of a "living sacrifice" in 12:1 suggests an alternative to the temple sacrifices, a sacrifice that Jews and gentiles can both perform, and perform

---

4. Phillips is echoed by N. T. Wright in his translation (KNT).

5. Martin Luther King Jr., "Transformed Nonconformist," in *Strength to Love* (Minneapolis: Fortress, 2010), 11–21.

together as God's temple (cf. 1 Cor 3:16). It is their spiritual, rational, or reasonable (the term *logikos* in 12:1 can mean any of these) worship: the appropriate response to receiving God's saving mercy. The singular form of the word "sacrifice" suggests both individual participation and a single, communal offering made by the "one body" (12:4–5). *This worship does not occur only in specific places or at specific times; it is, rather, the liturgy of life.* Worship for Christians is a 24-7 way of living.

The echoes of Rom 1 ("bodies," 1:21; "worship," 1:25) and Rom 6 ("present," or "offer" in some translations; 6:13, 16, 19) in 12:1–2 reveal that Paul wants the Roman communities in Christ to become the antithesis of the broken humanity we see in 1:18–3:20. The reappearance of the verb "present" reinforces Paul's emphasis on believers' personal and corporate responsibility to embody the truth of their situation in Christ. Resurrection and freedom can be experienced only as death to self and slavery, or absolute allegiance, to God. The body dominated by Sin (6:6; 8:13) has been given a new lease on life, life in the Spirit (8:1–13). Building on chapter 6, Paul says believers are constantly in a paradoxical state of dying yet living (see also Gal 2:19–20)—cruciformity suffused with the resurrection. Dead to Sin and alive to God (6:11), with the old self crucified (6:6), believers express their resurrection to new life (6:4) by presenting their bodies and bodily members as a living sacrifice to God. This is one of the great paradoxes of Christian existence: life in and through death.

Such a lifestyle is inherently holy, or alter-cultural, but even with the Spirit's presence, it does not happen automatically. That is why Paul can make transformation an imperative: "be transformed." Believers must take responsibility by allowing themselves to be transformed and thus to discern God's good will in order to do it and thus to please God (12:2; cf. 14:18). Such discernment requires community: "Iron sharpens iron" (Prov 27:17). Paul's goal in the following paragraphs of the letter is to assist the Roman church, as well as Christians today, in this process of individual and corporate transformation in order to do God's will—to faithfully embody the gospel in their lives, in their assemblies, and in the world.

12:3–21. LOVE AND GOODNESS TO ALL: THE GIFTED, MISSIONAL BODY OF CHRIST

Two main topics are addressed in the remainder of chapter 12: life within the graced and gifted community ("body"), and proper treatment of those outside it. In both aspects, Paul is talking about a missional God forming a missional people.

12:3–8. The Gifted Body of Christ

Echoing words penned originally for the Corinthians (1 Cor 12), Paul first counsels the Romans to live "with sober judgment" (12:3) as one unified body of Christ consisting of various "members" (12:4) and gifts (12:6–8). Paul clearly has in mind the factionalism and judgmentalism he will address in 14:1–15:13, as the phrase "according to the measure of faith that God has assigned" reveals (12:3; cf. 14:1, 22–23). The issue addressed beginning at 14:1 is one of attitude and judgment, and a renewed mind (12:2) would lead to humility rather than arrogance (12:3; cf. 12:16). This is the kind of mind the Spirit's transforming power will produce (8:5–7) because it is the mind of Christ (Phil 2:1–5). In a word (which will appear in 12:9), proper self-examination should lead to *love*.

The metaphor of a body for community or political life (12:4–5) was common in the ancient world, as it is today (e.g., "body politic"). Although the problems addressed in 14:1–15:13 are on the horizon, Paul does not restrict the discussion of Christ's one body to the Romans' factionalism. As in 1 Corinthians, he stresses unity in diversity (12:4–5a), as well as the interdependence and mutual belonging of the various members of the body: "we are members one of another" (12:5b). Moreover, all members have gifts of God's grace (Gk. *charismata*, from *charis*, "grace," as in 1 Cor 12:4, 9, 28, 30–31), and prophecy again ranks first among gifts given to those within the congregations.[6]

The seven gifts Paul enumerates in 12:6–8—the number seven probably being intentional and symbolic—are not meant to be an exhaustive but a significant representative list of the gifts of grace, suggesting that God provides all that the body needs:

- prophecy: speaking a specific, Spirit-inspired word to the assembly;
- ministry/service (*diakonia*): possibly referring to serving people's material and physical needs;
- teaching: general instruction in the faith, but also analysis and critique of the unchristian *habitus* of this age/world;
- exhortation, or possibly encouragement (*paraklēsis*): probably meaning general or specific moral instruction, but possibly spiritual support;
- giving: providing financial support to the assembly or its members, or both;

6. Technically, prophecy is second in 1 Corinthians, following only apostleship (1 Cor 12:28–29; 14:1). See also Eph 4:11, where "prophets" follows immediately after "apostles."

- leading, or having authority: providing oversight for the life of the community; and
- compassion (lit. "practicing mercy"): what the church would later call the works of mercy, including visiting the sick and imprisoned, sheltering the homeless, and so on.

Paul may be emphasizing the continuity of these gifts with those given throughout salvation history (cf. 11:29). What is new here vis-à-vis 1 Corinthians is the appearance of at least three gifts not specifically listed in the earlier letter: exhortation (though see 1 Cor 14:31 [NRSV, "encouraged"]), giving, and compassion or mercy.[7] Mercy is particularly noteworthy, as it implies the undoing of a particular form of Sin-dominated unmerciful human behavior (see 1:31) and a profound sharing in the character of the merciful God narrated in chapters 9–11.[8] Also distinctive in Romans is the stress on exercising whichever gift one has appropriately and responsibly, as an act of service to God and the church. This seems to be the upshot of the various qualifying phrases associated with each gift in 12:6b–8.

Missing from Romans, however, are most of the gifts listed in 1 Cor 12:8–10, 28–30, including the utterance/message of wisdom, the utterance/message of knowledge, faith, healing, working of miracles/deeds of power, discernment of spirits, various kinds of tongues, and the interpretation of tongues, as well as apostles. Does this mean that the Roman communities were less charismatic than the believers in Corinth? Or does Paul deliberately list gifts in Romans that highlight the exhortations about community life that immediately follow and extend to 15:13? We cannot know for sure.

In any event, this passage implies that because gifts are an operation of grace (and are therefore neither merited positions nor merely natural talents), they are distributed to all in the community: male and female, gentile and Jew, rich and poor. This means that the non-elite in the community are not only children of God and filled with the Spirit (ch. 8), they are also full members of the functioning body with gifts to exercise and contributions to make.[9] Implementing this reality would certainly prove to be a challenge in any culture,

7. Although the vocabulary is different, ministry/service (Gk. *diakonia*) and leading/authority in Rom 12:7–8 are similar to helping/assistance and leadership/guidance in 1 Cor 12:28. Prophecy/prophets appears in both letters.

8. The Greek word for "ruthless" (NRSV, ESV, RSV, NAB) at the end of 1:31 is better translated as "unmerciful" (NASB) or "without mercy" (CEB).

9. In contrast to 1 Corinthians, in Romans Paul does not specifically mention the Spirit in connection with the gifts (see 1 Cor 12:4–11) or call them *pneumatika* (Spirit-gifts; see

ancient or modern, where community participation is normally dominated by those with status or means, or both.

The use of these gifts is not only for the community's internal harmony and holiness. The mission of God in the world is accomplished primarily because gifted participants use their gifts for the edification of the community. This edification allows the community to function properly as peaceful, Spirit-filled, Christlike "weapons" of God's righteousness/justice (6:13) in the world, as well as in the church. This internal-external dynamic emerges more explicitly in the rest of the chapter.

12:9–21. Cruciform Love inside and outside the Community

The topic of exercising gifts soberly and graciously leads Paul, in 12:9–21, to write about relationships in the body. As in 1 Cor 12–14, but more succinctly, a discussion of love in very concrete terms follows a discussion of spiritual gifts. What does it mean, in real-life terms, to belong to one another (12:5)? Community requires mutual care, or "one-anothering"; it is a hallmark of the *ekklēsia* (12:10a, 12:10b, 12:16; 13:8).

But Paul writes not only about life within the community; he is also concerned about how the community engages those outside it. What does it mean to live in this world, or age, but not be conformed to it? It is tempting to read 12:9–13 as referring only to the treatment of believers and 12:14–21 to unbelievers, but 12:15–16 seems clearly to refer to relations within the church. This co-mingling of exhortations suggests that Paul is calling the Roman faithful to live the same way both internally and externally.

It has often been remarked that 12:9–21 has the appearance of a collection of maxims or proverbs, a list of (common early Christian?) exhortations (cf. 1 Thess 5:12–22) offered without development on any one topic, except non-retaliation (12:14, 19–21).[10] Although the Spirit is not specifically mentioned except in 12:11, this list is somewhat reminiscent of the fruit of the Spirit in Gal 5:22–23.

But this list of instructions is not random. The theme of love and goodness, though somewhat general, unites the maxims into a coherent and cruciform shape. Moreover, Paul seems to have done some grouping of the maxims into his

---

1 Cor 12:1; 14:1) as well as *charismata*. Nevertheless, we can safely assume he still believes the gifts come from the Spirit.

10. Most of the exhortations in 12:9–19 are actually expressed with Greek participles and infinitives, giving the whole section even more the flavor of a list.

own favorite categories of faith, hope, and love (see Gal 5:5–6; 1 Cor 13:13; 1 Thess 1:3; 5:8)—the theological virtues understood through the lens of the cross.

12:9–13. Love, Faith, and Hope

Paul's informal categorization of his first thirteen instructions, in 12:9–13, appears to be as follows: admonitions about love (12:9–10, 13), about faith (12:11), and about hope (12:12). The apostle is perhaps once again echoing the substance of 1 Corinthians (chs. 12–13; see esp. 13:13), in which a discussion of love (linked to faith and hope) follows the topic of gifts in the body.

Thus, Paul's admonitions in Rom 12:9–21 reveal a three-dimensional resurrectional cruciformity:

> *Love.* According to 12:9a, love must be "genuine" (NRSV) or "sincere" (NAB, NIV). Believers are to hate what is evil—not evil people—and hold fast to what is good (12:9b; cf. 1 Thess 5:21–22; Amos 5:14–15). (In 12:14, 21, this principle will be extended to outsiders as conquering evil with good rather than with retaliation.) Believers are to engage in "brotherly" (NJB) love *(philadelphia, philostorgoi),* or appropriate concern for fellow siblings in God's eschatological family (12:10a). Practically speaking, this is expressed in outdoing others in showing honor, that is, anticipating (see NAB) and meeting members' needs as one would those of family members, without selfish interest (12:10b). The typical Roman race to accumulate honor for self must be replaced with a steady granting of honors to others. This life-giving cruciform love is also expressed in contributing to fellow believers' material needs and in hospitably welcoming travelers, of which there were many in the early churches (12:13). These are concrete expressions of *koinōnia,* or Christian fellowship and solidarity.[11] Paul knows no other kind of Christian fellowship.
>
> *Faith/faithfulness.* The three admonitions in 12:11 depict the community's relationship to God, possibly enumerating each of the three persons of the Trinity. It needs to have zeal, or eagerness (toward God the Father?), which will be different from the misguided zeal noted in 10:2. It needs to be "on fire in the Spirit" (CEB).[12] And its service (enslavement, as in ch. 6) must be to the Lord, that is, to Jesus. Faith, then, though not named as such per se, is depicted here as zealous, inspired faithfulness.

11. Paul does not use that Greek word here, but he does in 15:26 in reference to sharing financial resources.

12. Many commentators interpret this phrase as a reference to God's Spirit, against most translations' reference to the ardor of the *human* spirit.

Hope. The vocabulary of 12:12 is that of hope in the midst of opposition and is reminiscent of 5:3–5 (cf. 1 Thess 5:16–18). Like 12:11, it has three components: believers should be joyful in hope, patient in suffering (recall 8:18–24, 31–39), and prayerful in order to persevere.

12:14–21. Internal and External Relationships of Harmony, Humility, and Peace

The exhortations to cruciform living continue in 12:14–21. Within the community, believers are expected to share in one another's sorrow and joy (12:15) and to embody a Christlike humility and concern for others, especially the "lowly" or humble, that creates harmony (12:16).[13] In contrast to normal Roman and generic human practice, Christians are expected to associate with and even honor those who are dismissed or despised, and those who have no status in this world but walk humbly with God (Mic 6:8). Believers are, once again, to give rather than pursue honor.[14]

The practice of associating with the lowly is grounded in the reality that "God chose what is foolish in the world to shame the wise; God chose what is weak in the world to shame the strong; God chose what is low and despised in the world, things that are not, to reduce to nothing things that are, so that no one might boast in the presence of God" (1 Cor 1:27–29). This divine preference for the weak is grounded still further in the reality that the weakness of Christ crucified is the power of God (1 Cor 1:18–25).

In these two verses (12:15–16), Paul amplifies what he has just said about being humble and giving honor (12:3, 10), and he echoes sentiments expressed in other letters (Phil 2:1–5; 1 Cor 12:22–26). He also further anticipates the problem of divisiveness that he will address in 14:1–15:13.

Wrapped around the call for internal harmony through humility in verses 15–16 is Paul's final set of exhortations in this chapter (12:14, 17–21). These appeals have to do with the treatment of outsiders—especially those who prove to be enemies by their persecution and other evil deeds: "Do not be overcome by evil, but overcome evil with good" (12:21).

A general instruction suggests that believers should attempt to live in peace and harmony with "all" (12:17)—that is, with nonmembers of the com-

---

13. Similar language appears in 15:5 and in Phil 2:2, 4—immediately before the poem of Christ's self-humbling and self-giving.

14. As noted in the introduction to the commentary, Paul uses one of his "co-" words in 12:16 ("co-join"; "associate with" in most translations), indicating the need for profound solidarity with the lowly—those of supposedly little or no status.

munity—thus preempting trouble (12:18).[15] They are to practice peace, to embody the shalom of God that they have been granted in Christ and the Spirit in their dealings with their nonbelieving neighbors, family members, friends, and associates. They are to practice Godlike enemy-love (see 5:6–11) in the world. Such peacemaking requires avoiding certain practices and embracing others. It is proactive, requiring discernment in order to fulfill the will of God (12:2).

When evil comes, however, in spite of all efforts at peace and goodwill, Christians must respond as their Lord did and taught. Romans 12:14 ("Bless those who persecute you . . .") is a clear reference to Jesus' teaching preserved in Luke 6:28, and all of 12:14–21 possesses the spirit of Luke 6:27–36 (Jesus' words) and Luke 23:32–43 (Jesus' example on the cross). These verses also echo the Sermon on the Plain in Luke (6:20–49) and the Sermon on the Mount in Matthew (esp. Matt 5:38–48).

But peaceful co-existence is not always possible, as it is dependent to some degree on the other party, as 12:18 implies. When peace becomes its antithesis, persecution, it is to be met with blessing rather than cursing (12:14). Vengeance, therefore, is not an option, as the Jewish wisdom tradition itself had said (e.g., Prov 20:22). And the Old Testament's Holiness Code had contrasted neighbor-love with vengeance, at least with respect to members of the community (Lev 19:18). For Christ-followers, retaliation not only violates the scriptural ethos and their Lord's teaching and example; it also usurps the future judgment of God that is central to the Scriptures (12:19, quoting Deut 32:35). Christians dare not take up swords (or guns) in self-defense, says Paul. *Violence is not the cruciform, life-giving way of God in Christ, who reconciled us while we were sinful enemies of God (5:6–8).*

Yet throughout the Bible, the unrepentant face the prospect of God's judgment, and Paul concurs. This certainty of future divine wrath—since in biblical thought the enemies of God's people are ultimately God's enemies—frees believers to deal in goodness with enemies. They can offer food and drink (12:20a; cf. Prov 25:21–22) and thereby "overcome [*nikaō*, "conquer"] evil with good" rather than being "overcome by evil" (12:21).[16] Nonretaliation is an essential part of being "more than conquerors"—super-conquerors (Gk. *hypernikōmen*) —"through him who loved us" (8:37).

Paul would not want believers to think that he believes this is ever easy;

---

15. "All" means outsiders in similar contexts in Gal 6:10 and 1 Thess 5:15.

16. The prophet Elisha stopped hostility by giving food and drink to enemies (2 Kgs 6:8–23). One is also reminded of the second-century bishop of Smyrna, Polycarp, who fed his captors a meal before being taken into custody (*Martyrdom of Polycarp* 7).

it requires the powerful presence of the Spirit. That is, the admonitions of chapter 12 of Romans make no sense without the basic presuppositions about the Spirit's ministry described in chapter 8.

But what about the puzzling phrase "heap burning coals on their heads" (12:20b)? Neither the present context nor the use of this phrase in antiquity suggests inflicting some kind of punishment. Rather, it seems to signify something like prompting repentance and turning the enemy into a friend. Repentance is, after all, the ultimate goal of God, who would prefer glorifying people rather than inflicting wrath on them (2:4–11). Moreover, God did not treat enemies with wrath but with love in sending Christ to die (5:6–8).

There is, however, no guarantee of success when love seeks to conquer evil, as both Jesus and Paul knew well. Thus, believers must be prepared to accept the possible consequences of the failure of nonretaliation to convert the oppressor. This was, for example, the perspective of the Rev. Dr. Martin Luther King Jr.

To sum up: practicing peace and doing good rather than engaging in evil and retaliation are grounded in several realities:

- scriptural teaching;
- Jesus' own teaching and example;
- God's love for enemies manifested in Jesus' death;
- the certainty of divine judgment for the unrepentant; and
- the hope of prompting enemies to change their hearts, minds, and lives.

13:1–7. A NONREVOLUTIONARY BUT SUBVERSIVE COMMUNITY

Romans 13:1–7 is among the most difficult, potentially disturbing, and even possibly dangerous of all Pauline texts. Over the centuries it has too often been used to support the divine right of kings, blind nationalism, and unquestioned loyalty to rulers—even tyrants. It is, however, neither a full-blown treatise on church-state relations nor the only passage in Paul with political overtones. Simply to confess Jesus as Lord and royal Messiah has political implications, especially in an imperial context, ancient or modern.

Some scholars have suggested that 13:1–7 is an interpolation, or later insertion, that does not fit the context or represent Paul's own beliefs. This thesis has not generally been accepted, however, and we must proceed on the dual assumption that Paul wrote it and placed it where he did for a reason.

Context

The difficulties of this text suggest that we must approach it carefully, with appropriate safeguards, in order to avoid the most egregious errors of interpretation. Still, the issues the text raises cannot be fully solved even by careful analysis, for they extend beyond Romans, Paul, and even the Bible itself into some of the most complex issues of theology and ethics. With respect simply to the text at hand, however, the following set of presuppositions seems appropriate. Romans 13:1–7 is related to, and should be interpreted in light of,

1. its immediate context;
2. the letter's larger context and overall purpose;
3. the political and religious situation of the Roman churches at the time of the letter; and
4. Paul's overarching theological perspectives and concrete practices.

These presuppositions hardly solve the interpretive problem, since each of them is itself disputed, but at least the interpretation offered here can be tested on the grounds of the plausibility of various aspects of the text's reconstructed contexts as well as the text itself.

1. The immediate context of 13:1–7 is 12:1–13:14, Paul's call to alter-cultural cruciformity (12:1–2) as the day of salvation approaches (13:11–14). Believers' minds and bodies belong to God (12:1–2), who is renewing them and calling them to participate in a spiritual, apocalyptic battle (13:11–14). This renewed, cross-shaped existence is to be expressed especially as loving care for all members and visitors (12:3–13, 15–16; 13:8–10), seeking peace with all outsiders (12:18), and returning good for any evil committed by enemies (12:14, 17–21).
2. Paul's overall purpose in Romans seems to be to proclaim the gospel of God's righteousness/justice for Jews and gentiles, to apply that gospel to the situation of the churches in Rome, and to solicit support for the spread of that gospel. This multidimensional purpose corresponds, as we have seen throughout the commentary, to the concrete situation at Rome.
3. Some of the opposition to the Roman house churches that Paul alludes to (e.g., 8:31–39; 12:14–21) had likely arisen during the course of synagogue disputes about the truthfulness of Jewish believers' claims that the Messiah (Gk. *Christos*) was Jesus. Claudius' expulsion of Jews from Rome (see the commentary's introduction, pp. 24–25) was clearly a political act designed

to break up a perceived political threat that, according to the Roman historian Suetonius (writing in Latin), involved one *Chrestus*. Jewish messianic expectation in general was anti-oppressor, and thus anti-Roman, since Rome was the supreme enemy of God's people at the time—at least for many Jews.

Actual Jewish opposition to Rome did exist in Paul's day, and sometimes took the form of tax protests and threats of revolt, especially in Palestine, but also in and around Rome. It is more likely than not that the earliest churches in Rome included members who were sympathetic to Jewish revolutionary or tax-resistance tendencies, and it is possible that these tendencies only increased with their conviction that the Messiah had come.

4.   Since the views expressed in Rom 13 are often labeled conservative, especially in comparison to Rev 13, it is important at the outset to recall what we have noted at various points in the commentary: that the gospel Paul proclaims had an inherently anti-imperial thrust: Jesus and Caesar cannot both rule the universe. *This dimension of the gospel will mean that Paul cannot in any way espouse blind nationalism, hyperpatriotism, or an uncritical stance toward political authorities.* In this respect, he agreed with all Jews that there is but one true Lord, and it is not any earthly political figure. Paul will also, however, agree with his fellow Jews—and many scriptural authors—that God poses and deposes human authority, using it as he sees fit (13:1–2).

What does all this mean for the interpretation of 13:1–7?

Interpretation: Paying Taxes

It is clear that the presenting issue at Rome that leads Paul to write these verses is taxation (13:6–7, naming both tribute [Gk. *phoron*] and custom taxes [Gk. *telos*]), and specifically the possibility of resistance by Roman believers to forms of Roman taxation (13:2, 4).[17] Paul's use of singular rather than plural forms of pronouns and verbs in 13:1–4 might simply be a rhetorical device, but it might also suggest that there is a minority resistance movement that Paul has in mind: "Let *every* person . . ." (13:1; emphasis added).

In any event, the primary purpose of this passage is narrow: a call for the believers—all the believers[18]—in Rome to pay their taxes (13:6–7) rather than

---

17. The tribute was a direct tax. Most translations render the word for tribute in 13:6–7 as "taxes" (but KJV has "tribute"), while the word for custom tax in 13:7 is translated as "revenue" (NRSV, NIV, NET, ESV), "toll" or "tolls" (NAB, NJB), or "custom" (NASB, KJV).

18. Paul returns to plural forms of the verbal imperatives in 13:6–7. (There is no main verb in the Greek of 13:5.)

resist paying them (13:2, 4). General statements about authorities, or (literally) "powers" (13:1-4), and about submission/subjection to them (13:1, 5), should be understood primarily as providing a Jewish, and Jewish-Christian, theological foundation for the concrete instruction. As divine servants, the powers are regarded in the Jewish tradition as accountable and answerable to God for their behavior, a point Paul undoubtedly assumes even if he does not mention it explicitly (see Prov 8:15–16).[19] Rulers may have a (limited) role in God's providential ordering of the world, including as instruments of divine wrath (as in 13:4).[20]

The role given to rulers includes bearing "the sword" (13:4). Contrary to popular interpretations of this phrase, it is not a blanket endorsement of any and every act of state violence (war, the death penalty, etc.). The sword in question is likely a reference to the policing sword. The image is simply, in context, a warning that those who fail to pay their taxes may incur the state-imposed consequences of their actions. This is because taxes, and those who impose them, are in principle aimed at "your good" (13:4) and thus at the common good God desires (cf. Prov 8:15–16).

Fundamentally, then, although Paul speaks in broad biblical, theological terms about the authority of authorities, practically speaking he portrays the Roman authorities as tax collectors.

Contrary to how participants in "this age" (12:2) think and act, Paul's perspective certainly does not make any Roman rulers—not even the emperors—divine. They are worthy of respect (13:7), but only inasmuch as they are God's tax-collecting servants for the common good. Paul, then, does not see the Roman authorities as all-powerful rulers enabled by God to pursue their power in any way, and at any cost to the people for whom they are supposed to do good. The gospel Paul proclaims therefore requires that believers in this situation follow the relevant laws and pay their taxes, seeking thereby to live at peace with all (12:18). But this gospel does not require much more.

19. See also Wis 6:1–21 (a text, probably written shortly before Romans, that is included in Catholic and Orthodox Bibles), where (Roman) rulers are acknowledged as established by God ("your dominion was given you from the Lord"; 6:3) and therefore subject to punishment for failing to act with justice: "Because as servants of his kingdom you did not rule rightly, or keep the law, or walk according to the purpose of God, he will come upon you terribly and swiftly, because severe judgment falls on those in high places" (Wis 6:4–5).

20. Paul does not even say that "the governing authorities" he has in mind execute God's justice—only God's wrath. That is because God's justice is revealed in and through Messiah Jesus. See Douglas Harink, *Resurrecting Justice: Reading Romans for the Life of the World* (Downers Grove, IL: IVP Academic, 2020), 177–78.

Interpretation: Submitting, Not Obeying, and Disobeying

It is critical to note in this regard that Paul does not urge his audience to *obey* the authorities but to *submit* to them. The Greek verb he uses (*hypotassō*) signifies being subject or subordinate to an authority. *Obedience* (Gk. *hypakouō*) *is reserved for God and the gospel* (6:15–22; 10:16; cf. 1:5; 16:26). Christians pledge believing allegiance and obedience to only one authority—their Lord. All of this suggests that if and when disobedience to the authorities were called for, submission would still be possible in the sense of submitting to the authorities' right to mete out consequences for such behavior.

The biblical tradition clearly indicates that God's people cannot follow the dictates of established authorities, religious or civil, should they require something opposed to God's will. Accordingly, when a civil authority is no longer a servant for God's good will for the world—when it engages in evil—disapproval will be, and disobedience may be, necessary for Christian individuals and churches. The stories of Shadrach, Meshach, and Abednego in the Old Testament (Dan 3), and Peter and the apostles in the New (Acts 5), just to name two instances, teach us that "we must obey God rather than any human authority" (Acts 5:29). Revelation 13 reminds us explicitly and vividly that civil authorities can become blasphemous enemies of God, not servants of God. Paul would not disagree, as even Rom 8:31–39 implies (cf. 1 Cor 2:6–8).

Thus, as with Jesus' teaching (e.g., Mark 12:13–17), Paul's words do not invite uncritical devotion to, or worship of, any political person or entity. Pay your taxes, but give your allegiance to God, not Caesar. That is the unified message of both Jesus and Paul. *They both ultimately challenge the authority of civil power and limit the relationship of disciples to it.* This is because, Paul would say, Christ-followers have already dedicated their minds and bodies to the service of God (12:1–2).

Combined with the immediate context of 13:1–7, which stresses neighbor-love and nonretaliation (i.e., enemy-love), this call for total self-dedication to God suggests that believers cannot offer their allegiance, or their minds and bodies, to civil powers for their wars, acts of retaliation, or other purposes that contradict the spirit and teachings of the gospel and the Lord of the gospel.[21] In this sense, those who are in Christ are more than nonrevolutionary; they are, paradoxically, also subversive, offering allegiance only to one Lord and

---

21. It is likely that Paul would find Christian participation in at least some aspects of political life (i.e., the powers) problematic since the execution of divine wrath is assigned in part to the powers (13:4) but forbidden for those in Christ (12:19).

his "empire." At the same time, if (some of) the Roman believers saw the Roman authorities as enemies, their tax resistance would be for them a form of retaliation, which Paul's gospel (the gospel of God) prohibits.

The Roman Believers and Rome

As Paul writes, the Romans have readmitted Jews to Rome and, it would seem, are not officially persecuting either the church or the Jewish community (though the possibility of such persecution in the future may lie, in part, behind Paul's concerns about not paying taxes). Roman officials are not now the objects, but rather the agents, of divine wrath (13:4–5), a point that may be intended to reinforce the reality of God's wrath in the world (1:18) as well as the prohibition of vengeance by believers (12:14–21).

If Paul has apparently turned an enemy of God's people (an oppressive power) into God's agent, he has done so in concert with his tradition, in which even God's enemies can be divine agents (e.g., Egypt, Assyria, and Babylon). Paul does not in any sense idolize Rome but places it in its proper place under God. His advice to the Roman believers does not displace YHWH or Jesus as the true Lord, and it does not call for blind obedience to the state. Furthermore, neither does it create a comprehensive political theology for all times and circumstances, or give blanket approval to any and every state policy and action. What it does, however, is redirect energy from resisting taxes to living in peace—something that may indirectly further the preaching of the gospel. And it simultaneously calls the church to be prepared for a day when the powers demand too much and must be resisted.

ROMANS 13 AND NONCONFORMITY TODAY:
THE CHRISTIAN COMMUNITY'S OBLIGATION TO OPPOSE
INHUMANE LAWS AND PRACTICES

Note: the points of this sidebar were first developed during the Trump years in response to certain claims of then–Attorney General Jeff Sessions (explicitly) and White House spokesperson Sarah Sanders (implicitly). They contended that Rom 13 (actually, only 13:1–7—and this point is important) was justification for calling those who take the Bible as a moral guide to support and follow all US immigration laws, policies, and practices. It was specifically cited in support of separating parents and children at the US border.

These ten points indicate why such actions that are instinctively morally repelling are also supported, not by Rom 13, but by a complete misreading of Rom 13. The main claim made here is number 8.

1. Various aspects of the meaning of Rom 13:1–7 are debated, but its main original intent was to tell the Roman Christians to pay their taxes (Rom 13:7). The text is not a call to blind obedience to all authorities and laws.

2. Whatever Rom 13:1–7 means, it can mean what it means only in light of its context. That is, it cannot be ripped from its place in the letter to the Romans. But this is what many have done, historically and recently.

3. Whatever Rom 13:1–7 means, it cannot be understood in a way that contradicts its context.

4. The immediate context of Rom 13:1–7 is the entirety of Rom 12 and 13. In those chapters, Paul sets out basic guidelines for the Christian communities in Rome, and for us.

5. Those guidelines begin with a call for *nonconformity to this age*, a radical transformation of attitudes and practices that is appropriate to those who have benefited from God's mercy in Christ (Rom 12:1–2). This spirit of nonconformity and transformation is the prerequisite for knowing and doing God's will. And it is the fundamental framework for everything that follows, including 13:1–7.

6. In Rom 12:9–21, after a brief discussion of various gifts in the body of Christ, Paul calls on the Christian community to practice a radical, genuine form of love that corresponds to the love they have received from God in Christ. This includes hating what is evil and practicing the good; showing hospitality to strangers; loving enemies; weeping with those who weep; associating with the lowly; blessing persecutors; not repaying evil for evil; practicing peace toward all; not seeking vengeance for harm done; and overcoming evil with good. The call to this lifestyle is what immediately precedes Rom 13:1–7.

7. Immediately after Rom 13:1–7 is the rest of the story: what Rom 13 says as a whole. Here we find another radical summons to neighbor-love and a call to avoid the works of darkness by putting on Christ (Rom 13:8–14).

8. This context for Rom 13:1–7 means that the Christian commu-

nity must not follow any authority or law that calls us to violate the basic Christian principles presented in the texts surrounding 13:1–7, because in so doing we would be failing to "put on the Lord Jesus Christ" (Rom 13:14). Rather than being a blanket call to obedience and allegiance, which is reserved for God alone, Rom 13:1–7—when read in context—actually supports Christian opposition to many laws and practices. *The Christian is free from the tyranny of obedience to political figures and entities but obligated to love and to work for the common good, even when doing so is an act of disobedience.*

9. Those who read "Rom 13" like Sessions and Sanders (including their predecessors and successors) have missed the point of the passage. If the practices and laws they defend manifest the opposite of the basic Christian ethic described in Rom 12–13, it is the duty of Christians to oppose—through prayer, protest, and possibly disobedience—those inhumane practices and laws that certain people justify, in part, by their misuse of Scripture.

10. Christians must also be prepared to try to offer humane alternatives to the practices and laws they oppose. And they must be prepared to suffer the consequences of "putting on" their Lord.

13:8–10. THE RULE OF LOVE

The mention of obligations in 13:7 ("what is due") leads Paul in 13:8–10 to return to his previous train of thought and name the most important debt of all—mutual love (Gk. *agapē*). Believers' only ultimate debt is not to the state but to God and others. (Paul has already spoken, in 8:12–13, of our debt to God to live in sync with the Spirit.) These three verses of chapter 13 both continue and summarize one of the two great interrelated themes of chapters 12–15: love (the other being holiness, to which Paul returns in 13:11–14). They also establish the principle of mutual love in the Christian community, about which Paul will speak at length in 14:1–15:13.

As he does in Gal 5:14,[22] Paul here summarizes the second table of the law (13:9, drawn from Exod 20 and Deut 5) in the words "Love your neighbor as yourself." *This summary does not negate or replace the more specific commandments but reveals what each is: a call to love.* Paul understands love positively

---

22. Echoing Jesus himself, according to Mark 12:31 and parallels.

as that which edifies and honors (12:9–13; cf. 1 Cor 8:1), and negatively as that which does no harm (13:10, reflecting the prohibitions in 13:9).[23]

Again, as in Gal 5:14, Paul also asserts that love, and thus the one who loves, fulfills the law (13:8, 10). This claim echoes 8:3–4, where Paul says God sent the Son so that "the just requirement of the law would be fulfilled" (MJG) in those who walk according to the Spirit, who creates love in the community (cf. Gal 5:22).[24] Thus, for Paul, the Son is both the source and the cruciform paradigm (as 15:3 will make clear) of love, yet only in connection with God the Father as the sender of both the Son and the Spirit. In other words, love is a Trinitarian work.

13:11–14. THE ESCHATOLOGICAL CONTEXT OF CHRISTIAN LIVING

To conclude the overview of life in Christ that started at 12:1, Paul offers a brief collage of images and instructions (cf. 1 Thess 5:11–22). These images draw on beliefs about the end (eschatology) that Paul shared with many other Jews, though they are reworked in light of Christ. These beliefs are not precise eschatological predictions, but a framework that leads naturally to a certain way of living. For Paul, as for Jesus (e.g., Mark 1:15), the new age of God's kingdom has already begun, though it is not here in its fullness. This already-but-not-yet dynamic drives Paul's concluding general exhortations.

Underlying all of these exhortations, then, is the conviction that the church is God's eschatological community, called to live in holiness (i.e., alter-culturally) in anticipation of the coming of Christ and the triumph of God (cf., e.g., 1 Thess 1:9–10). These verses make that assumption explicit and create an *inclusio* (a set of rhetorical bookends) with 12:1–2. The cultic, sacrificial image of holiness in 12:1–2 is transformed into a series of rich eschatological images in 13:11–14. Paul uses these images in the conviction that the salvation that will arrive on "the day [of the Lord Jesus]" is "near" (13:12; cf. 13:11). Even if Paul meant that day was imminent and, two thousand years later, we hesitate to

---

23. Some interpreters find in 13:10 a reference to the early Christian love feast, or the *agapē*, which would have included the Lord's Supper (see 1 Cor 11:17–34). Evidence for this is not solid here, but community meals are clearly in view, later, in 14:1–15:13, and "love does no wrong to a neighbor" is certainly applicable in that context.

24. As noted earlier, the NRSV and most translations actually have "might be fulfilled," but Paul intends to speak of God's purpose and its realization, rather than simply a possibility, as "might" could imply.

think that way, it is nonetheless true for all Christians that "salvation is nearer to us now than when we became believers" (13:11).

This conviction means that believers should wake up, not sleep (13:11), and they should change clothing—lifestyle—by taking off "works of darkness" and putting on "the armor of light" (13:12). The change-of-clothing image may derive from Christian baptism, though (ironically) it was also used by some pagans. Believers are to live in the light of the coming day, not the darkness of this age (13:12–13; recall 1:21). The reference to "armor" (NRSV) is actually "weapons" (CEB, NET), as in 6:13. Believers participate in a struggle against unseen but real powers (cf. Eph 6:10–18); this is what it means to share in the mission of God.

Such apocalyptic language for the moral life (13:13; cf. 1 Thess 5:4–11) is meant to extinguish any remnants of pagan revelry (CEB: "partying and getting drunk . . . sleeping around and obscene behavior") as well as internal dissension (cf. Gal 5:19–21). Both are instances of providing for, or walking according to, the flesh (13:14; cf. 8:3–17). The latter example ("quarreling and jealousy," 13:13) is mentioned as a segue into chapter 14.

The image of getting dressed reappears in 13:14: "put on the Lord Jesus Christ" (cf. Gal 3:27). *The "clothing" required for "walking" (living) as a Christian is ultimately nothing other than Jesus.* This is not just a matter of being clothed with divine power (see Luke 24:49), but with a specific divine presence having a particular shape—the cruciform shape of Jesus. Yet because the crucified Jesus is the living, resurrected Lord, this cruciformity is *resurrectional*—suffused with the transforming life of God.

The faithful, then, are to live out their community story freed from the deeds of the flesh, guided by the Spirit, and clothed in the narrative of cruciform, life-giving love found in Christ (cf. 15:1–3; 2 Cor 4:11), into whose death all were immersed in baptism (6:3). This lifestyle, which must be appropriated daily, is their means of spiritual warfare. Their lives bear witness to the gospel not only within the community but also in the presence of the outside world, the "all" named in 12:17–18.

Romans 12–13 ends where it began (12:1–2), with a call to exchange one mode of thinking and living for a new mode. These last two verses of Rom 13 were the catalyst for the conversion of Saint Augustine (354–430). After a life of philosophical and moral confusion, he was providentially drawn to this text by the voice of a small child calling, "Take and read," as Augustine tells us in book 8 of his *Confessions*. The summons to "put on the Lord Jesus Christ" is addressed to all, skeptic and believer alike.

REFLECTIONS AND QUESTIONS FOR 12:1–13:14

Spiritual, Pastoral, and Theological Reflections

1. **Worship** has to do with **minds and bodies**. Christians are not Gnostics; bodies matter. What we do with our bodies affects our spirituality—our relationship with God and others—and vice versa. Essential to Christian discipleship is the ongoing development of both a Christian worldview, or perspective on *everything*, and a Christian lifestyle, or way of doing *everything*. This is in large measure what John Barclay describes as the elements of a Christian *habitus*. "Everything" means precisely that: what we think about and practice concerning family life, sexuality, friendship, where and how we live, vocation, buying and giving habits, hobbies, travel, politics, the environment, and more. This sort of Christian perspective and practice—of becoming like Christ as an act of moment-by-moment worship—cannot be accomplished alone; it necessitates the power of the Spirit and participation in Christian community.

2. The **transformation** of individuals and communities into the shape of the gospel, the shape of Christ, is an **ongoing process** from justification/baptism to glorification. This is a process of unlearning and learning because we have been the victim—sometimes the willing victim, sometimes the unknowing victim—of powerful cultural and cosmic forces, in addition to our own propensity to prefer idols to God and our way to God's way. Many people are unaware of and unable to resist the various problematic cultural perspectives and practices that inevitably shape who they are. This is because these perspectives and practices are deemed normal by their culture or subculture: "this age." Finding the insight and courage to challenge these normal ways of thinking and doing requires, once again, the work of the Spirit and the gift of Christian community. But—and here is perhaps the greatest challenge—Christian communities themselves are also formed and malformed by the same spirit of this age. That is why every Christian community, whether local or global, needs prophets to speak words that have the potential to wake us up from our spiritual slumber.

3. One of the central aspects of a Christian *habitus* is a **fundamental option for the weak**, or a disposition of associating with "the lowly" (12:16)—"people who have no status" (CEB). (See also 12:3, 10.) This theme runs throughout Paul's letters because it is grounded in his proclamation of the gospel of God's identification with and as human weakness and poverty (see, e.g., 1 Cor 1:18–2:5; 2 Cor 8:9). Yet too often Christian communities are disposed precisely in the opposite direction: to seek out status and to honor those who

have attained it. This is one major area for the transformation of perspective and practice for many Christians and Christian communities. And it requires discernment and concrete, sometimes difficult, implementation, as Paul will demonstrate in 14:1–15:13 (see especially 14:1; 15:1–4).

4. Another basic characteristic of the Christian community is that it is **called to practice and to pursue peace**; it has a peacebuilding mission, internally and externally—what some have called "centripetally" and "centrifugally." Klaus Wengst called the early Christian community a "sphere of interrupted violence" in the midst of a violent world, the Roman Empire.[25] This is a high calling and, unfortunately, not always one that is realized. But for those who ask why peace work is required of Christians, there is one basic answer: *peacemaking is constitutive of the identity and mission of God displayed in Christ.* The God of peace is still in the business of effecting the peace of God. To practice Christlike, Godlike peacemaking energized by the Spirit is to participate in the mission and life of the triune God.

5. One of the **great tragedies of Christian history** has been the church's **complicity with evil** in the name of (allegedly) following the requirements of Rom 13:1–7. This complicity trickles down, of course, to the people in the pew, usually in the name of patriotism more than in the name of faith or faithfulness, or obedience to ecclesial leaders per se. But such blind patriotism, or nationalism, is far too often mixed with a perverted version of Christian faith and piety. As Robert Jewett has said, "Rom 13:1–7 has provided the basis for propaganda by which the politics of Mars and Jupiter have frequently been disguised as serving the cause of Christ."[26]

There are many issues related to this problem, but the central one is allegiance. Christian allegiance must always be to Jesus Christ—not the first allegiance among many, but the only allegiance. Allegiance means total and absolute commitment. All other commitments must be examined for their role in either aiding or hindering—or even threatening—our allegiance to Christ. Political commitments of various kinds, to nation or party or cause, are particularly dangerous to our allegiance to Jesus as Lord. We cannot "put on" both Christ and someone or something else as Lord.

6. Any Christian **protest and possible disobedience** must always be a part of discipleship, of participation in Christ, and not a secular act of hatred, retaliation, or violent revolution. In other words, when Christians criticize, protest,

25. Klaus Wengst, *Pax Romana and the Peace of Jesus Christ,* trans. John Bowden (Philadelphia: Fortress, 1987), 88.

26. Robert Jewett, *Romans,* Hermeneia (Minneapolis: Fortress, 2007), 803.

or disobey, they must do so in the cruciform power of the Spirit, whose work is righteousness/justice and peace (14:17), and "in accordance with Christ Jesus" (15:5), which means as an act of edification and love, especially for the weak. This way of faithful participation in Christ can be very costly, as even Peter and the apostles discovered—and accepted with joy (Acts 5:40–42). Paul himself was jailed as a political deviant and threat on numerous occasions, and he counted such suffering to be a grace he shared with other Christians (Phil 1:27–30).

Because human sinfulness can negatively affect our ability to see evil and to know how to respond to it, Christian disapproval and disobedience are matters in need of prayer, community wisdom, and discernment. In fact, **prayer itself can be a powerful and effective means of protest**, as Paul himself no doubt knew from the Scriptures:

> Why, O Lord, do you stand far off?
> Why do you hide yourself in times of trouble?
> In arrogance the wicked persecute the poor—
> let them be caught in the schemes they have devised. . . .
> O Lord, you will hear the desire of the meek;
> you will strengthen their heart,
> you will incline your ear to do justice for the orphan and the
> oppressed,
> so that those from earth may strike terror no more. (Ps 10:1–2, 17–18)

Questions for Those Who Read, Teach, and Preach

1. How can the body of Christ encourage its members, from youngest to oldest, to think about everything in light of the gospel?

2. How can the local Christian community embody the *habitus* (perspectives and practices) urged by Paul?

3. What are some specific contemporary manifestations of the gifts Paul lists, and of the instructions he offers, in his description of Christian community life in Rom 12?

4. What can be done to help the church overcome its propensity to excuse evil, and even participate in it, when it is legal, mandated by the state? How could or should the church, and your church, discuss the topic of civil disobedience as an expression of Christian discipleship?

5. In what ways might the gospel Paul offers in Romans challenge political powers and loyalties today? How would you respond to friends who profess Christian faith but find justification for nationalistic political obedience in Rom 13?

6. How might Rom 12–13 influence our understanding of appropriate participation in the government? Are there certain governmental activities in which Christians should not participate, such as carrying out the death penalty or participating in combat?

7. What would Christian peacemaking look like specifically in your church and community?

FOR FURTHER READING

Banks, Robert J. *Paul's Idea of Community: Spirit and Culture in Early House Churches.* 3rd ed. Grand Rapids: Baker Academic, 2020.

Bonhoeffer, Dietrich. *Life Together: The Classic Exploration of Christian in Community.* New York: Harper & Row, 1954.

Camp, Lee C. *Scandalous Witness: A Little Political Manifesto for Christians.* Grand Rapids: Eerdmans, 2020.

Cavanaugh, William T. *Migrations of the Holy: God, State, and the Political Meaning of Church.* Grand Rapids: Eerdmans, 2011.

Carroll R., M. Daniel. *The Bible and Borders: Hearing God's Word on Immigration.* Grand Rapids: Brazos, 2020.

Clapp, Rodney. *A Peculiar People: The Church as Culture in a Post-Christian Society.* Downers Grove, IL: InterVarsity, 1996.

Dawn, Marva J. *The Hilarity of Community: Romans 12 and How to Be the Church.* Grand Rapids: Eerdmans, 1992.

Dickson, John. *Humilitas: A Lost Key to Life, Love, and Leadership.* Grand Rapids: Zondervan, 2011.

Gorman, Michael J. *Becoming the Gospel: Paul, Participation, and Mission.* Grand Rapids: Eerdmans, 2015.

———. *Cruciformity: Paul's Narrative Spirituality of the Cross.* 20th anniversary ed. Grand Rapids: Eerdmans, 2021 (orig. 2001).

John, of Taizé, Brother. *Friends in Christ: Paths to a New Understanding of Church.* Maryknoll, NY: Orbis, 2012.

King, Martin Luther, Jr. *Strength to Love.* Minneapolis: Fortress, 2010.

Laytham, D. Brent, ed. *God Is Not . . . Religious, Nice, "One of Us," An American, A Capitalist.* Grand Rapids: Brazos, 2004.

Moore, Charles E., ed. *Called to Community: The Life Jesus Wants for His People.* Walden, NY: Plough, 2016.

Oakes, Peter. *Reading Romans in Pompeii: Paul's Letter at Ground Level.* Minneapolis: Fortress, 2009.

Pohl, Christine D. *Living into Community: Cultivating Practices That Sustain Us.* Grand Rapids: Eerdmans, 2012.

Sider, Ronald J. *If Jesus Is Lord: Loving Our Enemies in an Age of Violence*. Grand Rapids: Baker Academic, 2019.

Sire, James W. *The Universe Next Door: A Basic Worldview Catalog*. 6th ed. Downers Grove, IL: IVP Academic, 2020.

Smith, James K. A. *You Are What You Love: The Spiritual Power of Habit*. Grand Rapids: Brazos, 2016.

Swartley, Willard M. *Covenant of Peace: The Missing Peace in New Testament Theology and Ethics*. Grand Rapids: Eerdmans, 2006.

Williams, Rowan. *Being Disciples: Essentials of the Christian Life*. Grand Rapids: Eerdmans, 2016.

Yoder, John Howard. *The Politics of Jesus: Vicit Agnus Noster*. 2nd ed. Grand Rapids: Eerdmans, 1994 (orig. 1972).

14:1–15:13
Hospitality: A Community of Jews and Gentiles

On the surface, Rom 14:1–15:13 might look like a rather anticlimactic conclusion to the substance of this theologically powerful letter: words about a problem, or potential problem, concerning diet and calendar. Nothing could be further from the truth, however, at least in Paul's mind.

The Climax of the Letter

Rather than being anticlimactic, this section of Romans *is* the climax of the letter, the goal toward which the theme of Jew and gentile has been incessantly driving. This is not at all to say that the other parts of the letter are insignificant in their own right; quite the contrary. The other sections of the letter, with all their theological claims and promises, are coherent and critical aspects of Paul's gospel and theology in their own right. The climax of the letter does not detract from them, but it does demonstrate two things: (1) that Paul is a practical theologian whose theology always points toward real life, and (2) that the fairly general set of Christian practices we saw in chapters 12 and 13, all grounded in the gospel, must always be given concrete shape in concrete situations. Furthermore, the specific matter dealt with in 14:1–15:13 also has significance beyond the particularities of the situation in Rome.

The word that matters utterly to Paul in 14:1–15:13 is "welcome," that is, hospitality. It is both the starting point and the ending point of the letter's climax, grounded in the divine welcome given in the Messiah Jesus:

- **Welcome those who are weak in faith**, but not for the purpose of quarreling over opinions. . . . Those who eat must not despise those who abstain, and those who abstain must not pass judgment on those who eat; **for God has welcomed them.** (14:1, 3)
- **Welcome one another**, therefore, just as **Christ has welcomed you**, for the glory of God. (15:7)

This hospitality is an essential dimension of the Christian *habitus*—the array of dispositions and practices—that Paul has been proposing in Romans since chapter 5, and especially since chapter 12. Apart from that *habitus*, and the theological foundations on which it rests, such radical hospitality makes no sense.

Paul's mission among the nations, which he will discuss immediately after this section (15:14–33), is to proclaim the Messiah where he is not known (15:20). But this in no way excludes his fellow Jews, and it certainly is not intended to give either gentiles or Jews a superiority or inferiority complex. The gospel of welcome had, and still has, significant pastoral implications for life together. *Segregation was not, and is not, a Christian option.*

Christians of different cultures also constitute one culture in Christ, what some have called a third space that overcomes the distinctions we too often stress (Jew-gentile, Black-White, etc.). They should worship together, share meals—including the Lord's Supper (Communion)—together, engage in mission together. We cannot say for sure that Paul has the Lord's Supper specifically in mind here in Romans. But since the churches of Rome almost certainly had weekly meals that included worship similar to what is described in 1 Cor 11–14 (prayer, prophecy, singing, teaching, the Lord's Supper), then obviously the mutual welcome would implicitly include sharing the Lord's Supper together.

A community torn by intercultural strife subverts the gospel, as far as Paul is concerned, and he seeks to unify a fractured, inhospitable, multicultural community by reworking principles enumerated earlier for the Corinthians (1 Cor 8:1–11:1). Paul wants the Roman church(es) to live out the letter's theme of Jews and gentiles as one body in Christ (12:3–7), equally in need of God's grace and equally recipients of it. This will happen only if they lovingly welcome one another, including their cultural differences—matters that ultimately don't matter in Christ.[27] Then they will be able to worship God together

---

27. Theologically speaking, of course, the ongoing challenge for the church has always been deciding which matters matter, and which do not.

harmoniously as one body, a small but powerful example of God's intentions for the whole world (15:5–13). N. T. Wright offers this relevant description of Paul's view of the church:

> [Paul] saw the church as a *microcosmos*, a little world, not simply as an alternative to the present one, an escapist's country cottage for those tired of city life, but as the prototype of what was to come. That is why, of course, unity and holiness mattered. And, because this *microcosmos* was there in the world it was designed to function like a beacon: a light in a dark place . . . a place of reconciliation between God and the world; a place where humans might be reconciled to one another.[28]

THE SITUATION

There have been many attempts to identify the precise makeup and perspectives of the two groups described in these chapters, the "weak"/"weak in faith" (14:1–2; 15:1) and the "strong" or "powerful" (CEB; Gk. *dynatoi*, 15:1). That is, more neutrally, the observant and the nonobservant (of certain food and calendar practices). Some scholars deny that there was any concrete problem, making the passage a general admonition to avoid prejudice and practice tolerance, or a general theological statement about gentile-Jewish relations in the church. A very few scholars believe the "weak" are non-Christian Jews.

Most interpreters, however, find a specific problem in relations among two groups of believers at Rome. Paul refers to concrete issues and addresses the participants as siblings (14:10, 13, 15, 21) who serve the one Lord Christ (14:9) and are called to live in harmony with one another, as one family and one body, through Christlike love (15:5).

The general issue in play is sometimes described as a matter of boundary markers. Many scholars have identified circumcision, diet (kosher, avoiding unclean foods as prescribed in Scripture), and calendar observance (Sabbath, feasts, and holy days) as three practices that set Jews apart from gentiles. Paul's basic position is that these practices are not inappropriate for Jewish Christ-followers, but they are not to be imposed on gentiles. They are not, therefore, boundary markers of the Christian community as a whole. The boundary marker in question in Galatia was circumcision, about which Paul says, "neither circumcision nor uncircumcision is anything; but a new creation is everything!" (Gal 6:15). In Rome, the issue revolves around the other two boundary markers, diet and calendar.

---

28. N. T. Wright, *Paul and the Faithfulness of God* (Minneapolis: Fortress, 2013), 1492.

It seems likely that one group, the "weak" or powerless (observant) believers in Paul's description, abstain from meat and wine (14:2, 21) and "judge one day to be better than another" (14:5a). That is, they observe special (Jewish) dietary regulations and holy times. The other group eats and drinks anything (14:2, 21) and does not observe the holy times (14:5b).

It is true that the Judaism of Paul's day did not completely prohibit the consumption of (properly prepared) meat and wine, and that some non-Jews in antiquity abstained from meat or wine for various reasons. Nevertheless, the words about food and calendar observance (including especially the concern about unclean foods),[29] together with the naming of the "circumcised" and gentiles (15:8–12), strongly suggest that the groups to which Paul refers are divided primarily along Jewish and gentile lines and leanings. This division may have been manifested in differences between various house churches as well as within particular house churches.[30] If the split was along Jewish and gentile lines, then—given the arrogance some gentiles may have displayed (see ch. 11)—we might think of the weak and the strong in terms of those with and without status in the churches as a whole.

This is not to say, most scholars stress, that all the "weak" were ethnic Jews; it is quite possible that former Godfearers (gentiles who associated with the synagogue) and even pagan converts felt obliged to completely forsake pagan ways by observing a strict diet and calendar. Forsaking meat and wine may have been associated with the rejection of idolatry, in which context much meat and wine was consumed. It is also possible that some of the "strong" were ethnic Jews who felt that their freedom in Christ from the law included especially freedom from dietary and calendar regulations (perhaps like Paul himself). It is challenging to discern the precise situation and the reasons for the specific practices.

Despite this challenge, it is important to note what the nature of Paul's exhortation in this situation is not, as well as what it is. Paul does not simply say to the Roman churches, "Anything goes." *Paul is not the apostle of a modern or postmodern laissezfaire Christian ethic of tolerance of everything in the name of freedom and respect for diversity.*

Rather, what Paul addresses here is a matter that does not matter, an issue that the Stoics would include as part of the *adiaphora*—the nonessentials. Diet and calendar do not constitute the kingdom or gospel of God (14:17). Such things do not contribute to or detract from justification—right relationship

---

29. See 14:14, 20.

30. Rom 16:5 suggests the existence of multiple house churches addressed by this letter.

with God and membership in the community of the new covenant. Paul would have—and did have—quite different words for people who, in the name of freedom or tolerance, tried to impose something contrary to the gospel of Christ crucified (e.g., Galatians) or tried to confuse immorality or injustice for the work of the Spirit (e.g., 1 Cor 5–6). He has already made it quite clear that in Christ our minds and bodies—all aspects of our lives—are to be offered to God in total devotion (6:1–7:6; 12:1–2; 13:11–14). Putting on Jesus the Messiah and Lord (13:14) rules out living however one wishes, and Paul reinforces this here (14:7–9).

Neither is this passage an appropriate basis for the modern individualistic mantra of morality that says, "That's between me (or you) and God." That is a half-truth at best. Not only is Paul dealing with inconsequential issues, at least from his perspective, but even on these matters, he invokes a necessary concern for the community and for the glory of God that undercuts any self-centered or individualistic program. Romans 14:1–15:13 is fundamentally about respect for cultural differences within the sphere of multicultural community life, not individual rights. We most fully experience God's glory when we offer glory to God and give appropriate honor (not worship!) to others, rather than glorify ourselves or use others for our own ends or interests.

What Paul requires in this passage is threefold:

- multicultural cruciform hospitality that accepts diversity in matters that do not matter;
- cruciform self-denial for the edification of others; and
- attention in everything to the praise of God through obedience to Christ.

The primary burden of responsibility is on the strong, the powerful (14:1, 13–21; 15:1–4; cf. 1 Cor 8:1–13; 11:17–34), but the weak have obligations as well.

14:1–23. *ADIAPHORA*, JUDGMENTALISM, ACCOUNTABILITY, AND LOVE

14:1–12. *No to Judgmentalism, Yes to Accountability*

In the first half of chapter 14 (14:1–12), Paul weaves together a description of the two groups and their mutually judgmental attitudes with his views about service and accountability to the Lord. The "weak in faith," calendar-observant vegetarians (and perhaps teetotalers; see 14:21), condemn the strong who consume everything but observe nothing, while the strong despise (lit. "count as nothing") the weak (14:3, 10).[31] This weakness in faith is not vis-à-vis the gospel's essential claims, or commitment to Christ, but concerning convictions about disputed practices.

On the assumption that the matter at hand is not essential to the gospel message but is something about which deeply held but differing personal convictions are acceptable (14:5; cf. 14:22–23), Paul makes two main points in response:

- Such judgmental behavior, especially of the weak, does not reflect the welcome of God in Christ (14:3), a point to which Paul will return in chapter 15, especially 15:7–13. He no doubt expects us to recall that Christ died for us when we were weak (5:6; cf. 15:1–6).
- Each believer lives for and is accountable to his or her Lord. This principle is not a license to unbridled freedom but a call to deep, mutual respect within the Christian family.

14:1–6. Mutual Welcome, Not Mutual Judgment

Paul begins with an overview of the situation, his argument, and his appeal (14:1–4). Welcome is the first, and positive, exhortation he sets out (14:1), addressed especially to the nonweak, who are explicitly called the strong, or powerful, in 15:1. This must be a sincere, loving welcome, not a half-hearted one designed to exacerbate tensions or pass judgment. Paul then summarizes the two different cultures with reference to their food habits (14:2) before giving the second, and negative, exhortation. The differing cultures must refrain from mutual disdain and judgmentalism, because God has welcomed both groups (14:3). The implicit positive exhortation to welcome *one another* will come in 15:7.

The divine welcome requires imitation by those God has welcomed, just as God's enemy-love (5:6–8) requires imitation (12:14–21). Paul is once again issuing a call for Christlike Godlikeness, a participation in the hospitable life of God. A rhetorical question and answer completes the introduction (14:4), as Paul sets out the principle that the Christian life is about accountability to

---

31. For an interesting discussion of various reasons for ancient vegetarianism, see Charles H. Talbert, *Romans*, Smyth & Helwys Bible Commentary (Macon, GA: Smyth & Helwys, 2002), 314. A main reason for Jewish vegetarianism was to avoid gentile food, especially meat—which would often be connected to pagan sacrifices.

one's Lord (further developed in 14:7–12), who will take care of those in his service. This will rule out both judgmentalism toward others and any sense of autonomy regarding oneself.

Paul proceeds to note the second sort of cultural difference, which has to do with calendar observance (14:5). He does not side with either group at this point but rather urges each person to be "fully convinced" about their practice. He then states his own hospitable view, which he hopes every Christian in Rome will share (14:6): with respect to both food and calendar practices, he assumes that Christians do what they do with thanksgiving to God (the Father) and in order to honor the Lord (Jesus). This is a charitable view of cultural differences and is a springboard to further discussion in the following verses.

14:7–12. Accountability to the Lord

Spiritual accountability is the focus of 14:7–12. Paul develops this point at some length and from several angles; it becomes a summary of the fundamental character of "the obedience of faith"—allegiance to Jesus. Paul is not interested in defending libertinism, much less irresponsibility toward others, but in explaining devotion and responsibility to the Lord.

In 14:7–9, forms of the words for "live" and "die" occur eleven times, referring once to Christ's saving death and resurrection (14:9) and, emphatically, to our own life (and death) in response to his. Paul affirms in 14:7 that we do not live "to ourselves" (NRSV) or, better, "for ourselves" (NIV, CEB). Rather, we live to/for the Lord Jesus Christ (14:8–9), which is how we live to/for God (6:10–11) and under grace (6:14). Whatever Christians do, in even the most mundane aspects of life such as eating, they must seek to honor God with their behavior (cf. 1 Cor 10:31). To be a Christian is to live a God-oriented, Christ-oriented, Spirit-oriented life. (And, as we will soon see, this also means an others-oriented life.)

Having this mindset of devotion and accountability is absolutely fundamental to life in Christ; it is truly the only life-and-death issue for believers (14:8–9). Throughout all of life, right up to the point of death, everything Christians do is to be oriented toward pleasing the Lord to whom we belong. It is in fact the very reason Christ died and lived again: "so that he would be Lord of both the dead and the living" (14:9 NRSV alt; cf. 2 Cor 5:15).

On nonessential matters, therefore, what matters is that the behavior (e.g., eating or abstaining, observing a day or not) is done to glorify God in Christ. On this basis, and on this basis alone, will each believer one day give account to

God as Lord and judge (14:10b–12). Paul appeals both to rhetorical questions (14:10) and to Scripture (14:11) to drive home his point.[32]

The questions in 14:10 refer to those being condemned as brothers and sisters. Siblings in Christ are accountable both in life and in death to the Lord who has made them his own and for whom they live, paradoxically, as both the Lord's freedpersons and his slaves (cf. 1 Cor 6:19–20; 7:22–23). Christians are freed from judging their siblings in Christ with respect to cultural differences because they know that all will stand before God's judgment seat. Furthermore, the entire passage suggests that Christian siblings should assume that others' motives are the same as theirs: to please and praise God.

14:13–23. No to Judgmentalism, Yes to Love and Mutual Edification

The second half of chapter 14 continues the themes of not judging and of acting in sincere, full conviction. But it also adds a new, and critical, dimension: love for the other, and edification of the community, that might require some people—especially the strong/powerful—to refrain from certain practices even though they are not inherently wrong. This part of the chapter falls into two parts, 14:13–18 and 14:19–23, each beginning with an inclusive exhortation starting with the words "let us" and referring to "one another" (14:13, 19). Paul includes all the Roman believers and himself in these instructions. Implicitly, he also includes all who hear or read his words.

14:13–18. Love of Siblings as Service to Christ

Paul begins this half of the chapter with a general admonition ("let us") to nonjudgmentalism that repeats a main contention of the first half and is the logical ("therefore") conclusion to it (14:13a). But Paul moves quickly to a new exhortation (14:13b), a word directed, at least primarily, to the meat-eaters (the nonabstainers, the powerful): "resolve . . . never to put a stumbling block or hindrance in the way of another."

This exhortation is an echo of 1 Cor 8, where Paul urges the Corinthian Christians who eat meat in the precincts of pagan temples to refrain from doing so out of love for fellow siblings in Christ. Like the meat-eaters in Corinth, the strong in Rome may be putting a stumbling block or a "hindrance" (NIV,

---

32. The Scripture text in 14:11 is Isa 45:23, which Paul also cites in Phil 2:10–11.

CEB: "obstacle") in the way of Christian siblings, that is, the weak. Echoing Jesus, Paul prohibits such mistreatment of the weak.[33]

The strong could potentially harm or even ruin the weak (14:15)—that is, destroy their faith—by eating meat and drinking wine (14:20–21). Paul clearly sides with the strong in their more liberal convictions (see 15:1), even calling their practices a "good" (14:16). He emphasizes that in Christ, no food is inherently unclean (14:14, 20), again echoing the teaching of Jesus himself (Mark 7:18–19). Paul is in an interesting and, for him, quite unusual spot: he has two critical words from Jesus that make perfect sense as independent teachings but, when put together, seem to create a conflict. What is the apostle to say and do?

Paul maintains that Christians must not allow this good to be maligned (14:16) by their insistence on exercising a perceived right to eat and drink no matter the circumstances and the possible effects. Some Christians *do* find certain foods unclean. Eating should never be the cause of another's spiritual death. Paul calls such self-centered, harmful-to-others actions a failure to love (14:15), which is the absolute essential element of the Christian "walk" and of Christian community (12:10; 13:8–10). In effect, Paul says, *Do you want to be the cause of someone being separated from the love of Christ?* (8:35, 39). The brother or sister whose spiritual life is in jeopardy is someone for whom Christ died (14:15; cf. 5:8; 1 Cor 8:11). Thus, the theology behind Paul's call for self-restraint is especially his understanding of Christ's own sacrificial, non-self-pleasing love for us and for others, as he will say more fully in 15:1–4.

In addition, Paul insists that the kingdom of God—a term we don't see often in Paul's letters—is not a matter of eating and drinking, but of the following (14:17):

- righteousness, or justice, a major theme of the letter since 1:17;
- peace (cf. 1:7; 2:10; 3:17; 5:1; 8:6; 12:18; 14:19; 15:13, 33; 16:20); and
- joy in the Holy Spirit (cf. 12:12, 15; 15:13, 32; 16:19).

33. The word "stumbling block" (Gk. *proskomma*) also appears in 14:20, but most translations have a phrase such as "make others fall/stumble" (though see NAB). The word occurs as well in 9:32, 33 and 1 Cor 8:9. For "hindrance/obstacle" (Gk. *skandalon*), see 9:33; 11:9; 16:17 and, interestingly, Lev 19:14 LXX. Paul identifies the cross as a *skandalon* in 1 Cor 1:23 and Gal 5:11. Its verbal cousin, *skandalizō*, occurs twice in 1 Cor 8:13. This verb also appears in the Gospels, including several occurrences in Jesus' warnings in Mark 9:42–47 and parallels. The words of Jesus preserved in Mark 9:42, "If any of you put a stumbling block before [*skandalisē*] one of these little ones who believe in me, it would be better for you if a great millstone were hung around your neck and you were thrown into the sea," may be behind Paul's own warnings here in Rom 14.

To these Paul would certainly also add love, as he has just focused on it. To love in a Christlike way is rightly to embody the kingdom through service to the Lord Christ in the peace and joy of the Holy Spirit, which is acceptable, or pleasing to God (cf. 12:1–2) and to others (14:18). All three persons of the Trinity are named in the brief but significant statement about God's reign in 14:17–18.

As we saw in considering 5:1–11, psalmists and prophets had anticipated the day when righteousness and peace would kiss each other (Ps 85:10b; 84:11b LXX) and characterize the life of God's people in the world (e.g., Isa 32:16–18; 60:17b–18). Romans 14:17 suggests that Paul sees the church's life in the Spirit as the fulfillment of the psalmist's vision. *Because the righteousness, peace, and especially love of the triune God are demonstrated in the death of Christ (14:15), only the community that walks in cruciform love enjoys the blessing of that triune God's presence, joy, and peace.*

Before leaving this passage, we must note, somewhat ironically, that Paul actually *does* think that food and drink have something significant to do with the kingdom of God. In 12:20, he has said that Christians need to give their enemies food and drink. Such mundane but essential gifts should be a means of making peace, not creating dissension.

14:19–23. Pursuing Peace and Mutual Edification

Echoing the "let us" admonition of 14:13 in light of the word "peace" in 14:17, Paul urges the Roman believers and all Christians (including himself) to pursue peace and mutual edification (14:19; cf. 15:2), because "love builds up" (1 Cor 8:1); it does not "seek its own interests" (1 Cor 13:5 NAB).[34] Spirit-enabled peace, or shalom, is the antithesis of dissension and the pursuit of selfish ends (cf. Gal 5:13–26). Paul therefore reinforces his earlier instruction: don't let eating food "destroy the work of God"—probably a reference to the church, but possibly also to the individual brother or sister—or cause any Christian sibling to stumble or fall (14:20–21).[35]

The liberal actions that flow from one's convictions about nonessential matters such as food and drink are not sinful and are accepted by God as long as they are done in faith (i.e., as an expression of loyalty to one's Lord; 14:22–23). The rationale for such convictions is a matter of individual conscience before

---

34. Some important manuscripts of Romans have "we pursue" rather than "let us pursue," but the context makes that variant unlikely.

35. That is, "become a stumbling block [Gk. *proskomma*] by eating" (NAB).

God (14:22). But acting on those convictions must be curtailed if doing so could do serious harm to a brother or sister, or to the community at large. Each individual should have a firm "faith"—meaning conviction—about non-essential matters and therefore not eat, for instance, with qualms just because others are eating. That would be sin (14:23), because it does not proceed from faith, or faithfulness: single-minded devotion to one's Lord.

As Jesus said (and Paul seems to have known this part of the Jesus tradition too), evil is a matter of which actions proceed from the heart, not which foods go into the belly (Mark 7:20–23). Similarly, by implication, the mark of God's people is the love that comes from the circumcised heart of the renewed covenant, not the cultural food laws and other previous boundary markers. Neither practicing nor refraining from such cultural practices is essential to Christian faith. To paraphrase Paul's words to the Galatian communities, neither vegetarianism nor omnivorism is anything; but a new creation is everything! (see Gal 6:15).

15:1–13. CRUCIFORM HOSPITALITY AND THE GLORY OF GOD

Paul's admonition to the strong, or powerful, continues in 15:1–4 before merging back into a general call to harmony and hospitality in 15:5–6 and especially in 15:7–13. Both passages also have an implicit external, missional implication. The two halves of this section, verses 1–6 and verses 7–13, are structured in parallel form. Each part begins with an exhortation, which is followed by an appeal to Christ, a warrant from Scripture, and a closing prayer-wish, as follows:

PARALLELS BETWEEN ROMANS 15:1–6 AND 15:7–13

	ROM 15:1–6	ROM 15:7–13
Exhortation	15:1–2	15:7
Appeal to Christ	15:3a	15:8–9a
Scriptural warrant	15:3b–4	15:9b–12
Closing prayer-wish	15:5–6	15:13

15:1–6. Cruciform Hospitality

Identifying himself with the strong in 15:1, Paul calls on them not merely to "put up with the failings of the weak" (NRSV), or even to "bear with" their (alleged) failings (RSV, NIV, NET, ESV), but rather to "bear the weaknesses of the powerless" (MJG; cf. CEB). It is important to note that Paul speaks of *weaknesses*, not failings, and of *bearing them*, not putting up with them.

Identifying something as a weakness is a matter of perspective—the perspective of the powerful, among whom Paul includes himself. But the practices of the weak cannot be some sort of moral or spiritual failure, as Paul has stressed since 14:1. Furthermore, to "bear" is to take on, not merely to put up with; it signifies *solidarity* rather than a sense of *superiority*. Bearing, then, is the antithesis of "pleas[ing] ourselves." It is an obligation to practice cruciform love.[36]

The language of bearing and pleasing is typical of Paul's exhortations to unity through love:

- bearing others' burdens is how to fulfill the law, or narrative pattern, of Christ, the crucified Messiah (Gal 6:2);
- pleasing others (i.e., acting for their benefit and edification) is how one becomes an imitator of Paul and thus of Christ (1 Cor 10:33–11:1);
- loving others means not seeking one's own interests in the exercise of spiritual gifts but seeking the edification of the community (1 Cor 8:1; 13:5; ch. 14, esp. vv. 3–5, 12, 17);
- becoming a unified, loving community is possible only when, like Christ, believers seek the interests of others rather than their own (Phil 2:1–4).

This sort of love reflects and passes on the love of God demonstrated in Christ's death for us, when we were weak (5:6). *God did not merely put up with us!*

The verb "please" appears three times in 15:1–3. Paul is clear that pleasing one's neighbors means edifying and loving them (15:2; cf. 13:9–10; 14:19), not placating them or catering to their whims. Elsewhere, Paul says this is how he attempts to live: "just as I try to please everyone in everything I do, not seeking my own advantage, but that of many, so that they may be saved" (1 Cor 10:33). And as he does elsewhere (see especially Phil 2:1–11), Paul once again grounds his exhortation in the narrative of Christ crucified (15:3–4).[37]

Here the apostle calls on Ps 69, a text commonly associated with Christ's death in the early churches, to speak to the Romans (15:3).[38] Scripture al-

---

36. The word translated "ought" (NRSV) in 15:1 is the same verb as "owe" in 13:8 (as in "owe" love) and is related to the word "debtors" in 8:12.

37. As in the somewhat similar situation in Corinth involving disputes about food, Paul wants believers to be imitators of Christ by imitating his Christlike behavior (see 1 Cor 11:1).

38. Ps 69:21b, "for my thirst they gave me vinegar to drink," figures in all four Gospels.

ways speaks beyond its original audience to those who hear it as divine address (15:4); this is a fundamental interpretive principle for Paul and for us. The "God of steadfastness and encouragement" (15:5) is the one who speaks steadfastness and encouragement through the Scriptures (15:4). The God of Scripture is the God of hope (15:4; cf. 15:12–13).[39]

Rather than pleasing himself, Christ—as Ps 69:9 puts it—absorbed the insults of those who had insulted God. By reading this psalm text as an expression of Christ's freely chosen, prayerful attitude toward God, Paul encourages those who are strong to bear the burdens of others. Like Christ, who was powerful in position and status with God (2 Cor 8:9; Phil 2:6), the powerful can—indeed must, if they are to live "in accordance with Christ Jesus" (15:5)— bear, or take on, the weaknesses of the weak, or powerless, by abstaining from meat and wine even while believing that their own normal culinary habits are not wrong. The Greek phrase sometimes translated "harmony" in 15:5 (NRSV, NAB) echoes 12:16 and means the same (Christlike) attitude and practice.[40]

This pattern of Christ's action, and therefore of Christlike behavior, can be described as follows:

   although [x] not [y] but [z]

meaning

   although [x] = possessing status or rights
   not   [y] = exercising that status or rights for selfish purposes
   but   [z] = refraining from exercising the status or rights out of love for
            others

Such loving, others-oriented (others-pleasing) behavior is, in large measure, what Paul understands by clothing oneself in Christ (13:14). This is resurrectional cruciformity in action: a dynamic, cross-shaped, life-giving spirituality that tells a story: the story of Jesus. That story, as we saw in chapter 6, is constant yet never the same; it is creative, responding to the situation and the needs at hand.

It must be stressed that although Paul's words are directed *especially* at the powerful, they are not directed *only* at the powerful. "Each of us" (15:2) means all, powerful and powerless alike. In this way, Paul empowers the powerless

---

39. On hope, see also 4:18; 5:2–5; 8:19–25; 15:24.

40. In 15:5, Paul uses the same idiom for harmony, or same attitude and practice (see NIV, CEB), as in Phil 2:2, 4.

at Rome so that they can be, and are seen as, contributors to the community's life together.

Paul shifts to a prayer for the unity in life (15:5) and in liturgy, or worship (15:6), that will come to the community as they do, in fact, live according to the narrative pattern of the crucified Messiah he has just recounted (cf. 12:16). The theme of glory reappears here as we approach the letter's conclusion. In Christ, humanity's first sin, failure to glorify God (1:18–25), has been reversed. When gentiles and Jews join Paul (11:36; 16:25, 27) in glorifying God together in Christ, they also, like Christ and like their common father-in-the-faith Abraham (6:4; 4:20), share in God's promised glory that will soon come in fullness (2:7, 10; 5:2; 8:17–18, 21, 30). This concern will be continued in 15:7–13.

Humanity had relinquished the glory of God (divine presence) by failing to give glory to God (divine honor), as Paul had said early in the letter (see 1:21, 23; 3:23). The multicultural church(es) in Rome and elsewhere bear witness to the presence and power of God's glory when they live and worship in Christ-shaped harmony and love.

15:7–13. Mutual Welcome and the Glory of God

Paul's focus on the harmonious praise of God in 15:1–6 leads to the dramatic rhetorical and pastoral conclusion to the main part of the letter, its *peroratio*. We have in 15:7–13 (structurally parallel to 15:1–6) Paul's final exhortation to hospitality (15:7), grounded in the example of Christ and aimed at the glory (honor/worship) of God (a good summary of 15:1–6). This then explodes into a catena (chain) of scriptural citations about the plan of God for gentiles to join Jews in glorifying God.

The word "welcome" in 15:7 is a deliberate echo of 14:1 and 14:3 as Paul creates bookends for his instructions in 14:1–15:13. Now the welcome is mutual: all must practice hospitality. Christ, Paul claims (15:8), became a servant to the Jews both for their own benefit (in fulfilling the patriarchal promises) and also for the benefit of the gentiles. In other words, all of Romans—its various themes, its extended discourse on Jews and gentiles in chapters 9–11—is summarized here: God's faithfulness (lit. "truth," meaning fidelity to promises made; 15:8) to the Jews and mercy to the gentiles that creates a praise-filled, hospitable people.

The chain of texts witnessing to the inclusion of gentiles in the worship of God is from all parts of Paul's Bible:[41]

---

41. The word "gentiles," or "nations," appears six times in 15:9–12.

- the Greek version of Deut 32:43, a text from the Law (Rom 15:10);
- the Greek version of Isa 11:10, a text from the Prophets associated with the Messiah (Rom 15:12); and
- Ps 18:49 (Rom 15:9b) and Ps 117:1 (Rom 15:11), texts from the Writings.

Of particular importance is Paul's citation of Deut 32:43 in 15:10, which invites the gentiles/nations to "Rejoice . . . with his [God's] people"—but it does so only in the Greek text (LXX).[42] This is a picture of Jews and non-Jews together. Also highly significant is the citation of Isaiah's reference to "the root of Jesse"—that is, the Messiah—as the hope specifically of the gentiles (15:12).

If there is now to be a public witness to this divine economy, the members of the churches at Rome must embody these texts by accepting one another as different but equal participants in God's salvation. Through the Spirit, Paul prays, they will experience faith, joy, peace, and hope (cf. 14:17) from the God of hope, the God who gives hope (15:13). This will be the antithesis of Rom 1:18–3:20 and thus the fulfillment of God's "dream," God's intention for humanity: a righteous/just community enabled by the Spirit to live according to Christ and experience the glory of God as they glorify God.

Such a gift must be shared with others. This passage is not merely about the inclusion of the *believing* gentiles in Rome but also of the (as-of-now) *unbelieving* gentiles in Rome, and in Spain, and in every part of Paul's world—and ours. It is not merely about the unity of ancient gentiles and Jews in Christ but also about the unity of all Christians, then and now, who might be tempted to allow insignificant differences to separate them from one another.

REFLECTIONS AND QUESTIONS FOR 14:1–15:13

Spiritual, Pastoral, and Theological Reflections

1. For Paul **the church** is, and therefore must be, **both one and multicultural**. We learn from this episode, as from Galatians and 1 Corinthians—not to mention our own experience—how difficult it can be to embody this reality. Cultural differences in worship style, interpretations of baptism and Com-

---

42. For this reason, English translations, which are based on the Hebrew text, do not mention this invitation to the gentiles/nations.

munion, expectations of leaders, approaches to mission, political views, language, attitudes toward alcohol, and much more divide Christians more than they unite. But movements toward homogeneity in the church are theologically antithetical to the gospel of God that Paul preaches. Unity-in-diversity is not, therefore, an option to ponder but a reality with a mandate to heed.

2. Theologian Willie Jennings has a short but powerful essay entitled "**The Seduction of Segregation**" in his commentary on Acts 15.[43] Here are a few excerpts:

> The difference between Israel and the Gentiles and the differences among Gentile peoples does not occasion God's anger but God's delight, because the creation's multiplicity and variety signal the mystery of the creature that God embraces as its creator. . . . The single greatest challenge for disciples of Jesus is to imagine and then enact actual life together. . . . The dominant way of imaging people together has been forms of cultural and social parallelism (peoples living parallel lives) that underwrite segregationalist mentalities. . . . We are the inheritors of the legacy of segregation that has powerfully and successfully reduced the way we imagine church life. . . . Difference is best maintained, maintained in its life-giving realities, through communion with others. Only in life, shared, joined, and exchanged in desire of being made permanent, can differences emerge in their deepest beauty—as invitations to the expansion of life and love. . . . Segregated spaces are . . . places where [people] see and know themselves. . . . The seduction of segregation, however, hides the fact that such self-knowledge is facile and conceals our true calling—to be joined to another and then another.

3. Misunderstanding Paul's discussion in 14:1–15:13 as a form of **postmodern tolerance** of everything is not merely misguided; it (no less than homogeneity) is fundamentally antithetical to Paul's understanding of life in Christ as slavery to God and to one another. The freedom of conscience of which Paul speaks is only about the *adiaphora*, the nonessentials, of Christian life and thought. Consequently, the church cannot look for unity-in-diversity with respect to core beliefs such as the saving function of Jesus' death and resurrection, the present lordship of Christ, or the triune character of God. It cannot aim for unity-in-diversity regarding blatant evil, such as racism, nationalism, or sexually inappropriate behavior.

4. Three things make Rom 14:1–15:13 **challenging to embody today**.
   a. The first is the difficulty in knowing what is, and what is not, essential. This is probably more so the case for Christian behavior than for

43. Willie James Jennings, *Acts*, Belief: A Theological Commentary on the Bible (Louisville: Westminster John Knox, 2017), 145–49.

Christian doctrine, since there is no moral equivalent of the Christian creeds. Determining what is and is not essential to Christian sexual practice is particularly challenging in the contemporary ecclesial context. It is simply a truism to say that issues surrounding sex and gender are going to continue to divide the churches. The challenge is to maintain the goals of both identifying the essentials, the nonnegotiables, and acknowledging the reality that agreement on such matters is currently aspirational at best.

b.   The second challenge is knowing who should refrain from certain practices, and when. This is a question that few are willing to consider, especially in the realm of sexual behavior. But it is true in other dimensions of the church's life as well. What if, for instance, certain members of a congregation said something like, "Although we really prefer contemporary Christian music, out of love for more traditional approaches, we will yield our expression of this desire to the wishes of others." And what if, simultaneously, those in favor of traditional music expressed a similar sentiment of yielding to the wishes of others. What would be the result? A blended-music service? Or perhaps something not yet imagined.

     A similar challenge could present itself in a more explicitly multicultural context. What might happen, or should happen, when Black and White Christians decide they will worship together? Or Latinx and White Christians? What will be done about music? About preaching styles? About the presence or absence of alcohol at church social events?

c.   This leads to the third challenge: in any particular situation, who is to be identified as the strong/powerful and the weak/powerless? Is that not, for many reasons, a form of dangerous labeling that even an apostle should be concerned about, not to mention much more average church leaders and members?

5.   Although Rom 14:1–15:13 has sometimes figured in Christian discussions about the use of alcohol, it may especially be a resource for considering a **Christian approach to eating**. Although concerns about idolatry per se (if that was at least part of the issue for some Roman believers) may not be foremost in contemporary Christian thinking, what we eat and how we eat can have a significant impact not only on ourselves but also on others locally and globally. There is a justice dimension to food production and food consumption, and thus a spiritual dimension. In his book *Food and Faith*, Norman Wirzba

does not deal with Rom 14, but he does interpret Christian eating as a life/death matter in light of Rom 6.[44]

6. The **testimonial, or witness, value of a community life** such as that described in Rom 12:1–15:13 should not be underestimated. In many ways, this Christian *habitus* is alter-cultural, even countercultural. It is a different way, a unique way, of being human, of doing life together, especially in contexts of extreme individualism and polarization.

Questions for Those Who Read, Teach, and Preach

1. How does, or how should, the church distinguish between (a) matters that matter and (b) matters that don't matter?

2. What are some of the contemporary parallels to Rom 14:1–15:13 involving two different cultures in the Christian community as you have experienced it or been informed about them in other Christian communities?

3. What are some of the contemporary versions of judgmentalism (multicultural or other) about things that do not matter? Does Paul's perspective ultimately permit any and all beliefs and practices in the church?

4. How can the church encourage the sort of self-sacrificial, edifying love, especially for those without spiritual or social status, to be the norm in its life together?

5. How can the church work to overcome "the seduction of segregation"?

6. For Christians, what is the appropriate response to those of differing cultures and languages who migrate into their neighborhoods and churches?

For Further Reading

Jipp, Joshua W. *Saved by Faith and Hospitality*. Grand Rapids: Eerdmans, 2017.

Katongole, Emmanuel, and Chris Rice. *Reconciling All Things: A Christian Vision for Justice, Peace and Healing*. Downers Grove, IL: InterVarsity, 2008.

McKnight, Scot. *Reading Romans Backwards: The Gospel of Peace in the Midst of Empire*. Waco: Baylor University Press, 2019.

Pohl, Christine D. *Making Room: Recovering Hospitality as a Christian Tradition*. Grand Rapids: Eerdmans, 1999.

44. Norman Wirzba, *Food and Faith: A Theology of Eating*, 2nd ed. (New York: Cambridge University Press, 2019).

Robert, Dana L. *Faithful Friendships: Embracing Diversity in Christian Community*. Grand Rapids: Eerdmans, 2019.

Sutherland, Arthur. *I Was a Stranger: A Christian Theology of Hospitality*. Nashville: Abingdon, 2006.

Tisby, Jemar. *How to Fight Racism: Courageous Christianity and the Journey Toward Racial Justice*. Grand Rapids: Zondervan, 2021.

Webb, Stephen. *Good Eating*. Grand Rapids: Brazos, 2001.

Wirzba, Norman. *Food and Faith: A Theology of Eating*. 2nd ed. New York: Cambridge University Press, 2019.

Works, Carla Swafford. *The Least of These: Paul and the Marginalized*. Grand Rapids: Eerdmans, 2020.

I f it is true that Romans reaches a climax in 14:1–15:13, focusing on the theme of Jews and gentiles in Christ for the glory of God, then in 15:14–33 Paul describes his own mission and his relationship with the faithful in Rome as one aspect—one highly significant aspect—of the outworking of God's plan in the world, particularly the evangelization of the gentiles and the unification of Jews and gentiles in the Messiah. The content of this last substantive section of the letter contains echoes of Paul's introductory remarks in his thanksgiving (1:8–15).

In 15:14–21, Paul relates his mission to his letter to the Roman faithful. In 15:22–29, he relates his mission to his failure, thus far, to visit Rome and his hope to finally realize his long-term desire to do so on his way to Spain. But first he must do something terribly important: go east, rather than west, to deliver a financial gift from the (largely) gentile churches to the poor among the Jewish believers in Jerusalem. Accordingly, this section of Romans focuses on Paul's ministry itinerary: Jerusalem—Rome—Spain. Paul then closes with a request for prayer for the Jerusalem trip and a peace-benediction (15:30–33) before proceeding to greetings and a final doxology in chapter 16.

15:14–21. THE NATURE OF PAUL'S MISSION AND THE WRITING OF THIS LETTER

This short passage tells us a lot about Paul's ministry:

- its *source* is God's grace, and its means is the Spirit's power;
- its *focus* is the gentiles' obedience to the gospel;
- its *scope* is wherever Christ is not known;
- its *mode* is both words and deeds, including signs and wonders.

How does this mission relate to the letter his Roman audience is engaging?

In the letter, Paul has occasionally, not least in 14:1–15:13, written "rather boldly" (15:15) to these believers, even though he does not know most of them and has never been to Rome.[1] He wants them to understand the letter as a

---

1. Another rather bold move on Paul's part is ch. 11, where he confronts gentile believers' arrogance.

"reminder" (15:15), not as an assault on their character or spiritual maturity. Paul has every confidence in them—their character, knowledge, and ability to instruct one another (15:14). The letter is part of his grace-enabled ministry (15:15b), his "priestly service" (15:16). It is a friendly pastoral prompt rather than a scolding (in contrast to, say, his missive to the Galatians).

Priests, of course, make offerings to God, but the Greek of 15:16 can be interpreted in at least two main ways. Does "the offering of the Gentiles" refer to (1) *Paul's* offering of the gentiles, or to (2) something that the *gentiles* offer? If the answer is (1), Paul probably means that he envisions his ministry of evangelizing and encouraging the gentiles as offering them to God, "sanctified by the Holy Spirit." If the answer is (2), Paul could be referring to the gentiles' self-offering to God as they respond in obedient faithfulness to the gospel (see also 15:18). He could also possibly be alluding to the collection for the poor Jerusalem saints that the gentile believers are now, through Paul, about to offer to God and to those Jerusalem saints. Paul will bring up this specific ministry starting in 15:25.

The immediate context (15:17–22) suggests that Paul's primary reference is to his own ministry of offering the gentiles to God. But we cannot rule out a deliberate double entendre here. If Paul's priestly ministry is his work among the gentiles, then one aspect of that ministry is the gentiles' collection of an offering for Jerusalem—which Paul also calls "my ministry" (or "service") to Jerusalem (15:31). In fact, Paul's wish in 15:16 that the offering of the gentiles be acceptable (Gk. *euprosdektos*) to God is echoed in his prayer that his ministry of taking the collection to the Jerusalem saints be acceptable (*euprosdektos*) to them (15:31).

An essential part of Paul's ministry, then, is to ensure that the gentiles themselves, as well as their participation in Paul's mission, constitute an acceptable and holy sacrifice to God (15:16b). The present letter fits within this responsibility, as Paul indicates with the similar language of a holy, God-pleasing sacrifice in 12:1–2. If the Roman believers become an acceptable, transformed living sacrifice to God, Paul's priestly "gospelizing" of them will have been acceptable to God as well. He would then have another reason to "boast" in the success of his work (15:17). But any confidence of pride he has is grounded in God's grace (15:15). It is focused on "what Christ has accomplished" through him to bring about the gentiles' "obedience" (15:18; cf. 1:5; 10:16; 16:19, 26) by "the power of the Spirit of God" (15:19).

This missional activity of the triune God, in which Paul is privileged to participate, includes for him not only proclamation in words but also "signs and wonders" (15:18–19; cf. 2 Cor 12:12). Specifically, Paul sees his gift ("grace,"

15:15) to be proclaiming the gospel to those who have not heard (15:20–21), in fulfillment of Isa 52:15 (LXX), quoted in 15:21: "Those who have never been told of him shall see, and those who have never heard of him shall understand." He does not wish to add to the work of other architects of Christian community (15:20b), which also helps to explain his nonvisit, so far, to Rome.[2]

Rather, Paul has faithfully executed the unique mission given to him by God from its point of origin to the east in Jerusalem all the way westward (from his location in Corinth) to Illyricum (15:19).[3] Paul has a sense of mission accomplished—and yet there is more to do, as we will now hear. And the Romans are, Paul hopes, an essential part of that new mission, which further explains the writing of this letter.

15:22–29. PAUL'S RELATIONSHIP WITH ROME, JERUSALEM, AND SPAIN

What we have seen in 15:14–21 is the nature of Paul's priestly mission to the gentiles and how his letter to Rome fits into that mission. We have also seen that the specific character of that mission—to unbelieving gentiles—explains the lack, thus far, of a personal visit to Rome, despite years of Paul's trying to go (15:22, 23b; cf. 1:10–14). But his failure to visit has not been a personal decision: "I have so often been hindered" (15:22; cf. 1:13; Acts 16:6). Paul here summarizes the sentiments expressed at the start of the letter (1:8–15). As in 1:13, the source of this hindrance is more likely God than humans or Satan.[4]

Sensing that his mission to the region east of Italy was complete (15:23), Paul now expresses his hope of passing through Rome on his way to Spain, the western edge of the empire (15:24, 28). He seems confident that taking the gospel to Spain is God's will for him. His goal in going to Rome, then, would not merely be a bit of preaching, teaching, and fellowship (as 1:11–13 and even 15:32 might suggest) but also a sending by the Roman Christians (15:24). This suggests that Paul has in mind the provision of a mission base, financial support, and perhaps companions. This subtle (or not-so-subtle) request for

---

2. Paul emphasizes a similar point in 2 Cor 10:13–18, indicating that he does not want to step on the toes of other workers in the field.

3. Illyricum was on the east coast of the Adriatic Sea and across the water from Italy. About Paul's work there nothing specific is known, but see 2 Tim 4:10 (Dalmatia = Illyricum).

4. In 1 Thess 2:18, Paul does speak of being hindered by Satan, but there Paul seems to have been in despair about that blockage. Here, however, he seems to be attributing the hindrance to his vocation and to God's will.

money should not, however, be blown out of proportion and turned into the sole reason for the letter, as a few interpreters have suggested.

Yet generosity to fellow believers and to apostolic work is very important, and Paul wants the Roman faithful to be aware of yet another delay in his visit to them: a trip to Jerusalem—which is not on the way from Paul's current base in Corinth to Rome or Spain!—for the benefit of the "poor among saints" there (15:26). It is possible, unfortunately, to read Paul's letters and miss the critical and symbolic importance of this effort to him. Because he sees his mission as an integral part of God's plan to unite Jews and gentiles in Christ, Paul believes that the sharing of resources for the spiritual benefit of gentile nonbelievers or the material welfare of poor Jewish believers is also integral to God's work (15:25–27). His concern for the poor among the believers in Jerusalem is also an expression of his general promise to "remember the poor" throughout his ministry (Gal 2:10).

Convincing largely gentile congregations in Asia Minor (what is now Turkey) or Greece, themselves consisting primarily of people on the financial margins, to give money for Jewish believers in Jerusalem was not always an easy task. In 15:26, Paul mentions two success stories: gifts from churches in Macedonia (northern Greece, including the community at Philippi and other churches) and Achaia (southern Greece, including primarily Corinth), who were "pleased" to participate (15:26, 27). But collecting funds from the Corinthians was a hard-fought battle (see 2 Cor 8–9), and it is not known for sure whether an effort in Galatia (1 Cor 16:1–4), unmentioned here, was successful.

The hard-fought-for collection to some extent consumed Paul for years. Its imminent delivery to Jerusalem, he seems to have thought, was symbolic of several things:

- the successful completion of his work in Asia Minor and Greece, the Aegean mission;
- the unity of gentiles and Jews in the Messiah;
- the debt (15:27) gentiles owe to Jews for their salvation;
- the nature of Christian *koinōnia* (sharing, solidarity) as both spiritual and material (15:27); and
- the need for economic "fair balance" (NRSV, NJB) or "equality" (NAB, NIV, NET, CEB, RSV) among the churches (2 Cor 8:13–15).[5]

---

5. My former student Hunter Brown summarizes Paul's collection mission as an act

Paul, then, plans to bring his ministry-to-date to completion by going to Jerusalem and then heading for Spain via Rome (15:28). He is certain he will arrive at Rome with Christ's fullest blessing (15:29), probably meaning with Christ's approval for his completed Aegean mission, his Jerusalem trip, his arrival in Rome, and his plans for an upcoming Spanish mission.

15:30–33. AN APPEAL FOR PRAYER AND A BLESSING OF PEACE

Despite his certainty of Christ's blessing, Paul is concerned about how the collection will be received. So he appeals to the Roman Christians to co-struggle with him in prayer (15:30).[6] Significantly, like his perspective on his mission, Paul's prayer request in 15:30 reflects a Trinitarian spirituality.

The request is twofold (15:31). First, he wants prayer for protection from the "disobedient" (NAB, NET), probably referring to any Jewish Christ-followers in Jerusalem who oppose him and his gentile mission.[7] This request reflects his sense of apostolic, Christlike self-sacrificial giving—risking his life in a potentially dangerous mission. Second, and closely related, he requests prayer that "my ministry" or "service" (Gk. *diakonia*) will be well received by the Jerusalem saints (15:31). It is interesting, as noted above, that Paul sees the gentiles' gift as part of *his* ministry.

If the prayers of Paul and the Roman faithful result in the success of the Jerusalem mission, Paul will arrive in Rome full of joy and ready for an experience of mutual spiritual refreshment, or co-rest (15:32), as he had stated in 1:11–12. Paul's sense of solidarity with believers he hardly knows is apparent; it is reinforced with the titles, like "co-worker," he gives to people in chapter 16.

Paul concludes the body of the letter and its travel plans with a benediction (15:33) that echoes 15:13 and anticipates 16:20: the God of the gospel is the God of shalom.

---

of "ecumenical charity." We might also call it an act of ecumenical justice. See esp. 2 Cor 9:6–10.

6. See NIV, NAB, CEB for translations that rightly convey the struggle element in Paul's language. The verb used here is reminiscent of the verbs used in 8:22 and may allude to the prayer-ministry of the Spirit in 8:26.

7. The translation "unbelievers" (NRSV, NIV), which would almost certainly mean non-Christ-followers, is less likely than "disobedient." However, according to Acts, Paul does, in fact, face opposition from nonbelievers in Jerusalem (Acts 21:27–39; 23:12–35; 25:1–5; cf. 1 Thess 2:14–16), though not in connection to the collection. Acts, in fact, does not explicitly mention the collection, though some find an allusion in 24:17.

REFLECTIONS AND QUESTIONS FOR 15:14–33

Spiritual, Pastoral, and Theological Reflections

1. Christian ministry and mission require **sensitivity to contextual needs** that requires, in turn, sensitivity to the leading of the Spirit.

2. It is critical that Christian ministers, both lay and ordained, humbly **attribute the success of their ministries to God.** Doing so is not only a sign of humility but also a sign of truth-telling. Thinking we are the means of our own ministerial accomplishments is the first step toward moving outside both the will and the mission of God.

3. The **global Christian church** is a fellowship of **mutual support and solidarity** (*koinōnia*), both spiritual and material. It is the responsibility of all Christians and churches to contribute to the expression of this solidarity in appropriate ways.

Questions for Those Who Read, Teach, and Preach

1. How would you characterize the mission of God, Paul, and the church according to Romans? What help might Romans offer for the contemporary church in understanding its mission?

2. Should all Christian ministry be imaged as priestly in character? If so, in what sense? (For traditions in which clergy are designated priests, how is their priestly ministry both similar to and different from the priestly ministry of all Christians?)

3. How can a local Christian community express the reality that it is part of a global fellowship?

4. How can a Christian community with significant means share its surplus with other communities as a partner in a mutually beneficial relationship—that is, without taking on the role of patron or even oppressor?

5. What benefits and insights might the poor, both inside and outside the church, have to contribute to it? Is giving to the poor simply an act of charity that serves to reduce the assets of the giver, or is there a circle of reciprocity that returns a genuine benefit back to the giver? How does this seem to work in Paul's theology and ministry?

FOR FURTHER READING

Anderson, Gary A. *Charity: The Place of the Poor in the Biblical Tradition.* New Haven: Yale University Press, 2013.

Barram, Michael. *Missional Economics: Biblical Justice and Christian Formation.* Grand Rapids: Eerdmans, 2018.

Blomberg, Craig. *Christians in an Age of Wealth: A Biblical Theology of Stewardship.* Grand Rapids: Zondervan, 2013.

Burke, Trevor J., and Brian S. Rosner, eds. *Paul as Missionary: Identity, Activity, Theology, and Practice.* Library of New Testament Studies 420. London: T&T Clark, 2011. (more technical)

Downs, David J. *The Offering of the Gentiles: Paul's Collection for Jerusalem in Its Chronological, Cultural, and Cultic Contexts.* Grand Rapids: Eerdmans, 2016. (more technical)

Griffin, Michael, and Jennie Weiss Block, eds. *In the Company of the Poor: Conversations with Dr. Paul Farmer and Fr. Gustavo Gutierrez.* Maryknoll, NY: Orbis, 2013.

Johnson, Luke Timothy. *Sharing Possessions: What Faith Demands.* 2nd ed. Grand Rapids: Eerdmans, 2011.

Longenecker, Bruce. *Remember the Poor: Paul, Poverty, and the Greco-Roman World.* Grand Rapids: Eerdmans, 2010. (more technical)

16:1–27
Closing

In the final chapter of the letter, Paul greets the surprising number of believers he knows at Rome, adds some final instructions, and closes with a doxology. It is easy to gloss over these verses, but they disclose some quite interesting and significant things about Paul and about the diverse Christian community at Rome, and about Christian ministry.

Romans 16 reveals Paul's personal connections to the house churches in Rome that he has not visited. There is one specifically named house church (16:5) and hints of other small congregations (see 16:10, 11, 14, 15).[1] The chapter also reveals Paul's collaborative style of ministry, including ministry with women. As for the churches in Rome, the chapter informs us, through its names, that there was great socioeconomic diversity and, of course, both Jews and gentiles.[2]

16:1–23. Greetings, Commendations, and Final Instructions

16:1–16. Greetings

The fascinating list of people and their designations in 16:1–16 is full of tidbits about Paul's relationships, and especially about his positive estimation of the role of women (at least nine are mentioned) in the early churches. Paul uses the verb "greet" sixteen times. The following table summarizes the verses containing these greetings, after which there are a few additional comments:

---

1. As noted in the introduction to the commentary, Rom 16:10 and 16:11 imply households (see NIV, CEB, NET, NJB), while 16:14 and 16:15 imply small communities that are not members of a household. The term "house church" can refer to houses of various sorts (from tenement apartments to villas), but early Christian groups may also have met elsewhere: in workshops, in restaurants and taverns, and so on.

2. Although the manuscript evidence suggests to some that this chapter was not original to the letter, that is not the conclusion of the majority of scholars.

PEOPLE IN ROMANS 16

Name	Designation	Other Biographical Details
Phoebe (vv. 1–2)	servant/minister/deacon (Gk. *diakonos*) of the church at Cenchreae; benefactor (patron) of many, including Paul	gentile woman; almost certainly the letter bearer, and quite probably its interpreter
Prisca and Aquila (vv. 3–5a)	co-workers in Christ	Jewish tentmaking couple from Rome who met Paul in Corinth (Acts 18:1–3); risked their necks for Paul; esteemed by gentile churches; hosted house church in Rome
Epaenetus (v. 5b)	Paul's beloved; first convert in Asia (Asia Minor)	gentile man
Mary (v. 6)	hard worker in Rome	Jewish (probably) woman (possibly Miriam)
Andronicus and Junia (not the male form Junias) (v. 7)	co-family-members (ethnic relatives? spiritual relatives?); co-prisoners with Paul; prominent apostles; older in Christ than Paul	possibly a Jewish couple
Ampliatus (v. 8)	Paul's beloved in the Lord	gentile man; possibly slave/freedperson
Urbanus (v. 9)	Paul's co-worker	gentile man; possibly slave/freedperson*
Stachys (v. 9)	Paul's beloved	gentile man; possibly slave/freedperson
Apelles (v. 10)	approved (tested?) in Christ	gentile or Jewish man
those of Aristobulus (v. 10)	—	family members or slaves, or both, of a (probably nonbelieving) gentile male
Herodion (v. 11)	co-family-member (ethnic relative? spiritual relative?)	Jewish male
family/household of Narcissus (v. 11)	those in the Lord	unbelieving gentile man with believing family/household
Tryphaena and Tryphosa (v. 12)	workers in the Lord	gentile or Jewish women; possibly sisters or slaves, or both, or freed slaves

NAME	DESIGNATION	OTHER BIOGRAPHICAL DETAILS
Persis (v. 12)	beloved, hard worker in the Lord	gentile woman; possibly a slave or freed slave
Rufus and his mother (v. 13)	chosen in the Lord; also a "mother" to Paul	gentile man, possibly the son of Simon of Cyrene (Mark 15:21), and his mother
Asyncritus, Phlegon, Hermes, Patrobas, Hermas, and the brothers with them (v. 14)	—	gentile males, possibly slaves or freed-persons; members together of a house church
Philologus, Julia (v. 15)	—	possibly a gentile couple
Nereus and his sister (v. 15)	—	gentiles
Olympas (v. 15)	—	gentile man
all the saints with them (v. 15)	—	likely a gentile house church

* Here and below a number of the names were frequently given to slaves.

This table illustrates how the several house churches of Rome embody the Pauline vision of an inclusive community: gentiles and Jews; slave, free, and freedpersons (former slaves); elite and non-elite; men and women; from all corners of the empire (cf. Gal 3:28; 1 Cor 1:26–28). Paul has relations of intimacy, collegiality, gratitude, and admiration with these people. Many are leaders in the spread of the gospel: fellow apostles (the term obviously referring to more than Paul and the Twelve), co-workers, and even co-prisoners. They exemplify the cruciform life Paul tries to live and preaches. No wonder he wants the church at Rome to be united in love.

As noted above, especially telling is Paul's esteem for women; of the twenty-six named persons, nine are women. They are among the most hardworking, and they have served in the role of minister/deacon (servant of some kind), benefactor, and even apostle. Furthermore, although Paul actually rarely uses the Greek word for "sister" (*adelphē*), it occurs twice in the greetings (16:1, 15).[3]

3. Elsewhere in the Pauline letters, we find it only in 1 Cor 7:15; 9:5; 1 Tim 5:2; Phlm 2. Some English translations introduce the words "and sisters" when it is clear that "brothers" (Gk. *adelphoi*) includes women.

Phoebe is identified as a servant, minister, or deacon (*diakonos*) and Christian benefactor/patron (16:1–2). Some translations (e.g., RSV, NJB) have mistakenly rendered *diakonos* as "deaconess," but there is no such gender designation in Paul's description. She is a minister from the church at Cenchreae, near Paul's base in Corinth, and is commended because Paul is sending the letter with her. She shares in his own ministry/service (*diakonia*; 15:31), which is also to share in the ministry of Christ (15:8).

It is likely also that Paul is expecting Phoebe to interpret Romans—the longest and most important letter he ever wrote—to the church(es) in Rome as they have it read. (It is impossible to pass over the irony in this situation, since so many people have accused Paul of restricting, if not disparaging, women.) And Paul expects the Roman believers to welcome and assist her in this ministry.

Other women of note in this chapter include the "workers in the Lord" Tryphaena and Tryphosa (16:12) as well as the hardworking Mary (16:6) and Persis (16:12). Particularly touching is the mention of Rufus' unnamed mother, who was also a surrogate or spiritual mother to Paul (16:13).

Christian couples are also among those Paul greets and respects for their shared ministry. The couple Prisca, or Priscilla, and Aquila (16:3–4) we know from 1 Corinthians and from Acts.[4] They must have done something remarkable in the way of risking their necks for Paul, as did Epaphroditus (Phil 2:29–30). Known and respected among the gentile churches, they also have a church meeting in their house.

There are two other possible couples. Philologus and Julia, joined in Greek with "and" (as in CEB, NET, NJB), are briefly noted in 16:15. Longtime believers Andronicus and Junia (16:7), possibly husband and wife, were once co-prisoners with Paul and are identified as "prominent among the apostles." Some older translations and interpretations, based in part on poorer manuscripts, misidentify Junia as a male with the name Junias, but this is incorrect.

By "apostle," Paul probably means someone like him who has seen the resurrected Lord and has been called and commissioned to take the gospel into the world (1 Cor 9:1–2; 15:7–10). Including Andronicus and Junia in the category of "apostle" may be surprising, but we see already in 1 Corinthians that the term can designate both the twelve (1 Cor 15:7; "all the apostles") and someone like Paul's partner Barnabas (1 Cor 9:5–6).[5] But Junia is the only woman to be called an apostle in the New Testament.

---

4. 1 Cor 16:19; Acts 18:1–3, 18, 26; see also 2 Tim 4:19. "Priscilla" is the name used in Acts.

5. "Apostles" is one of the gifts of the Spirit (1 Cor 12:28–29), which means also of Christ (Eph 4:11).

Paul's affection and respect for the believers and ministers he does know in Rome is clear; he uses the word "beloved" four times (16:5, 8, 9, 12). Several times he expresses his solidarity with them in Greek words beginning with the prefix "co-" (Gk. *syn-*): co-worker(s) (16:3, 9; cf. 16:21); co-family-members (16:7, 11; cf. 16:21) and co-prisoners (16:7).[6]

Also significant is how Paul repeatedly describes people and their work as "in the Lord" (16:2, 8, 11, 12, 13; cf. 16:22) or "in Christ" (16:3, 7, 9. 10). This is the essential description of a Christian for Paul: a person who inhabits and is shaped by the crucified and resurrected Messiah and Lord Jesus. Solidarity and participation with one another are grounded in Christians' participation in and solidarity with Christ.

After sending his own personal greetings to individuals, in 16:16 Paul instructs the Roman faithful to greet one another with the holy kiss and, acting as a spokesperson for the church universal, passes on greetings from "all the churches of Christ" (in Achaia, where he is located? everywhere?).

16:17–20. Appeals and a Blessing

Paul next issues final appeals (echoing 15:30) as he begins to wrap up the letter. He warns the Roman believers to watch out for troublemaking teachers who cause dissension and offense (16:17), contradicting the teaching they have received (cf. 6:17). Such teachers serve not Christ but themselves and their appetites (cf. Phil 3:18–19) and deceive the gullible (16:18).

It is likely that Paul has in mind people who misinterpret the gospel and mislead people down a path that does not embody Christlike "newness of life" (6:4). He may also be referring to those who have maligned him and his teaching in advance of his potential visit (3:8). Another likely reference would be to those who have provoked the judgmentalism and separations Paul addresses in 14:1–15:13. This warning is, once again, a relatively gentle pastoral reminder, since Paul is joyfully confident in their obedience, as their reputation indicates (16:19).

The warning and the words of confidence lead to both a promise and a blessing (16:20). Paul puts the Roman situation and struggle in apocalyptic perspective, promising that God will soon defeat Satan, the ultimate cosmic

---

6. English translations do not always capture the full sense of collegiality and solidarity conveyed by these words. For example, "co-prisoners" in 16:7 is usually rendered as "fellow prisoners" (RSV, NAB, CEB, NET, ESV) or even simply "in prison with me" (NRSV, NIV).

enemy of the church and all humanity (16:20a; cf. "the god of this world" in 2 Cor 4:4). As Ephesians puts it, "our struggle is not against enemies of blood and flesh, but against the rulers, against the authorities, against the cosmic powers of this present darkness, against the spiritual forces of evil in the heavenly places" (Eph 6:12). But at the same time, as Martin Luther declared (in his famous hymn "A Mighty Fortress"), echoing Paul, "for lo! his doom is sure." The certainty of this defeat is therefore paired with a benediction of grace for sustenance in the struggle (16:20b).

16:21-23. More Greetings

Returning briefly to greetings, Paul passes on hellos from several people (16:21-23), among whom are his beloved co-worker Timothy; Tertius, his amanuensis (scribe, secretary), who offers his personal greeting; Gaius, the patron/host of the "whole church" in Corinth, suggesting he is likely a man of means with a villa (cf. 1 Cor 1:14); and Erastus, a Corinthian public servant, possibly the "city treasurer" (NRSV) or "director of public works" (NIV).[7]

16:25[24]-27. DOXOLOGY

Although some ancient manuscripts lack the letter's final doxology or locate it elsewhere in the letter, it is a fitting end to Romans and ably sums up the letter's focus in a prayerful spirit. It links the prophets to Paul's apostleship and gospel, and both to the gentiles.

The doxology is offered to God, who is able to strengthen the Roman believers and all Christians, according to what Paul describes as the gospel, the proclamation of Christ, and the revealed mystery promised by the biblical prophets and now finally disclosed (16:25-26). This "mystery" is the will, or command, of God that gentiles—like Jews—be summoned to covenant relationship with God: "the obedience of faith" (16:26). With this phrase, Paul repeats the purpose of his own mission and of this letter, with which Romans opened (1:5; see also 15:18; 16:19).

So, what is this "obedience of faith"? As stated earlier in the commentary, it is essentially sharing in the faithful obedience (3:22, 26) of the Messiah: that is, Christlikeness. Paul's mission was to bring about resemblance to the obedient and faithful Son of God among the nations, restoring humanity's lost glory and righteousness so that gentiles and Jews alike could fully participate in the life

---

7. For Erastus, see also Acts 19:22; 2 Tim 4:20.

of the triune God, Father, Son, and Spirit—the life God intended for them. They are called and enabled to be communities of Spirit-enabled, Christlike Godlikeness, of righteousness and (cruciform) glory, in anticipation of God's final glory and their participation in it as whole, resurrected persons in eternal celebration with the entire creation.

For this grace, Paul reminds us, God is truly wise and truly worthy of praise through Jesus Christ!

REFLECTIONS AND QUESTIONS FOR 16:1–27

Spiritual, Pastoral, and Theological Reflections

1. Christians may be anywhere geographically: in Rome or Corinth or New York or Mumbasa or. . . . But their **primary and fundamental location** is always and everywhere *in Christ*, in the Lord.
2. **Christian ministry** is most faithful and effective when it is **collaborative**, and that collaboration should include both men and women as well as people from different ethnic and socioeconomic contexts. The **Christian church** is also most faithful and effective when it includes **people from different ethnic and socioeconomic contexts.**
3. Many Christians in many parts of the world, either by necessity or by choice, have recently learned or relearned **the value of house churches.** Such small Christian communities sometimes supplement and sometimes—again by necessity or choice—replace larger churches and Christian communities. Many Christian practices are, in fact, difficult or impossible to observe without participation in smaller groups of disciples. In larger churches and parishes, many Christians say, the key to vital Christian growth and service is participating in these groups. In places of persecution, house churches are frequently the only viable form of corporate Christian existence.
4. **Hospitality is a critical and central part** of the Christian church's life, both locally and globally. As one of my students once asked, "Where would we be today if Phoebe had been outright rejected?"[8]
5. Worth pondering carefully, as we come to the end of Romans and Paul's words about the revelation of the mystery, are **Dietrich Bonhoeffer's words about mystery.** These include the following:

> That . . . Jesus of Nazareth, the carpenter, was himself the Lord of glory [cf. 1 Cor 2:8–10]: that was the mystery of God. It was a mystery because God

8. The student was Rev. Dion Thompson.

became poor, low, lowly, and weak out of love for humankind, because God became a human being like us, so that we would become divine, and because he came to us so that we would come to him. . . . That it is the one God, the Father and Creator of the world, who in Jesus Christ loved us unto death, who in the Holy Spirit opens our hearts to him, that we love him, that there are not three gods but that God is one, who embraces, creates, and redeems the world from the beginning to the end—that is the depth of the Deity, whom we worship as mystery and comprehend as mystery.[9]

Questions for Those Who Read, Teach, and Preach

1. What does Rom 16 communicate about the character of Christian ministry and community?
2. In what ways does ministry in your context reflect, or not reflect, the vision of ministry implied in Rom 16?
3. In what ways does the church in your context reflect, or not reflect, the vision of the church implied in Rom 16?
4. At the end of your study, teaching, or preaching of Romans, what are the most important takeaways for you in your context?

For Further Reading

Burroughs, Presian R., ed. *Practicing with Paul: Reflections on Paul and the Practice of Ministry in Honor of Susan G. Eastman.* Eugene, OR: Cascade, 2018.

Campbell, Joan Cecelia. *Phoebe: Patron and Emissary.* Collegeville, MN: Liturgical, 2009.

Epp, Eldon Jay. *Junia: The First Woman Apostle.* Minneapolis: Augsburg Fortress, 2005.

Finger, Reta Halteman. *Paul and the Roman House Churches: A Simulation.* Eugene, OR: Wipf & Stock, 2006.

———. *Roman House Churches for Today: A Practical Guide for Small Groups.* 2nd ed. Grand Rapids: Eerdmans, 2007.

Gombis, Timothy G. *Power in Weakness: Paul's Transformed Vision for Ministry.* Grand Rapids: Eerdmans, 2021.

Gooder, Paula. *Phoebe: A Story.* Downers Grove, IL: IVP Academic, 2018.

Hellerman, Joseph H. *Embracing Shared Ministry: Power and Status in the Early Church and Why It Matters Today.* Grand Rapids: Kregel, 2013.

9. Dietrich Bonhoeffer, *I Want to Live These Days with You: A Year of Daily Devotions,* trans. O. C. Dean Jr. (Louisville: Westminster John Knox, 2007), 149.

Lee, Dorothy A. *The Ministry of Women in the New Testament: Reclaiming the Biblical Vision for Church Leadership*. Grand Rapids: Baker Academic, 2021.

Thompson, James W. *Pastoral Ministry according to Paul: A Biblical Vision*. Grand Rapids: Baker Academic, 2006.

Westfall, Cynthia Long. *Paul and Gender: Reclaiming the Apostle's Vision for Men and Women in Christ*. Grand Rapids: Baker Academic, 2016.

SUMMARY OF ROMANS 12–16

Chapters 12–16 lay out Paul's understanding of faithful living for gentiles and Jews in the community of the new covenant in Christ.

- Believers offer themselves to God as a "living sacrifice."
- The church is a holy and hospitable community in which gifts are appropriately exercised, and where love and honor are offered to all, including outsiders and even enemies.
- The gospel requires gentiles, Jews, and all multicultural groups within the church to live without mutual judgmentalism concerning matters that do not matter, for the justified live for their Lord in their own distinctive ways.
- There is a special burden placed on the strong, or powerful (those less scrupulous about nonessential matters), not simply to put up with the scruples of the weak, or powerless, but to bear, or take on, their weaknesses in Christlike fashion.
- The goal of God's plan and Paul's mission work is the salvation of Jews and gentiles, and the creation of multicultural communities in which they welcome and respect one another as God in Christ has welcomed them; this is symbolized in the collection for Jerusalem.
- Paul is assisted in this work by various kinds of service by both men and women with various gifts in collaborative, respectful ministry.

Index of Subjects and Names

Claudius, Caesar, 24, 25, 218, 253–54
co-crucifixion with Christ, 41, 145, 166, 167, 169–73. *See also* cruciformity; participation/sharing: in Christ's death and resurrection
collection, for Jerusalem, 27, 286, 288–89, 300
commandment(s), 102, 184–85, 259–60; fulfillment of, 198; Noahide, 81n10; Ten, 97; two great, 80–82, 84. *See also* law
communion, 16, 207, 267, 281. *See also* fellowship; participation/sharing
community. *See* church
condemnation: absence of God's, 98, 195, 196, 200, 209–11, 223; God's, 98, 105–6, 161, 162; of pride, 101–2; of self, 95; of sin, 195, 196. *See also* judgment, God's; judgmentalism; mercy, God's
confession of Christ, 13, 14, 46, 99, 169, 212, 218, 227–28, 230, 235, 237, 241, 252
conformity. *See* Christoformity; cruciformity
congregation. *See* church
co-resurrection with Christ: future, 208; present, 145, 167, 169–73. *See also* participation/sharing: in Christ's death and resurrection
cosmic powers. *See* powers
covenant: with Abraham/Israel, 11, 201, 218, 220, 228, 232–36, 239; breaking of, 83, 101–2, 124, 195; gentiles and, 127, 139, 297; justification and, 4, 128, 227; nature/obligations of, 41, 72, 76, 80–82, 84, 95, 97–98, 103–4, 201; new, 10, 11, 13, 35–36, 49, 60, 98, 103–4, 151, 167, 181, 191–92, 236, 242, 270, 300; relations, 11, 15, 60, 67, 77–78, 112, 118, 125; renewal of, 227–28, 236, 276. *See also* church: as covenant community; circumcision; dysfunctionality, covenant; faith/faithfulness: of God; justification; law
covetousness, 42, 185, 190
creation: 61, 149, 162; care of, 46, 215; God's work of, 82, 83n15, 85, 97, 121, 281; new, 10, 13, 15, 28, 99, 104, 136, 171, 268, 276; redemption of, 36n13, 46, 149, 192,

203–7, 213, 217, 298; suffering of, 156, 203–7, 212, 213–14; witness of, 82–84. *See also* nature
creator. *See* God: as creator
creature, 83, 85, 204, 244, 281
crucifixion. *See* co-crucifixion with Christ; Christ: death of
cruciformity, 16, 23, 36, 150, 171–72, 174, 213, 220, 243–44, 248–52, 270, 294; resurrectional character of, 13, 122n58, 172, 178–79, 191–212, 215, 217, 242–45, 249–51, 261, 278. *See also* co-crucifixion with Christ; hospitality; love
curse, 205, 219–20

David/Davidic line, 36, 62, 127, 130, 132, 134
death: Adam and, 158–59; Abraham, Sarah, and, 131, 137–38; believer's, 150, 272; defeat of, 14, 171, 196; eschatological, 89, 175, 239; to/of flesh/self, 166, 170, 171, 184, 193, 200, 203, 212, 217, 245; to the law, 176, 184; versus life, 144–45, 157, 195, 199; as power (Death), 11, 14, 40n18, 110, 116, 157n23, 158–60, 162–63, 171, 173, 191; present life as, 11, 15, 89, 112–13, 116, 125, 157, 173, 185–86; reign of, 159, 161–62, 174, 183, 216; rescue/resurrection from, 38, 135–41, 145, 148, 164, 171, 173, 180, 195, 199; to Sin, 169–72, 184, 200, 203, 212, 216, 245; spiritual, 274; as wages of Sin, 11, 35, 37, 175. *See also* baptism: as participation; Christ: death of; co-crucifixion with Christ; life/new life
deed(s). *See* work(s)/deeds
deification. *See* theosis
deliverance: future, 67, 236; of Israel, 67, 236; from pain, 214; from Sin and Death, 76, 115, 124, 128, 172, 196–97, 227. *See also* justification; liberation; salvation
deliverdict, 128
desire(s), disordered, 83, 85, 110–11, 173, 181, 185–86, 188, 190, 198
diatribe, 33, 93–95, 100, 109, 126, 131, 165, 218

138, 142, 152, 160, 163, 196–97, 235–36; need for, 11, 89, 112, 115

freedom: believers', 143, 245, 261, 269–71, 273, 281; from God, 85, 175, 184; God's, 219, 221–23, 230; as idol, 156, 163–64, 177, 179; from the law, 175–77, 184, 269; need for, 124; from sin and death, 125, 128, 145, 172–74, 184, 200. *See also* liberation

Gaventa, Beverly Roberts, 100n33, 112n49

gentiles: condition of, 11, 77–90; covenant and, 127, 139, 297; immorality of, 11, 78n5, 81–84, 87–89, 92; mercy to, 12, 223–24, 230–39; Paul's mission to, 8, 48, 64, 285–89, 292–94, 297–98; in Roman church, 24–27, 218, 237–38, 253, 267–70, 279–81; sacrifice of, 286; unwritten law and, 97–99. *See also* circumcision; Jews and gentiles/Greeks

gift. *See* grace

glorification, 25, 29, 121–26, 147–51, 179, 192–94, 202–4, 207–11, 215–17, 223, 262. *See also* glory

glory, 37–39, 41, 78, 88–89, 96–97, 107, 114, 148–51, 206, 214, 222, 238, 242, 297–98; cruciform, 122n58, 204, 208, 214, 298; of God, 16, 39, 41, 82–83, 121–26, 147, 173, 175, 243, 244, 267, 270, 276, 279–80, 285; restoration of humanity's, 29, 38, 39, 41, 115, 121–22, 124, 125, 126, 194, 208, 242, 297. *See also* glorification

God: blessing of, 11, 67, 122, 134, 199, 232, 275, 289; as creator, 11, 82–83, 85, 88, 97, 121, 125, 137, 281, 299; faithfulness of, 10, 12, 35–36, 68–73, 76, 106–7, 117–29, 136, 142, 148, 153, 211, 218–40; 279; as father, 15, 193–95, 201, 207, 213–14; freedom of, 219, 221–23, 230; glory of, 16, 39, 41, 82–83, 121–26, 147, 173, 175, 243, 244, 267, 270, 276, 279–80, 285; holiness of, 41, 60, 103, 123; of hope, 278, 280; impartiality of, 11, 29, 35, 48, 77–78, 93–98, 103, 106–7, 125, 127, 142; judgment of, 25, 67, 77–80, 89, 99, 100, 103, 114, 127–28, 218, 223, 227n13, 238–39,

251–52, 273; justice of, 12, 31, 42–43, 63, 65–74, 76, 105–7, 118, 120–21, 123–24, 218, 221–23, 241, 253, 255n20; love of, 12, 32, 40n17, 73, 146, 148, 150–55, 203, 206, 209–11, 252, 277; mercy of, 10, 12, 27, 35, 73, 76–77, 98–99, 107, 117–26, 138, 211, 218–24, 228, 230–40; mission of, 46, 101, 173, 177, 179, 228–29, 239, 248, 261, 263, 290; peace of, 10, 14, 16, 29, 31, 38–39, 41–43, 46, 60–61, 63, 73–74, 146–50, 156, 199, 205, 264, 274–75, 285, 289; revelation of, 10, 12, 66, 67, 73, 110, 117, 234; righteousness of, 29, 36, 44, 68–69, 71, 73–74, 118; as sender of Son and Spirit, 195, 260; truthfulness of, 69, 105–6, 279; will of, 95, 184, 245, 251, 256, 258

Godfearers, 8, 269

godlessness. *See* idolatry; ungodliness

gospel: for all, 8, 48–49, 79, 96–97, 141, 224–28, 233–34, 239; as challenge to Rome, 29, 30–32, 38–39, 63, 254, 264; content of, 10–11, 29–30, 36, 50, 59–63, 65–74, 115–16; misinterpretation of, 106, 162, 169, 174, 179, 296; obedience to the, 11, 62, 96n28, 175, 228–29, 237, 285–86; response to the, 11, 13, 14–16, 99, 104, 127, 151, 192, 227–28, 235–36, 242–43, 256, 300; Rome's, 4, 10. *See also* embodiment of the gospel; peace; Rome: ideology/practices of

government. *See* authorities

grace: Abraham and, 133–36, 138–39; age of, 118; cheap, 155, 156, 169, 177, 179; Christ's death as, 125, 127, 142, 148, 151–53, 157–58, 161–62; and deeds, 95, 99; definition of, 61, 152–53; as gift of God, 113, 124–25, 152–53, 161, 211, 212–13, 223, 230–33, 237, 239; gifts of, 246–47; and human response, 14, 15, 38, 119; justification by, 48, 72, 77, 95, 120, 125, 133–36, 138–39, 147–48, 153; Paul's ministry and, 285–86, 297; as power, 40n18, 158, 162, 164; reign/empire of, 144–45, 157, 162, 164–65, 170, 174, 216; and sin, 168–69, 174–75, 179; as theme in Romans, 25,

Irenaeus, 41–42

Isaac, 131, 137–38, 199, 210n80n, 221–22

Israel: advantages of, 67, 105–7, 109, 122, 220; belief of, 230, 232–38; calling/ election of, 11, 67, 86, 207, 221–23, 236; covenant with, 11, 103, 201, 218, 220, 228, 232–36, 239; disobedience/sin of, 11, 84–85, 106, 223–24, 229–31, 236; exodus of, 143n1; God's faithfulness/ mercy toward, 10, 12, 68–69, 218–41; holiness of, 86, 87, 232; hope for, 38, 49, 230–32, 235; judgment of, 78, 100, 104, 106; mission of, 11; Paul's attitude toward, 49, 103–5, 221–22; Paul's prayer for, 219–21, 224–26, 239; promises to, 13, 38; relation to gentiles, 231–34, 281; remnant of, 224, 229–32, 235–36, 241; salvation of, 67, 230–38, 241; stumbling of, 49, 223, 226, 231, 241; unbelief of, 219–25, 228–38, 241. *See also* Jews; Jews and gentiles/Greeks; Judaism, Paul's relation to

Jackson, Daniel W., xxi, 83n16

Jacob, 101, 222, 236

Jennings, Willie James, 281

Jenson, Robert W., 138n74

Jerusalem, 6–7, 23, 27, 48, 236, 285–89

Jesus. *See* Christ (Jesus the Messiah)

Jewett, Robert, 32n12, 263

Jews: in Christ, 49, 105, 109, 176, 207, 235, 239, 244, 266–80, 285, 288, 292; condition of, 100–102; gospel/grace for, 23, 25, 29, 35, 48, 65, 66, 76, 124, 136, 139, 141–42, 218, 226, 230, 239, 242, 253; messianic, 239; priority of, 48; in Roman churches, 24–25, 253–54, 257, 266–70, 279–80, 292–94; in Rome, 24–25, 218, 253–54, 257; situation of, 77, 98, 110, 124, 141–42, 231; as theme in Romans, 26, 29n10, 33, 41, 64n9, 66, 223–24, 237. *See also* Israel; Jews and gentiles/Greeks; Judaism, Paul's relation to

Jews and gentiles/Greeks: in Christ, 49, 105, 109, 176, 207, 235, 239, 244,

266–80, 285, 288, 292; gospel/grace for, 23, 25, 29, 35, 48, 65, 66, 76, 124, 136, 139, 141–42, 218, 226, 230, 239, 242, 253; situation of, 77, 98, 110, 124, 141–42, 231; as theme in Romans, 26, 29n10, 33, 41, 64n9, 66, 223–24, 237

Johnson, Luke Timothy, 203n69

joy, xix, 16, 27, 41, 63, 145, 150, 192, 204, 212, 250, 264, 274–75, 280, 289, 296

Judaism, Paul's relation to, 3–4, 48–49, 81n10, 100n33, 102. *See also* Israel; Jews

judgment, God's, 25, 67, 77–80, 89, 99, 100, 103, 114, 127–28, 218, 223, 227n13, 238–39, 251–52, 273; basis of, 48, 77, 93–98, 107; final, 14, 16, 95, 98. *See also* acquittal; forgiveness; wrath

judgmentalism, 26, 77, 94, 107, 108, 129, 198, 238, 240, 242, 246, 270–76, 283, 296, 300

Junia, 60, 293, 295

justice/righteousness: in Christ's death, 117–21, 123–24, 144; eschatological, 13–14, 205–6, 238; God's saving/restor- ative, 12, 31, 42–43, 63, 65–74, 76, 105–7, 118, 120–21, 123–24, 218, 221–23, 241, 253, 255n20; practice of, xix, 46, 129, 179, 214, 248, 264, 274, 280, 282–83, 288n5; restoration of humanity's, 29, 38, 39, 41, 115, 121–22, 124, 125, 126, 194, 208, 242, 297; Roman, 30–31, 63; vocabulary for, 43, 69–70, 80, 106, 117, 120–21, 143–44, 160

justification: Abraham and, 77, 119, 120n56, 130–35, 144, 148, 150; baptism and, 165–70, 172, 178, 262; through Christ's death, 117–26, 146–56, 159, 163, 209–10; circumcision and, 134–35, 138–39, 140; covenant and, 4, 128; definition of, 15, 72, 126, 128, 129, 132–33, 134, 135–40, 144–45, 162, 216–17, 227; as deliverdict, 128; faith/faithfulness and, 29, 65–67, 72, 118–20, 124–27, 131–40, 142, 148, 151, 153, 166–67, 225, 227, 229; forgiveness and, 125, 126, 131–32, 134, 138–42; glory and, 121–22, 208; grace and, 48, 72, 77, 95, 120, 125, 133–36,

219, 223–24, 228, 236–38; in Christ, 73, 76, 123, 124, 234, 242; to gentiles, 12, 233; to Israel, 218–24, 230–40; practice of, 247; response to, 234, 238, 241, 279

mercy seat, 124

messiah: crucified, 7, 10, 12–13, 66–67, 128, 212, 225–26, 231, 279; debates about, 24, 253–54; Jesus as, 29, 42, 49, 62–63, 73, 218. *See also* Christ (Jesus the Messiah)

metamorphosis. *See* transformation

mind: of Christ, 16, 246; dedication of the, 253, 256, 262, 270; faith and the, 67; set on the flesh, 42, 200; Sin and the, 82, 84, 85, 88–90, 96, 112, 115, 116, 188–89, 198, 244; set on the Spirit, 42, 200; transformation of, 16, 115, 116, 243–45

mission. *See* church: mission of; God: mission of; Paul: apostleship of; Paul: mission of

Moses, 122, 220, 222, 227, 229. *See also* law

nationalism, 84, 91, 190, 252, 254, 263, 281. *See also* idolatry; patriotism

nations. *See* gentiles; Jews and gentiles/ Greeks

nature, 85–86, 90, 204–6, 213. *See also* creation

Nee, Watchman, 180n42

neighbor, love of, 11, 80–81, 85, 128, 243, 251, 256, 258–60, 277

nonretaliation, 173, 248–52, 256–57, 263

obedience: of Abraham, 131; of Christ, 12, 120, 123, 125, 128, 144, 157, 160, 162, 167, 175, 216, 229; and/of faith, 15, 29, 35, 50, 61–62, 67, 72–73, 76, 118, 120, 127, 162, 175, 228–29, 242, 272, 297–98; to God/righteousness, 11, 39, 84, 173–75, 184, 199, 201, 256; to the gospel, 11, 62, 96n28, 175, 228–29, 237, 285–86; to in- justice/Sin/passions, 184, 96; to Jesus, 13, 15, 62, 228–29, 244, 270, 272; of the Jews, 230, 235, 236; political authorities and, 256–59, 263–64; as theme in Ro-

mans, 29n8, 61, 74. *See also* allegiance; disobedience; faith/faithfulness; slav- ery: to God/Christ/righteousness

obedience of faith. *See* obedience: and/ of faith

offering, to God, 17, 85, 167–69, 171, 243. *See also* collection, for Jerusalem

Origen, xvii, 239

outside Christ. *See* human condition

outsiders, treatment of, 249–51, 253, 261, 290, 300. *See also* love: of enemies

parousia. *See* Christ (Jesus the Messiah): second coming of

participation/sharing: in Christ's death and resurrection, 5, 13–15, 29, 36, 38, 62, 121, 125–26, 135, 138, 140, 148, 165–72, 176, 178; and community life, 250, 267; in faith/obedience of Christ, 62, 119, 120, 124–25, 148, 162–63, 165, 175, 297; in faith of Abraham, 120, 135–36, 139, 148, 222n9; and finances, 249n11, 288, 290; in God's character, 39, 60, 68, 69, 123, 207, 247; in God's glory, 123, 147, 201, 202, 205, 206, 217, 279; in God's holiness, 41, 60, 103, 123; in God's mission, 46, 173, 177, 179, 228–29, 239, 248, 261, 263, 295; and transformation, 16, 28, 29n9, 38, 41, 42, 50, 171, 178. *See also* Christ (Jesus the Messiah): "in Christ"; co-crucifixion with Christ; co-resurrection with Christ; fellowship; Holy Spirit: indwelling of; Holy Spirit: life in; indwelling, mutual; solidarity

patriotism, 156, 254, 263. *See also* nationalism

Patterson, Jane, 162n30

Paul: apostleship of, 7–9, 17, 27, 36, 59–60, 64, 138–39; call/conversion/ transformation of, 7–9, 121n57; inter- pretive perspectives on, 3–5; as letter writer, 9–10, 77; life of, 5–10; mission of, 8–9, 46, 48, 64–65, 77, 285–90, 292–94, 297–98; as pastor, 11, 17, 77; spirituality of, 16–18, 171, 183–84, 212, 240, 262, 278, 289; suffering of, 9, 66n11,

Index of Scripture and Other Ancient Sources

For Romans, only citations that are out of their natural order in the commentary are included.